FREE Test Taking Tips DVD Offer

To help us better serve you, we have developed a Test Taking Tips DVD that we would like to give you for FREE. **This DVD covers world-class test taking tips that you can use to be even more successful when you are taking your test.**

All that we ask is that you email us your feedback about your study guide. Please let us know what you thought about it – whether that is good, bad or indifferent.

To get your **FREE Test Taking Tips DVD**, email freedvd@studyguideteam.com with “FREE DVD” in the subject line and the following information in the body of the email:

a. The title of your study guide.

b. Your product rating on a scale of 1-5, with 5 being the highest rating.

c. Your feedback about the study guide. What did you think of it?

d. Your full name and shipping address to send your free DVD.

If you have any questions or concerns, please don’t hesitate to contact us at freedvd@studyguideteam.com.

Thanks again!

FTCE Elementary Education K-6 Book

FTCE Test Prep Review Team

Table of Contents

Quick Overview

As you draw closer to taking your exam, effective preparation becomes more and more important. Thankfully, you have this study guide to help you get ready. Use this guide to help keep your studying on track and refer to it often.

This study guide contains several key sections that will help you be successful on your exam. The guide contains tips for what you should do the night before and the day of the test. Also included are test-taking tips. Knowing the right information is not always enough. Many well-prepared test takers struggle with exams. These tips will help equip you to accurately read, assess, and answer test questions.

A large part of the guide is devoted to showing you what content to expect on the exam and to helping you better understand that content. Near the end of this guide is a practice test so that you can see how well you have grasped the content. Then, answer explanations are provided so that you can understand why you missed certain questions.

Don't try to cram the night before you take your exam. This is not a wise strategy for a few reasons. First, your retention of the information will be low. Your time would be better used by reviewing information you already know rather than trying to learn a lot of new information. Second, you will likely become stressed as you try to gain a large amount of knowledge in a short amount of time. Third, you will be depriving yourself of sleep. So be sure to go to bed at a reasonable time the night before. Being well-rested helps you focus and remain calm.

Be sure to eat a substantial breakfast the morning of the exam. If you are taking the exam in the afternoon, be sure to have a good lunch as well. Being hungry is distracting and can make it difficult to focus. You have hopefully spent lots of time preparing for the exam. Don't let an empty stomach get in the way of success!

When travelling to the testing center, leave earlier than needed. That way, you have a buffer in case you experience any delays. This will help you remain calm and will keep you from missing your appointment time at the testing center.

Be sure to pace yourself during the exam. Don't try to rush through the exam. There is no need to risk performing poorly on the exam just so you can leave the testing center early. Allow yourself to use all of the allotted time if needed.

Remain positive while taking the exam even if you feel like you are performing poorly. Thinking about the content you should have mastered will not help you perform better on the exam.

Once the exam is complete, take some time to relax. Even if you feel that you need to take the exam again, you will be well served by some down time before you begin studying again. It's often easier to convince yourself to study if you know that it will come with a reward!

Test-Taking Strategies

1. Predicting the Answer

When you feel confident in your preparation for a multiple-choice test, try predicting the answer before reading the answer choices. This is especially useful on questions that test objective factual knowledge or that ask you to fill in a blank. By predicting the answer before reading the available choices, you eliminate the possibility that you will be distracted or led astray by an incorrect answer choice. You will feel more confident in your selection if you read the question, predict the answer, and then find your prediction among the answer choices. After using this strategy, be sure to still read all of the answer choices carefully and completely. If you feel unprepared, you should not attempt to predict the answers. This would be a waste of time and an opportunity for your mind to wander in the wrong direction.

2. Reading the Whole Question

Too often, test takers scan a multiple-choice question, recognize a few familiar words, and immediately jump to the answer choices. Test authors are aware of this common impatience, and they will sometimes prey upon it. For instance, a test author might subtly turn the question into a negative, or he or she might redirect the focus of the question right at the end. The only way to avoid falling into these traps is to read the entirety of the question carefully before reading the answer choices.

3. Looking for Wrong Answers

Long and complicated multiple-choice questions can be intimidating. One way to simplify a difficult multiple-choice question is to eliminate all of the answer choices that are clearly wrong. In most sets of answers, there will be at least one selection that can be dismissed right away. If the test is administered on paper, the test taker could draw a line through it to indicate that it may be ignored; otherwise, the test taker will have to perform this operation mentally or on scratch paper. In either case, once the obviously incorrect answers have been eliminated, the remaining choices may be considered. Sometimes identifying the clearly wrong answers will give the test taker some information about the correct answer. For instance, if one of the remaining answer choices is a direct opposite of one of the eliminated answer choices, it may well be the correct answer. The opposite of obviously wrong is obviously right! Of course, this is not always the case. Some answers are obviously incorrect simply because they are irrelevant to the question being asked. Still, identifying and eliminating some incorrect answer choices is a good way to simplify a multiple-choice question.

4. Don't Overanalyze

Anxious test takers often overanalyze questions. When you are nervous, your brain will often run wild, causing you to make associations and discover clues that don't actually exist. If you feel that this may be a problem for you, do whatever you can to slow down during the test. Try taking a deep breath or counting to ten. As you read and consider the question, restrict yourself to the particular words used by the author. Avoid thought tangents about what the author *really* meant, or what he or she was *trying* to say. The only things that matter on a multiple-choice test are the words that are actually in the question. You must avoid reading too much into a multiple-choice question, or supposing that the writer meant something other than what he or she wrote.

5. No Need for Panic

It is wise to learn as many strategies as possible before taking a multiple-choice test, but it is likely that you will come across a few questions for which you simply don't know the answer. In this situation, avoid panicking. Because most multiple-choice tests include dozens of questions, the relative value of a single wrong answer is small. Moreover, your failure on one question has no effect on your success elsewhere on the test. As much as possible, you should compartmentalize each question on a multiple-choice test. In other words, you should not allow your feelings about one question to affect your success on the others. When you find a question that you either don't understand or don't know how to answer, just take a deep breath and do your best. Read the entire question slowly and carefully. Try rephrasing the question a couple of different ways. Then, read all of the answer choices carefully. After eliminating obviously wrong answers, make a selection and move on to the next question.

6. Confusing Answer Choices

When working on a difficult multiple-choice question, there may be a tendency to focus on the answer choices that are the easiest to understand. Many people, whether consciously or not, gravitate to the answer choices that require the least concentration, knowledge, and memory. This is a mistake. When you come across an answer choice that is confusing, you should give it extra attention. A question might be confusing because you do not know the subject matter to which it refers. If this is the case, don't eliminate the answer before you have affirmatively settled on another. When you come across an answer choice of this type, set it aside as you look at the remaining choices. If you can confidently assert that one of the other choices is correct, you can leave the confusing answer aside. Otherwise, you will need to take a moment to try to better understand the confusing answer choice. Rephrasing is one way to tease out the sense of a confusing answer choice.

7. Your First Instinct

Many people struggle with multiple-choice tests because they overthink the questions. If you have studied sufficiently for the test, you should be prepared to trust your first instinct once you have carefully and completely read the question and all of the answer choices. There is a great deal of research suggesting that the mind can come to the correct conclusion very quickly once it has obtained all of the relevant information. At times, it may seem to you as if your intuition is working faster even than your reasoning mind. This may in fact be true. The knowledge you obtain while studying may be retrieved from your subconscious before you have a chance to work out the associations that support it. Verify your instinct by working out the reasons that it should be trusted.

8. Key Words

Many test takers struggle with multiple-choice questions because they have poor reading comprehension skills. Quickly reading and understanding a multiple-choice question requires a mixture of skill and experience. To help with this, try jotting down a few key words and phrases on a piece of scrap paper. Doing this concentrates the process of reading and forces the mind to weigh the relative importance of the question's parts. In selecting words and phrases to write down, the test taker thinks about the question more deeply and carefully. This is especially true for multiple-choice questions that are preceded by a long prompt.

9. Subtle Negatives

One of the oldest tricks in the multiple-choice test writer's book is to subtly reverse the meaning of a question with a word like *not* or *except*. If you are not paying attention to each word in the question, you can easily be led astray by this trick. For instance, a common question format is, "Which of the following is...?" Obviously, if the question instead is, "Which of the following is not...?," then the answer will be quite different. Even worse, the test makers are aware of the potential for this mistake and will include one answer choice that would be correct if the question were not negated or reversed. A test taker who misses the reversal will find what he or she believes to be a correct answer and will be so confident that he or she will fail to reread the question and discover the original error. The only way to avoid this is to practice a wide variety of multiple-choice questions and to pay close attention to each and every word.

10. Reading Every Answer Choice

It may seem obvious, but you should always read every one of the answer choices! Too many test takers fall into the habit of scanning the question and assuming that they understand the question because they recognize a few key words. From there, they pick the first answer choice that answers the question they believe they have read. Test takers who read all of the answer choices might discover that one of the latter answer choices is actually *more* correct. Moreover, reading all of the answer choices can remind you of facts related to the question that can help you arrive at the correct answer. Sometimes, a misstatement or incorrect detail in one of the latter answer choices will trigger your memory of the subject and will enable you to find the right answer. Failing to read all of the answer choices is like not reading all of the items on a restaurant menu: you might miss out on the perfect choice.

11. Spot the Hedges

One of the keys to success on multiple-choice tests is paying close attention to every word. This is never more true than with words like *almost*, *most*, *some*, and *sometimes*. These words are called "hedges" because they indicate that a statement is not totally true or not true in every place and time. An absolute statement will contain no hedges, but in many subjects, like literature and history, the answers are not always straightforward or absolute. There are always exceptions to the rules in these subjects. For this reason, you should favor those multiple-choice questions that contain hedging language. The presence of qualifying words indicates that the author is taking special care with his or her words, which is certainly important when composing the right answer. After all, there are many ways to be wrong, but there is only one way to be right! For this reason, it is wise to avoid answers that are absolute when taking a multiple-choice test. An absolute answer is one that says things are either all one way or all another. They often include words like *every*, *always*, *best*, and *never*. If you are taking a multiple-choice test in a subject that doesn't lend itself to absolute answers, be on your guard if you see any of these words.

12. Long Answers

In many subject areas, the answers are not simple. As already mentioned, the right answer often requires hedges. Another common feature of the answers to a complex or subjective question are qualifying clauses, which are groups of words that subtly modify the meaning of the sentence. If the question or answer choice describes a rule to which there are exceptions or the subject matter is complicated, ambiguous, or confusing, the correct answer will require many words in order to be expressed clearly and accurately. In essence, you should not be deterred by answer choices that seem excessively long. Oftentimes, the author of the text will not be able to write the correct answer without offering some qualifications and modifications. Your job is to read the answer choices thoroughly and completely and to select the one that most accurately and precisely answers the question.

13. Restating to Understand

Sometimes, a question on a multiple-choice test is difficult not because of what it asks but because of how it is written. If this is the case, restate the question or answer choice in different words. This process serves a couple of important purposes. First, it forces you to concentrate on the core of the question. In order to rephrase the question accurately, you have to understand it well. Rephrasing the question will concentrate your mind on the key words and ideas. Second, it will present the information to your mind in a fresh way. This process may trigger your memory and render some useful scrap of information picked up while studying.

14. True Statements

Sometimes an answer choice will be true in itself, but it does not answer the question. This is one of the main reasons why it is essential to read the question carefully and completely before proceeding to the answer choices. Too often, test takers skip ahead to the answer choices and look for true statements. Having found one of these, they are content to select it without reference to the question above. Obviously, this provides an easy way for test makers to play tricks. The savvy test taker will always read the entire question before turning to the answer choices. Then, having settled on a correct answer choice, he or she will refer to the original question and ensure that the selected answer is relevant. The mistake of choosing a correct-but-irrelevant answer choice is especially common on questions related to specific pieces of objective knowledge, like historical or scientific facts. A prepared test taker will have a wealth of factual knowledge at his or her disposal, and should not be careless in its application.

15. No Patterns

One of the more dangerous ideas that circulates about multiple-choice tests is that the correct answers tend to fall into patterns. These erroneous ideas range from a belief that B and C are the most common right answers, to the idea that an unprepared test-taker should answer "A-B-A-C-A-D-A-B-A." It cannot be emphasized enough that pattern-seeking of this type is exactly the WRONG way to approach a multiple-choice test. To begin with, it is highly unlikely that the test maker will plot the correct answers according to some predetermined pattern. The questions are scrambled and delivered in a random order. Furthermore, even if the test maker was following a pattern in the assignation of correct answers, there is no reason why the test taker would know which pattern he or she was using. Any attempt to discern a pattern in the answer choices is a waste of time and a distraction from the real work of taking the test. A test taker would be much better served by extra preparation before the test than by reliance on a pattern in the answers.

FREE DVD OFFER

Don't forget that doing well on your exam includes both understanding the test content and understanding how to use what you know to do well on the test. We offer a completely FREE Test Taking Tips DVD that covers world class test taking tips that you can use to be even more successful when you are taking your test.

All that we ask is that you email us your feedback about your study guide. To get your **FREE Test Taking Tips DVD**, email freedvd@studyguideteam.com with "FREE DVD" in the subject line and the following information in the body of the email:

- The title of your study guide.
- Your product rating on a scale of 1-5, with 5 being the highest rating.
- Your feedback about the study guide. What did you think of it?
- Your full name and shipping address to send your free DVD.

Introduction

Function of the Test

In order to become a certified teacher in the state of Florida, a candidate must pass the Florida Teacher Certification Examinations (FTCE). In 2001, the No Child Left Behind Act began the administration of the FTCE. These exams are part of a teacher's certification process in the state of Florida. The Bureau of Educator Certification (BEC) determines the specific exams that a candidate needs to take to teach and become certified in Florida. The required tests depend on certifications that a candidate holds in other states or countries, his or her change of career status, and whether the candidate graduated from a teaching institute in Florida. In order to determine which tests to take, a candidate must submit an application to the BEC, whom will then determine a candidate's testing requirements.

The Elementary Education K-6 Exam assesses content knowledge and pedagogy in four subtests: Language Arts and Reading, Social Science, Science, and Mathematics. All four subtests must be passed in order to successfully pass the Elementary Education exam. Test takers who are attempting the exam for the first time are required to take all four subtests. On subsequent attempts, any or all subtests can be attempted in one testing appointment.

Test Administration

After the BEC determines which tests a candidate needs to take, an applicant can then register for a test. Admission tickets are sent via email and must be presented at the test appointment along with proper identification. Test sites are available throughout the state of Florida as well as nationwide. Appointments can be made year-round.

A candidate must report to the test site 30 minutes before the appointment time on the admission ticket in order to complete pre-administration activities, such as an identity verification procedure, which includes a photo and palm scan. If a candidate wears glasses, a visual inspection is conducted, but the candidate's glasses will not be handled or touched. All personal items are kept in a secure storage area and a candidate receives an erasable notepad and pen. Then, a tutorial is given on how to take a computer-based test, as well as a test agreement and waiver. These processes need to be completed in 5 minutes. If the waiver is not accepted within 5 minutes, the candidate will be required to wait 31 calendar days before a retest, and he or she will not be given a refund. Breaks for the restroom are counted as part of the test time, unless scheduled breaks are provided; test takers attempting at least three subtests are allowed a 15-break. Candidates with disabilities need to complete an Alternative Testing Arrangements Request Form. The form must be submitted to FTCE customer service as soon as possible because test appointment cannot be made until approval.

Test Format

The FTCE Elementary Education is a computer-based exam. A reference sheet is provided for the math subtest. The breakdown of the number of questions and allotted time for each of the four subtests is provided in the table below:

Test	Number of Questions	Allotted Time
Subtest 1: Language Arts and Reading	60 multiple-choice questions	65 minutes
Subtest 2: Social Studies	55 multiple-choice questions	65 minutes
Subtest 3: Science	55 multiple-choice questions	70 minutes
Subtest 4: Mathematics	50 multiple-choice questions	70 minutes

It is important to note that the exam may include evaluation questions that the administrators use to assess for future inclusion. These questions are unscored.

Scoring

A minimum scaled score of 200 on each of the four subtests is required to achieve a passing score on the FTCE Elementary Education exam. Candidates wishing to take a retest must wait 31 calendar days after the most recent attempt before reattempting the exam. Scores are posted to a candidate's online account on Tuesdays after 10:00p.m. Eastern Standard Time on the score report date, which is within 4 weeks after the test date. As long as the test is not under current revision or getting redeveloped, the unofficial passing status will be displayed on the computer screen upon completion prior to leaving the testing site. Otherwise, a candidate will just receive a receipt of test completion until scores are released.

Language Arts and Reading

Reading Process

Blending, Segmenting, Substituting, and Deleting Phonemes, Syllables, Onsets, and Rimes

The ability to break apart a word into its individual phonemes is referred to as *segmenting*. Segmenting words can greatly aid in a child's ability to recognize, read, and spell an entire word. In literacy instruction, *blending* is when the reader connects segmented parts to create an entire word. Segmenting and blending practice work together like pieces of a puzzle to help children practice newly-acquired vocabulary. Educators can approach segmenting and blending using a multi-sensory approach. For example, a child can manipulate letter blocks to build words and pull them apart. An educator may even ask the child to listen to the word being said and ask him or her to find the letter blocks that build each phoneme, one at a time:

/m/ /u/ /g/

/b/ /a/ /t/

/r/ /u/ /n/

Once children are able to blend and segment phonemes, they are ready for the more complex skill of blending and segmenting syllables, onsets, and rimes. Using the same multi-sensory approach, children may practice blending the syllables of familiar words on a word wall, using letter blocks, paper and pencil, or sounding them out loud. Once they blend the words together, students can then practice segmenting those same words, studying their individual syllables and the letters and sounds that create the words. Educators may again read a word out loud and ask children to write or build the first syllable, followed by the next, and so on. The very same practice can be used to identify the onset. Children can work on writing and/or building this sound followed by the word's rime. Word families and rhyming words are ideal for this type of exercise so that children can more readily see the parts of each word. Using words that rhyme can turn this exercise into a fun and engaging activity.

Once children have demonstrated the ability to independently blend and segment phonemes, syllables, onsets, and rimes, educators may present a more challenging exercise that involves *substitutions* and *deletions*. As these are more complex skills, children will likely benefit from repeated practice and modeling. Using word families and words that rhyme when teaching this skill will make the activity more enjoyable, and it will also greatly aid in a child's overall comprehension.

Substitution and Deletion Using Onset and Rime				
Word	**Onset Deletion**	**Rime Deletion**	**Onset Substitution**	**Rime Substitution**
run	un	r	fun	rat
bun	un	b	gun	bat
sun	un	s	nun	sat

Substitution and Deletion Using Phonemes		
Word	**Phoneme Substitution**	**Phoneme Deletion**
sit	sat	si
bit	bat	bi
hit	hat	hi

Substitution and Deletion Using Syllables		
Word	**Syllable Substitution**	**Syllable Deletion**
cement	lament or, cedar	ce
moment	statement, or motive	mo
basement	movement, or baseball	base

Stages of Language Acquisition

There are many factors that influence a child's language acquisition. A child's physical age, level of maturity, home and school experiences, general attitudes toward learning, and home languages are just some of the many influences on a child's literacy development. However, a child's *language acquisition* progresses through the following generalized stages:

Stage	Examples	Age
Preproduction	does not verbalize/ nods yes and no	zero to six months
Early production	one to two word responses	six to twelve months
Speech emergence	produces simple sentences	one to three years
Intermediate fluency	simple to more complex sentences	three to five years
Advanced fluency	near native level of speech	five to seven years

While this applies to language acquisition in one's home language, the very same stages apply to English language learners (ELLs). Since effective communication in any given language requires much more than a mere collection of vocabulary words that one can accurately translate, paying particular attention to each stage in language acquisition is imperative. In addition to vocabulary knowledge, language acquisition involves the study and gradual mastery of intonation, a language's dialects—if applicable—and the various nuances in a language regarding word use, expression, and cultural contexts. With time, effort, patience, and effective instructional approaches, both students and educators will begin to see progress in language acquisition.

Second language acquisition does not happen overnight. When educators take the time to study each stage and implement a variety of effective instructional approaches, progress and transition from one stage to the next will undoubtedly be less cumbersome and more consistent. In the early stages of language acquisition, children are often silently observing their new language environment. At these early stages, listening comprehension should be emphasized with the use of read alouds, music, and visual aids. Educators should be mindful of their vocabulary usage by consciously choosing to speak slowly and to use shorter, less complex vocabulary. Modeling during these beginning stages is also very effective. If the educator has instructed the class to open a book for instance, they can open a book as a visual guide. If it is time to line up, the educator can verbally state the instruction and then walk to the door to begin the line.

During the *pre-production stage*, educators and classmates may assist ELLs by restating words or sentences that were uttered incorrectly, instead of pointing out errors. When modeling the correct language usage instead of pointing out errors, ELL learners may be less intimidated to practice their new language.

As students progress into the *early production stage*, they will benefit from exercises that challenge them to produce simple words and sentences with the assistance of visual cues. The educator should ask students to point to various pictures or symbols and produce words or sentences to describe the images they see. At the early production and speech emergent stages, ELL students are now ready to answer more diverse questions as they begin to develop a more complex vocabulary. Working in heterogeneous pairs and small groups with native speakers will help ELL students develop a more advanced vocabulary.

At the *beginning and intermediate fluency stages*, ELLs may be asked questions that require more advanced cognitive skills. Asking for opinions on a certain subject or requiring students to brainstorm and find ways to explain a given phenomenon are other ways to strengthen language proficiency and increase vocabulary.

When a child reaches the *advanced fluency stage*, he or she will be confident in social and academic language environments. This is an opportune time to introduce and/or increase his or her awareness of idiomatic expressions and language nuances.

World-Class Instructional Design and Assessment (WIDA) is a consortium of various departments of education throughout the United States that design and implement proficiency standards and assessments for English language learners and Spanish language learners. Primarily focusing on listening, speaking, reading, and writing, WIDA has designed and implemented English language development standards and offers professional development for educators, as well as educational research on instructional best practices. The five English language proficiency standards according to WIDA are as follows:

English Language Proficiency Standards—WIDA
1. Within a school environment, ELL students require communication skills for both social and instructional purposes.
2. Effective communication involving information, ideas, and concepts are necessary for ELL students to be academically successful in the area of Language Arts.
3. Effective communication involving information, ideas, and concepts are necessary for ELL students to be academically successful in the area of Mathematics.
4. Effective communication involving information, ideas, and concepts are necessary for ELL students to be academically successful in the area of Science.
5. Effective communication involving information, ideas, and concepts are necessary for ELL students to be academically successful in the area of Social Studies.

According to WIDA, mastering the understanding, interpretation, and application of the four language domains—listening, speaking, reading, and writing—is essential for language proficiency. Listening requires ELL students to be able to process, understand, interpret, and evaluate spoken language. Speaking proficiently allows ELL students to communicate their thoughts, opinions, and desires orally in a variety of situations and for a variety of audiences. The ability to read fluently involves the processing, understanding, interpreting, and evaluating of written language with a high level of accuracy, and writing proficiency allows ELL students to engage actively in written communication across a multitude of disciplines and for a variety of purposes.

Since language acquisition involves the ELL students, their families, their classmates, educators, principals and administrators, as well as test and curriculum developers, WIDA strives to ensure that the English Language Proficiency Standards reflect both the social and academic areas of language development.

Communicating with Diverse Partners

Communication is never one-sided. There are always at least two individuals engaged in a conversation, and both acts of speaking and listening are often interchangeable. In the classroom, educators communicate with all students, and students communicate with one another. Some forms of communication are intended for instructional purposes, while other forms may be solely for entertainment. To be an effective communicator, it is critical that the purpose for speaking is clear to both the presenter and the audience. It is also important that the mode of communication is culturally sensitive and age appropriate. The presenter should use language that best suits his or her audience. For example, if an educator wishes to speak to a primary class about the importance of homework, domain-specific language may not be appropriate, but that same conversation with educational colleagues may require domain-specific language. Here are some key techniques to consider when developing strong communication skills:

Effective Speaking	Effective Listening
Check for understanding and interest—ask key questions	Offer relevant information to the topic
Repeat important information in a variety of ways	Ask poignant questions, clarify understanding
Use nonverbal forms of communication—body language for effect	Use nonverbal forms of communication—body language for effect
Remain observant—maintain eye contact	Remain observant—maintain eye contact
Develop a healthy sense of humor	Develop a healthy sense of humor
Strive for honesty	Strive for honesty
Consider language choices	Develop active listening skills—not simply waiting to respond
Develop cultural sensitivity	Strengthen patience

Engaging Oral Presentations

Oral presentations can cause panic in a classroom as children scramble to figure out how, when, where, why, and what to speak about. However, if given proper guidance, appropriate time, and constructive feedback, the panic will soon fade, and in turn, students will learn how to give powerful oral presentations.

In order to be effective, educators should follow best practices, including sharing a well-designed rubric with the class, discussing the importance of each skill listed, answering any questions the children might have, and providing ongoing and constructive feedback while children develop their presentations.

Key areas to develop oral presentations:

Volume

Children should consider where the presentation would be held. Will it be indoors, outdoors, in an auditorium, or in the classroom? Learning to match the volume of the presentation with the location and size of the audience will greatly improve the presentation.

Articulation

Pronouncing words clearly is another aspect of effective communication, especially during an oral presentation. Slurred words, rushed words, mumbling, or leaving out the beginning or ending of sentences will have a negative impact on the message, and the presenter risks losing the interest of the audience.

Awareness of Audience

Facing the audience at all times is paramount to the success of an oral presentation. If possible, walking around the room and maintaining eye contact with the audience have proven to be effective techniques. Welcoming questions from the audience, restating questions for everyone to hear, and providing honest and thoughtful responses, also play a key role in ensuring a successful oral presentation.

Phonological Awareness

Well before children are able to read and write, they begin to develop basic listening skills and gradually begin to imitate and produce the sounds they hear. Since language is used to communicate one's needs, react to situations, share experiences, and develop an understanding of the surrounding world, these beginning stages form the foundation of a child's literacy development. Before a child reaches the preschool years, they begin to develop the ability to recognize and manipulate the sounds in their environment.

Generally speaking, *phonological awareness* is the ability to identify and manipulate specific units of oral language, including words, syllables, onsets, and rimes. The beginning stages of phonological awareness occur when a child is able to listen to and understand the words that people speak and read and when they are further able to recognize the various sounds within these words. Phonological awareness is also defined as the ability to sound out various words by connecting the sounds heard to familiar sounds and to manipulate those sounds in order to create new sounds and words. A child is demonstrating phonological awareness when they are able to do the following:

- Appropriately recognize and apply words that rhyme—*cat, bat, sat*
- Identify initial letters—the *c* in *cat*
- Identify middle letters—the *a* in *cat*
- Identify ending letters—the *t* in *cat*
- Separate simple words into their individual sounds or phonemes—c/a/t *cat*

There are many strategies educators can use to strengthen a child's phonological awareness. One effective strategy to strengthen a child's awareness of word units is clapping out the number of syllables in a word. Familiar and enjoyable songs, such as "Bingo," help children to identify individual phonemes within a word and strengthen their spelling skills, listening comprehension, and rhythm. Other strategies may include word games that challenge children to think of rhyming words or words that share the same initial, middle, or ending sounds. Creating fun and engaging ways for children to strengthen their phonological awareness will build the framework for future literary success.

Phonemes, Syllables, Onsets, and Rimes

A *phoneme* is commonly referred to as a sound or a group of sounds that differentiate one word from another in a spoken language. Phonemes are language-specific sound units that do not carry inherent meanings, but are simply known as the smallest unit in a language. For example, there are phonemes unique to the English language that do not necessarily exist in other spoken languages. In English, although there are only twenty-six letters, there are forty-four phonemes:

Forty-Four Phonemes in English			
Consonant Sounds		**Vowel Sounds**	
/b/	boy	/a/	bat
/d/	desk	/e/	head
/f/	fall	/i/	dish
/g/	game	/o/	rock
/h/	hand	/u/	muck
/j/	joy	/a/	bake
/k/	king	/e/	meet
/l/	life	/i/	like
/m/	map	/o/	moat
/n/	nail	/yoo/	cube
/p/	park	/e/	alarm
/r/	run	/oo/	doom
/s/	sock	/oo/	nook
/t/	tail	/ou/	mouse
/v/	veil	/oi/	toy
/w/	water	/o/	call
/y/	yawn	/u/	herd
/z/	zebra	/a/	hair
/ch/	chalk	/a/	star
/sh/	shallow		
/th/	thorn		
/hw/	whale		
/zh/	leisure		
/ng/	sing		

Mastery of all forty-four phonemes in oral and written communication is a strong predictor of future reading readiness.

Syllables are defined as one complete unit of pronunciation. Every syllable contains only one vowel sound that can be created by one or more than one vowel. Syllables can consist of vowels that stand alone or combine with consonants. The study of syllables and how they operate help children to become stronger readers and will aid in spelling proficiency. Educators will often introduce new words that contain more than one syllable by teaching children to say and write the syllable. Segmenting a word into its individual syllables, as well as blending syllables into whole words, allows children to see the key parts of a word and provides opportunities for them to strengthen their reading skills.

In the English language, there are six different types of syllables, four of which are syllable combinations:

- Closed syllables: syllables that end in a consonant, as in *bat*, or *it*
- Open syllables: syllables that end with a vowel, as in *he*, *she*, or *we*
- Vowel-consonant-e syllables: syllables that end with a silent *e*, as in *ate*, *wife*, or *mile*
- Vowel team syllables: syllables that work in combination to create a new sound, as in *mouth* or *join*
- Consonant + le syllables: syllables that contain a consonant and end with an *le*, as in *turtle*
- R-Controlled syllables: syllables that contain a vowel followed by the letter *r*, where the *r* controls how the vowel is pronounced, as in *bird* or *word*

A word is broken up into two pieces: onset and rime. The *onset* is the initial phonological unit of any word, whether it is a consonant or a consonant cluster. The *rime* is the string of letters that follows the onset, usually consisting of a vowel or variant vowels along with one or more consonants. Many words in the English language share common features or patterns. These *word families* often share the same letter combinations that form the same or similar sounds. When introducing word families, educators will often initiate activities involving onsets and rimes to help children accurately recognize, read, and spell simple words. The study of onsets and rimes has shown to improve a child's overall literacy skills, increase reading fluency, and strengthen spelling skills. The following word family list illustrates words separated into onset and rime:

Word	Onset	Rime
sun	s	Un
sunny	s	unny
sunshine	s	unshine

Common Phonics and Word-Recognition Approaches for ELLs

Phonics instruction and word-recognition exercises involve a number of skills, including print awareness, alphabetic knowledge, phonological and phonemic awareness, the alphabetic principle, decoding, the memorization of high-frequency words, and reading practice. As language acquisition is highly complex, there seems to be some debate in the educational field regarding the best instructional approaches for ELL students. Some educators argue that phonics should be taught in isolation and not in context, while others stress the need for a more integrated approach. When faced with what instructional approach to implement, educators who take the time to learn about each child's home language, literacy development, and exposure to the English language will be in the best position to decide on whether a student would benefit from an isolated phonics approach or one that is more integrated. The following are the three different instructional approaches to phonics:

Synthetic Phonics
Educators implement an explicit approach, teaching individual letter-sound correspondence and helping students to blend letters into words.

Embedded Phonics
Educators teach letter-sound correspondence during the reading of a text.

Analogy-Based Phonics

Educators teach students to use parts of words that they already know to help decode words that they don't know. Analogy-Based phonics involves the use of story time, tutoring in small groups, and various language-based activities. Educators share various books and stories with decodable words with students and provide opportunities for children to spell words and write simple sentences with letter-sound correspondence.

The amount of time allotted for phonics and word recognition instruction varies greatly from classroom to classroom. Educators who pay particular attention to the ages of the ELL students and their current level of English language proficiency will be in the best position to decide on an appropriate approach to phonics instruction. However, generally speaking, younger ELL students in the primary grades will benefit from explicit practice with phonemic awareness and the alphabetic principle. Exposure to print awareness will increase in complexity as the child progresses in his or her understanding and application of phonemic awareness skills. Decoding practice, exposure to word families, spelling patterns, onsets and rimes, and structural analysis—including affixes and root words—should be gradually introduced as the child becomes more able to read simple words and simple sentences independently.

When working with ELL students, educators must be sensitive to each child's background knowledge, home language, and experiences involving literacy. In order to become proficient in the English language, ELL students must develop a clear understanding of the relationship that exists between letters and sounds in the English alphabetic system, and this may be in complete opposition to the rules they have already mastered in their home language. For example, some languages use the same or similar alphabet as English, but some of the phonemes might be pronounced differently, causing confusion. The English language may also have letter combinations that do not exist in the student's home language, adding to the confusion. Complicating matters even further, some languages do not utilize an alphabetic writing system, such as the Chinese language, which is *logographic*, relying on characters that represent a word or idea, rather than relying on letters to produce a sound. Therefore, a formal study of phonics is critical to ELL students' literacy development.

One approach for educators to consider is the highlighting of similarities and differences between the student's home language and that of English. For instance, many *cognates* exist between English and Spanish that can act as a bridge to strengthen a child's English language acquisition. Since cognates share the same or similar meaning, spelling, and pronunciation in two different languages, ELL students can quickly add these new words to their vocabulary inventory. Some effective approaches to integrate cognate awareness into lessons include read alouds, student reading activities, and word sorts.

As children read aloud, ELL students are encouraged to raise their hand when they think they've come across a cognate. The reading can momentarily stop while the class discusses the similarities and differences between the pronunciation, spelling, and meaning of each cognate. During a student reading activity, ELL students are encouraged to locate two, three, or more cognates they encounter in their reading and to write them down in their notebooks. These cognates can then be added to the classroom's word wall and further explored. In pairs, students can be given a number of cards with Spanish and English cognates. The students then sort the cards appropriately and discuss their meaning, spelling, and pronunciation. These approaches not only build vocabulary knowledge and confidence for ELL students by actively including their home language in lessons, but they also help to build social bonds in the classroom. Since language acquisition is also very social, when children develop and strengthen positive friendships within and outside the classroom, language acquisition will likewise develop and strengthen. Other effective classroom approaches to help ELL students with phonics and word-recognition skills include the use of word walls and posters throughout the classroom.

As children progress with their phonemic awareness skills, educators may introduce word studies by helping children classify and sort words according to the same or similar spelling patterns. Word study increases children's vocabulary and acts as a bridge from reading to writing as children transfer their newly-acquired words into print. Introducing children to a variety of reading and writing genres and formats will also help to strengthen their reading and writing skills. For example, learning to follow recipes provides children with opportunities to read and engage in hands-on activities to demonstrate their understanding by following a recipe's steps. Personal journals continue to be an effective practice that stimulates creative writing and helps children to express their thoughts and opinions in writing, without worrying too much about grammar, spelling, and punctuation. Personal journals can also be used as reading practice as children pick and choose sections to read aloud to the entire class, in pairs, or in small groups.

It is important for educators to recognize that some written languages are not read from left to right, and some are not even read from top to bottom. Therefore, it is also important for educators to teach print conventions and book awareness, including the direction in which the words in books are read and how to handle and hold a book. These lessons can be taught explicitly or may be simply modeled by the educator during shared reading time.

Phonics and Word Analysis

Phonics is the study of sound-letter relationships in alphabetic writing systems, such as the English language, and it is paramount to a child's future ability to read and write. Phonics helps children recognize and identify letter symbols and translate these symbols into their corresponding sound units, phonemes. The study of phonics concerns itself with the *Alphabetic Principle*—the systematic relationships that exist between letters and sounds—as well as with *Phonemic Awareness*—the understanding that letters correspond with distinct sounds and that there are specific rules governing the placement of letters in the English language.

As children become more familiar with recognizing the names and shapes of each letter, called *graphemes*, they begin to verbally practice their corresponding sounds—the phonemes. Although this sounds straightforward, it can pose significant challenges to both the children and teachers.

For example, when children learn that the letter *y* is pronounced /wigh/, but that it can make other various sounds, including /ee/, /i/, and /igh/—depending on letter placement—it may take repeated practice in order for children to pronounce and read this one letter accurately. Some examples would be the words, *happy, gym,* and *cry.* Although each word contains the same vowel, *y*, the placement of the *y* in each word differs, which affects the letter's pronunciation.

For this reason, there is an ongoing debate in literacy circles regarding the appropriate instructional approach for teaching phonics. Should educators teach letter shapes with their corresponding names or letter shapes with their corresponding sound or sounds? Is it possible to combine instruction to include shapes, names, and sounds, or should each of these skills be taught in isolation with a cumulative approach—shape, sound/s, and name? Some experts believe that when children are introduced to letter names and shapes in isolation of their corresponding sounds, children can become quickly confused, which can delay reading acquisition. Therefore, the answer to what approach to take lies with a keen understanding of a student's background knowledge in English and each child's specific needs. In order to create effective phonics instruction and help students strengthen literacy development, it is strongly suggested that educators are sensitive and aware of these unique challenges to English language acquisition.

It is widely accepted that letter-sound relationships are best taught systematically, introducing one relationship at a time and gradually increasing in complexity. Effective instruction in the initial stages of phonics awareness involves explicit introduction of the most important and the most frequently used letter-sound relationships. For instance, short vowels should be introduced and practiced ahead of long vowels, and lower case letters should be introduced ahead of upper case as they occur the most often. Letters that frequently appear in simple words, such as /a/, /m/, and /t/ would be logical starting points, followed by letters that look similar but carry different sounds, as in /b/ and /d/. The following guide offers an introduction of phonics instruction:

Introduction	**Examples**
Initial consonants	s, t, m, n, p
Short vowel and consonant	-it, -in, -at, -an
Consonant blends	-st, -bl, -dr
Digraphs	-th, -ph, -sh, -ch
Long vowels	ear, eat, oar, oat
Final (silent) e	site, mine, lane
Variant vowels and dipthongs	-au, -oo, -ow, -ou, -oi
Silent letters and inflectional endings	-kn, -gn, -wr, es, s

Effective phonics instruction begins with focusing on the overall literacy experiences of the students and connecting these experiences to further their literacy development. Best practices in teaching will work to establish a student's prior phonics knowledge, if there is any at all. Educators can differentiate their instruction based on their students' unique needs and background knowledge of phonics. Creating phonics activities that ensure students are actively engaged and motivated is key to overall success in literacy development.

Once children have mastered the relationship that exists between the names, shapes, sounds of letters, and letter combinations, educators may begin a more implicit instructional approach by incorporating the children's current phonics awareness with simple basal readers that focus on basic monosyllabic words. Grouping monosyllabic words according to their initial sounds continues to be an effective approach to instruction as the students advance in their understanding and application of phonics. When educators combine or further this practice with that of identifying the names of the initial letters in the words, children are likely to have more success with overall literacy development.

A word wall with simple consonant-vowel-consonant words in alphabetical order acts as a visual reference to help strengthen a child's literacy development:

Word Wall

A	B	C
add	ball	car
age	bean	clean
ant	black	cub

At this stage, educators begin laying the foundation for reading readiness. Children begin listening to others read and start to recognize familiar sounds within the words being read. They independently practice sounding out words and will soon learn how to independently segment, blend, and manipulate the individual sounds in each newly acquired word.

When a child demonstrates phonological awareness and a clear understanding of how phonics works, they are ready to further their literacy development with *word analysis*. Word analysis is an effective study that helps students acquire new vocabulary. *Morphemes* are when words are broken down into their smallest units of meaning. Each morpheme within words carry specific meanings, therefore adding to children's understanding of entire words. When children begin to recognize key morphemes—especially prefixes and suffixes—they are beginning to demonstrate word analysis skills, which is a critical foundation in literacy development.

Word analysis helps children to read and comprehend complex reading materials, including informational texts. It is essential for vocabulary development. Word analysis skills also help children clarify the meaning of unknown words, figurative language, word relationships, and nuances in word meaning with the use of context clues.

Some effective instructional strategies to teach word analysis skills include Universal Design for Learning (UDL), studying words according to a subject theme, using diagrams and graphic organizers, and pre-teaching and reviewing new vocabulary on a regular basis. UDL involves the modeling of how to analyze new words by breaking them down into their individual morphemes and studying each morpheme separately. Once each morpheme in a given word has been identified and defined, students put the morphemes back together in order to understand the word in its entirety.

The following is a word analysis study of the word *astronaut*:

Word	**Morpheme 1**	**Morpheme 2**	**Word Meaning**
astronaut	astro—Greek origin, roughly translates to anything relating to the stars and outer space	naut—Greek origin, roughly translates to "sailor"	a sailor of outer space

Studying words according to a shared theme is another effective word analysis strategy. For instance, when studying mathematics, educators may focus on words that contain the same prefix, such as *kilometer*, *kilogram*, and *kilowatt*. Common suffixes in science include *microscop*e, *telescope*, and *macroscope*.

Diagrams and graphic organizers provide students with visual clues to contrast and compare word meanings. From organizational charts and mind maps to Venn diagrams and more, visual aids help students readily see and analyze the similarities and differences in various word meanings.

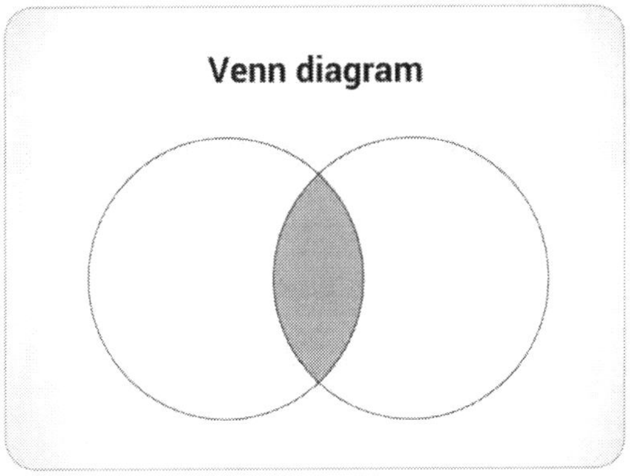

With the introduction to new topics of discussion or a new theme to any subject area, it is likely that there will also be an introduction to new, unfamiliar words. Both educators and students will benefit from a formal introduction to these new words prior to the lesson. Pre-teaching new vocabulary increases vocabulary acquisition and allows children to become comfortable and familiar with new terms ahead of the lesson. Pre-teaching new vocabulary has also been shown to reduce unnecessary stress and time that would otherwise be taken to stop lessons in order to explain unfamiliar words.

Key Details and the Central Idea of an Informational Text

Informational texts appear in several forms, including expository texts, persuasive texts, procedural texts, and nonfiction narratives. As early as kindergarten, children are encouraged to read a variety of informational texts. Placing an assortment of texts in the classroom library, hanging posters on classroom walls that promote a wide range of topics, and providing children with ample time and opportunity to explore any number of subjects, has shown to have a very positive impact on reading comprehension and overall literacy skill development. Informational texts provide children an opportunity to explore and develop a better understanding of the world around them. Taking this one step further, by allowing children to choose topics of informational texts that pique their curiosity, educators help children develop a more positive attitude toward reading and writing.

All informational texts typically include five key elements:

- The author's purpose(s)
- A major idea(s)
- Supporting detail(s)
- Visual or graphic aid(s)
- Vocabulary

Author's Purpose

Expository texts typically share information about a given topic. *Persuasive texts* aim to convince readers to think or act a certain way, and *procedural texts* generally give step-by-step or "how-to" instructions in a given discipline. *Nonfiction narratives* tell a true story, perhaps to inspire, educate, bring awareness to a subject, or simply chronicle an important historical event. In order for students to become independent readers and draw their own conclusions about what they read, it is critical that they learn to discern the *author's purpose*.

One obvious approach to teaching children how to reveal an author's purpose is to simply ask children why they think the author wrote this information. These types of open-ended class discussions allow children to express their ideas, explore theories, and consider what others have to say on the subject. Educators can record various answers and then ask the children to return to the text as detectives, looking for clues that support each theory.

Another approach to uncovering the author's purpose is for students to take a closer look at the written structure of the text and the vocabulary usage. For example, is the text's structure written in chronological order, simply listing events as they occurred? Does the text open up with a problem that is then resolved? Is the author using cause/effect or compare/contrast vocabulary? Learning about the structure of the text gives great insight into the author's purpose.

When children develop reading fluency, they are able to read a text with minimal to no errors, with consistent speed, and with appropriate expression, and they learn to connect with what they are reading on a personal level. As children read through an informational text, educators may ask how the students are feeling. Did they begin feeling one way and end up feeling another by the end of the text? When children examine their own personal feelings with regard to what they have read, they will be in a better position to explore the author's purpose.

Once children have had several opportunities to explore the author's purpose using a variety of informational texts, prompting them to write their own informational texts will help them to develop and strengthen a better understanding about writing with a purpose. Perhaps they can write a procedural text that lists the steps in how to ride a bike, or they can write a persuasive paper to try to convince their teacher that extra free time during the school day stimulates learning.

Learning to identify an author's purpose connects children with their reading on a deeper level. Instead of believing everything they read, they will begin to understand that there are many reasons why authors write, and they will further understand that they possess the ability to draw their own conclusions and make their own decisions on any given topic.

Major Idea

Some children struggle with identifying the main idea of an informational text. Identifying the main idea of a text requires that the reader understand the entire text and is able to zero in on one central, overarching idea amongst a sea of other information. The ability to sort through the entire text and arrive at the main idea takes a considerable amount of effort and practice for beginning readers.

Before prompting students to locate the main idea of a given text or passage, educators must first explain what the main idea actually is. Here are some guidelines, tips, and tricks to follow that will help children identify the main idea:

Identifying the Main Idea
The most important part of the text
Text title and pictures may reveal clues
Opening sentences and final sentences may reveal clues
Key vocabulary words that are repeatedly used may reveal clues

Providing students with simple lists of related vocabulary may be a logical starting point when teaching how to recognize a main idea. For instance, on a large chart, educators may list several fruits, vegetables, snacks, and meals, and then prompt the children to explain what they have in common. This also works well with a set of images, pictures, or photographs that all represent the same idea. After repeated practice, children will begin to strengthen their ability to center in on the main idea that connects all the elements on the list.

Once children begin to identify and demonstrate a clear understanding of the main idea in simple lists, educators may wish to introduce simple texts that gradually increase in complexity.

Supporting Details

Supporting details of texts are defined as those elements of a text that help readers make sense of the main idea. They either qualitatively and/or quantitatively describe the main idea, strengthening the reader's understanding.

Using simple sentences is an effective instructional approach when introducing children to supporting details. Educators may write out a simple sentence and ask the children to underline the main idea, as in the sentence that follows:

The *apple* is hard, red, and juicy.

Once the main idea, the apple, is accurately identified, educators can now ask children to locate words that describe or support this main idea and highlight/circle each supporting word:

The *apple* is hard, red, and juicy.

Simple sentence exercises will gradually become simple paragraphs and, eventually, full texts in which children are challenged with the task of locating the main idea and the supporting details. Children must learn to differentiate between trivial and supporting details by evaluating whether or not the detail in question further quantifies or qualifies the main idea. If the detail does neither, it is likely not important enough to be considered a supporting detail and can be left alone.

Graphic organizers can also be a helpful tool when working with main ideas and supporting details. There are many graphic organizers that help students to organize their analysis into clear and visible representations. The following are examples of graphic organizers that are commonly used when teaching the main idea and supporting details.

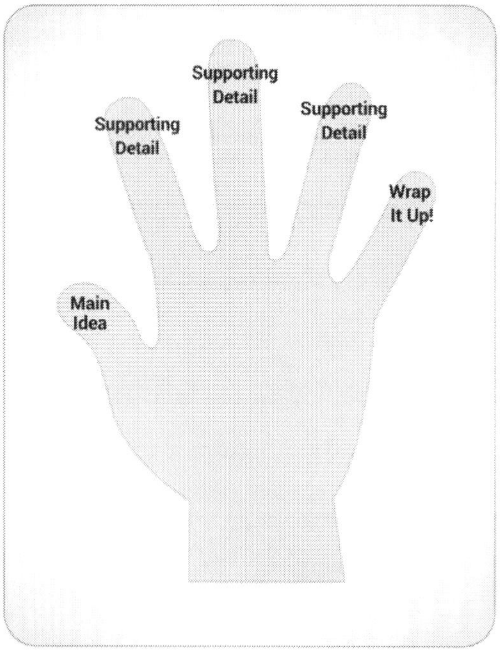

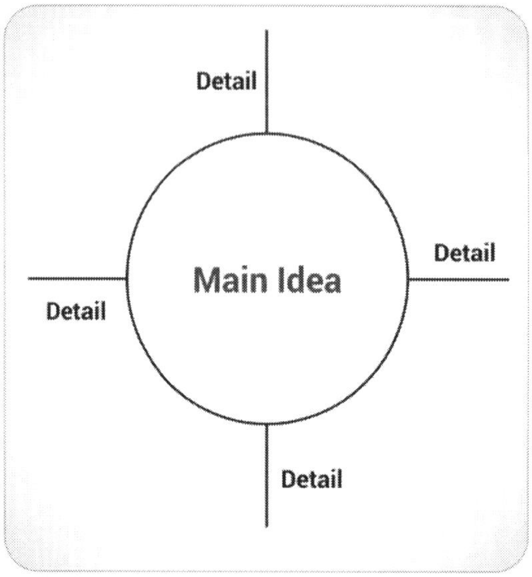

Children who demonstrate the ability to accurately identify a text's main idea and supporting details can further strengthen these skills by attempting to write their own texts with a main idea and supporting details. Likewise, graphic organizers can be used as tools that help children to organize their thoughts and ideas before they begin this writing process.

Visual or Graphic Aids

Authors of informational texts will often employ the use of visual or graphic aids in strategic locations throughout the text in order to strengthen the reader's understanding of the topic at hand. Visual aids can provide an overview of key information, illustrate relationships among important text elements, and summarize the main idea. Visual aids are generally colorful and catch students' attention; they help to simplify what could be potentially complicated information. There are a multitude of visual aids that are frequently used in informational texts, including models, graphs, charts, tables, maps, drawings, photographs, and time lines. Some visual aids also involve a side bar, which defines key vocabulary necessary to understand the topic.

In most instances, children merely need to look at the visual aid to make an instant connection. The implementation of graphic aids in writing reduces instructional time and strengthens comprehension. During read alouds and guided reading sessions, educators may wish to model how to extract meaning from visual aids by connecting the graphic to specific elements in the text. Before reading begins, educators have students skim through the pages to find the visual aids and predict what the text may be about based on the text's graphics. Therefore, visual aids may often help students to identify the text's main idea.

The time it requires to read and process the written text is considerably longer than the time it takes to derive meaning from the graph. Helping students to identify and derive meaning from visual aids will help to strengthen their reading comprehension skills and overall literacy development.

Vocabulary

Vocabulary used throughout informational texts is generally quite different than vocabulary found in fictional print. For this reason, it is imperative that educators help children strengthen and increase their vocabulary inventory so that they can eventually become successful at reading and understanding informational text.

For instance, educators can point out *signal words* throughout texts to help children more readily and accurately identify the author's purpose. There are specific vocabulary words that authors employ that spotlight the author's intent. For instance, if authors wish to list examples to support a main idea, they may use vocabulary such as *for example*, *such as*, or *as illustrated*. When displaying the chronological order of events, authors may use *first*, *lastly*, *before*, and *finally*. Some common compare and contrast vocabulary words include *but*, *same as*, *similar to*, *as opposed to*, and *however*. There are several key phrases that signal cause and effect relationships, including *because of*, *as a result of*, and *in order to*.

Using word walls and personal dictionaries, sorting vocabulary words according to theme, introducing text maps, and teaching children to become familiar with sidebars and glossaries in informational texts, educators will help expand their students' vocabulary and strengthen their ability to read and comprehend informational texts successfully.

Inferences Made from Text Supported with Appropriate Evidence

Although related to predictions and the finding of factual information, *inferences* refer to the ability to make logical assumptions based on contextual clues. People of all ages make inferences about the world around them on a daily basis but may not be aware of what they are doing. Even young children may infer that it is likely cold outside if they wake up and their bedroom is chilly or the floor is cold. While being driven somewhere on the highway and a child notices a person at the side of the road with a parked car, that child will likely infer that the individual is having car problems and is awaiting some assistance. Therefore, the challenge for educators is not necessarily teaching children how to infer, but rather demonstrating how this skill they already use can be transferred into the study of various texts.

One effective introductory strategy may be to set up scenarios within the classroom and challenge the children to infer what is happening. For instance, the educator may arrive at school pretending to have a cold without saying anything. By placing a personal box of tissues on the desk along with a nasal spray and frequently sneezing, the teacher is challenging the students to infer that he or she not feeling well. Once the children begin to understand that making inferences is indeed similar to detective work by collecting key evidence, the educator can now introduce more inanimate objects like photographs, pictures, or diagrams void of explanatory language. The children's task would be to study the visual aids to try to infer what the subject is about. Educators can assist the children initially by asking questions aloud, modeling how to arrive at a logical inference. For example, the teacher might hold up a picture of a school in which all children are gathered in the playground and grouped according to their classes. Upon closer examination, the children might spot a fire truck parked at the side of the road and may infer that the school had a fire drill or an actual fire.

As the children progress in their ability to infer based on picture clues, it is time to transfer their new skill to texts. Educators may wish to begin with inference challenges in which students are prompted to write short stories about specific events—without directly mentioning the event. For instance, if a child is interested in swimming, they may write about the ideal temperature of the water, backstroke, freestyle, full laps, and so on without ever mentioning the word *swimming*. Other children in the class will then be prompted to read the short story and infer what the text is about. The children must examine the clues in the text, make an inference, and support the inference with evidence from the text:

> In the second paragraph, it says that the water was relatively warm, so it was easy to finish a full lap. This must mean that the person was swimming in the water.

The more initial practice children receive before moving into more complicated texts, the most success they will have in making accurate inferences and, in turn, the more fun they will have acting as text detectives.

Key Claims from Textual Evidence

The ability to identify significant claims made by the author and to support those claims with evidence found within the text is integral to the development of reading comprehension and critical thinking skills. Educators need to introduce key vocabulary words and phrases that authors use when stating and supporting claims. These vocabulary terms can be added to an ever-changing and expanding classroom word wall, incorporated into personal dictionaries and captured on charts to further classroom discussions. Once children begin to identify key words and phrases as indicators of claims and claim evidence, they are ready to begin the more complex task of evaluating these claims.

When children can identify claims and show evidence that supports the claims, educators may wish to initiate a class discussion on whether or not these claims are valid. For instance, prompting a reader's background knowledge and personal experiences on the topic, examining the author's expertise on the subject, weighing any possible cultural or personal bias the author may have, and comparing/ contrasting the author's claims to claims made by other authors on the same subject will help children develop objectivity as they read.

Summarization of Information

While summarizing information from a text seems like an easy concept at first, it is more complex than one thinks. *Summarizing* involves the ability to extract the most important elements in writing, to eliminate elements of lesser importance, to reorganize the information, to rewrite information in one's own words, and, finally, to condense the writing into a significantly smaller text than that of the original. Thus, learning to summarize consists of many individual skills that all converge and overlap. There are two forms of summary: (1) summaries that aid the reader in understanding the text and (2) summaries that aid others in their understanding of the text.

Summarizing should be explicitly taught beginning in the primary school years with continual reinforcement and gradual introduction to more complex texts as students progress. In order to summarize effectively, children need to demonstrate the following abilities:

- Text comprehension
- Identification of main idea
- Elimination of inconsequential information
- Ability to condense
- Ability to paraphrase
- Ability to organize writing in a logical order

Personal Summaries

Educators are encouraged to first assist children in summarizing texts as a means to strengthen personal comprehension. For instance, when children are able to identify a text's main idea, state that idea in their own words, and back up that main idea with supporting evidence, they are learning to summarize, and their comprehension undoubtedly strengthens.

Summarizing for oneself is also an invaluable tool for studying and memorizing, which children will use throughout their academic careers. When students summarize for themselves, the goal is to strengthen overall comprehension of the text, arrive at the author's point of view, and isolate the main idea. Since the summary is intended to be only for the student, there is no need to pay particular attention to spelling, grammar, or sentence structure. Students are learning to make personal notes for the purpose of comprehension strengthening and, possibly, memorization for upcoming tests.

Summaries for Others

Once children have demonstrated a clear ability to summarize a variety of texts for their own understanding, educators may begin to introduce them to the skill of *summarizing for others*. This involves a more complex approach to summarization. Now that students have ownership of the given text, they inherit the challenge of explaining the text's meaning to an audience. In addition to extracting the main idea, eliminating unimportant text elements, reorganizing and condensing the text, and paraphrasing, students must now pay close attention to the summary's length, the mechanics of writing, and the audience. For example, are students writing to classmates to help them better understand the text? Are they writing the summary for their teacher, in an effort to demonstrate their ability to summarize? Since this type of summarization involves a polished finish, children must also employ proofreading and revision skills.

Educators who are introducing summarization for the first time should focus on less complex texts that involve familiar subject matter, and the texts should be well organized, with titles, possible subtitles, and easily identifiable main ideas. Allowing children to refer to the text as often as possible while learning to summarize is also an important teaching strategy. Children at the early stages of summarizing should not be expected to have memorized and clearly understood what they have read. Sometimes children need to reread the same text several times before beginning a summarization. By explicitly teaching children how to recognize signaling devices, educators help them summarize and isolate a text's main idea. Some signaling devices may be found in an introductory or summary statement or specific words or phrases that have been placed in italics, bold print, or are underlined.

The more advanced students become with summarizing texts, the greater their comprehension and ability to apply what they learn will be.

Literary Analysis and Genres

Structural Elements of Literature Across Genres

There are several *genres* of literature including poetry, fiction, nonfiction, and drama. Each genre has specific structural elements. Although there are elements that are shared by more than one genre of literature—such as character, setting, and plot, which are found in both fiction and drama—there are also clear differences in other genres. For instance, the structural elements in nonfiction often consist of cause and effect, sequence, or compare and contrast.

<u>Structural Elements in Drama</u>
A drama, or a play, is almost exclusively delivered as a dialogue and performed live on a stage. The audience observes the story unfolding as opposed to reading it in a book. The actors or actresses in a drama follow written scripts, which are divided into acts and further divided into scenes. The only written material generally given to the audience is the cast of characters, which lists all the character names with an accompanying brief description of their role in the play. This is the only written assistance the audience will receive, so it is imperative that they read through the cast of characters and then carefully follow each scene in the play to understand the story.

Stage directions in a drama refer to the directions or descriptions given to the actors in each scene. They are often presented in italics or in parentheses to differentiate the directions from the dialogue. Stage directions may tell actors where to stand, what direction to face, how to deliver lines, and whom to address.

<u>Structural Elements in Poetry</u>
Generally speaking, *rhyme* goes hand and hand with the study of poetry and involves the repetition of similar sounds. Sounds may rhyme at the end of every two or more lines, referred to as *end rhyme*, or may even rhyme in the middle of a line, referred to as *internal rhyme*. The following offers examples of both:

> I went to school *today*,
>
> Not wanting to leave the *house*,
>
> And as I passed the *day*,
>
> I remained as quiet as a *mouse*.
>
> In rain or *shine*, your house or *mine*,
>
> We'll meet *again*, my dear *friend*.

The first poem demonstrates the example of end rhyme. The second example demonstrates internal rhyme.

Meter is the rhythm of the syllables within a poem. Each type of meter equates to the specific number of syllables and, possibly, the way the syllables are stressed. There are five basic meters: *iambic*, *trochaic*, *spondaic*, *anapestic*, and *dactylic*. Recognizing the meter within poetry helps readers understand the poem's rhythm and guides the reader in how to read the poem with the poet's intended emphasis. Meter also helps poets develop and maintain the structural elements within the poem.

Organizational Structures of Informational Text

Organizational structures found in informational text differ from structures found in fictional works. It is important for educators to teach children how to recognize and use these structures to further their knowledge of a given discipline.

<u>Cause and Effect</u>
When an author unfolds a cause and effect relationship within a given text, readers must work to uncover what has happened and why. Sometimes, the cause and effect relationships are melancholy, but they can also be positive. Before asking children to locate the cause and effect relationship within an informational text, it is first important to define the terms and then provide key examples with which the students can relate. For instance, a teacher might ask the children what happens after it rains. There will undoubtedly be a variety of responses, from *the ground becomes wet* to *the flowers grow*. From this simple exercise, educators can begin to model the relationship between the *cause*—why something happened—and the *effect*—what happened as a result.

Showing pictures, photographs, and other visual aids, and gradually encouraging children to use key graphic organizers will also help them solidify their understanding of cause and effect relationships. Teaching key vocabulary words that specifically relate to cause and effect are also effective instructional strategies. Educators should ensure that these vocabulary lists become incorporated into classroom word walls and personal dictionaries.

<u>Problem and Solution</u>
Similar to cause and effect, the *problem and solution pairing* that often appears in informational texts refers to something that has happened that requires a solution. Although both cause and effect and problem and solution involve related events that occur before and after, cause and effect situations do not necessarily seek a solution to a problem. They seek to identify the impact one or more events have had on something else. In contrast, the problem and solution pairing in a text refers specifically to a problem that has occurred that requires a solution:

Problem	**Solution**
Scraped a knee	Wash, dry, and apply bandage
Unprepared for upcoming test	Practice and study
No clean clothes to wear	Do some laundry

Figurative Language

Figurative language is a specific style of speaking or writing that uses tools for a variety of effects. It entertains readers, ignites imagination, and promotes creativity. Instead of writing in realistic terms or literal terms, figurative language plays with words and prompts readers to infer the underlying meaning. There are seven types of figurative language:

Type	**Definition**	**Example**
Personification	Giving animate qualities to an inanimate object	The tree stood tall and still, staring up at the sky.
Simile	The comparison of two unlike things using connecting words	Your eyes are as blue as the ocean.
Metaphor	The comparison of two unlike things without the use of connecting words	She was in the twilight of her years.
Hyperbole	An over-exaggeration	I could eat a million of these cookies!
Alliteration	The patterned repetition of an initial consonant sound	The bunnies are bouncing in baskets.
Onomatopoeia	Words that are formed by using the very sound associated with the word itself	"Drip, drip, drip" went the kitchen faucet.
Idioms	Common sayings that carry a lesson or meaning that must be inferred	That math work was a piece of cake!

Interpretation

Since idioms and hyperboles are commonly used in everyday speech, educators may wish to introduce them early.

> I'm so tired that I could sleep forever!—Hyperbole
>
> He's not playing with a full deck!—Idiom

Other forms of figurative language can be found in poetry and in children's stories. As educators come across figurative speech, they can prompt children's critical thinking skills by asking what they think the author meant by those words or that particular sentence. Giving concrete examples of each style and challenging children to attempt writing their very own creative sentences will strengthen their understanding and application of figurative language.

Multicultural Texts

Awareness of multicultural education is vital in the fast-changing demographics of United States education. Multicultural education seeks to ensure that all students have a fair and equal chance at education. Educators should keep in mind the importance of teaching various historical perspectives and an awareness of global issues and cultural consciousness. Educators should always seek to display cultural sensitivity when implementing activities or assigning multicultural texts.

In addition to different cultures, multicultural education also seeks to include all those who are considered to be in underrepresented groups, such as girls, students of different ethnicities, and students with disabilities. Taking assessment of the students in the classroom and their various needs are essential in developing a multicultural curriculum.

There is a multitude of options to choose from for educators looking to incorporate multicultural reading in their classrooms. Below is a brief list of possible texts that deal with multicultural sensitivity:

Preschool:

- *I Love Saturdays y Domingos* by Alma Flor Ada
- *Wild Berries* by Julie Flett
- "My People" by Langston Hughes
- *Niño Wrestles the World* by Yuyi Morales
- *Cradle Me* by Debby Slier
- *Pecan Pie Baby* by Jacqueline Woodson
- *The Twins' Blanket* by Hyewon Yum

Ages Five to Seven:

- *Little Roja Riding Hood* by Susan Middleton Elya
- *Honey, I Love, and Other Poems* by Eloise Greenfield
- *Take Me Out to the Yakyu* by Aaron Meshon
- *Shades of Black: A Celebration of Our Children* by Sandra L. Pinkney
- *Jingle Dancer* by Cynthia Leitich Smith
- *What Can You Do With a Paleta?* by Carmen Tafolia

Ages Seven to Nine:

- *My Name is Maria Isabel* by Alma Flor Ada
- *Shin-chi's Canoe* by Nicola Campbell
- *The Year of the Book* by Andrea Cheng
- *Crouching Tiger* by Ying Chang Compestine
- *The People Could Fly: American Black Folktales* by Virginia Hamilton
- *Wings* by Christopher Myers
- *Rickshaw Girl* by Mitali Perkins
- *Indian Shoes* by Cynthia Leitich Smith
- *Diego Rivera: His World and Ours* by Duncan Tonatiuh

Ages Nine to Twelve:

- *The Birchbark House* by Louise Erdrich
- *Inside Out & Back Again* by Thanhha Lai
- *Where the Mountain Meets the Moon* by Grace Lin
- *Ninth Ward* by Jewell Parker Rhodes
- *Star in the Forest* by Laura Resau
- *Boys without Names* by Kashmira Sheth
- *The Composition* by Antonio Skarmeta
- *One Crazy Summer* by Rita Williams-Garcia

Student Response to Text

When educators introduce a text within a classroom, there are a few ways to identify and evaluate appropriate techniques for students to respond to that text. Giving students a chance to respond to readings helps them feel included in the classroom setting and inspires them to administer focus into the reading and instruction. Below are a few different techniques to incorporate student response to text in the classroom.

Think-Pair-Share
Think-pair-share is a reading response technique that educators use to allow every student a chance to voice their ideas. After the teacher reads a few pages of a text, the teacher asks the students to think about a concept that was just read, or may have the students compare those few pages with another text that was read before in class. After the students think about their ideas, they turn to a partner and share their ideas with their partner. The teacher goes around the room and asks each of the students what their ideas were. This technique allows all children to share their ideas to each other and the teacher, and does not put pressure on the students less reluctant to share in front of a group. This technique also motivates students to think about a topic independently as well as build oral communication skills.

Reading Response Journals
Educators use reading response journals in order to increase reading comprehension amongst their students. These journals give students the freedom and confidence to respond to the text in their own way, enhancing their reading capacity as well as writing capacity. Journals can be anything from a few papers sewn together to a store-bought notebook. Some teachers have students write or take notes as they read, and some teachers use the letter format. The letter format is where students write a letter to the author or character in their journal. This facilitates student response to text and allows them to critically think about the content they've read.

Evidence-Based Discussion
Evidence-based discussion is a strategy used in the classroom to facilitate student response to a topic using objective data to back up that response. For example, let's look at a class of fourth graders. The students are given a topic with a research question, and then they are asked to do some research on that topic and focus on the research question. The students go to the library and write down facts and examples they learn about their topic on note cards. Once they come back to class, they share their responses with the class one at a time using the information they've gathered from the library. Evidence-based discussion provides students with the ability to confidently share their ideas with facts and allows students to participate in a discussion where they built upon one another's ideas.

Language and the Writing Process

Developmental Stages of Writing

Developmental stages of writing are stages students go through when learning to write fluently. Not all students will be on the same stage as their peers. The developmental stages of writing are fluid, and the stages have been merged over the years.

Below is a list of stages that are the most common in writing development.

- Scribbling: Younger students use scribbling to express their ideas. This is a mock-writing stage, and represents a random assortment of lines and marks on paper. These marks may resemble drawing, although students at this stage do not have the coordination to form letters.
- Letter-Like Symbols: At this stage, students write symbols that look similar to letters and numbers. Spacing between letters is non-existent at this stage.
- Strings of Letters: In the strings-of-letters stage, students begin to write capital letters side-by-side without spacing, although the letters usually do not form actual words. Students at this stage are becoming aware of the sound-to-symbol relationship.
- Beginning Sounds Emerge: Though students may not use spacing in this stage, they start seeing the differences between letters and words.
- Consonants Represent Words: At this stage, the letters may have spaces between them, and the writing, though it may still be illegible, begins to look like small sentences strung together. Uppercase and lowercase letters may be mixed together.
- Initial, Middle, and Final Sounds: Student writing at this stage is legible. Familiar words may be spelled out, such as names of family members or pets. Most words are written the way they sound, instead of the way they are actually spelled.
- Transitional Phases: At this stage, writing is legible and looks more like conventional spelling.
- Standard Spelling: Students at this stage in their writing spell most words correctly and understand that root words, compound words, and contractions can be used in other similar wording.

Producing Clear and Coherent Writing Using the Stages of the Writing Process

<u>Writing Skills Development</u>
Children who receive regular and consistent encouragement to write and whose environment is rich with writing materials and resources will be more apt to strengthen their writing proficiency. Research suggests that at least an hour a day of writing practice, including skilled instruction, is necessary. Writing projects should be chosen that also involve the subjects of science, social studies, reading, or mathematics to give students well-rounded views of the purposes for writing. Piece by piece, students practice writing skills in all subjects, and collectively it should add up to more than an hour a day.

<u>POWER Strategy for Teaching the Writing Process</u>
The POWER strategy helps all students to take ownership of the writing process by prompting them to consciously focus on what they are writing.

The POWER strategy is an acronym for the following:

- Prewriting or Planning
- Organizing
- Writing a first draft
- Evaluating the writing
- Revising and rewriting

Prewriting and Planning
During the Prewriting and Planning phase, students learn to consider their audience and purpose for the writing project. Then they compile information they wish to include in the piece of writing from their background knowledge and/or new sources.

Organizing
Next, students decide on the organizational structure of their writing project. There are many types of organizational structures, but the common ones are: story/narrative, informative, opinion, persuasive, compare and contrast, explanatory, and problem/solution formats. Often graphic organizers are an important part of helping students complete this step of the writing process.

Writing
In this step, students write a complete first draft of their project. Educators may begin by using modeled writing to teach this step in the process. It may be helpful for beginning writers to work in small groups or pairs. Verbalizing their thoughts before writing them is also a helpful technique.

Evaluating
In this stage, students reread their writing and note the segments that are particularly strong or need improvement. Then they participate in peer editing. They ask each other questions about the piece. The peers learn to provide feedback and constructive criticism to help the student improve. Scoring rubrics are a helpful tool in this phase to guide students as they edit each other's work.

Revising and Rewriting
Finally, the student incorporates any changes she or he wishes to make based on the evaluating process. Then students rewrite the piece into a final draft and publish it however it best fits the audience and purpose of the writing.

<u>6+1 Traits Strategy for Teaching Writing</u>
6+1 Traits is a model for teaching writing that uses a common language to explain the standards for what good writing looks like. Students learn to evaluate whether these expectations have been met in their own writing and then edit, revise, and rewrite accordingly. The 6+1 Traits are the characteristics that make writing readable and effective no matter what genre of writing is being used. The 6+1 Traits are as follows:

- Ideas
- Organization
- Voice
- Word choice
- Sentence fluency
- Conventions
- Presentation

The Ideas Trait
This trait is the content of the writing. This is where students learn to select an important topic for their writing. They are taught to narrow down and focus their idea. Then they learn to develop and elaborate on the specific idea. Finally, they investigate and discover the information and details that best convey the idea to others.

The Organization Trait

This trait teaches students how to build the framework for their writing. They choose an organizational strategy or purpose for the writing and build the details upon that structure. There are many purposes for writing, and they all have different frameworks. However, there are commonalities that students can learn to effectively organize their writing so it makes sense to the reader. Students learn to invite the reader into their work with an effective introduction. They are taught how to create thoughtful transitions between ideas and key points in their writing and how to create logical and purposeful sequencing of ideas. Finally, students are taught how to create a powerful conclusion to their piece that summarizes the information but leaves the reader with something to think about. Many students are inclined to jump into their writing without a clear direction for where it is going. The organization trait teaches them to plan and purpose their writing toward excellence.

The Voice Trait

This is the trait that gives the writing a sense of individuality and connection to the author. It shows that the writing is meaningful and that the author cares about it. It is what makes the writing uniquely the author's own. It is how the reader begins to know the author and what she or he "sounds like." Students learn to recognize "voice" in some writing samples and find their own "voice" to apply to their work. Students are taught to speak on an emotional level directly to their readers. Students experiment with matching their style to the audience and the purpose of the writing. Students are taught to enjoy taking risks and putting their personal touch into their work.

The Word Choice Trait

This trait gives writing a sense of functional communication through precise language that is rich and enlightening. If the work is narrative, the words create images in the mind's eye; if the work is descriptive, the words clarify and expand thoughts and ideas. If the work is persuasive, the words give new perspective and invite thought. Students learn not only to choose exceptional vocabulary, but also to hone their skills for using ordinary words well. Students are taught to describe things using striking language. They learn to use exact language that is accurate, concise, precise, and lively.

The Sentence Fluency Trait

When sentences are built to fit together and move with one another to create writing that is easy to read aloud, the author has written with fluency. Students learn to eliminate awkward word patterns that otherwise would encumber the reader. Sentences and paragraphs start and stop in precisely the right places so that the writing moves well. Students are taught to establish a flow, develop a rhythm, and give cadence to their work. They edit their sentences to vary the structure and length. Educators can teach fluency through reading aloud beautifully written examples and contrasting them with less fluent work.

The Conventions Trait

Here the focus changes from creation of the piece to preparation for the reader. Instead of revision that the first five traits teach, this trait teaches editing skills. The students learn to make their writing clear and understandable through the use of proper grammar, spelling, capitalization, and punctuation. Students are taught the differences between revision and editing. They learn basic editing marks and symbols. Teachers can assist students to learn conventions through guided editing and regular practice. Expectations for correctness need to be kept developmentally appropriate. If immediate correctness is expected, students may shy away from experimenting and taking risks.

The Presentation Trait
This trait focuses on the final appearance of the work. Presentation is not a concern during the process of the other six traits, nor must perfect presentation be expected for every work a student does. Students are taught to make their work inviting and accessible to the reader of the end product. They learn to show they care about their writing when it is neat and readable. Students are taught about uniform spacing, legible handwriting, appropriate use of fonts and sizes, and how to use bullets, numbers, headings, charts, graphs, and pictures to help make the work visually appealing. Students are taught about the publishing process and are given opportunities to showcase their finished products.

<u>Purposeful Writing</u>
Purposeful writing practices have a significant effect on writing development. Purposeful writing refers to intentional writing practices for the purpose of communicating. Through learning to write well, students can begin to use writing as a method of thinking through issues and solving problems. They become more adept with questioning and investigation. Students learn to accurately convey and critique information. They can more readily express real or imagined experiences to others. Through the varied writing purposes, students learn to focus on what the audience understands, while at other times, they focus on the topic and what information they are trying to impart. Other situations call for focus on their own thinking and feelings. Writing as a whole becomes more effective and accessible as students glean skills for writing with purpose. Some of the writing purposes are as follows:

- Letter writing
- Poetry and Songs
- Creative and Narrative writing
- Informative writing
- Opinion writing
- Persuasive writing
- Compare and Contrast writing
- Explanatory/Expository writing
- Problem and Solution writing

Common Types of Writing

<u>Opinion/Argument</u>
In the early elementary grades, students begin to write simple *opinion pieces*. Acting as a precursor to argumentative and persuasive writing, opinion pieces allow children to express how they feel on a certain subject based on preferences, express their likes and dislikes, and use personal knowledge, without relying too heavily on supporting evidence. Educators encourage children to write opinion pieces with the use of personal journals as well as reflective pieces, connecting personal experiences to various stories read.

In the middle school years and beyond, students will be required to write *argumentative* or *persuasive* pieces of writing, which must involve logical and relevant proof for a claim or an assertion. Regarded as a more sophisticated form of writing, argumentative or persuasive writing works to change the point of view of the readers or ignite a call-to-action response. This form of writing does not shy away from contradicting points of view but, instead, brings them to light and then works to disprove or discredit each opposing claim. Some examples of argumentative or persuasive writing include essays, reviews, and letters to the editor.

Informative

Informative writing comes in many forms, including directions, instructions, definitions, summaries, and more. *Informative writing* works to relay information and advance the reader's understanding of a given subject. If written correctly, the vast majority of informative writing is written in third person to distance the author from relying on personal bias, instead relying on objective facts, historical evidence, and statistics.

Narrative

Almost always written in first person, *narratives* include autobiographies, memoirs, and even fictional stories. Their general purpose is to entertain readers, but some also focus on morals, values, or life lessons. By conveying personal experiences on a given subject or by opening up one's life to the audience, narrative writers create a more intimate connection with readers.

Purpose, Key Components, and Subgenres of Writing

Effective writing, whether for the purpose of persuading, entertaining, or advancing a reader's knowledge, must be well planned and organized. In order to create a powerful piece of writing, authors must adhere to specific structural designs, apply a functional and logical order to their writing, and employ key elements.

The following chart outlines three types of writing and their respective purposes, the structural elements unique to each type of writing, and some examples of subgenres:

	Opinion/Persuasive	**Narrative**	**Informative**
Purpose	To persuade, influence, or prompt a call-to-action response	To entertain or to share a moral when writing fictional narratives To share factual information when writing nonfiction narratives	To convey information and advance a reader's knowledge of a given topic
Key components	Opening statement and point of view Well organized paragraphs with supportive evidence and/or examples Strong concluding statement that reinforces point of view	Fictional narratives: plot, characters, setting, point of view, tone Nonfictional Narratives: introductory paragraph Body: including details and descriptions of events and individuals Conclusion	Introduction Headings and Subheadings Body Conclusion Works Cited
Subgenres	Speeches, letters, reviews, advertisements, essays	Fictional narratives: folktales, fantasy, science-fiction, mystery, drama Nonfictional narratives: autobiographies, biographies, memoirs	How-to books, cookbooks, instructional manuals, textbooks

Effectiveness of Writing Samples

The ultimate goal in every English language arts classroom is to advance students' ability to write coherently and effectively with relative ease. The process of writing begins in the very primary stages and continues throughout a student's academic career. With each passing year, students who receive effective writing instruction and constructive feedback will be able to practice and apply their writing skills to more complex writing assignments. To help students advance in their writing skills, evaluation and assessment of a student's writing should be ongoing and occur during and after instruction of each writing unit.

In order to evaluate the effectiveness of a student's writing, educators should continuously focus on formative and summative assessments that outline clear expectations for the student and the educator. Formative assessments allow both the student and the educator to monitor the student's writing progress with ongoing feedback, discussion, and guidance. For example, after formative assessments, educators may recognize that some students need further instruction on a given skill or would benefit from a modified writing assignment. Summative assessments should only be employed at the very end of an instructional unit and should be used to evaluate how well the student was able to apply specific writing skills to the assigned and completed task. Praising each student's writing progress and allowing time for one-to-one conferences are also valuable instructional techniques that build a student's confidence in the writing process.

The following are examples of assessment practices that help drive instruction and strengthen a student's understanding and application of writing skills for different types of writing.

Effective writing assessments:

- Rating scales and rubrics
- Student logs: student evaluation of writing exercises
- Small groups and peer evaluations
- POWER method: Plan, Organize, Write, Edit, Rewrite (self-assessment)
- Standardized and diagnostic assessments
- Formative assessments
- Summative assessments

Educators who give clear expectations at the beginning, throughout, and at the end of a writing task help students advance their writing skills and become more proficient writers across a number of disciplines and genres. Since there are different types of writing, and considering that writing occurs in all subjects and disciplines, all educators should plan and develop several opportunities for students to practice various types of writing. For example, depending on the students' age and grade level, short, creative, daily writing exercises at the beginning or end of class can be used as an effective opening or closing routine. One day, students can practice narrative writing and the next, persuasive. Teachers can offer an author's chair in which children can read excerpts of their informative, persuasive, or narrative writing, and answer questions from peers relevant to their writing.

Dedicating time to the writing process—with a variety of writing exercises and assignments that occur in every discipline—is paramount to a child's writing acquisition. Effective instructional and assessment practices help foster an appreciation of writing that will continue throughout a student's lifetime.

Writing Pieces for Specific Purposes

Aristotle's Rhetorical Triangle is perhaps the best visual representation to demonstrate the importance of effective writing. Three key areas require the writer's full attention and should be balanced accordingly throughout the writing process:

Ethos refers to the writer's credibility: What are the writer's qualifications regarding the subject of the writing? Is the author using an objective or subjective approach? Are the sources, evidence, and examples in the writing relevant and credible?

Pathos refers to the writer's ability to engage and connect with the intended audience: What details and imagery does the author use to ignite and excite the emotions, imagination, values, and beliefs of the audience?

Logos refers to the validity of the author's message: Is the author's message clearly discernible? Is it logical and well organized?

Each of these three areas are critical to the quality of the writing and require the author's full attention and consideration throughout the writing process, from the preliminary stages to the final published work. Writers are tasked with the responsibility of choosing appropriate language to connect with an audience and choosing a style that maintains interest, which helps the audience understand the writer's purpose and accept the writer's intent. Did the writer succeed, for instance, in entertaining, informing, or persuading the audience?

Conventions of Standard English Grammar, Usage, Mechanics, and Spelling

When learning to speak, listen, read, or write in any language, students are tasked with multiple challenges. The study of the English language is no exception. The conventions of Standard English are complex and require comprehensive study and continual practice.

<u>Parts of Speech</u>

Words within the English language play very unique roles in the formation of coherent sentences. Each English word is categorized into a specific part of speech that carries a unique function. For instance, in order to create simple English language sentences, writers are required to incorporate a noun and a verb. However, when sentences become more complex, additional parts of speech are required. The following chart outlines the parts of speech, along with a brief description of their function within an English sentence and concrete examples.

Part of Speech	Function	Examples
Noun	Identifies a person, place, or thing—can be concrete or abstract	Love, thought, man, woman, child, school, home, integrity, America
Pronoun	Replaces a noun	He, she, it, they
Verb	Depicts an action or state of being	Run, jump, fly, is, are
Adjective	Modifies nouns	Great idea, interesting thought, tall girl
Adverb	Modifies verbs, other adverbs, and adjectives	He has an extremely shy demeanor. She quickly ran away. They walked very clumsily together.
Preposition	Almost always combined with other key words in a sentence in order to indicate a time, location, or movement	At nine o'clock, beside the nightstand, toward the door
Conjunction	Connects words, clauses, or sentences, with related meaning	She and I have similar tastes in food. The teacher handed us the assignment, but we refused to accept it. The dogs ran and played, while the cats sat and stared.
Interjection	Brief exclamations that are added to sentences for emphasis or effect	Wow! I had no idea you could sing! "Boo!" she screamed, as she jumped out from behind the door.

Although an explicit approach to teaching the various parts of speech plays an integral role in the primary grades, it is equally as important that a child learns to recognize these parts of speech when reading and gradually learn to apply them to writing tasks. Being able to recognize and appropriately use various parts of speech demonstrates a growing command of the English language and its conventions.

Correction of Errors

Usage and mechanics are often mistakenly used as interchangeable terms in the educational field. In writing, *usage* refers to a student's ability to choose appropriate words that clearly express an idea, thought, or opinion, or accurately summarize information. Therefore, usage is a very important component of learning to be an effective writer. *Mechanics* involve the writer's ability to use capitalization, ending punctuation, apostrophes, and commas properly. For writing to be both coherent and fluent, mechanics play an important role. *Spelling* is a little less complicated to understand, as it refers to the student's ability to spell decodable and non-decodable words accurately. Learning how and when to correct errors in usage, mechanics, and spelling can be a source of frustration for educators, but it need not be. By creating a logical balance and manageable plan for correcting student writing, educators will help children to be more effective, lifelong writers. The key is balance.

Traditionally, English language educators have focused a great deal of evaluation and feedback on correcting mistakes in usage, mechanics, and spelling alone. Although it is widely accepted that these components are necessary in order to write fluent and coherent sentences, too much focus on correcting these areas—and not enough attention paid to the creative side of writing—may have a negative impact on the writing process.

For example, instead of emphasizing or highlighting every spelling error, educators should ensure that their corrections reflect the task. In other words, if children are given a writing assignment that must incorporate their spelling words, they will undoubtedly expect the educator to correct and evaluate how well they spelled these key words. However, since the assignment also asked the children to use a creative approach to this writing assignment, educators would be doing students a disservice if they did not also offer praise and feedback on the children's writing creativity.

Developing a writing checklist with well-defined goals and sharing this checklist with the class helps educators keep the correction process clear and specific, and it provides children with the opportunity to self-correct and edit their work prior to submission. Using a standardized system of symbols that helps children focus on spelling, capitalization, or word choice is also an effective strategy. Displaying these symbols in a readily accessible place in the classroom will allow them to self-correct and help their peers with the correction process.

For writing to be meaningful and for students to advance in their writing skills, educators should follow a balanced approach to correcting student work with frequent, timely, and appropriate feedback that reflects the task.

Sentence Types

When children begin to connect letters to words and, gradually, words to sentences, those sentences are generally very simple, consisting of one subject and one verb. However, as children advance in their writing fluency, it is paramount to introduce more complex sentences.

Simple sentences are sentences that consist of one subject and one verb:

> I run.
>
> She eats.
>
> They play.

At this stage, educators may prompt children to add some more detail to the simple sentences with adjectives or adverbs:

I run *quickly*.

She eats *very well*.

They play *together*.

Compound sentences contain two independent clauses connected by a conjunction:

I run, but she runs marathons.

I run is an *independent clause*. *She runs marathons* is another independent clause. Each clause could be a complete sentence that stands on its own. However, they are connected with the coordinating conjunction, *but*.

Complex sentences are structures in which two clauses exist, but one clause is *dependent* on the other—that is, it cannot form a sentence in its own right and requires the assistance of the independent clause in order for the sentence to be coherent. Here's an example:

Although he passed the exam, he remained very sad.

He remained very sad is an independent clause, but *Although he passed the exam* is not, as it is dependent on the second part of the sentence in order for the sentence to be coherent.

Compound-complex sentences are structures that employ two or more independent clauses along with at least one dependent clause:

Though I preferred long distance running, I started speed walking, and I enjoyed it very much.

Though I preferred long-distance running is a dependent clause that relies on the independent clause *I started speed walking*. The second independent clause is *I enjoyed it very much*, making this sentence compound-complex.

<u>English Used in Stories, Dramas, or Poems</u>

Register

Despite the fact that a standardized form of English is used in published academic and scientific language, several varieties of spoken and written English also exist. There are differences in how one speaks at home, with friends, to teachers, and to colleagues. In each social setting, a person's *register*—his or her level of formality—will likely change in order to appropriately address the audience. Written registers also vary, depending on a number of factors. For instance, when writing a research paper for professional purposes, formal language will be used, but when writing a letter to a friend, a person is more apt to employ a more casual register. The following statements indicate differences in register:

Call me back when you get this message.

I look forward to hearing back from you at your earliest convenience.

Although both statements express the writer's desire to further communicate with the receiver of the message, the degree of formality, the register, is strikingly different.

Dialect
A language also has several dialects, which are dependent on a great many factors. *Dialects* have specific grammatical rules and patterns that often differ from the standard rules of the language. For instance, within Britain, Canada, and the United States, there are several dialects of the English language. One need only travel from Newfoundland, in eastern Canada, to Louisiana, in the southern United States, to witness a striking difference in how the English language is spoken.

Written dialects and registers also exist. They vary, based on the type of written work, when it was created, where it was written, by whom it was written, for what purposes, and for what audience it was intended. Authors of dramas, stories, and poetry employ the use of dialect for a multitude of reasons. For instance, when authors wish to develop a clear picture of the setting and characters within a drama, dialect plays a significant role. Here are some examples of dialect:

> "Bess, you is my woman now . . ."—from George Gershwin's opera, *Porgy and Bess*

> "That ain't no matter."—from Mark Twain's novel, *Huckleberry Finn*

With the careful and skillful placement of written dialect, the author conveys the character's personality, situation, and social class.

Literal Meaning of Unknown Words

As children advance in their reading fluency, written material will likewise become more complex. Students transition from reading works in which the meaning is literal and direct, to works that require a more critical thinking approach. Educators can facilitate this transition by modeling and demonstrating how to use context clues, syntax, roots, and suffixes to derive meaning from texts.

Context Clues
There are many types of clues found within sentences that help to clarify the meaning of unfamiliar words. Sometimes sentences provide a clear and direct definition of an unfamiliar word:

> Anglophones, *also known as native English speakers,* are found in every corner of the globe.

Teaching children phrases that are used to compare and contrast can also be an effective instructional approach:

> The workday today was laborious *as opposed to* yesterday, which was relaxed and easy going.

If children were unfamiliar with the word *laborious*, they would quickly decipher that it means the opposite of *relaxed* and *easy going*, thanks to the use of the phrase *as opposed to*.

Syntax
There is a certain order to the way in which words are placed in a sentence. For instance, many English sentences follow the pattern of noun + verb + object. The more acquainted children become with syntax, the stronger their ability to recognize parts of speech and how they are interrelated.

Roots and Affixes

Having even a rudimentary understanding of root words and affixes can greatly increase a reader's ability to decipher unknown words. The study of word origins helps children to understand that words are not just arbitrarily put together, but they are often formed like pieces of a puzzle. The following are examples:

- Astronaut
  - Astro: star or celestial body (Greek)
  - Naut: sailor (Greek origin)
- Portable
  - Port: carry
  - Able: ability, capacity

Relationship Between Word Choice and Tone

The words authors choose to use must always be well thought out. Although words carry specific meanings, they also carry *connotations*—emotional feelings that are evoked by the words. Connotation creates the tone of the writing. Some words can be said to be loaded words or trigger words that ignite strong emotional responses in readers. These two sentences offer examples:

My grandfather is a robust, elderly man.

My grandfather is a chubby, old man.

In the first sentence, the adjectives used to describe the grandfather instill positive emotions in the reader. However, in the second sentence, the adjectives instill negative emotions. The *mood* of a writing piece refers to the emotions—positive or negative—the reader feels during and after reading. *Tone* refers to the author's purposeful choice of words, designed to evoke those feelings.

Tiers of Vocabulary

Language is used for effective communication and can be thought of as a social tool. However, since communication is also used in educational and professional circles, language must be flexible enough to meet the challenges of each social structure.

Conversational language is the everyday language spoken at home, with family, and with friends. It is a relaxed form of communication that may carry regional dialects, slang, and even sayings that may only be known by those who are part of those intimate social circles.

Academic language refers to the understanding and application of key vocabulary terms in order to achieve academic success. From their introduction to formal education, students become acquainted with this language tier. It prompts higher-level thinking and challenges students to research, analyze, and push the boundaries of thought, belief, and imagination.

Domain-specific languages are now widely used to refer to computer-based languages—called DSLs—but they are also known as any language system that has been specifically designed to perform a task in a given domain. In domain-specific languages, people are able to communicate concepts unique to that particular domain, avoid redundancy, and stay focused and on target.

Word Choice, Order, and Punctuation

Language is a powerful communication tool that advances thought and facilitates social change. Some features of language that play key roles in communication include word choice, order, and punctuation.

For example, an author can write two sentences that carry a similar meaning but evoke opposing emotions based on word choice. For instance, to write that a person is *intelligent* is a compliment, but to rewrite that sentence and replace *intelligent* with *smart aleck* changes the compliment to an insult. The order of words can also be effective in writing. Instead of beginning a sentence with the subject, authors can begin with the predicate, which instills a sense of mystery and wonder in the reader. The same can be true of fictional stories in which the author begins at the end or in the middle and works backward to unravel the tale. These writing styles create a powerful, dramatic effect on the stories.

Punctuation can also play a key role in how a reader interprets a passage:

> He did do his homework?
>
> He did do his homework!

With the mere change in ending punctuation, the author changes the reader's interpretation of the sentence. Although both sentences use identical words and order, the first sentence infers nothing more than an innocent inquiry, whereas the second infers an emotional, perhaps defensive response.

Literacy Instruction and Assessments

Fostering Students' Participation in Collaborative Conversations with Diverse Partners

<u>Effective and Responsible Practices in Communication with Children</u>

The foundation of a child's academic, social, and emotional success in any classroom lies directly in the educator's ability to use effective communicative interactions. DAP, or Developmentally Appropriate Practice, was designed by researchers who took into consideration what is known about how children develop, as well as what is known about effective early education instruction. Classrooms with effective communication techniques will generally see enthusiastic, engaged children. DAP focuses on these 10 basic principles that aim to help educators build an effective foundation of communication:

- Acknowledgement
- Encouragement
- Immediate and beneficial feedback
- Modeling
- Demonstrating
- Challenging
- Questioning
- Providing effective assistance
- Providing valuable information
- Giving appropriate directions

Acknowledgement

Students are not simply little subjects for educators to enlighten. They are intellectual, social, and emotional beings worthy of recognition and appreciation. Acknowledgement of students begins with understanding where they are coming from and the experiences they bring with them. When a teacher considers prior knowledge before beginning instruction, they are being considerate of the student's time and intellect. They are acknowledging that the student already has the capacity for learning and brings valid experiences and aptitudes that are useful for assimilating new information. The teacher doesn't waste time re-teaching what students have already mastered. Review is necessary, of course, but not to the extent that there is a risk of losing student engagement and interest.

Students come to learn at various stages of intellectual development. In the early stages, there is a duplicity of black-and-white thinking. Multiplicity should come next, where there is some understanding of opinion and perspective. Finally, learning to value evidence and validity helps students understand topics at various complexity levels of complexity. When teachers take this into account, they are acknowledging the students' individuality and honoring their learning needs.

Significant differences exist in the way teaching and learning is conceptualized for various cultures. Values for particular types of learning, the beliefs about best practices, and the role of the teacher/student relationship may be strikingly different from culture to culture. The value of learning itself is a bridge for multicultural connection. When teachers recognize and celebrate cultural differences, they are acknowledging the students at the level of their individual identity.

The social trends and expectations of students and teachers grow and change over generations. The topics and ways that students are learning and teachers are teaching are likely quite different from what they were even a decade ago. Educators cannot expect students to learn the same way from generation to generation. Awareness of generational differences acknowledges the student and his or her perception of the world.

Encouragement

Ideally, students come into classrooms hopeful and willing to take risks. With this in mind, teachers have to develop the kind of classroom that fosters participation and motivation. Here are some ways that teachers can encourage classroom participation:

- Students should be praised. This helps them know they are at the center of learning. They need to feel cared for and valued. Positive behavior should be rewarded and progress acknowledged.
- Students should be allowed to have some control in their lives. Choices should be offered and mistakes forgiven.
- Excellence should be expected from students. High but realistic expectations should be held for them. The effort they put forth should be respected. The learning process, over the end product, should be valued.
- Children should be allowed to be children. There should be much activity and collaboration.
- The fun of learning should be shown to students. They should be encouraged by taking part in the planning of field trips, guest speakers, and other extraordinary activities.
- Students should be made aware of how learning relates to their lives. Teachers should teach to the interests of the students and understand where they are coming from.
- Clear and simple lessons should be presented at a pace they can all follow. Teachers should communicate clearly and enunciate understandably so students do not have to struggle to follow along. Teachers should regularly check on the students' level of understanding.

- A pleasant and comfortable environment free from obvious distractions should be created.

Immediate and Beneficial Feedback
Students need to know what they are doing well and what needs improvement. There should be no mystery about the learning targets. They need a positive self-image fostered by repeated success. Feedback should be positive and specific. Giving clear and effective feedback communicates to the student that her or his work is worthwhile, and that someone cares enough to review and consider it.

Informal feedback is part of formative assessment and should let students know where they are in the learning process and what they should do next. They should be able to formulate a plan for improvement and a vision of the next success they can achieve. Informal feedback is often oral and interactive.

Formal feedback is driven by objectives and rubrics that students should be given prior to a learning task. This gives them a clear goal for the activity and outlines expectations. Formal feedback should be presented in writing or another tangible format. Formal feedback is often summative in nature and may or may not be tied to grades and final assessments.

Feedback strategies are variable. Individualized adjustments can be made regarding timing, amount, mode, and audience. The timing may be immediate or delayed and given frequently or infrequently. Feedback might describe progress on many points or just a few, and it may go into great detail or be generalized. It may be oral, written, or demonstrative. It might be addressed to the individual, a small group, or the entire class. Feedback content is also infinitely variable. Feedback might focus on the work itself, the process, or the student's self-regulation but never on the student personally. Feedback comparisons might be criterion-, norm-, or self-referenced. It may function as a description of the work or an evaluation of the work but should not be judgmental. It can be both positive and negative, but any negative comments should be accompanied by suggestions for improvement. Feedback should be understandable to the student and developmentally appropriate. In some cases, feedback can be too specific so that it becomes difficult for a student to apply it to other situations. It can also be overly general, which does not give the student enough information to help with correction. Finally, feedback should communicate respect, activate motivation, and inspire thought.

Modeling, Explaining, and Demonstrating
In order to learn to read and write well, all children need effective modeling and demonstration. Educators often are content to assign reading and writing tasks and ask students to answer questions about the task in lieu of quality direct interactive instruction.

Modeling is when teachers engage in the activity of reading or writing and the children observe and imitate the procedures and strategies. Children can pick up many skills by simply watching and attempting to copy adult behaviors. Reading aloud is one of the most powerful strategies for teaching in the classroom. When being read to, students are given a model for how reading should sound and how stories are constructed. Talking about the reading selection during and after reading models an appropriate response to text. It also fosters comprehension strategies that children need in order to become effective readers. Writing down main points of the reading selection and taking notes models a function of writing. Designating a time each day for reading aloud highlights the importance of reading. High-quality literature with rich text and content should be chosen to read in the classroom. This models the evaluation of literature and the selection of quality reading material. Response groups should be formed so children have a model for collaboratively comprehending text. Modeling is an essential component of any classroom. However, modeling is not sufficient to give children enough information about how to accomplish the tasks that readers and writers actually need to be proficient.

Explanation is also a key component of classroom instruction. Adults in classrooms spend much time explaining reading and writing methods to students. Unfortunately, students often miss key messages because their attention span isn't long enough to follow wordy explanations. Explanations often involve specialized vocabulary that students may not be able to use to comprehend the instruction. Giving excellent explanations is an essential skill for teachers. Seeing teachers and other children model reading and writing and being told how to read and write is still not sufficient for teaching literacy to many struggling learners. This is where *demonstration* comes into play.

Demonstration is when a teacher not only models and explains how to do a task but also engages in thinking through the task with the students. Effective teachers narrate their thinking processes when modeling a strategy. An effective demonstration includes opportunities for the student to try the strategy with immediate feedback from the teacher. Demonstration is teaching and learning in real-time. Effective demonstration occurs in four steps: preparation, presentation, application, and evaluation.

During *preparation*, a teacher puts the students at ease with the impending learning task. He or she assesses students for prior knowledge of the information. Explaining the importance of the learning task is essential. This step may include an attention-getter or motivational strategy. Finally, preparation includes getting the students ready to observe, ensuring they can see and hear well and have appropriate note-taking supplies.

During *presentation*, the teacher tells, shows, illustrates, explains, questions, and models the task. By carefully and patiently narrating the process step-by-step, stressing key points and learning goals, the teacher presents all information and models all skills needed.

Application is guided practice. It includes students attempting the task and then having the teacher give them immediate feedback. Repetition is often used to solidify the skills. The teacher's job is to narrate the steps taken, to ask questions for a measure of understanding, and to prevent errors.

Evaluation is following up with the learning that occurred during the demonstration. The teacher reviews the objectives and evaluates whether they were covered effectively. Checking for readiness and making sure the students know how to get help if they need it are parts of this step.

Challenging and Questioning

Educators are constantly asking questions. This is because questioning serves a wide range of functions in the classroom. Teachers ask questions to involve and engage students in a lesson. Questions increase interest and motivation. A teacher asks questions to assess prior knowledge and readiness for learning. Questioning can help check for completion of learning tasks. It is key for developing critical thinking skills. Questions might be asked to review or assess mastery of learning goals. Asking questions stimulates independent and collaborative learning and invites insight and forethought.

When questioning, it is important to consider how many questions to ask. During the lesson, it is vital to know when the questions are the most appropriate. Will the questions lend meaning to the instruction? Will the questions cause students to focus on all the information presented or only on the parts that help them answer the question? Will the questions lead away from the topic? It is also important to consider how much wait-time to give students to answer the question before the teacher elaborates or asks a new question. Typically, students need to be afforded at least three seconds to formulate an answer to a question. The way a teacher responds to answers is just as important as the questions themselves. The teacher can affirm a correct response, probe the student for more information, or redirect him if the answer is wrong or misinterpreted.

It can be difficult for teachers to give lessons at the appropriate level of difficulty in a classroom of students who are at varying levels of academic readiness. How does a teacher reach a student who is struggling and one who is above grade level in the same lesson? Knowing the appropriate challenge level is essential for learning in the classroom. If a lesson is too challenging, some students will give up. Conversely, if a lesson is not challenging enough, some students will get bored.

There are many strategies that teachers can use to differentiate lessons for varying challenge levels including:

- Allowing choices
- Integrating technology
- Allowing collaboration
- Accommodating pace
- Assessing prior knowledge
- Encouraging goal setting
- Providing creative teaching
- Allowing independent learning
- Allowing students to explore their interests
- Using self-assessment

Providing Effective Assistance and Valuable Information
Students need assistance and guidance in a classroom; however, knowing how much help to offer is always a balancing act. If teachers give too much assistance, they end up doing the work for students, who then do not learn. If teachers do not offer enough assistance, students become lost, overwhelmed, and do not learn. What does the right amount of help look like for each student? Giving effective assistance to students is a foundational teaching strategy. The goal is to help students become as self-motivated and autonomous as possible.

Autonomy in the classroom begins with establishing clear and consistent classroom procedures. Students should be taught how the classroom runs and how to manage themselves. If a student knows what to do to solve simple problems such as sharpening pencils, teachers do not need to waste valuable teaching time with disruptions. Educators can continue to build autonomy by allowing freedom of choice and giving students some power.

Related to autonomy is the concept of self-motivation. Teachers can help students become self-motivated learners by making learning individualized and accessible to all. Instruction should be differentiated for levels of readiness, for personal interests and aptitudes, and for varied learning styles and multiple intelligences. Offering students choices of learning activities and methods of assessment helps individualize education. Educators should have knowledge of the Universal Design for Learning, which promotes differentiation through considering the following three premises:

- Content should be presented in multiple ways: visual, oral, kinesthetic, etc.
- Students should be able to show their learning in multiple ways: writing, speaking, drawing, acting, etc.
- Engaging students should occur in multiple formats: videos, technology, group work, etc.

Teachers can also foster self-motivation by holding high expectations of students and giving them a sense of competence. When adults expect excellence from students, the students often rise to the occasion. Care must be taken that expectations are developmentally appropriate and attainable, but they should always stretch students to the top of their capabilities. Giving students a sense of competence means learning effective praise techniques. It is best to praise effort (something students can control) over intelligence (something out of their control). Students will gain a sense that they learn through their own hard work.

Giving Appropriate Directions
One of the biggest obstacles to learning is when students do not understand or cannot remember the directions they are given. Present directions in auditory and visual formats and assess for understanding by having students retell them to each other or to the teacher. Some tips for teachers to give good directions include:

- Providing directions in story form. Students can often remember stories, since they are typically more interesting and therefore, better than other forms of communication for multi-step directions.

- Starting with *"when I say go,"* which gets them to listen for all the directions before moving, then telling students what they're *"going to"* do for each step of the process. Students create pictures of themselves doing the steps in their mind's eye and assume they can do it without help.

- Being silly! Throwing in some funny character voices, different facial expressions, or random silly instructions for things they should do between steps of the real task adds interest and increases the desire of students to listen more closely.

- Asking students to speak up if they don't understand all the steps. Teachers should inform students that they want to know of any questions before the students begin the task, rather than find out in the middle of the activity that the students didn't hear or understand all the instructions at the beginning. This makes students responsible for knowing what to do.

- Begin with requiring students to only do a few things at a time. However, as they get used to working with provided instructions, they will be able to take on much more lengthy activities and remember more directions.

<u>The Abecedarian Approach</u>
The Abecedarian Approach is primarily concerned with a child's behavioral and intellectual successes from birth to adulthood. There are four main components of the Abecedarian Approach: 1) learning games; 2) conversational reading; 3) language priority; and 4) enriched caregiving. Two areas explicitly involve literacy development: conversational reading and language priority. They both involve playful, responsive approaches to rich language instruction.

The Abecedarian Approach to Conversational Reading
The Abecedarian Approach to conversational reading has been demonstrated to have significant benefits in the areas of reading fluency and comprehension. Conversational reading involves a conversational-style of reading instruction in which the educator plays an active role by partnering in shared reading activities. Conversational reading gets its name from being a back-and-forth reading conversation. During the reading process, educators prompt the children to "see, show, and say" what they are reading. This is referred to as the *3S Strategy*. Children may be encouraged to identify the

words they know on a given page, look for rhyming words, or draw pictures that correspond to the reading. Educators take an active role in the reading process by running their fingers along the words, asking questions about the reading, prompting conversations, and strengthening comprehension, as well as pointing out interesting ideas about the reading to encourage a dialogue.

The Abecedarian Approach to Language Priority
The Abecedarian Approach uses language priority to focus on rich language stimulation. By emphasizing language throughout the day, the language priority strategy creates endless occasions for meaningful conversations. Educators work to extend conversations from a variety of different angles, promoting higher cognitive thinking and engagement. Educators will also use the *3N Approach* by *noticing* the student's current reading level, *nudging* or encouraging the student to go one step beyond this level, and *narrating* the student's activities.

Communication and Media Literacy

Letter-Sound Correspondences

When children begin to learn the various letter-sound correspondences, their phonemic awareness begins to overlap with their awareness of orthography and reading. One of the widely accepted strategies to employ when introducing children to letter-sound correspondences is to begin with those correspondences that occur the most frequently in simple English words. In an effort to help build confidence in young learners, educators are encouraged to introduce only a few letter-sound combinations at a time and provide ample opportunities for practice and review before introducing new combinations. Although there is no formally established order for the introduction of letter-sound correspondences, educators are encouraged to consider the following general guidelines, but they should also keep in mind the needs, experiences, and current literacy levels of the students.

The following is intended as a general guide only:

a
m
t
p
o
n
c
d
u
s
g
h
i
f
b
l
e
r
w
k
x
v
y
z
j
q

As a generally accepted rule, short vowels should be introduced ahead of long vowels, and lowercase letters should be mastered before the introduction of their upper case counterparts.

Spelling conventions in the English language are primarily concerned with three areas: mechanics, usage, and sentence formation.

Mechanics

For primary students who are just beginning to master the alphabetic principle, educators should first concentrate on proper letter formation, the spelling of high-frequency words and sight words, and offer classroom discussions to promote the sharing of ideas. When children begin to write in sentences to share their thoughts and feelings in print, educators may consider the introduction of an author's chair, in which students read their writing out loud to their classmates.

Although the phonetic spelling or invented spelling that primary students employ in these early stages may not be the conventional spelling of certain words, it allows primary students to practice the art and flow of writing. It works to build their confidence in the writing process. This is not the time for educators to correct spelling, punctuation, or capitalization errors as young learners may quickly lose interest in writing and may lose self-confidence.

One strategy to employ early on to help students with proper spelling is to ensure there is an easily accessible and updated word wall that employs high-frequency words and sight words. Students should be encouraged to refer to the word wall while they write.

Usage

Usage concerns itself with word order, verb tense, and subject-verb agreement among other areas. As primary children often have a basic knowledge of how to use oral language effectively in order to communicate, this area of spelling conventions may require less initial attention than the mechanics of spelling. During read-aloud and shared reading activities, educators may wish to point out punctuation marks found in print, model how to read these punctuation marks, and periodically discuss their importance in the reading and writing process.

When children begin to engage in writing exercises, educators may wish to prompt self-editing skills by asking if each sentence begins with a capital and ends with a period, question mark, or exclamation point.

Sentence Formation

Verbs, nouns, adverbs, and adjectives all play significant roles in the writing process. However, for primary students, these concepts are fairly complex to understand. One instruction approach that may prove effective is to categorize a number of simple verbs, nouns, adverbs, and adjectives on index cards by color coordination. Educators can then ask one child to choose a noun card and another student to choose a verb card. The children can then face the class and read their words starting with the noun and then the verb. The students can even try reading the verb first followed by the noun. A class discussion can follow, analyzing whether or not the sentences made sense and what words might need to be added to give the sentence more meaning.

Active Listening

To develop active listening skills, several important areas require focus and conscious effort. Before a speech or dialogue even begins, removing any distractions sets a positive and respectful tone. Those with active listening skills offer undivided attention, acknowledge the presenter's message by asking relevant questions and provide encouraging feedback when appropriate. Maintaining eye contact, smiling, and using posture that signifies respect are also effective characteristics of active listening, but perhaps one of the most important ways to improve active listening skills is to keep an open mind and defer judgment until the speaker has completed the entire message.

Active listening skills are an important part of children's family, social, and academic life, and they will eventually become an equally important part of their professional lives. Recognizing the importance of active listening and strengthening these skills assists students in achieving personal, academic, and professional success.

Developing Skills Necessary for Speaking, Listening, and Presenting

<u>Instructing Children to Enhance Their English Language Literacy Development</u>
Speaking, listening, reading, and writing are all intimately connected as essential elements of literacy development. As social beings, children begin to recognize that with effective literacy skills, their social, emotional, and physical needs can be met, and their curiosity can be satisfied. They also begin to learn that they can develop communication skills to answer questions that others pose. This can be an exciting and self-affirming realization for young children. In order to encourage literacy development, educators should ensure that all activities in the classroom involve meaningful language and literacy experiences. Each child learns at a unique pace and in a unique way. With this sensitivity in place, classroom activities should be as differentiated as possible.

Developing Listening Skills
Actively teaching good listening skills is essential in the classroom. Behaviors should not be expected that have not been taught. Students need to learn the difference between what an excellent listener does and what poor listening behaviors are. Good listening skills that should be taught include:

- Focusing on the speaker, looking them in the eye, and choosing not to interrupt.
- Looking at the speaker to indicate that the student is ready to hear what the speaker has to say and to pick up body language cues and facial expressions.
- Giving nonverbal signals that the student is listening (e.g., nods, smiles).
- Giving verbal signals that indicate interest in the speaker (e.g., repeating back what is heard to indicate understanding).
- Subtly matching the energy and emotional level of the speaker to indicate understanding.
- Choosing not to make side comments or to focus on other things occurring in the room.

Some strategies for teaching these skills in the classroom include, but are not limited to:

- Providing pre-listening activities, such as teaching new vocabulary words, outlining what students will be hearing, distributing study guides or pre-listening questions, and teaching students the objectives of the listening activity beforehand.
- Avoiding repeating directions multiple times. Teachers are often inclined to repeat steps and directions several times before allowing students to begin working. This is counterproductive because it teaches students that they do not have to listen the first time. Students should be taught that the teacher will say things only once and they are expected to listen, but they may ask for clarification. Students should also be taught to seek other sources of finding the instructions.

- Modeling good listening and speaking skills in the classroom because students learn by watching and emulating others. Teachers need to consistently model choosing not to interrupt and focusing their full attention on the speaker. They also need to model speaking clearly with proper grammar and foster an environment in the classroom of good peer modeling as well.

- Teaching students to take notes, write down questions, and report on or paraphrase what they have heard the speaker say. Students should be given active listening activities to complete during and after the listening task.

- Giving students multiple methods to contribute to conversations. Some students are not inclined to speak in front of others. In such cases, it may be helpful to allow them to give other signals of understanding such as "thumbs up," "thumbs sideways," "thumbs down," or sign language for "yes" and "no" answers.

- Encouraging the use of technology in the classroom to allow students to blog, tweet, or use quiz show-style games to indicate understanding of what they heard.

Developing Speaking Skills

Similar to listening skills, students also need to be taught speaking and presenting skills. Students need to learn such skills as:

- How to introduce themselves effectively
- How to make appropriate eye contact with listeners
- How to begin a conversation and keep it going
- How to interact with various types of audiences
- How to answer questions in an interview
- How to stand and deliver a speech with confidence
- How to ask for and answer questions during a presentation

The following strategies can help teach conversational and speaking skills:

- Students can be taught to use "conversation enhancers" when working with others. Some examples are: "Really?" "Wow!" "That's interesting" "Tell me more about ..." "Can you say that in another way?" "Tell me what you are thinking ..." and "Can you add to my idea?"

- Good conversational skills can be modeled as frequently as possible in one- to two-minute one-on-one dialogues with students. This is especially important for the introverted and shy students.

- A safe speaking environment can be fostered by teaching good manners to listeners, and by challenging students who are disrespectful listeners to act in a different way.

- Students should be asked open-ended questions that have no right or wrong answer and that invite lengthy answers instead of just "yes" or "no" responses.

- "I don't know" should not be accepted for an answer. Students should be taught that their thinking is valued rather than whether they *know* something.

- Students should be taught how to take turns in the classroom fairly and to not interrupt one another.

- Students should be instructed not to read their presentations word for word, and to speak toward the audience instead of toward the project or PowerPoint slide.

- Videos of good and poor presentations can be shown as models for students to critique.

- Students should be taught to build in humor and good non-verbal communication into their presentations.

- Students should be shown how to curb involuntary habits such as repeating themselves or saying "um" or "like" too much.

Task, Purpose, and Audience
Teaching students to present and speak to an audience involves teaching them how to structure a presentation so that it is appropriate for the task, purpose, and audience. *Task* is what the students are required to do with their presentation. *Purpose* is the reason for the presentation and how it will achieve the outcome of the task. *Audience* is whom the presentation is for, the population it is trying to reach, and why it is specifically for that group. Some presentation tips that teachers should impart to students are as follows:

- During student preparation, students should ask themselves: "Why am I giving this presentation?" "What do I want people to take away from the presentation?" and "How much does my audience already know about the topic?"

- Presentations should be structured with an effective introduction, covering each item on their agenda succinctly, and wrapping up with a memorable conclusion.

- Presentations should be given with clarity and impact. The audience won't remember everything a student presents, so he or she needs to highlight the key points clearly and concisely and then expand and illustrate as needed.

- Visual aids should be used to enhance the presentation without causing distractions—such as useless images and animated transitions between slides—from the information.

- Presentations should be given without memorization. Students should be charged with becoming more familiar with their content and to "test drive" the presentation beforehand.

- Appropriate pauses should be used during presentations to help the audience better absorb the information.

- Various techniques can be employed if there is a "stumbling point" or a piece of information is forgotten during the presentation.

Written, Visual, and Oral Information from Texts and Multimedia Sources

Students in a modern classroom have access to a wide variety of instructional resources. From teacher-led instruction and classroom activities, traditional textbooks, encyclopedias, nonfiction magazines, and customized classroom libraries to desktop computers, iPads, tablets, laptops, online tutorials, and smart boards, there is a plethora of information waiting to be discovered. Learning how to integrate traditional written, visual, and oral information to other information provided on a multimedia platform can prove challenging, but it is well worth the effort. Since the vast majority of children from the primary school years and older are well equipped at using a variety of technology-based resources, educators who integrate technology in the classroom will likely succeed in helping children to progress both academically and socially. The classroom is as much a social setting as it is academic, and as society changes, so must the instructional approaches.

Time management is one of the initial tasks facing educators when setting up their academic year. Educators are responsible for teaching a wide range of subjects, specific domains within each subject, and numbers of skills within each domain. Designing long-range plans that take all of this into account and forming a framework for the academic year is the most logical starting point.

From this framework, educators can determine how to teach each discipline with an effective, time management approach. Taking the number of students, the possible varying academic and social levels, socioeconomic differences, and language barriers into account, teachers can begin to develop differentiated instructional approaches that cater to all the needs in the classroom. It is at this stage that both traditional resources and technology must find a way to complement each other in the classroom.

For instance, one effective approach is to instruct children to ensure that every research project involves a minimum of two textbook sources as well as a minimum of two technology-based sources. When introducing new topics or reinforcing a lesson, educators are still highly encouraged to use visual aids in the classroom, including word walls, personal dictionaries, and classroom labels. Modeling the effective use of hand-held books, reference guides, and magazines also provides children the opportunity to see how valuable written information continues to be in the world of education.

In order for children to experience a well rounded, quality education, instructional days should be divided between effective, quality instruction, independent exploration and learning, and positive social interaction. Since the needs of children vary in each classroom, as well as their academic and social levels, each educator's decision on how to divide instructional time will also vary. However, having access to technology is paramount in every classroom and at every grade level.

Technology in the classroom helps children to become more actively engaged and encourages independent learning with the use of student-centered, project-based activities. From virtual math tools to collaborative class blogs, there are many ways for students to effectively engage in technology in the classroom.

Although technology plays an important role in the modern classroom, it is still important for educators to guide children, helping them use the technology in an effective, efficient, and responsible manner. Teaching children about cyber-bullying, copyright, plagiarism, and digital footprints will inevitably strengthen their ability to responsibly and safely conduct themselves online.

Educators also use technology for lesson planning, assessments, and evaluation. With a number of online programs available, educators are able to provide students, colleagues, administration, and parents with effective feedback and to develop and evaluate high-quality formative and summative assessments in an efficient manner.

By combining the use of technology along with teacher-centered instruction and traditional textbooks, educators will undoubtedly help to create a classroom with children who are actively engaged throughout the instructional day.

Primary and Secondary Sources

Primary sources refer to first-hand accounts of events, a subject matter, an individual, or a time period. Primary sources also include original works of art. They can also be non-interpretive, factual pieces of information. Some examples include diaries, journals, letters, government records, maps, plays, novels, and songs.

Secondary sources refer to the analysis or interpretation of primary sources and are, therefore, usually considered more subjective than objective. In other words, researchers may discover contradictory information on the same subject from different secondary sources. Some examples include literary and film reviews, newspaper articles, and biographies.

Both primary and secondary sources of information are useful. They both offer invaluable insight that helps the writer learn more about the subject matter. However, researchers are cautioned to examine the information closely and to consider the time period as well as the cultural, political, and social climate in which accounts were given. Learning to distinguish between reliable sources of information and questionable accounts is paramount to a quality research report.

Reliable and Unreliable Sources

When conducting research, students must be able to distinguish between reliable and unreliable sources in order to develop a well-written research report. When choosing print sources, typically published works that have been edited and clearly identify the author or authors are considered credible sources. Peer-reviewed journals and research conducted by scholars are likewise considered to be credible sources of information.

When deciding on what Internet sources to use, it is also a sound practice for researchers to look closely at each website's universal resource locator, the *URL*. Generally speaking, websites with.edu, .gov, or .org as the Top Level Domain are considered reliable, but the researcher must still question any possible political or social bias. Personal blogs, tweets, personal websites, online forums, and any site that clearly demonstrates bias, strong opinions, or persuasive language are considered unreliable sources.

Paraphrasing and Plagiarizing

Paraphrasing: The restating of one's own words, text, passage, or any information that has already been heard, read, or researched

Plagiarizing: The copying of a text, passage, or any other information in print or digital format, and claiming the work as one's own

Credible Print and Digital Sources

Credible print sources are those that have been edited and published, reveal the author or authors, and clearly identify their expertise on the subject matter. Scholarly reviews are typically very reliable sources as they are written by experts in the field and, more often than not, have been evaluated by their respective peers. Credible digital sources may sometimes prove a little more difficult to discern, and researchers must employ due diligence to ensure the sources are reliable. Distinguishing between biased and unbiased websites, objective versus subjective information, as well as informative versus persuasive writing can prove confusing at times. By paying attention to a website's URL and carefully considering the language and tone applied to the writing, researchers should be able to evaluate the website's reliability.

Learning how to locate key information within sources requires a basic understanding of written structure. If the source of information is written well, there should be titles, subtitles, headings, and subheadings that researchers can use to zero in on key information. Additionally, informational texts often employ the use of an index and table of contents, which helps them locate specific information. Similarly, digital sources often employ titles, subtitles, headings, and subheadings, and they will generally offer a search box to look for specific information or key terms within the website.

Citing sources at the end of a research paper is critical to the overall quality of work. If sources are not cited or poorly cited, a researcher's work risks losing credibility. There are various accepted methods to use when citing information. The method used often depends on the preferences of the authority that has assigned the research. The most generally accepted methods for citing sources are MLA, APA, and Chicago style. Although each citation format is distinct in structure, order, and requirements, they all identify key information. Citation formats also ensure that published authors of given works receive full credit.

Practice Questions

1. When children begin to negotiate the sounds that make up words in their language independently, what skill/s are they demonstrating?
   a. Phonological awareness
   b. Phonemes
   c. Phoneme substitution
   d. Blending skills

2. What is phonics?
   a. The study of syllabication
   b. The study of onsets and rimes
   c. The study of sound-letter relationships
   d. The study of graphemes

3. Word analysis skills are NOT critical for the development of what area of literacy?
   a. Vocabulary
   b. Reading fluency
   c. Spelling
   d. Articulation

4. What area of study involves mechanics, usage, and sentence formation?
   a. Word analysis
   b. Spelling conventions
   c. Morphemes
   d. Phonics

5. How do the majority of high-frequency sight words differ from decodable words?
   a. They do not rhyme.
   b. They do not follow the Alphabetic Principle.
   c. They do not contain onsets.
   d. They contain rimes.

6. Reading fluency involves what key areas?
   a. Accuracy, rate, and prosody
   b. Accuracy, rate, and consistency
   c. Prosody, accuracy, and clarity
   d. Rate, prosody, and comprehension

7. When students study character development, setting, and plot, what are they studying?
   a. Word analysis
   b. Points of view
   c. Literary analysis of fictional texts
   d. Fluency

8. The author's purpose, major ideas, supporting details, visual aids, and vocabulary are the five key elements of what type of text?

a. Fictional texts
b. Narratives
c. Persuasive texts
d. Informational texts

9. When students use inference, what are they able to do?

a. Make logical assumptions based on contextual clues
b. Independently navigate various types of text
c. Summarize a text's main idea
d. Paraphrase a text's main idea

10. Story maps, an effective instructional tool, do NOT help children in what way?

a. Analyze relationships among characters, events, and ideas in literature
b. Understand key details of a story
c. Follow the story's development
d. Read at a faster pace

11. Which text feature does NOT help a reader locate information in printed or digital text?

a. Hyperlink
b. Sidebar
c. Glossary
d. Heading

12. Read the following sentence to answer the question below:

> *He is a kind and generous man who wants nothing more than the best for his community*, thought Michael as the board members discussed the nominees for head of council. Lana June, however, was far more critical. *He is just saying those things to get elected*, she thought.

What is the author's point of view?

a. First person
b. Third person limited
c. Third person omniscient
d. Objective

13. What do *quantitative*, *qualitative*, and *reader* and *task* measure?

a. Text complexity
b. Genres of writing
c. Points of view
d. Reading comprehension

14. Autobiographies and memoirs are examples of what form of writing?

a. Fiction
b. Narrative
c. Informational text
d. Research papers

15. Rating scales, student logs, and the POWER method are effective assessment practices for what area of literacy development?

a. Reading
b. Writing
c. Spelling
d. Listening

16. Which effective writing area engages and connects with the audience, igniting emotion?

a. Ethos
b. Logos
c. Pathos
d. Kairos

17. When children begin to leave spaces between words with a mixture of uppercase and lowercase letters, what developmental stage of writing are they demonstrating?

a. Emergence of beginning sound
b. Strings of letters
c. Words represented by consonants
d. Transitional phase

18. First-hand accounts of an event, subject matter, time period, or an individual are referred to as what type of source?

a. Primary sources
b. Secondary sources
c. Direct sources
d. Indirect sources

19. The following is an example of what type of sentence?

> Although I wished it were summer, I accepted the change of seasons, and I started to appreciate the fall.

a. Compound
b. Simple
c. Complex
d. Compound-Complex

20. Read the following sentence to answer the question below:

> The teacher directed the children's attention to the diagram, but the children couldn't understand the information.

This is an example of what type of sentence?

a. Complex
b. Compound
c. Simple
d. Compound-Complex

21. Read the following sentences to answer the question below:

Give me a shout back when you can.

Please return my call at your earliest convenience.

What is the main difference in these two sentences?

a. Point of view
b. Dialect
c. Accent
d. Register

22. What type of literary device is being used in this sentence?

I worked a billion hours this week!

a. Idiom
b. Metaphor
c. Hyperbole
d. Alliteration

23. What are the three tiers of vocabulary?

a. Conversational, academic, and domain-specific language
b. Informal, formal, and academic
c. Social, professional, and academic
d. Phonics, fluency, and rate

24. Volume, articulation, and awareness of audience help with what practice?

a. Effective instruction
b. Communication
c. Active listening
d. Oral presentations

25. Offering a presenter with undivided attention and asking relevant and timely questions are examples of what skill set?

a. Active listening skills
b. Effective speaking
c. Formal communication
d. Informal communication

26. What is the method called that teachers use before and after reading to improve critical thinking and comprehension?

a. Self-monitoring comprehension
b. KWL charts
c. Metacognitive skills
d. Directed reading-thinking activities

27. When a student looks back at a previous reading section for information, he or she is using which of the following?
  a. Self-monitoring comprehension
  b. KWL charts
  c. Metacognitive skills
  d. Directed reading-thinking activities

28. Which choice of skills is NOT part of Bloom's Taxonomy?
  a. Remembering and understanding
  b. Applying and analyzing
  c. Listening and speaking
  d. Evaluating and creating

29. When a student looks at a word and is able to tell the teacher that the letters spell C-A-T, but the student cannot actually say the word, what is the spelling stage of the student?
  a. Alphabetic Spelling
  b. Within Word Pattern Spelling
  c. Derivational Relations Spelling
  d. Emergent Spelling

30. Predicting, Summarizing, Questioning, and Clarifying are steps of what?
  a. Reciprocal teaching
  b. Comprehensive teaching
  c. Activation teaching
  d. Summative teaching

31. When a student asks, "What do I know?" "What do I want to know?" and "What have I learned?" and records the answers in a table, he or she is using which of the following?
  a. Self-monitoring comprehension
  b. KWL charts
  c. Metacognitive skills
  d. Directed reading-thinking activities

32. What technique might an author use to let the reader know that the main character was in a car crash as a child?
  a. Point of view
  b. Characterization
  c. Figurative language
  d. Flashback

33. A graphic organizer is a method of achieving what?
  a. Integrating knowledge and ideas
  b. Generating questions
  c. Determining point of view
  d. Determining the author's purpose

34. A student is trying to decide if a character is telling the truth about having stolen candy. After the student reads that the character is playing with an empty candy wrapper in her pocket, the student decides the character is guilty. This is an example of what?

a. Flashback
b. Making inferences
c. Style
d. Figurative language

35. What is the method of categorizing text by its structure and literary elements called?

a. Fiction
b. Non-Fiction
c. Genre
d. Plot

36. A reader is distracted from following a story because they are having trouble understanding why a character has decided to cut school, so the reader jumps to the next page to find out where the character is headed. This is an example of what?

a. Self-monitoring comprehension
b. KWL charts
c. Metacognitive skills
d. Directed reading-thinking activities

37. Phonemic Awareness, Phonics, Fluency, Vocabulary, and Comprehension are the five basic elements of what?

a. Bloom's Taxonomy
b. Spelling instruction
c. Reading education
d. Genre

38. A child reads the story Little Red Riding Hood aloud. He easily pronounces the words, uses an apprehensive tone to show that the main character should not be leaving the path, adds a scary voice for the Big Bad Wolf, and reads the story at a pace that engages the class. What are these promising signs of?

a. Reading fluency
b. Phonemic awareness
c. Reading comprehension
d. Working memory

39. A student is trying to read the word "preferred." She first recognizes the word "red" at the end, then sounds out the rest of the word by breaking it down into "pre," then "fer," then "red." Finally she puts it together and says "preferred." This student is displaying what attribute?

a. Phonemic awareness
b. Phonics
c. Fluency
d. Vocabulary

40. A class silently reads a passage on the American Revolution. Once they are done, the teacher asks who were the two sides fighting, why were they fighting, and who won. What skill is the teacher gauging?

a. Orthographic development
b. Fluency
c. Comprehension
d. Phonics

41. Poems are often an effective device when teaching what skill?

a. Fluency
b. Spelling
c. Writing
d. Word decoding

42. What allows readers to effectively translate print into recognizable speech?

a. Fluency
b. Spelling
c. Phonics
d. Word decoding

43. A teacher wants to help her students write a nonfiction essay on how the Pueblos built their homes. Before they write, she helps the students make clay from cornstarch and water, draw a plan for the house with a ruler, and build it using the clay and leaves from the schoolyard. These exercises are examples of what?

a. Proficiency
b. Collaboration
c. Constructive writing
d. Cross-curricular integration

44. A student has quickly written a story and turned it in without reading it. To help reinforce the POWER strategy, the teacher tells the student go back and read his story. This POWER stage is called what?

a. Prewriting
b. Evaluating
c. Organizing
d. Revising

45. During which stage of the POWER strategy are graphic organizers used?

a. Pre-writing
b. Organizing
c. Writing
d. Evaluating

46. A teacher wants his students to write a story over two weeks. They are instructed to write a draft the first day. On each of the following days, he asks the students to develop and edit the story for one of the following: ideas, organization, voice, word choice, sentence fluency, conventions, and presentation. What does this teaching technique incorporate?

a. Ideas
b. POWER strategy
c. Cross-curricular integration
d. 6+1 Traits

47. Which trait teaches students to build the framework of their writing?

a. Conventions
b. Word choice
c. Ideas
d. Organization

48. Which trait ultimately forms the content of the writing?

a. Conventions
b. Word choice
c. Ideas
d. Voice

49. Which trait is most commonly associated with giving individuality and style to writing?

a. Voice
b. Word choice
c. Presentation
d. Ideas

50. A teacher asks a student to describe a beautiful day. The student says the flowers were pretty, the air was warm, and animals were running. The teacher asks the student to specify how many flowers there were—just a few hopeful buds or an abundance of blossoms? Was the air still or breezy? How did it feel? The teacher is developing which trait in the student?

a. Voice
b. Word choice
c. Organization
d. Presentation

51. Writing practice for the sole purpose of communicating refers to what kind of writing?

a. Persuasive
b. Informational
c. Narrative
d. Purposeful

52. A second-grade student brings a book to read to a group. It is about a caterpillar counting its food each day of the week before becoming a butterfly. Realizing the group is very familiar with their days and numbers, the teacher uses the story to explore the "moral" of the story and proper nutrition. This is an example of what?

a. Modeling
b. Encouragement
c. Acknowledgement
d. Challenging

53. A student is struggling with reading, especially aloud. When it is his turn to read to the class, the teacher offers an easier book she knows the student likes and is very familiar with. When the student reads aloud well and with enthusiasm, the teacher praises him to the class, then gives a more challenging book the next time. What is this called?

a. Acknowledgement
b. Providing feedback
c. Encouragement
d. Effective assistance

54. Preparation, Presentation, Application, and Evaluation are the four steps of what?

a. Demonstration
b. Modeling
c. Explanation
d. Challenging

55. Students are asked to pretend to prepare a meal. At various classroom stations, they must draw a picture, engage in pretend play, or write a list of instructions: one for grocery shopping, cooking, and cleanup. The teacher helps each student choose which task to pair with which station, encouraging autonomy and self-motivation. This is an example of what instruction technique?

a. Challenging
b. Modeling
c. Giving feedback
d. Giving assistance

56. Throughout the day, a teacher used language priority, beginning each subject by asking students to volunteer five related words that start with the letter "P." Then, during a reading exercise, the teacher partnered with a small group to turn their words from the day into a cover illustration for a story. This is an example of what?

a. Giving directions
b. The Abecedarian Approach
c. Developmentally appropriate practice
d. Autonomy

57. Speaking, listening, reading, and writing are four essential elements of what?

a. Developmentally appropriate practice
b. The Abecedarian Approach
c. Literacy development
d. Task, purpose, and audience

58. A teacher is about to read a story. He tells the class they will be quizzed and need to pay attention. He instructs them to focus by clearing everything else from their desks, to look at his face for clues about the story's tone, and to think about the adjectives used to describe the characters to learn more about them. What skill is he teaching?

a. Writing
b. Reading
c. Speaking
d. Listening

59. Since teachers must be communicators, educators, evaluators, models, and agents of socialization, this is considered to be mastery of what?

a. Conventions
b. Spelling
c. Speaking
d. Listening

60. Synonyms, Antonyms, and Homonyms are examples of what?

a. Syntax relationships
b. Pragmatic relationships
c. Semantic relationships
d. Morphology relationships

Answer Explanations

1. A: Phonological Awareness refers to a child's ability to understand and use familiar sounds in his or her social environment in order to form coherent words. Phonemes are defined as distinct sound units in any given language. Phonemic substitution is part of phonological awareness—a child's ability to substitute specific phonemes for others. Blending skills refers to the ability to construct or build words from individual phonemes by blending the sounds together in a unique sequence.

2. C: When children begin to recognize and apply sound-letter relationships independently and accurately, they are demonstrating a growing mastery of phonics. Phonics is the most commonly used method for teaching people to read and write by associating sounds with their corresponding letters or groups of letters, using a language's alphabetic writing system. Syllabication refers to the ability to break down words into their individual syllables. The study of onsets and rimes strives to help students recognize and separate a word's beginning consonant or consonant-cluster sound—the onset—from the word's rime—the vowel and/or consonants that follow the onset. A grapheme is a letter or a group of letters in a language that represent a sound.

3. D: Breaking down words into their individual parts, studying prefixes, suffixes, root words, rimes, and onsets, are all examples of word analysis. When children analyze words, they develop their vocabulary and strengthen their spelling and reading fluency.

4. B: Spelling conventions is the area of study that involves mechanics, usage, and sentence formation. Mechanics refers to spelling, punctuation, and capitalization. Usage refers to the use of the various parts of speech within sentences, and sentence formation is the order in which the various words in a sentence appear. Generally speaking, word analysis is the breaking down of words into morphemes and word units in order to arrive at the word's meaning. Morphemes are the smallest units of a written language that carry meaning, and phonics refers to the study of letter-sound relationships.

5. B: Although some high-frequency sight words are decodable, the majority of them are not, so they do not follow the Alphabetic Principle, which relies on specific letter-sound correspondence. High-frequency sight words appear often in children's literature and are studied and memorized in order to strengthen a child's spelling and reading fluency. High-frequency sight words, as well as decodable words, may or may not rhyme and may or may not contain onsets and rimes.

6. A: Reading fluency involves how accurately a child reads each individual word within a sentence, the speed at which a child reads, and the expression the child applies while reading. Therefore, accuracy, rate, and prosody are the three key areas of reading fluency.

7. C: Literary analysis of a fictional text involves several areas of study, including character development, setting, and plot. Although points of view refer to a specific area of study in literary analysis, it is only one area. Word analysis does not involve the study of elements within a fictional text.

8. D: Informational texts generally contain five key elements in order to be considered informative. These five elements include the author's purpose, the major ideas, supporting details, visual aids, and key vocabulary. Narratives are accounts—either spoken or written—of an event or a story. Persuasive texts, such as advertisements, use persuasive language to try to convince the reader to act or feel a certain way. Informational texts strive to share factual information about a given subject in order to advance a reader's knowledge.

9. A: When a person infers something, he or she is demonstrating the ability to extract key information and make logical assumptions based on that information. The information provided is not direct, but implied. Being able to navigate a variety of texts independently has nothing to do with inference; it demonstrates a student's reading comprehension and fluency. Successfully summarizing and paraphrasing texts are advanced literacy skills that demonstrate a student's reading comprehension and writing proficiency.

10. D: Story maps are a specific type of visual aid that helps younger children develop a clearer understanding of a story being read. Story maps may represent the beginning, middle, and ending of a story, or they may be used to develop a clearer picture of each character's personality and traits, unfold the story's plot, or establish the setting.

11. C: Informational texts organized with headings, subheadings, sidebars, hyperlinks and other features help strengthen the reader's reading comprehension and vocabulary knowledge. A glossary defines terms and words used within a text.

12. C: Third person is a term used to refer to a specific point of view in literature. A third person omniscient point of view develops the point of view of each character within a given story and allows the reader to understand each character's feelings as well as their interpretation of a story's events. Third person limited only offers insight into one character, usually the main character. Character analysis is the intimate study of one character within the story—the character's physical characteristics, personality traits, and relationships to the story's elements and other characters. The story's plot refers to the story's main events; it usually reveals the problem and how it might be resolved. A genre of writing is the specific style of writing the author employs—fiction, non-fiction, mystery, narrative, or informational text.

13. A: These are all measures of a text's complexity. Quantitative measures determine a text's level of difficulty. There are several ways to measure this level of difficulty, some of which are sentence length, number of unfamiliar words, and even syllable count within words. Qualitative measures examine a text's attributes, including clarity of language, figurative versus literal language, and a text's overall meaning. Since each reader has unique background knowledge, skill set, and level of reading motivation, reader and task refers to how likely a reader is to engage in and comprehend a given text. Thus, all three of these components comprise a text's complexity. A genre of writing is simply the style of writing that the author employs. Authors will always reveal a given point of view in fictional writing. Sometimes, the author offers readers several points of view, and sometimes, the points of view are limited. Reading comprehension refers to how well a student demonstrates understanding or mastery of the text.

14. B: Narratives are personal accounts of a time period, event, or an individual, with the purpose of documenting, recording, or sharing such factual information. By contrast, fiction is a genre of writing that is fabricated. Informational texts are academic texts used to further a student's mastery of a given subject, and research papers are written reports students write to demonstrate their understanding of a given area of study that has been researched.

15. B: There are several effective assessments to evaluate a child's overall writing progress. Rating scales, student logs, and the POWER method are just some of these assessment methods. Although educators can create rating scales and student logs to assess and help students assess reading and spelling, the POWER method is specific to writing:

P—Prewriting

O—Organizing

W—Writing a rough draft

E—Evaluating

R—Revise and Rewrite

16. C: Pathos refers to the author's appeal to the audience or reader's emotions. Ethos refers to the level of credibility of a piece of writing. Logos refers to the author's appeal to the audience or reader's logic. Kairos refers to the most opportune moment to do something. Therefore, the correct answer is pathos.

17. C: There are eight developmental writing stages:

- Scribbling
- Letter-like symbols
- Strings of letters
- The emergence of beginning sounds
- Words represented by consonants
- Initial, middle, and final sounds
- Transitional phase
- Standard spelling

When children begin to leave visible spacing between words, even if those words are incorrectly spelled or if there is a mixture of upper and lower case letters, they are considered to be at the *Words represented by consonants* stage.

18. A: Firsthand accounts are given by primary sources—individuals who provide personal or expert accounts of an event, subject matter, time period, or of an individual. They are viewed more as objective accounts than subjective. Secondary sources are accounts given by an individual or group of individuals who were not physically present at the event or who did not have firsthand knowledge of an individual or time period. Secondary sources are sources that have used research in order to create a written work. Direct and indirect sources are not terms used in literary circles.

19. D: Since the sentence contains two independent clauses and a dependent clause, the sentence is categorized as compound-complex:

Independent clause: *I accepted the change of seasons*

Independent clause: *I started to appreciate the fall*

Dependent clause: *Although I wished it were summer*

20. B: Since the sentence contains two independent clauses connected by a conjunction, it is referred to as a compound sentence.

Independent clause: *The teacher directed the children's attention to the diagram*

Independent clause: *The children couldn't understand the information*

Conjunction: *But*

21. D: The first sentence is written quite informally and gives a clear impression that the exchange is on a socially relaxed level. The second sentence is written quite formally and gives a clear impression that the exchange is academic or professional in nature. Although both sentences carry the same message—to respond to the messenger as quickly as possible—the register, or level of formality, is very different.

Accent refers to the way in which certain words are pronounced by an individual and is usually dependent on where a person resides. Dialect refers to how groups of people from a specific geographical region manipulate their language. Point of view refers to a person's interpretation of or feelings toward an event. In literature, a point of view refers to a character's interpretation of or feelings toward an event.

22. C: When authors use hyperbole, they are using extreme exaggeration to strongly state a point or evoke a specific emotion in the reader. Idioms can be in the form of words, phrases, or sentences that are expressed figuratively, but they carry a literal meaning that readers must infer. Metaphors are literary devices that compare two unlike entities, as in "The United States is a melting pot." Alliteration is a poetic device that repeats the beginning consonant sound throughout a sentence or phrase strictly for entertainment—"The **b**all **b**ounced along the **b**lue **b**alcony."

23. A: The three tiers of vocabulary are as follows:

Conversational: informal, more relaxed

Academic: more professional, with vocabulary intended to challenge critical thinking skills

Domain-specific language: a unique vocabulary inventory that focuses around a given discipline or computer language

24. D: In order for oral presentations to be effective, the presenter's volume should match the size of audience and the location of the presentation. The presenter should also practice articulation—how clearly the words are being said. The third most important element of oral presentations is how well the presenter is engaging the audience. Making eye contact, moving around the room, and involving the audience, when appropriate, are all part of audience awareness skills.

25. A: Active listening skills are very important in all forms of communication, whether one is at home, among friends, in school, or at work. An active listener is one who pays close attention to what is being said, maintains eye contact, uses body language to indicate respect, asks relevant questions, and shares information that directly pertains to the subject.

26. D: Teachers use directed reading-thinking activities before and after reading to improve critical thinking and reading comprehension. Metacognitive skills are when learners think about thinking. Self-monitoring is when children are asked to think as they read and ask themselves if what they have just read makes sense. KWL charts help guide students to identify what they already know about a given topic.

27. C: Asking oneself a comprehension question is a metacognition skill. Readers with metacognitive skills have learned to think about thinking. It gives students control over their learning while they read. KWL charts help students to identify what they already know about a given topic.

28. C: Listening and speaking are not part of Bloom's Taxonomy. The six parts are remembering, understanding, applying, analyzing, evaluating, and creating.

29. D: During the Emergent Spelling stage, children can identify letters but not the corresponding sounds. The other choices are all fictitious.

30. B: Reciprocal teaching involves predicting, summarizing, questioning, and clarifying. The other choices are all fictitious.

31. A: KWL charts are an effective method of activating prior knowledge and taking advantage of students' curiosity. Students can create a KWL (*Know/Want to know/Learned*) chart to prepare for any unit of instruction and to generate questions about a topic.

32. D: Flashback is a technique used to give more background information in a story. None of the other concepts are directly related to going back in time.

33. A: Graphic organizers are a method of integrating knowledge and ideas. These include many different visual tools for connecting concepts to help students understand information.

34. B: Making inferences is a method of deriving meaning in writing that intended by the author but not explicitly stated. A flashback is a scene set earlier than the main story. Style is a general term for the way something is done. Figurative language is text that is not to be taken literally.

35. C: Genre is a means of categorizing text by its structure and literary elements. Fiction and non-fiction are both genre categories. Plot is the sequence of events that make a story happen.

36. A: Scanning future portions of the text for information that helps resolve a question is an example of self-monitoring. Self-monitoring takes advantage of a natural ability of students to recognize when they understand the reading and when they do not. KWL charts are used to help guide students to identify what they already know about a given topic. Metacognitive skills are when learners think about thinking. Directed reading-thinking activities are done before and after reading to improve critical thinking and reading comprehension.

37. C: The five basic components of reading education are phonemic awareness, phonics, fluency, vocabulary, and comprehension.

38. A: If a child can accurately read text with consistent speed and appropriate expression while demonstrating comprehension, the child is said to have reading fluency skills. Without the ability to read fluently, a child's reading comprehension (Choice *C*) will be limited.

39. B: Phonics is the ability to apply letter-sound relationships and letter patterns in order to accurately pronounce written words. Phonemic awareness is the understanding that words are comprised of a combination of sounds. Fluency is an automatic recognition and accurate interpretation of text. Vocabulary is the body of words known to a person.

40. C: Comprehension is the level of content understanding that a student demonstrates after reading. Orthographic development is a cumulative process for learning to read, with each skill building on the previously mastered skill. Fluency is an automatic recognition and accurate interpretation of text. Phonics is the ability to apply letter-sound relationships and letter patterns in order to accurately pronounce written words.

41. A: Poems are an effective method for teaching fluency, since rhythmic sounds and rhyming words build a child's understanding of phonemic awareness.

42. C: Phonics allows readers to effectively translate print into recognizable speech. It essentially enables young readers to translate printed words into recognizable speech. If children lack proficiency in phonics, their ability to read fluently and to increase vocabulary will be limited.

43. D: Cross-curricular integration is choosing to teach writing projects that include the subjects of science, social studies, mathematics, reading, etc.

44. B: Students should carefully read what they've written during the Evaluating stage of the POWER strategy.

45. B: Graphic organizers are used during the Organizing stage of the POWER strategy. They help students to examine, analyze, and summarize selections they have read and can be used individually or collaboratively in the classroom. Graphic organizers may be sequencing charts, graphs, Venn diagrams, timelines, chain of events organizers, story maps, concept maps, mind maps, webs, outlines, or other visual tools for connecting concepts to achieve understanding.

46. D: 6+1 Traits is a model for teaching writing that uses common language to explain writing standards. The 6+1 Traits are the characteristics that make writing readable and effective no matter what genre of writing is being used. These seven traits are ideas, organization, voice, word choice, sentence fluency, conventions, and presentation.

47. D: Organization is the trait that teaches students how to build the framework of their writing. Students choose an organizational strategy or purpose for the writing and build the details upon that structure. There are many purposes for writing, and they all have different frameworks.

48. C: Ideas ultimately form the content of the writing. The Ideas Trait is one of the 6+1 Traits model and is where students learn to select an important topic for their writing. They are taught to narrow down and focus their idea before further developing it.

49. A: Voice is the primary trait that shows the individual writing style of an author. It is based on an author's choice of common syntax, diction, punctuation, character development, dialogue, etc.

50. B: Word choice is the trait that teaches the use of precise language. Teachers can enhance this trait in students by helping them to use exact language that is accurate, concise, precise, and lively.

51. D: Intentional writing practice for the purpose of communicating refers to purposeful writing. Students can use this as a method of thinking through issues and solving problems related to writing.

52. C: Considering prior knowledge before instruction is part of Acknowledgement. For teachers, it begins with understanding where students are coming from and the experiences they bring with them to the classroom. When a teacher considers prior knowledge before beginning instruction, they are being considerate of each student's time and intellect.

53. B: Providing feedback is a way to build positive self-image and encourage success. A positive self-image is fostered by repeated success. Giving clear and effective feedback communicates to the student that her or his work is worthwhile, and that someone cares enough to review and consider it.

54. A: Demonstration includes the four steps: Preparation, Presentation, Application and Evaluation. Demonstration is when a teacher not only models and explains how to do a task but also engages in thinking through the task with the students. Effective teachers narrate their thinking processes when modeling a strategy.

55. D: Autonomy and self-motivation are the goals of giving assistance. Students need assistance and guidance in a classroom; however, knowing how much help to offer is always a balancing act. If teachers give too much assistance, they end up doing the work for students, who then do not learn. If teachers do not offer enough assistance, students become lost, overwhelmed, and do not learn.

56. B: Conversational reading and language priority are premises of the Abecedarian Approach. Conversational reading involves a conversational-style of reading instruction in which the educator plays an active role by partnering in shared reading activities. By emphasizing language throughout the day, the language priority strategy creates endless occasions for meaningful conversations. Educators work to extend conversations from a variety of different angles, promoting higher cognitive thinking and engagement.

57. C: Speaking, Listening, Reading, and Writing are the four elements of literacy development. As social beings, children begin to recognize that with effective literacy skills, their social, emotional, and physical needs can be met, and their curiosity can be satisfied.

58. D: Four concepts that teach listening skills are focusing, looking, non-verbal cues, and verbal cues. Behaviors that enable good listening skills should not be expected. They need to be taught. Students need to learn the difference between what an excellent listener does and what poor listening behaviors are.

59. A: Teachers must master conventions because they are communicators, educators, evaluators, models, and agents of socialization. Teachers serve several key roles in the classroom. Students will not be able to learn properly unless their teachers have mastered these conventions.

60. C: Synonyms, Antonyms, and Homonyms are examples of semantic relationships. There are five types of semantic relationships, including the three noted in the question. The other two are Hyponyms and Meronyms.

Social Science

Effective Instructional Practices and Assessment of the Social Sciences

Instructional Delivery of Social Science Concepts

Teachers should strive to move beyond textbooks in the classroom, introducing students to a variety of primary and secondary sources. Written secondary sources can include professional monographs, popular histories, historical fiction, magazines, newspapers, and scholarly journals and articles. Written primary sources can include journals, diaries, newspaper clippings, government documents, context-specific literature, letters, biographies and autobiographies, folklore, and cultural mythology. Students should also be exposed to visual sources such as political cartoons, artwork, ads, signs, graphs, charts, tables, photographs, and videos. Students can also be introduced to relevant musical works. As digital archives and histories are becoming more relevant in 21st century classroom, it's important that students are exposed to computer-based resources.

Planning for Instruction of Social Science Concepts

Besides traditional lectures, textbook work, PowerPoints, and direct instruction, teachers can diversify pedagogical methods in their classrooms by incorporating inquiry-based practices, project-based learning, field work, role plays, sociodramas, skits, simulations, field trips, student-specific academic interventions, debates, and identity-based social-emotional learning activities into social science courses. The goal is to differentiate sources, instruction, and assessments so all students have access to social science content.

Assessing Social Science Concepts

Differentiated assessments are crucial for tailoring the educational environment for individual learning types. Teachers must be aware and sensitive to the neurodiversity in their classrooms. When designing social science assessments, teachers should keep in mind the unique learning types and cognitive skills of English Language Learners (ELLs), Section 504 students, Gifted and Talented (GT) students, and Special Education (SPED) students. In addition, teachers in K-6 social science classrooms must be sensitive to cultural. Whenever possible, social science teachers should make their materials and assessments personally and culturally relevant.

Students should be comfortable exploring and expressing their identities in social science classrooms. For students to excel at historical inquiry, it's important that they understand their own genders, sexual orientations, races, ethnicities, political affiliations, religious beliefs, and socioeconomic statuses to better understand how these categories drive the decisions of historical actors and even their peers. The TEKS performance standards act as a means for assessing the needs of each student; moreover, the TEKS performance standards encourage cultural diversity. Contrary to popular belief, these standards don't limit one's ability to implement varied assessments; rather, the TEKS were created as guideposts for implementing diverse assessments that account for the varied interests and skills present in every classroom. Whenever possible, use the TEKS for direction, and employ kinesthetic-, auditory-, oral-, written-, and visual-based assessments for every student. Also try to vary assessments by incorporating design-thinking, inquiry-based learning, project-based learning, and student voice and choice. Inevitably, a good teacher will respond to student needs and concerns and offer alternative assessments without diminishing the crucial nature of the TEKS.

Learning Environments for Social Science

Besides direct classroom instruction, teachers can take students on field trips to different communities, historical sites, and museums. Teachers should introduce students to the notion that history exists in all settings, finding opportunities for students to carry out research projects, project-based learning, and experiential learning in surrounding communities. Students should recognize that all materials—buildings, streets, schools, antiques, common objects—possess some semblance of historical agency. Each material item has a unique biography. By "taking to the streets," students will be more prepared for interdisciplinary scholarship and field research in higher education. Students can also be encouraged to explore their own communities to collect formal and oral histories for the classroom.

History

Connections Between Causes and Effects

When examining the historical narratives of events, it is important to understand the relationship between causes and effects. A cause can be defined as something, whether an event, social change, or other factor, that contributes to the occurrence of certain events; the results of causes are called effects. Those terms may seem simple enough, but they have drastic implications on how one explores history. Events such as the American Revolution or the Civil Rights Movement may appear to occur spontaneously, but a closer examination will reveal that these events depended on earlier phenomena and patterns that influenced the course of history.

For example, although the battles at Concord and Lexington may seem to be instantaneous eruptions of violence during the American Revolution, they stemmed from a variety of factors. The most obvious influences behind those two battles were the assortment of taxes and policies imposed on the Thirteen Colonies following the French and Indian War from 1754 to 1763. Taxation without direct representation, combined with the deployment of British soldiers to enforce these policies, greatly increased American resistance. Earlier events, such as the Boston Massacre and the Boston Tea Party, similarly stemmed from conflicts between British soldiers and local colonists over perceived tyranny and rebelliousness. Therefore, the start of the American Revolution progressed from preceding developments.

Furthermore, there can be multiple causes and effects for any situation. The existence of multiple causes can be seen through the settling of the American West. Many historians have emphasized the role of manifest destiny—the national vision of expanding across the continent—as a driving force behind the growth of the United States. Yet there were many different influences behind the expansion westward. Northern abolitionists and southern planters saw the frontier as a way to either extend or limit slavery. Economic opportunities in the West also encouraged travel westward, as did the gradual pacification of Native American tribes.

Even an individual cause can be subdivided into smaller factors or stretched out in a gradual process. Although there were numerous issues that led to the Civil War, slavery was the primary cause. However, that topic stretched back to the very founding of the nation, and the existence of slavery was a controversial topic during the creation of the Declaration of Independence and the Constitution. The abolition movement as a whole did not start until the 1830s, but nevertheless, slavery is a cause that gradually grew more important over the following decades. In addition, opponents of slavery were divided by different motivations—some believed that it stifled the economy, while others focused on moral issues.

On the other end of the spectrum, a single event can have numerous results. The rise of the telegraph, for example, had several effects on American history. The telegraph allowed news to travel much quicker and made events, such as the sinking of the USS *Maine,* which sparked the Spanish-American War, into immediate and national news. In addition, the telegraph helped make railroads run more efficiently by improving the links between stations. The faster speed of both travel and communications led to a shift in time itself, and localized times were replaced by standardized time zones across the nation.

The importance of grasping cause-and-effect relationships is critical in interpreting the growth and development of the Civil Rights Movement. Historical narratives of the movement often focus on charismatic individuals, such as Martin Luther King Jr., and they certainly played a key leadership role. Even so, elements of the movement had already emerged in previous decades through the growth of the National Association for the Advancement of Colored People (NAACP) and other organizations. Several factors proved critical to the formation of civil rights organizations during the 1950s. African American veterans returning from World War II, as well as those continuing to serve in the military, called for equal rights. Furthermore, the United States' role as a key member of the United Nations, which included African countries, required the federal government to take racial discrimination seriously.

A specific example in the Civil Rights Movement is the sit-ins during 1960, in which black and white students defied segregation policies in restaurants and other establishments. The wave is often thought to originate from spontaneous activism by students in Greensboro, North Carolina. However, there had already been other sit-ins, such as at Royal Ice Cream Parlor in Durham, North Carolina, in 1957. In fact, the sit-ins would not have spread as quickly without a preexisting network of activists across the nation, which in part stemmed from the growth of organizations through various local and national movements. By looking at such cases closely, it becomes clear that no event occurs without one—if not multiple—causes behind it, and that each historical event can have a variety of direct and indirect consequences.

One of the most critical elements of cause-and-effect relationships is how they are relevant not only in studying history but also in contemporary events. Much of the current political debate about social security and health care stems from FDR's New Deal in the 1930s, and at the time some people criticized the programs for being too extensive, while others argued that he did not go far enough with his vision. Current environmental concerns have their origins in long-term issues that reach back centuries. The United States' mixed history of global isolation and foreign intervention continues to influence foreign policy approaches today. Most of all, people must realize that events and developments today will likely have a number of consequences later on. Therefore, the study of cause and effect remains vital in understanding the past, the present, and the future.

Sequential Nature of Historical Events

Timelines are useful tools that teachers and students of history use to understand the sequential nature of events. Timelines are essential for listing events in chronological order. Knowing the chronology of events can help teachers and students understand relationships between events, and how historical context can affect human decisions. Often, in a social studies classroom, timelines assist students in understanding cause and effect. There are two basic types of chronologies that teachers can highlight for students: absolute chronology and relative chronology. Timelines are examples of absolute chronologies that arrange events in a specific order based on the dates that events occurred. Relative chronologies are less structured than absolute chronologies and merely list events in order without regarding specific dates.

Primary and Secondary Source Documents

Traditionally, historical documents have been separated into two major categories: primary sources and secondary sources. Understanding the features of each is crucial for building foundational historical inquiry skills in the K-6 classroom. Students must learn to deconstruct primary and secondary sources to gain a better understanding of historical context and personal perspective.

Primary sources contain firsthand documentation of a historical event or era. Primary sources are provided by people who have experienced an historical era or event. Primary sources capture a specific moment, context, or era in history. They are valued as eyewitness accounts and personal perspectives. Examples include diaries, memoirs, journals, letters, interviews, photographs, context-specific artwork, government documents, constitutions, newspapers, personal items, libraries, and archives. Another example of a primary source is the Declaration of Independence. This historical document captures the revolutionary sentiment of an era in American history.

Authors of secondary sources write about events, contexts, and eras in history with a relative amount of experiential, geographic, or temporal distance. Normally, secondary source authors aren't firsthand witnesses. In some cases, they may have experienced an event, but they are offering secondhand, retrospective accounts of their experience. All scholars and historians produce secondary sources—they gather primary source information and synthesize it for a new generation of students. Monographs, biographies, magazine articles, scholarly journals, theses, dissertations, textbooks, and encyclopedias are all secondary sources. In some rare instances, secondary sources become so enmeshed in their era of inquiry that they later become primary sources for future scholars and analysts.

Teachers and students alike must spend a great deal of time analyzing the relationships between primary sources, secondary sources, and their historical scopes. Juxtaposing primary sources with secondary sources helps teachers and students attain a deeper understanding of the material they are studying.

Cultural Contributions and Technological Developments

<u>Cultural Contributions and Technological Developments in Africa</u>

Between the 1500s and 1800s, over 12 million African slaves were shipped across the globe as free labor for agricultural markets. Slavery had a cultural impact not only on Africa, but also the entire globe, especially the developing colonies and nations of North and South America. The spread of African languages and cultures to the New World (called the African Diaspora) created an entirely new culture in the Americas.

Africa is also responsible for exporting important agricultural and animal domestication techniques, textile creation skills, and other technological advances to the rest of the world in antiquity. North Africans shared shipbuilding techniques with Greek and Roman civilizations, and they became leaders in mathematics and engineering. Ethiopians were the first to cultivate coffee and recognize its energizing properties. The Nile River Valley region is also believed to be one of the first to develop cotton as a textile and agricultural export.

Cultural Contributions and Technological Developments in the Americas

During the Age of Exploration, indigenous Americans taught European explorers how to cultivate such plants as maize (corn), beans, pumpkins, squash, cacao, beans, vanilla, sweet potatoes, peppers, peanuts, pineapples, sunflowers, gourds, plums, and tobacco. Native American agricultural techniques and harvesting technologies transformed the diets of people around the world. Native Americans also exported domestication techniques for turkeys and certain dog breeds, transforming the trade market for household and farm animals. Additionally, the Native American civilizations advanced studies in mathematics, engineering, and astronomy. In the United States, indigenous culture and mythology still pervades the national psyche even though many Native Americans were slaughtered by the colonial and revolutionary governments of the New World.

Revolution, in and of itself, is also one of the greatest exports of the Americas. The American Revolution, the first of its kind in the New World, became a focal point of later revolutions. Today, many revolutionary forces still look to the American Revolution for inspiration.

Cultural Contributions and Technological Developments in Europe

Much of the West's political and philosophical heritage is owed to the Greek and Roman civilizations of European antiquity. The Greeks established democracy, and the Romans established the framework of republicanism. During the Enlightenment, these classical values helped shape the revolutionary sentiments of the Founding Fathers of the United States. Christianity is another essential European export. Europe adopted the religion during Late Antiquity and the Middle Ages. Eventually, Christianity was dispersed throughout the world during the Age of Exploration. During the Enlightenment and Age of Exploration, Europe also became a leader in science, mathematics, and technology, thanks in part to the influences of North Africa, the Middle East, and the Arab world. Europeans became expert shipbuilders and explorers, refining such exploratory tools as the astrolabe and compass.

Cultural Contributions and Technological Developments in the Middle East

The Middle East has always been a hub of early civilization. Middle Easterners helped develop early mathematical principles (number systems, algebra, geometry) as well as advanced mathematics (trigonometry and calculus). Likewise, Middle Easterners were leaders in engineering and architecture during Late Antiquity and the Middle Ages. Their architectural styles influenced European and American buildings. The Middle East is also the epicenter of monotheistic religion, as the original home of Judaism, Christianity, and Islam.

Cultural Contributions and Technological Developments in Asia

Asia was responsible for dispersing gunpowder, silk, fireworks, tea, and spices throughout the world during the Age of Exploration. Following the success of overland travels across the Silk Road in the 1200s and 1300s, Europeans began to develop a fascination with the Far East. This Orientalism drove explorers to find faster sea routes to China and Japan. In many ways, the Far East's grip on the European consciousness is, perhaps, the driving force of the Age of Exploration.

Twentieth-Century Development in World History

At the turn of the twentieth century, imperialism had led to powers, such as France, the United States, and Japan, to establish spheres of influence throughout the world. The combination of imperial competition and military rivalries led to the outbreak of World War I when Archduke Ferdinand of Austria was assassinated in 1914. The war pitted the Allies, including England, France, and Russia, against the Central Powers of Austria-Hungary, Germany, and the Ottoman Empire—a large Islamic realm that encompassed Turkey, Palestine, Saudi Arabia, and Iraq. The rapid advances in military technology turned the war into a prolonged bloodbath that took its toll on all sides. By the end of the war in 1918, the Ottoman Empire had collapsed, the Austrian-Hungarian Empire was split into multiple countries, and Russia had descended into a civil war that would lead to the rise of the Soviet Union and Communism.

The Treaty of Paris ended the war, but the triumphant Allies also levied heavy fines on Germany, which led to resentment that would be accentuated by the Great Depression of the 1930s. The Great Depression destabilized the global economy and led to the rise of fascism, a militarized and dictatorial system of government, in nations such as Germany and Italy. The rapid expansion of the Axis Powers of Germany, Italy, and Japan led to the outbreak of World War II. The war was even more global than the previous conflicts, with battles occurring in Europe, Africa, and Asia. World War II encouraged the development of new technologies, such as advanced radar and nuclear weapons, that would continue to influence the course of future wars.

In the aftermath of World War II, the United Nations was formed as a step toward promoting international cooperation. Based on the preceding League of Nations, the United Nations included countries from around the world and gave them a voice in world policies. The formation of the United Nations coincided with the independence of formerly colonized states in Africa and Asia, and those countries joined the world body. A primary goal of the United Nations was to limit the extent of future wars and prevent a third world war; while the United Nations could not prevent the outbreak of wars, it nevertheless tried to peacefully resolve them. In addition to promoting world peace, the United Nations also helped protect human rights.

Even so, the primary leadership in the early United Nations was held by the United States and its allies, which contributed to tensions with the Soviet Union. The United States and the Soviet Union, while never declaring war on each other, fueled a number of proxy wars and coups across the world in what would be known as the Cold War. Cold War divisions were especially noticeable in Europe, where communist regimes ruled the eastern region and democratic governments controlled the western portion. These indirect struggles often involved interference with foreign politics, and sometimes local people began to resent Soviet or American attempts to influence their countries. For instance, American and Soviet interventions in Iran and Afghanistan contributed to fundamentalist Islamic movements. The Cold War ended when the Soviet Union collapsed in 1991, but the conflict affected nations across the globe and continues to influence current issues.

Another key development during the twentieth century, as noted earlier with the United Nations, was that most colonized nations broke free from imperial control and asserted their independence. Although these nations achieved autonomy and recognition in the United Nations, they still suffered from the legacies of imperialism. The borders of many countries in Africa and Asia were arbitrarily determined by colonists with little regard to the arrangement of native populations. Therefore, many former colonies have suffered conflicts between different ethnic groups; this was also the case with the British colony in India, which became independent in 1947. Violence occurred when it split into India and Pakistan because the borders were largely based on religious differences. In addition, former colonial powers continue to assert economic control that inhibits the growth of native economies. On the other hand, the end of direct imperialism has helped a number of nations, such as India and Iran, rise as world powers that have significant influence on the world as a whole.

Additionally, there were considerable environmental reforms worldwide during the twentieth century. In reaction to the growing effects of industrialization, organizations around the world protested policies that damaged the environment. Many of these movements were locally based, but others expanded to address various environmental threats across the globe. The United Nations helped carry these environmental reforms forward by making them part of international policies. For instance, in 1997, many members of the United Nations signed a treaty, known as the *Kyoto Protocol*, that tried to reduce global carbon dioxide emissions.

Most significantly, the twentieth century marked increasing globalization. The process had already been under way in the nineteenth century as technological improvements and imperial expansions connected different parts of the world, but the late twentieth century brought globalization to a new level. Trade became international, and local customs from different lands also gained prominence worldwide. Cultural exchanges occur on a frequent basis, and many people have begun to ponder the consequences of such rapid exchanges. One example of globalization was the 1993 establishment of the European Union—an economic and political alliance between several European nations.

European Exploration in North America and Factors that Shaped British Colonial America

Early Exploration

European exploration in North America dates back to around 1000 AD when Scandinavian Vikings, led by Leif Eriksson, first made their way to Greenland and then journeyed on to modern-day Newfoundland. They settled briefly in an area now known as L'Anse Meadows. However, clashes with the Native American people living nearby caused them to return to Greenland a few years later. The first permanent settlements in North America began after Italian sailor Christopher Columbus landed in the Caribbean in 1492. This was a significant breakthrough since most Europeans did not know that this huge landmass even existed. It initiated a period of discovery, conquest, and colonization of the Americas by the Europeans. Often referred to as the *Columbian Exchange*, this period allowed people who had been cut off from each other for 15,000 years to share knowledge, ideas, culture, food, plants and animals, technology, and religion; this led to significant changes and enhancements for both regions.

European Expansion and Influence

Other European cultures quickly followed, sending sailors across the Atlantic to find new passages to the East and lay claim to new lands. Explorers typically hailed from countries with a seafaring reputation. Spain, France, and England were the major forces, whereas Portugal, Holland, Russia, and Sweden played lesser roles. This merging of cultures had an unfortunate effect on the Native American people who were not immune to the diseases the new arrivals brought with them. Millions died from deadly diseases; others were killed or enslaved in territorial encounters when some Europeans sought to conquer the Indians. Over the next few centuries, this led to a 90 percent population decline among the Native Americans.

England and Spain waged the biggest struggle to claim the most land in North America. Spain took the initial lead in the early 1500s, exploring or establishing settlements in the southern portion of what is now the United States. Spain settled in present-day Florida, Texas, California, Arizona, New Mexico, Mexico, and a good portion of Central America and South America. Up until the 1840s, Spain, and later Mexico, controlled large expanses of the area now known as the southwestern United States.

Colonization

The British first established a presence in 1585 when Sir Walter Raleigh founded the Roanoke colony in what was then called Virginia, but later became North Carolina. It is now known as the *Lost Colony* because John White, the colony's leader, went back to England for supplies in 1587 and later returned to find that all of the colonists had mysteriously disappeared. In 1607, the British established their first permanent settlement in Jamestown, Virginia. In 1620, a group of approximately one hundred people sailed from England on the *Mayflower* and landed at a site they named Plymouth. Many were Pilgrims seeking religious freedom. They founded the first permanent European settlement in New England. Within seventy-five years, England had established thirteen British colonies along the east coast of North America, laying the foundation for the future United States of America.

French Influence

The French gained a stronghold in Canada in 1534 when Jacques Cartier sailed up the St. Lawrence River and claimed the territory for France. In 1608, French explorer Samuel de Champlain further explored the region and later founded Quebec. By 1673, France expanded their claim from Canada to the Gulf of Mexico when Father Jacques Marquette and Louis Joliet journeyed down the Mississippi River, naming the territory Louisiana after King Louis XIV.

Key People, Events, and Developments in the History of the United States between 1860 and 1945

Slavery

Slavery was an issue for America from its early days when Africans were brought to Virginia to work in the tobacco fields. In the 1800s, the Underground Railroad was a secret network of tunnels and safe houses that helped slaves escape slavery in the South and gain freedom in the North. Escaped slave Harriet Tubman was its most famous "conductor." Slave owners and abolitionists bitterly debated slavery, and southern leaders began to threaten secession. Slavery became the major focus of the 1860 presidential election, particularly since the South was convinced that Abraham Lincoln would abolish slavery if elected. Lincoln won the election, which only further increased tensions. Southern states began to secede in late 1860. By February 1861, they had formed the new nation of the Confederate States of America, electing Jefferson Davis as their president in November of that year.

Civil War

In April 1861, Confederate soldiers fired upon a Union-held ship seeking to reinforce Fort Sumter in Charleston, South Carolina. This signaled the beginning of the Civil War and divided the U.S. into the North (Union) and South (Confederates). The two sides battled for four years, and the smaller Confederate Army surprised the Union Army with their tenacity. The Confederate Army claimed various victories throughout Virginia from 1861-1863 under the leadership of General Robert E. Lee. These victories included the Battle of Bull Run, Fredericksburg, and Chancellorsville. The turning point was the Battle of Gettysburg in Pennsylvania, which resulted in 51,000 troops on both sides being killed, wounded, or declared missing. The Confederate Army suffered a loss of one-third of its soldiers. In 1864, Union General William T. Sherman marched through Georgia, burning Atlanta and devastating much of the landscape. In 1865, he then moved through the Carolinas to Richmond, Virginia where General Lee, who was facing the determined assaults of future president Ulysses S. Grant, surrendered. Five days later, John Wilkes Booth shot President Lincoln who was watching a play at Ford's Theatre in Washington, D.C.; Lincoln died the next morning.

Reconstruction

During the Reconstruction period following the Civil War, the North and South continued to wage power and economic struggles. Many African Americans from the South moved north and west to seek more fair treatment. The American frontier provided opportunities for immigrants and others seeking new prospects. Many people made their way west, farming the land and finding jobs in industries such as mining, forestry, and oil. This forced Native Americans to fight for their land or pick up and move to reservations. In the 1876 conflict known as *Custer's Last Stand*, Colonel George Custer's troops were killed by a group of Sioux Indians led by Chiefs Crazy Horse and Sitting Bull. This defeat angered the U.S.

government and caused them to increase their efforts against the Indians, which put an end to the Indian Wars. The introduction of the railroad in the mid-nineteenth century provided many jobs and allowed people and goods to travel the vast landscape of North America at a much quicker pace.

Industrial Revolution

Author Mark Twain deemed the period of business and industrial growth from 1876 through the turn of the twentieth century as the *Gilded Age* since it appeared shiny and golden on the surface, but was fueled by undercurrents of corruption led by big businessmen known as robber barons. They controlled many of America's booming new industries, including steel (Andrew Carnegie), steamships and railroads (Cornelius Vanderbilt), oil (John D. Rockefeller), and banking (J.P. Morgan). None of the U.S. Presidents during this period were particularly strong leaders and practiced a hands-off approach to business. High tariffs were another issue supported by businesses and Congress. In 1890, Congress passed the McKinley Tariff, named after future President and then Representative William McKinley. This tariff raised duties over 48 percent on average.

U.S. Expansion

The U.S. continued to seek out and acquire new lands, a tactic often referred to as *Manifest Destiny*. This practice led to the purchase of Alaska from Russia in 1867 and the annexation of Hawaii in 1898. The Spanish-American War in 1898 lasted just a few weeks, but helped Cuba gain its independence from Spain and helped the U.S. gain a strategic foothold in many distant locales that were formerly Spanish territories. These included Guam and the Philippines. Future president Theodore Roosevelt became a hero when his troops defeated the Spanish fleet at the Battle of San Juan Hill.

World War I

World War I began in 1914 when a Serbian assassin killed Archduke Franz Ferdinand of Austria, which prompted Austria-Hungary to declare war on Serbia. Due to protective alliances they had forged, other European countries soon joined the war. If one country was attacked, the country's allies were obliged to defend it.

Most Americans supported the Allies, particularly after German submarines sank the passenger ship *Lusitania* in 1915, killing 128 Americans. In 1917, news leaked that Germany was trying to turn Mexico against the U.S. As a result, President Woodrow Wilson declared war on Germany. American troops helped defeat the German army in September 1918. Fighting ended in November of that year after Germany signed a peace agreement. President Woodrow Wilson's plan for peace was the League of Nations, which was adopted as part of the Treaty of Versailles in 1919, but then rejected by the U.S. Senate.

Prohibition and The Great Depression

Prohibition (the 18th Amendment to the U.S. Constitution) was passed in 1919 and prohibited the production and sale of alcoholic beverages. This amendment fueled corruption since people made, sold, and transported liquor illegally. The 21st Amendment repealed it in 1933. Women had been campaigning for the right to vote since the 1840s, and these suffragettes used the outbreak of World War I to leverage their fight, stating they would help support the war if they were granted the right to vote. The 19th Amendment, which guaranteed women the right to vote in federal elections, was finally passed by Congress in 1919 and ratified the following year. On October 29, 1929 (referred to as Black Tuesday) the stock market crashed, marking the beginning of the Great Depression that lasted through the 1930s. President Franklin Delano Roosevelt's solution was the *New Deal*—a variety of new programs and laws to provide government funding to help rebuild America's economy.

World War II

In 1939, after Adolf Hitler began to invade and occupy several European nations, World War II broke out in Europe and many countries declared war on Germany. Germany aligned with Italy and Japan in 1940 to form the Axis Alliance. Their goal was to establish a German empire in Europe and place Japan in control over Asia. When Germany invaded the Soviet Union in June 1941, the Soviets immediately allied with Britain. The U.S. entered the war when Japan bombed Pearl Harbor in Hawaii on December 7, 1941. Battles raged in Europe and the Pacific, and the Allied forces won an important victory in June 1942 at the Battle of Midway. At this battle, the U.S. stopped the Japanese from advancing and prevented the invasion of Australia. In 1943, Axis troops in North Africa surrendered to the Allies, who then began to invade Italy, and finally France on June 6, 1944 (known as D-Day), which resulted in severe losses on both sides. In early 1945, President Roosevelt met with British Prime Minister Winston Churchill and Soviet director Joseph Stalin in Yalta, Crimea to plan their final assault on Germany and discuss postwar strategies. The Allies continued their attack, liberating Nazi death camps. This forced Hitler to commit suicide, and Germany surrendered in May. However, Japan did not yield, even after the capture of Okinawa in June. As a result, the U.S. dropped an atomic bomb on the Japanese cities of Hiroshima and then Nagasaki, forcing Japan to surrender in early September.

Key People, Events, and Developments in the United States between 1950 and the Present

In the years following World War II, the U.S. and Soviet Union arose as the two dominant world forces. But because the countries had very different political systems—democracy (the U.S.) and Communism (the Soviet Union)—a feeling of mistrust developed between the two. This was heightened by the fact that both countries had developed nuclear weapons. This became known as the Cold War. The Soviet Union introduced Communism into Eastern Europe, which it had occupied since World War II. This led to the formation of the North Atlantic Treaty Organization (NATO) between Western Europe, Canada, and the U.S. in defense of Soviet hostility. The Soviet Union countered by creating the Warsaw Pact.

United Nations

Toward the end of World War II, a group of fifty nations (including the U.S. and the Soviet Union) formed the United Nations as a peacekeeping group. However, Communism still continued to spread throughout the world, including to Latin America, Africa, and Asia. When Communist North Korea invaded South Korea in June 1950, the U.N. sent a group of troops led by the U.S. to help South Korea. This action led to a three-year conflict that ended in a cease-fire in 1953. Although war was never officially declared and neither side won, the fighting showcased President Truman's hard stance against Communism.

Baby Boom

The 1950s were generally a prosperous time for Americans. Many Americans took advantage of college loan programs and the G.I. Bill, which gave military veterans a free education. Mortgage programs provided more affordable housing, which enabled many people to move to the suburbs. The population surged during this *baby boom*, labor unions helped workers increase their wages, and people were able to afford more expensive items, such as cars and television sets.

Civil Rights Movement

During this time, African Americans were still repressed, particularly in the southern U.S., and segregation was rampant in many public places. When the Supreme Court ruled that school segregation was illegal in 1954 in the revolutionary case *Brown vs. the Board of Education*, the Civil Rights Movement was set in motion. This movement continued throughout the 1950s and 1960s and included dozens of nonviolent protests, such as the Montgomery bus boycott in Alabama. The boycott was organized after Rosa Parks was arrested because she refused to give up her seat on the bus to a white man. The Southern Christian Leadership Conference (SCLC) was soon formed as a way to bring African Americans together to help fight segregation in a peaceful way. The Reverend Dr. Martin Luther King, Jr. was its first president. Dr. King and his supporters kept up the fight throughout the 1960s, staging sit-ins at segregated lunch counters, *Freedom Rides* on segregated buses, and marches and protests in segregated cities, such as Birmingham, Alabama. The demonstrations often ended in violence and police brutality, which served to aid the cause and led to the passage of the Civil Rights Act in 1964.

U.S. Conflicts

The Cold War between the U.S. and Soviets continued as both countries tried to assert their dominance through technological and military advances. This spawned events such as the creation of the Berlin Wall by the Russians in 1961, which was devised to separate the sector of Berlin they occupied from the area controlled by the Western allies (France, Britain, and the U.S.). The Cuban Missile Crisis in 1962 was sparked by the failed invasion of Cuba by the U.S. a year earlier. After the invasion, the Soviets placed nuclear missiles aimed at the U.S. in Cuba. However, when U.S. spy planes spotted them, President John F. Kennedy demanded the dismantling and removal of the missile sites, and as a concession agreed to go forward with the planned removal of U.S. missile sites in Turkey. A year later on November 22, 1963, President Kennedy was assassinated in Dallas by Lee Harvey Oswald.

Space Race

The Cold War prompted the *space race* between the U.S. and Soviets, each attempting to outdo the other with different space exploration milestones. In 1957, the Russians launched *Sputnik*, the first satellite, into space. This prompted President Eisenhower to establish the National Aeronautics and Space Administration (NASA) in 1958. Although the Soviets were also the first nation to send a human into space in 1961, the U.S. quickly caught up. President Kennedy vowed to land an American on the moon by 1969—a feat that was accomplished by astronaut Neil Armstrong on July 20, 1969.

Vietnam War

In 1954, rebels seized control of Vietnam from France. The country was split into two regimes with the northern part under Communist leadership. As the threat of communism continued to loom, the U.S. sent advisors and weapons to South Vietnam beginning in 1955. The U.S. got more directly involved in the 1960s during the presidency of Lyndon B. Johnson, who sent troops in great numbers to help South Vietnam win the fight. Many Americans opposed the war, which caused anti-war protests and unrest. A cease-fire was signed in 1973, and the last U.S. forces pulled out in 1975.

Women's Rights Movement

Due to the Women's Liberation Movement and the creation of the National Organization for Women (NOW) in 1966, the 1960s and 1970s were an important time for women. Women gained the right to vote in 1920, but still were not on equal terms with men in many areas. Suffragist leader Alice Paul had introduced the Equal Rights Amendment (ERA) in 1923 to help bridge this gap. Congress finally passed the ERA in 1972 and sent it to the states for ratification. However, not all states ratified the amendment, and to date only a total of thirty-five have ratified it, which is three less than the thirty-eight required to pass. In the controversial 1973 court case *Roe vs. Wade*, the Supreme Court gave women the right to legally obtain abortions within the first three months of pregnancy.

1970s and Watergate

U.S. diplomatic relations with the Communist nations of China and the Soviet Union improved a bit in the 1970s. President Richard Nixon paid visits to both countries in 1972. The Strategic Arms Limitation Talks (SALT I and II), negotiated between 1972 and 1979, resulted in limits on nuclear weapons for both the U.S. and Russia. In 1974, Nixon became the first and only U.S. president to resign from office as a result of the Watergate scandal. The scandal erupted when five of his staff members were caught stealing information from the Democratic Party headquarters in Washington, D.C. In 1973, a group of Arab nations tried to regain land seized by Israel in the 1967 Six-Day War. The U.S. was a main Israeli ally, and the Arab-controlled Organization of Petroleum Countries (OPEC) cut off oil shipments to the U.S. Because the U.S. was highly dependent on imports of oil from the Middle East, this energy crisis resulted in a huge surge in gas prices and long lines at the pumps.

The Reagan Years

In his role as U.S. president from 1980-1988, Ronald Reagan was against big government and supported industry deregulation, fewer social programs, lower taxes, and bigger military spending. A scandal referred to as the Iran-Contra Affair emerged during Reagan's presidency, involving the secret sale of weapons to Iran in exchange for American hostages. Profits from the sale were then sent to aid Nicaraguan Contras in their cause to overthrow the communist Sandinista government. Reagan opposed Communism and advocated *peace through strength*, building up the U.S. military and launching the Strategic Defense Initiative (SDI), also called *Star Wars*, designed to shield the U.S. from nuclear attack. Reagan worked with Soviet President Gorbachev to put controls on nuclear weapons after Gorbachev launched the policies of *glasnost* (political openness) and *perestroika* (economic restructuring). This led to the breakup of the Soviet Union, and the end of the Cold War.

Desert Storm

In 1990, Iraqi dictator Saddam Hussein invaded Kuwait in order to take possession of the tiny country's huge oil fields. A few months later, U.S. President George H.W. Bush launched Operation Desert Storm with a coalition of several Middle Eastern and European countries. This Gulf War started with air bombings and ended in a five-day ground war that drove Hussein out.

The Clinton Years

Democratic President William (Bill) Clinton was elected in 1992. Unlike Reagan, he supported social programs, although his plan for a national health care system never passed through Congress. He negotiated the North American Free Trade Agreement (NAFTA) with Canada and Mexico in 1993. In 1996, he was impeached for lying under oath about his relationship with a young White House intern, Monica Lewinsky, but the Senate did not think his crimes were severe enough to remove him from office.

1990s and Technology Boom

IBM had introduced personal computers in 1981, and the early 1990s marked the public adoption of the Internet, an interconnected communications network that changed the way people accessed information. The 1990s were also a time of violence. This violence included bombings on New York's World Trade Center in 1993 by an Islamic Fundamentalist group, the bombing of the Murrah Federal Building in Oklahoma City in 1995 by antigovernment extremists, race riots, and school shootings.

September 11th Terrorist Attacks

On September 11, 2001, terrorists led by Islamic fundamentalist Osama bin Laden hijacked four airplanes. Terrorists flew two planes into the World Trade Center in New York City, bringing down both buildings, and flew one plane into the Pentagon in Washington, D.C. The other plane crashed into a Pennsylvania field when passengers tried to overthrow the terrorists. The terrorist attack killed over three thousand people. This led President George W. Bush to wage a *war on terror* and resulted in bombing raids on various locations in Afghanistan where bin Laden and his al-Qaeda network were purportedly hiding. When Iraqi dictator Saddam Hussein defied terms of the truce agreed upon in 1991 after the Gulf War, Bush was convinced that the country possessed *weapons of mass destruction* (WMDs) and invaded Iraq in 2003.

Obama's Presidency

Barack Obama, America's first African American President, was elected in 2008. Fighting in the Iraq region continued between groups with differing political and religious views. Obama pulled U.S. troops from the region in 2011, but many have been trickling back into the country in efforts to help maintain order. In 2011, Obama gave the order to launch a raid on bin Laden's compound in Pakistan, which resulted in a group of Navy SEALs finding and killing the al-Qaeda leader. In December 2010, a revolution in Tunisia kicked off a series of democratic uprisings and protests throughout the Middle East. These uprisings are often referred to as the *Arab Spring*. The U.S. pledged support and military aid, but tensions continue to escalate particularly in Syria. The militant group Islamic State of Iraq and al-Sham (ISIS) has taken advantage of the Syrian civil war by launching a series of terrorist attacks there and in areas outside the Middle East. Domestically, one of Obama's pledges was to launch a health care reform plan providing affordable and accessible health care for all Americans. He signed the Affordable Care Act, sometimes referred to as *Obamacare*, into law in 2010.

Immigration and Settlement Patterns that have Shaped the History of the U.S.

Constant immigration meant that land prices in the eastern United States rose, and people sought new economic opportunities on the frontier where land was cheaper. The United States government tried purchasing land from Native Americans, but most refused to relinquish their territories. Native Americans continued to defend their land until Tecumseh was defeated in the War of 1812. This defeat helped secure the Northwest Territory, and more settlers began pouring in. After the Louisiana Purchase, Lewis and Clark paved the way for expansion into the Great Plains and further west.

Several important laws also stimulated western expansion during the second half of the 19th century. Congress passed the Homestead Act in 1862, which allowed citizens to claim 160 acres for only $1.25 per acre. The settler also had to live on the land for five years and make improvements. That same year, Congress also passed the Pacific Railroad Act, which supported the construction of a transcontinental railroad. The United States government provided land and financial support to railroad companies and the first transcontinental link was established in 1869. This facilitated trade and communication between the eastern and western United States.

As Americans poured westward, conflict again broke out between settlers and Native Americans. The discovery of gold in the Black Hills of South Dakota caused prospectors to flood into the area although the U.S. government had recognized the territory belonged to the Sioux. General George Armstrong Custer brought in troops to try and take possession of the Black Hills. This led to disaster when Custer and more than 250 soldiers died at the Battle of Little Big Horn in 1876.

The U.S. government continued its efforts to control Native American tribes. The Dawes Act of 1887 encouraged Native Americans to settle on reservations and become farmers in exchange for U.S. citizenship. Chief Joseph was a leader of the Nez Perce tribe who refused to live on a reservation and tried to flee to Canada. However, the U.S. captured Chief Joseph and his tribe and forced them onto a reservation. Reformers also required Native Americans to send their children to boarding schools where they had to speak English and dress like Caucasians instead of maintaining their traditional culture. The schools were often crowded, and students were also subjected to physical and sexual abuse.

In 1890, the Lakota Indians tried to preserve their traditional beliefs by performing a special ceremony called a Ghost Dance. U.S. government officials felt threatened and sent soldiers to try and disarm the

Lakota. This led to the Massacre at Wounded Knee in 1890 where at least 150 Lakota, including many women and children, were slaughtered. It was the last major conflict between Native Americans and U.S. forces.

Cultural Contributions to Florida

The historical development of Florida can be broken into eight major categories: 1) Florida's prehistory, 2) exploration and colonization, 3) the 18th century, 4) American possession and Indian removal, 5) antebellum slavery and the Civil War era, 6) Reconstruction and railroads, 7) 20th century advances, and 8) postwar immigration and the allure of the Sun Belt.

Florida's Prehistory

Around 12,000 years ago, Florida's coastline extended further into the Atlantic Ocean and the Gulf of Mexico. In fact, the peninsula was twice as large as modern-day Florida. During this time, Florida's first inhabitants settled there after migrating from eastern Asia to North America. Following the Ice Age, these Paleo-Indians, as they are now called, altered their nomadic lives to accommodate the warmer climates. Around 700-500 BCE, the Paleo-Indians of Florida began creating more stable political and social institutions, adopting the technological and environmental changes spawned by the wider Agricultural Revolution. Natives began to cultivate corn in the northern half of modern-day Florida.

Exploration and Colonization (Pre-Statehood)

Juan Ponce de Leon became the first European explorer to arrive on the Florida peninsula. In 1513, the adventurer docked his ships at the modern city of St. Augustine, naming the land *la Florida* after the Feast of Flowers in his home nation of Spain. Attacks from the natives stifled any attempts at immediate colonization. Over twenty years later, Spanish explorer Hernando de Soto explored the Tallahassee region of Florida in search of treasure, but he did not establish a colony.

Between the 1550s and 1560s, Spanish and French settlers tried to establish colonies in Florida, but with little success. By the 1570s and 1580s, as colonization accelerated for the major European powers, Florida became a sought-after prize for the Spanish, French, and English. While English explorers like Sir Francis Drake successfully attacked Spanish forts, Spain remained the unassailable power of the Caribbean region. Even with English colonies sprouting in the north and French colonies expanding in the west, Spain held on to Florida throughout most of the 17th century.

18th Century

Florida fell into different colonial hands on several occasions during the 18th century. On several occasions, English colonists attacked Spanish forts and missions, including a failed siege on the Castillo de San Marcos at St. Augustine in 1740. Following the Seven Years' War of 1756-1763, Florida briefly became a British colony. Nevertheless, by 1781, Florida returned to Spanish control following the treaty that ended the American War for Independence. Throughout this time, Native Americans in Florida, specifically the Seminoles of Creek descent, fought for their homeland, adding to the conflict in the region.

American Possession and Indian Removal

In 1821, Spain ceded Florida to the United States government. President Andrew Jackson, who had already fought in the First Seminole War in 1818, had a vested interest in the region, establishing it a territory of the United States. The new territory diversified the United States, adding more Spanish colonists, African-American slaves, and Native Americans to the growing nation. In 1845, Florida gained admission into the union as the 27th state. As more Anglo-Americans moved to Florida in the antebellum period to establish plantations, many residents started to pressure the President to remove the lingering Native American tribes. Between 1835 and 1842, the U.S government waged a war with the remaining Seminoles. Jackson allocated millions of dollars to remove the Seminoles to Oklahoma (then called Indian Territory). Seminoles who resisted were forced onto confining reservations in Florida if they didn't accept relocation to Oklahoma.

Antebellum Slavery and the Civil War Era
Sometimes labeled the "Forgotten State of the Civil War," Florida remained tied to slavery in the antebellum and Civil War eras. Nearly half of the population in the antebellum period—almost 60,000 people—were slaves. Most Floridian plantation owners refused to accept abolition, leading to Florida's secession from the Union on January 10, 1861. Thousands of white residents joined the Confederate army, heading North for battle, as no decisive Civil War skirmishes were fought in Florida.

Reconstruction and Railroads
Farming remained vital to the agricultural economy of Florida during the Reconstruction era. During Reconstruction, white and black sharecroppers moved to Florida to develop the farming sector. Railroad construction provided access to the remote state, catalyzing citrus production and tourism. By the late 19th century, Florida became a major player in the American tourism industry as businessmen drained swamps for lavish hotels. By the time the Spanish-American War rolled around, Florida had become a key port state for the growing U.S. military.

Twentieth Century Advances
Thanks to the growth of the railroad, agricultural, and tourism industries, population and wealth were booming in Florida by the end of World War I. Yet a combination of local environmental disasters (hurricanes and the introduction of the Mediterranean fruit fly) and national economic disaster (the Great Depression) stifled economic growth in the late 1920s-1940s. Women gained the right to vote in this era, and by 1944, whites-only primary elections were outlawed in Florida. The expanding U.S. military industrial complex reached well into Florida, further diversifying the populace.

Postwar Immigration and the Allure of the Cold War Sunbelt
The U.S. Immigration and Nationality Act of 1965 transformed the ethnic fabric of the United States, eliminating many of the previous quotas on immigration from the Middle East and East Asia. Consequently, the Act helped to diversify states such as Florida during the Cold War. During this time, highway construction and the invention of air conditioning brought many to Florida. Northern laborers and retirees migrated to the Sunshine State to escape the harsh winters and economic desolation of the Rust Belt. This era also witnessed the desegregation of schools and the expansion of the universities in Florida. Community colleges and state university systems surrounded the burgeoning U.S. Space Program at Cape Canaveral. The arrival of the National Aeronautics and Space Administration in the 1950s and 1960s brought a sort of "brain boom" during the Cold War, which witnessed Florida becoming the home of immigrants seeking to aid in the ongoing space race with the Soviet Union. Tourist attractions such as Walt Disney World also brought millions of people to Florida. In this era, Florida became home for Cuban, Caribbean, and Latin America refugees seeking escape from hostile governments.

Major Contributions of Classical Civilizations

There were a number of powerful civilizations during the classical period. Mesopotamia was home to one of the earliest civilizations between the Euphrates and the Tigris rivers in the Near East. The rivers provided water and vegetation for early humans, but they were surrounded by desert. This led to the beginning of irrigation efforts to expand water and agriculture across the region, which resulted in the area being known as the Fertile Crescent.

The organization necessary to initiate canals and other projects led to the formation of cities and hierarchies, which would have considerable influence on the structure of later civilizations. For instance, the new hierarchies established different classes within the societies, such as kings, priests, artisans, and workers. Over time, these city-states expanded to encompass outside territories, and the city of Akkad became the world's first empire in 2350 B.C. In addition, Mesopotamian scribes developed systemized drawings called pictograms, which were the first system of writing in the world; furthermore, the creation of wedge-shaped cuneiform tablets preserved written records for multiple generations.

Later, Mesopotamian kingdoms made further advancements. For instance, Babylon established a sophisticated mathematical system based on numbers from one to sixty; this not only influenced modern concepts, such as the number of minutes in each hour, but also created the framework for math equations and theories. In addition, the Babylonian king Hammurabi established a complex set of laws, known as the Code of Hammurabi, which would set a precedent for future legal systems.

Meanwhile, another major civilization began to form around the Nile River in Africa. The Nile's relatively predictable nature allowed farmers to use the river's water and the silt from floods to grow many crops along its banks, which led to further advancements in irrigation. Egyptian rulers mobilized the kingdom's population for incredible construction projects, including the famous pyramids. Egyptians also improved pictographic writing with their more complex system of hieroglyphs, which allowed for more diverse styles of writing. The advancements in writing can be seen through the Egyptians' complex system of religion, with documents such as the *Book of the Dead* outlining not only systems of worship and pantheons of deities but also a deeper, more philosophical concept of the afterlife.

While civilizations in Egypt and Mesopotamia helped to establish class systems and empires, other forms of government emerged in Greece. Despite common ties between different cities, such as the Olympic Games, each settlement, known as a polis, had its own unique culture. Many of the cities were oligarchies, in which a council of distinguished leaders monopolized the government; others were dictatorships ruled by tyrants. Athens was a notable exception by practicing an early form of democracy in which free, landholding men could participate, but it offered more freedom of thought than other systems.

Taking advantage of their proximity to the Mediterranean Sea, Greek cities sent expeditions to establish colonies abroad that developed their own local traditions. In the process, Greek merchants interacted with Phoenician traders, who had developed an alphabetic writing system built on sounds instead of pictures. This diverse network of exchanges made Greece a vibrant center of art, science, and philosophy. For example, the Greek doctor Hippocrates established a system of ethics for doctors called the Hippocratic Oath, which continues to guide the modern medical profession. Complex forms of literature were created, including the epic poem "The Iliad," and theatrical productions were also developed. Athens in particular sought to spread its vision of democratic freedom throughout the world, which led to the devastating Peloponnesian War between allies of Athens and those of oligarchic Sparta from 431 to 404 B.C.

Alexander the Great helped disseminate Greek culture to new regions. Alexander was in fact an heir to the throne of Macedon, which was a warrior kingdom to the north of Greece. After finishing his father's work of unifying Greece under Macedonian control, Alexander successfully conquered Mesopotamia, which had been part of the Persian Empire. The spread of Greek institutions throughout the

Mediterranean and Near East led to a period of Hellenization, during which various civilizations assimilated Greek culture; this allowed Greek traditions, such as architecture and philosophy, to endure into the present day.

Greek ideas were later assimilated, along with many other concepts, into the Roman Empire. Located west of Greece on the Italian peninsula, the city of Rome gradually conquered its neighbors and expanded its territories abroad; by 44 B.C., Rome had conquered much of Western Europe, northern Africa, and the Near East. Romans were very creative, and they adapted new ideas and innovated new technologies to strengthen their power. For instance, Romans built on the engineering knowledge of Greeks to create arched pathways, known as aqueducts, to transport water for long distances and devise advanced plumbing systems.

One of Rome's greatest legacies was its system of government. Early Rome was a republic, a democratic system in which leaders are elected by the people. Although the process still heavily favored wealthy elites, the republican system was a key inspiration for later institutions such as the United States. Octavian "Augustus" Caesar later made Rome into an empire, and the senate had only a symbolic role in the government. The new imperial system built on the examples of earlier empires to establish a vibrant dynasty that used a sophisticated legal code and a well-trained military to enforce order across vast regions. Even after Rome itself fell to barbarian invaders in fifth century A.D., the eastern half of the empire survived as the Byzantine Empire until 1453 A.D. Furthermore, the Roman Empire's institutions continued to influence and inspire later medieval kingdoms, including the Holy Roman Empire; even rulers in the twentieth century called themselves Kaiser and Tsar, titles which stem from the word "Caesar."

In addition, the Roman Empire was host to the spread of new religious ideas. In the region of Israel, the religion of Judaism presented a new approach to worship via monotheism, which is the belief in the existence of a single deity. An offshoot of Judaism called Christianity spread across the Roman Empire and gained popularity. While Rome initially suppressed the religion, it later backed Christianity and allowed the religious system to endure as a powerful force in medieval times.

Geography

Six Spatial Elements of Geography

Spatial Terms

Earth is an incredibly large place filled with a variety of different land and water *ecosystems*. *Marine ecosystems* cover over 75 percent of the Earth's surface and contain over 95 percent of the Earth's water. Marine ecosystems can be broken down into two primary subgroups: *freshwater ecosystems*, which only encompass around 2 percent of the earth's surface; and *ocean ecosystems*, which make up over 70 percent. On land, *terrestrial ecosystems* vary depending on a variety of factors, including latitudinal distance from the equator, elevation, and proximity to mountains or bodies of water. For example, in the high latitudinal regions north of the Arctic Circle and south of the Antarctic Circle, frozen *tundra* dominates. Tundra, which is characterized by low temperatures, short growing seasons, and minimal vegetation, is only found in regions that are far away from the direct rays of the sun.

In contrast, *deserts* can be found throughout the globe and are created by different ecological factors. For example, the world's largest desert, the Sahara, is almost entirely within the tropics; however, other deserts like the Gobi in China, the Mojave in the United States, and the Atacama in Chile, are the result of the orographic effect and their close proximity to high mountain ranges such as the Himalayas, the

Sierra Nevada, and the Andes, respectively. In the Middle Latitudes, greater varieties of climatological zones are more common due to fluctuations in temperatures relative to the sun's rays, coupled with the particular local topography. In the Continental United States, *temperate deciduous forest* dominates the southeastern portion of the country. However, the Midwestern states such as Nebraska, Kansas, and the Dakotas, are primarily *grasslands*. Additionally, the states of the Rocky Mountains can have decidedly different climates relative to elevation. In Colorado, Denver, also known as the "Mile High City," will often see snowfalls well into late April or early May due to colder temperatures, whereas towns and cities in the eastern part of the state, with much lower elevations, may see their last significant snowfall in March.

In the tropics, which are situated between the Tropics of Cancer and Capricorn, temperatures are generally warmer, due to the direct rays of the sun's persistence. However, like most of the world, the tropics also experience a variety of climatological regions. In Brazil, Southeast Asia, Central America, and even Northern Australia, tropical rainforests are common. These forests, which are known for abundant vegetation, daily rainfall, and a wide variety of animal life, are absolutely essential to the health of the world's ecosystems. For example, the *Amazon Rain Forest* is also referred to as "the lungs of the world," as its billions of trees produce substantial amounts of oxygen and absorb an equivalent amount of carbon dioxide—the substance that many climatologists assert is causing climate change or *global warming*. Unlike temperate deciduous forests whose trees lose their leaves during the fall and winter months, *tropical rain forests* are always lush, green, and warm. In fact, some rainforests are so dense with vegetation that a few indigenous tribes have managed to exist within them without being influenced by any sort of modern technology, virtually maintaining their ancient way of life in the modern era.

The world's largest ecosystem, the *taiga*, is found primarily in high latitudinal areas, which receive very little of the sun's indirect rays. These forests are generally made up of *coniferous* trees, which do not lose their leaves at any point during the year as *deciduous* trees do. Taigas are cold-climate regions that make up almost 30 percent of the world's land area. These forests dominate the northern regions of Canada, Scandinavia, and Russia, and provide the vast majority of the world's lumber.

Overall, it is important to remember that climates are influenced by five major factors: elevation, latitude, proximity to mountains, ocean currents, and wind patterns. For example, the cold currents off the coast of California provide the West Coast of the United States with pleasant year-round temperatures. Conversely, Western Europe, which is at the nearly the same latitude as most of Canada, is influenced by the warm waters of the *Gulf Stream*, an ocean current that acts as a conveyor belt, moving warm tropical waters to the icy north. In fact, the Gulf Stream's influence is so profound that it even keeps Iceland—an island nation in the far North Atlantic—relatively warm.

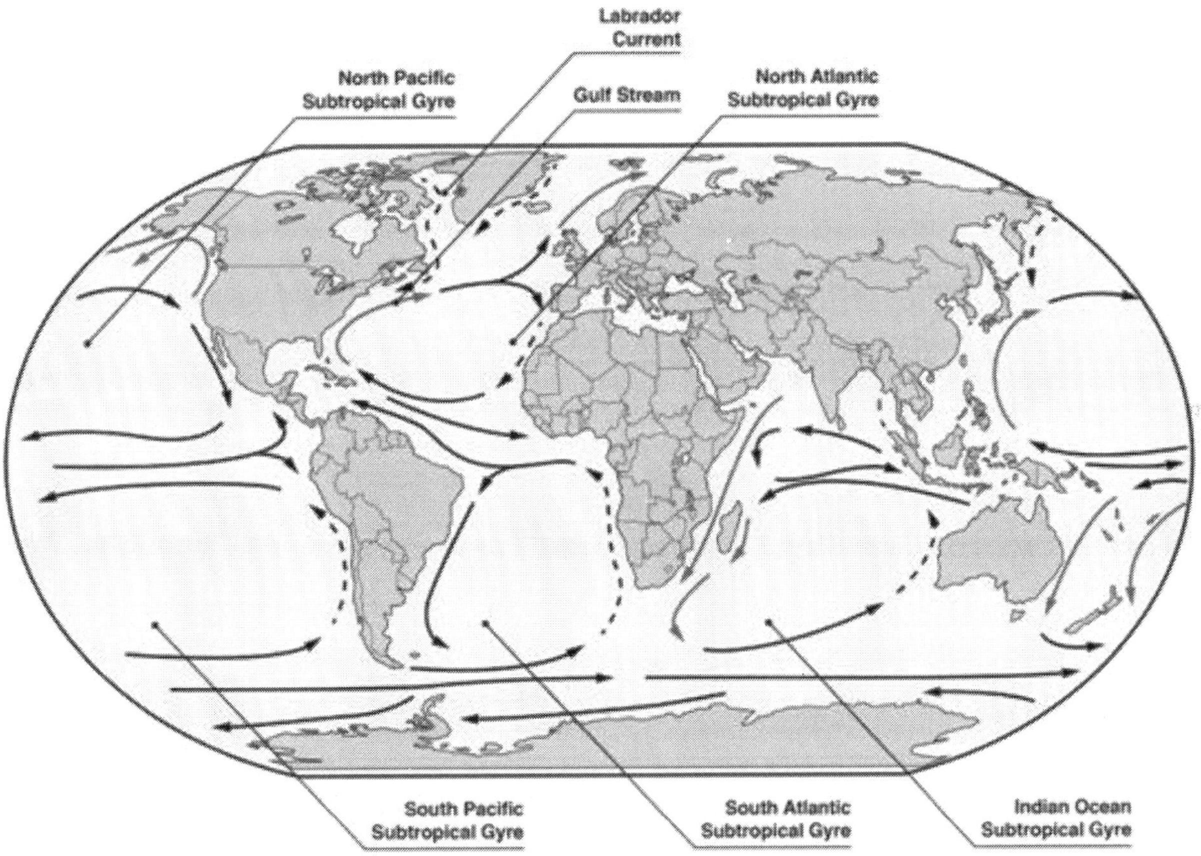

Places and Regions

Both absolute and relative location help humans understand their sense of place. Place is a simple concept that helps to define the characteristics of the world around us. For example, people may create *toponyms* to further define and orient themselves with their sense of place. Toponyms are simply names given to locations to help develop familiarity within a certain location. Although not always the case, toponyms generally utilize geographical features, important people in an area, or even wildlife commonly found in a general location. For example, many cities in the state of Texas are named in honor of military leaders who fought in the Texas Revolution of 1836 (such as Houston and Austin), while other places, such as Mississippi and Alabama, utilize Native American toponyms to define their sense of place.

Regions

Geographers divide the world into regions in order to more fully understand differences inherent with the world, its people, and its environment. Lines of latitude such as the Equator, the Tropics, and the Arctic and Antarctic Circles already divide the Earth into solar regions relative to the amount of either direct or indirect sunlight that they receive. Although not the same throughout, the middle latitudes generally have a milder climate than areas found within the tropics. Furthermore, tropical locations are usually warmer than places in the middle latitudes, but that is not always the case. For example, the lowest place in the United States—Death Valley, California—is also home to the nation's highest-ever recorded temperature. Likewise, the Andes Mountains in Peru and Ecuador, although found near the Equator, are also home to heavy snow, low temperatures, and dry conditions, due to their elevation.

Formal regions are spatially defined areas that have overarching similarities or some level of *homogeneity* or *uniformity*. Although not exactly alike, a formal region generally has at least one characteristic that is consistent throughout the entire area. For example, the United States could be broken down into one massive formal region due to the fact that in all fifty states, English is the primary language. Of course, English isn't the only language spoken in the United States, but throughout that nation, English is heavily used. As a result, geographers are able to classify the United States as a formal region; but, more specifically, the United States is a *linguistic region*—a place where everyone generally speaks the same language.

Functional regions are similar to formal regions in that they have similar characteristics, but they do not have clear boundaries. The best way to understand these sorts of regions is to consider large cities. Each large city encompasses a large *market area*, whereby people in its vicinity generally travel there to conduct business, go out to eat, or watch a professional sporting event. However, once anyone travels farther away from that *primate city*, they transition to a different, more accessible city for their needs. The functional region, or *area of influence*, for that city, town, or sports team transitions, depending upon the availability of other primate cities. For example, New York City has two primary professional baseball, basketball, and football teams. As a result, its citizens may have affinities for different teams even though they live in the same city. Conversely, a citizen in rural Idaho may cheer for the Seattle Seahawks, even though they live over 500 miles from Seattle, due to the lack of a closer primate city.

Physical Systems

Earth is a complex system of the atmosphere (air), hydrosphere (water), as well as continental land (land). All work together to support the biosphere (life).

The atmosphere is divided into several layers: the troposphere, stratosphere, mesosphere, and thermosphere. The troposphere is at the bottom and is about seven and a half miles thick. Above the troposphere is the 30-mile-thick stratosphere. Above the stratosphere is the mesosphere, a 20-mile layer, followed by the thermosphere, which is more than 300 miles thick.

The troposphere is closest to Earth and has the greatest pressure due to the pull of gravity on its gas particles as well as pressure from the layers above. 78 percent of the atmosphere is made of nitrogen. Surprisingly, the oxygen that we breathe only makes up 21 percent of the gases, and the carbon dioxide critical to insulating Earth makes up less than 1 percent of the atmosphere. There are other trace gases present in the atmosphere, including water vapor.

Although the stratosphere has minimal wind activity, it is critical for supporting the biosphere because it contains the ozone layer, which absorbs the sun's damaging ultra-violet rays and protects living organisms. Due to its low level of air movement, airplanes travel in the stratosphere. The mesosphere contains few gas particles, and the gas levels are so insignificant in the thermosphere that it is considered space.

Visible light is colors reflecting off particles. If all colors reflect, we see white; if no colors reflect, we see black. This means a colored object is reflecting only that color—a red ball reflects red light and absorbs other colors.

Because the thermosphere has so few particles to reflect light rays (photons), it appears black. The troposphere appears blue in the day, and various shades of yellow and orange at sunset due to the angle of the sun hitting particles that refract, or bend, the light. In certain instances, the entire visible spectrum can be seen in the form of rainbows. Rainbows occur when sunlight passes through water droplets and is refracted in many different directions by the water particles.

The hydrosphere, or water-containing portion of the Earth's surface, plays a major role in supporting the biosphere. In the picture below, a single water molecule (molecular formula H_2O) looks like a mouse head. The small ears of the mouse are the two hydrogen atoms connected to the larger oxygen atom in the middle.

Each hydrogen atom has one proton (positively charged, like the plus end of a magnet) in its nucleus (center), while oxygen has eight protons in its center. Hydrogen also has only one electron (negatively charged, like the minus end of a magnet) orbiting around the nucleus. Because hydrogen has only one proton, its electron is pulled more toward the oxygen nucleus (more powerful magnet). This makes hydrogen exist without an electron most of the time, so it is positively charged. On the other hand, oxygen often has two extra electrons (one from each hydrogen), so it is negatively charged. These bonds between the oxygen and hydrogen are called covalent bonds.

This charged situation is what makes water such a versatile substance; it also causes different molecules of water to interact with each other.

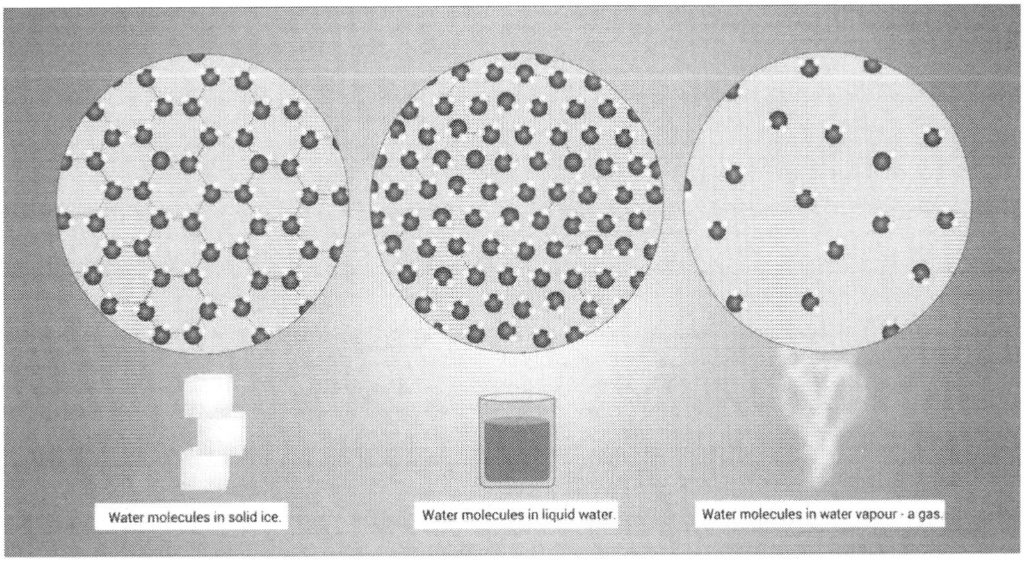

In a solid form (ice), water lines up in a crystal structure because the positive hydrogen atoms prefer to be next to the negative oxygen atoms that belong to other water molecules. These attractions are represented by the blue lines in the molecular picture of ice above. As heat is added and the ice melts, the water molecules have more kinetic energy and move faster; therefore, they are unable to perfectly arrange in the lattice structure of ice and turn into liquid. If enough heat is added, the water molecules will have so much kinetic energy they vaporize into gas. At this point, there are no bonds holding the water together because the molecules aren't close enough.

Notice how ice in its intricate arrangement has more space between the particles than liquid water, which shows that the ice is less dense than water. This contradicts the scientific fact that solids are denser than liquids. In water's case only, the solid will float due to a lower density! This is significant for the hydrosphere, because if temperatures drop to lower than freezing, frozen water will float to the surface of lakes or oceans and insulate the water underneath so that life can continue in liquid water. If ice was not less dense than liquid water, bodies of water would freeze from the bottom up and aquatic ecosystems would be trapped in a block of ice.

The hydrosphere has two components: seawater and freshwater (less than 5 percent of the hydrosphere). Water covers more than 70 percent of the Earth's surface.

The final piece of the biosphere is the lithosphere, the rocky portion of earth. Geology is the study of solid earth. Earth's surface is composed of elemental chunks called minerals, which are simply crystallized groups of bonded atoms. Minerals that have the same composition but different arrangements are called polymorphs, like graphite and diamonds. All minerals contain physical properties such as luster (shine), color, hardness, density, and boiling point. Their chemical properties, or how they react with other compounds, are also different. Minerals combine to form the rocks that make up Earth.

Earth has distinct layers—a thin, solid outer surface, a dense, solid core, and the majority of its matter between them. It is kind of like an egg: the thin crust is the shell, the inner core is the yolk, and the mantle and outer core that compose the space in between are like the egg white.

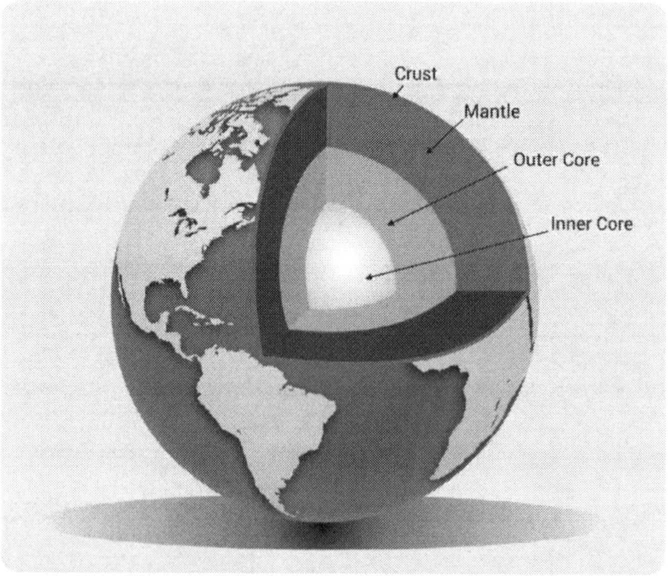

The outer crust of Earth consists of igneous or sedimentary rocks over metamorphic rocks (dense compacted rock underneath). The crust, combined with the upper portion of the mantle, forms the lithosphere, which is broken into several different plates, like puzzle pieces.

Human Systems

Migration is governed by two primary causes: *push factors*, which are reasons causing someone to leave an area, and *pull factors*, which are factors luring someone to a particular place. These two factors often work in concert with one another. For example, the United States of America has experienced significant *internal migration* from the industrial states in the Northeast (such as New York, New Jersey, Connecticut) to the Southern and Western states. This massive migration, which continues into the present-day, is due to high rents in the northeast, dreadfully cold winters, and lack of adequate retirement housing, all of which are push factors. These push factors lead to migration to the *Sunbelt*, a term geographers use to describe states with warm climates and less intense winters.

In addition to internal migrations within nations or regions, international migration also takes place between countries, continents, and other regions. The United States has long been the world's leading nation in regard to *immigration*, the process of having people come into a nation's boundaries. Conversely, developing nations that suffer from high levels of poverty, pollution, warfare, and other violence all have significant push factors, which cause people to leave and move elsewhere. This process, known as *emigration*, is when people in a particular area leave in order to seek a better life in a different—usually better—location.

Demography, or the study of human populations, involves a variety of closely related stimuli. First, economic factors play a significant role in the movement of people, as do climate, natural disasters, or internal unrest. For example, in recent years, millions of immigrants from the war torn country of Syria have moved as far as possible from danger. Although people are constantly moving, some consistencies remain throughout the world. First, people tend to live near reliable sources of food and water, which is why the first human civilizations sprung up in river valleys like the Indus River Valley in India, the Nile River Valley in Egypt, and the Yellow River Valley in Asia. Second, extreme temperatures tend to push people away, which is why the high latitudinal regions near the North and South Poles have such few inhabitants. Third, the vast majority of people tend to live in the Northern Hemisphere, due to the simple fact that more land lies in that part of the Earth. In keeping with these factors, human populations tend to be greater where human necessities are easily accessible, or at least more readily available. In other words, such areas have a greater chance of having a higher population density than places without such characteristics.

Demographic patterns on earth are not always stagnate. In contrast, people move and will continue to move as both push and pull factors fluctuate along with the flow of time. For example, in the 1940s, thousands of Europeans fled their homelands due to the impact of the Second World War. Today, thousands of migrants arrive on European shores each month due to conflicts in the Levant and difficult economic conditions in Northern Africa. Furthermore, people tend to migrate to places with a greater economic benefit for themselves and their families. As a result, developed nations such as the United States, Germany, Canada, and Australia have a net gain of migrants, while developing nations such as Somalia, Zambia, and Cambodia generally tend to see thousands of their citizens seek better lives elsewhere.

It is important to understand the key variables in changes regarding human population and its composition worldwide. Religion and religious conflict play a role in where people choose to live. For example, the Nation of Israel won its independence in 1948 and has since attracted thousands of people of Jewish descent from all over the world. Additionally, the United States has long attracted people from all over the world, due to its promise of religious freedom inherent within its own Constitution. In contrast, nations like Saudi Arabia and Iran do not typically tolerate different religions, resulting in a decidedly uniform religious—and oftentimes ethnic—composition. Other factors such as economic opportunity, social unrest, and cost of living also play a vital role in demographic composition.

Environment and Society

When gas prices are high, prices on virtually everything increase. After all, there are very few products that humans can buy that are not transported by either a gasoline- or diesel-powered engine. As a result, an increase in fuel prices leads to an increase in the price of food, goods, or other cargo. Recently, there has been considerable debate regarding the reliance on *nonrenewable resources* like oil, natural gas, and coal. These resources, which are also known as *fossil fuels*, are quite common throughout the world and are generally abundant, and cheaper to use than *renewable resources* like solar, wind, and geothermal energy. While solar energy is everywhere, the actual means to convert the sun's rays into energy is not. Conversely, coal-fired power plants and gasoline-powered engines, which are older technologies in use during the industrial revolution, remain quite common throughout the world. In fact, reliance on non-renewable resources continues to grow, due to the availability coupled with the existing infrastructure. However, use of renewable energy is increasing, as it becomes more economically competitive with nonrenewable resources.

In addition to sources of energy, nonrenewable resources also include anything that can be exhausted. These can include precious metals like gold, silver, and platinum, freshwater underground aquifers, and precious stones such as diamonds, emeralds, and opals. Although abundant, most nonrenewable sources of energy are not sustainable because their creation takes millions of years and can therefore not be reproduced. Renewable resources are sustainable, but must be properly overseen so that they remain renewable. For example, the beautiful African island of Madagascar is home to some of the most amazing rainforest trees in the world. As a result, logging companies cut, milled, and sold thousands of them in order to make quick profits without planning how to ensure the continued health of the forests. As a result of severe deforestation on the island, mudslides became more and more common as the forests gradually shrank from widespread logging. In this case, renewable resources were mismanaged, and thus essentially became nonrenewable, due to the length of time for growth for the replacement of rainforest trees. In the United States, paper companies harvest pine trees to create paper; and because it can take almost twenty years for a pine tree to reach maturity, most of the companies utilize planning techniques to ensure that mature pine trees will always be available. In this manner, these resources remain renewable for human use in a sustainable fashion.

Renewable sources of energy are relatively new in the modern economy. Even though electric cars, wind turbines, and solar panels are becoming more common, they still do not provide enough energy to power the world's economy. As a result, reliance on older, reliable forms of energy continues, which has a devastating effect on the environment. Beijing, China, which has seen a massive boom in industrial jobs, is also one of the most polluted places on Earth. Furthermore, developing nations with very little modern infrastructure also rely heavily on fossil fuels, due to the ease in which they are converted into usable energy. Even the United States, which has one of the most developed infrastructures in the world, still relies almost exclusively on fossil fuels, with only ten percent of the required energy coming from renewable sources.

Uses of Geography

Two primary realms exist within the study of geography. The first realm, *physical geography*, essentially correlates with the land, water, and foliage of the Earth. The second realm, *human geography*, is the study of the Earth's people and how they interact with their environment. Like land and water on Earth, humans are also impacted by different forces such as culture, history, sociology, technological advancement and changes, and access to natural resources. For example, human populations tend to be higher around more reliable sources of fresh water. The metropolitan area of New York City, which has abundant freshwater resources, is home to nearly 20 million people, whereas Australia, both a continent and a country, has almost the same population. Although water isn't the only factor in this disparity, it certainly plays a role in a place's *population density*—the total number of people in a particular place divided by the total land area, usually square miles or square kilometers. Australia's population density stands at 8.13 people per square mile, while the most densely populated nation on Earth, Bangladesh, is home to 2,894 people per square mile.

Population density can have a devastating impact on both the physical environment/ecosystem and the humans who live within the environment/ecosystem of a particular place. For example, Delhi, one of India's most populated cities, is home to nearly five million gasoline-powered vehicles. Each day, those vehicles emit an enormous amount of carbon monoxide into the atmosphere, which directly affects the quality of life of Delhi's citizens. In fact, the problem of the smog and pollution has gotten so severe that many drivers are unable to see fifty feet in front of them. Additionally, densely populated areas within third-world nations, or developing nations, struggle significantly in their quest to balance the demands of the modern economy with their nation's lack of infrastructure. For example, nearly as many automobiles operate every day in major American cities like New York and Los Angeles as they do in Delhi, but they create significantly less pollution due to cleaner burning engines, better fuels, and governmental emission regulations.

Due to improvements in transportation and communication, the world has become figuratively smaller. For example, university students on the Indian Subcontinent now compete directly with students all over the world to obtain the skills employers desire to move their companies forward. Additionally, many corporations in developed nations have begun to *outsource* labor to nations with high levels of educational achievement but lower wage expectations. The process of opening the marketplace to all nations throughout the world, or *globalization*, has only just started to take hold in the modern economy. As industrial sites shift to the developing world, so does the relative level of opportunity for those nation's citizens. However, due to the massive amounts of pollution produced by factories, the process of globalization also has had significant ecological impacts. The most widely known impact, *climate change*, which most climatologists assert is caused by an increase of carbon dioxide in the atmosphere, remains a serious problem that has posed challenges for developing nations, who need industries in order to raise their standard of living, and developed nations, whose citizens use a tremendous amount of fossil fuels to run their cars, heat their homes, and maintain their ways of life.

Interpreting Maps

Geography is essential in understanding the world as a whole. This requires a study of spatial distribution, which examines how various locations and physical features are arranged in the world. The most common element in geography is the region, which refers to a specific area that is separate from surrounding ones. Regions can be defined based on a variety of factors, including environmental, economic, or political features, and these different kinds of regions can overlap with each other.

It is also important to know the difference between location and place. A location, defined either through its physical position or through its relation to other locations, determines where something is, and this characteristic is static. A place, on the other hand, describes a combination of physical and human elements in relation to each other; the determination of place is therefore changeable depending on the movement of individuals and groups.

Geography is visually conveyed using maps, and a collection of maps is called an atlas. To illustrate some key points about geography, please refer to the map below.

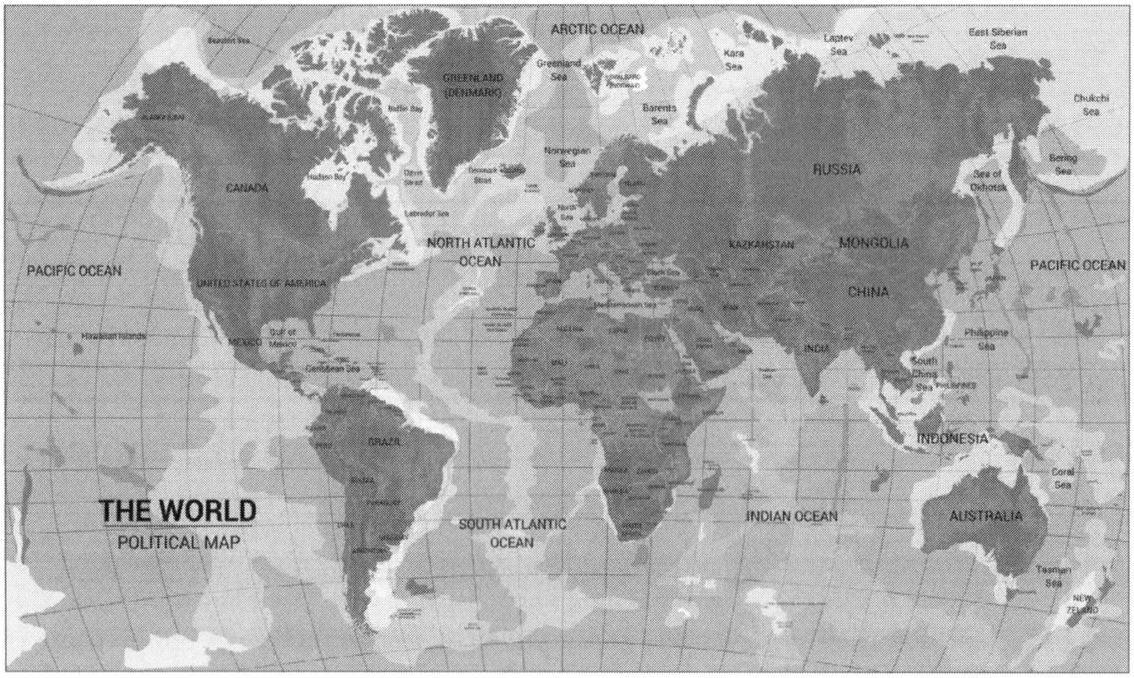

This is a traditional map of the world that displays all of the countries and six of the seven continents. Countries, the most common approach to political regions, can be identified by their labels. The continents are not identified on this map, with the exception of Australia, but they are larger landmasses that encompass most of the countries in their respective areas; the other five visible continents are North America, South America, Europe, Africa, and Asia. The seventh continent, Antarctica, is found at the South Pole and has been omitted from the map.

The absence of Antarctica leads into the issues of distortion, in which geographical features are altered on a map. Some degree of distortion is to be expected with a two-dimensional flat map of the world because the earth is a sphere. A map projection transforms a spherical map of the world into a flattened perspective, but the process generally alters the spatial appearance of landmasses. For instance, Greenland often appears, such as in the map above, larger than it really is.

Furthermore, Antarctica's exclusion from the map is, in fact, a different sort of distortion—that of the mapmakers' biases. Mapmakers determine which features are included on the map and which ones are not. Antarctica, for example, is often missing from maps because, unlike the other continents, it has a limited human population. Moreover, a study of the world reveals that many of the distinctions on maps are human constructions.

Even so, maps can still reveal key features about the world. For instance, the map above has areas that seem almost three-dimensional and jut out. They represent mountains and are an example of topography, which is a method used to display the differing elevations of the terrain. A more detailed topographical map can be viewed below.

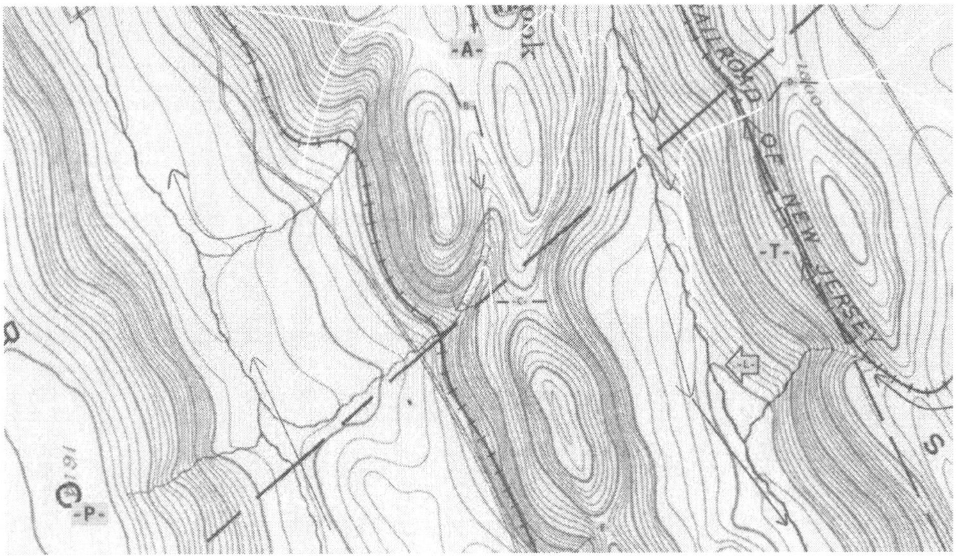

On some colored maps, the oceans, represented in blue between the continents, vary in coloration depending on depth. The differences demonstrate *bathymetry*, which is the study of the ocean floor's depth. Paler areas represent less depth, while darker spots reflect greater depth.

Please also note the many lines running horizontally and vertically along the map. The horizontal lines, known as *parallels,* mark the calculated latitude of those locations and reveal how far north or south these areas are from the equator, which bisects the map vertically. Generally, with exceptions depending on specific environments, climates closer to the equator are warmer because this region receives the most direct sunlight. The equator also serves to split the globe between the Northern and Southern hemispheres.

Longitude, as signified by the vertical lines, determines how far east or west different regions are from each other. The lines of longitude, known as meridians, are also the basis for time zones, which allocate different times to regions depending on their position eastward and westward of the prime meridian. As one travels west between time zones, the given time moves backward accordingly. Conversely, if one travels east, the time moves forward.

There are two particularly significant longitude-associated dividers in this regard. The prime [Greenwich] meridian, as displayed below, is defined as zero degrees in longitude, and thus determines the other lines. The line, in fact, circles the globe north and south, and it therefore divides the world into the Eastern and Western hemispheres. It is important to not confuse the Greenwich meridian with the International Date Line, which is an invisible line in the Pacific Ocean that was created to represent the change between calendar days. By traveling westward across the International Date Line, a traveler would essentially leap forward a day. For example, a person departing from the United States on Sunday would arrive in Japan on Monday. By traveling eastward across the line, a traveler would go backward a day. For example, a person departing from China on Monday would arrive in Canada on Sunday.

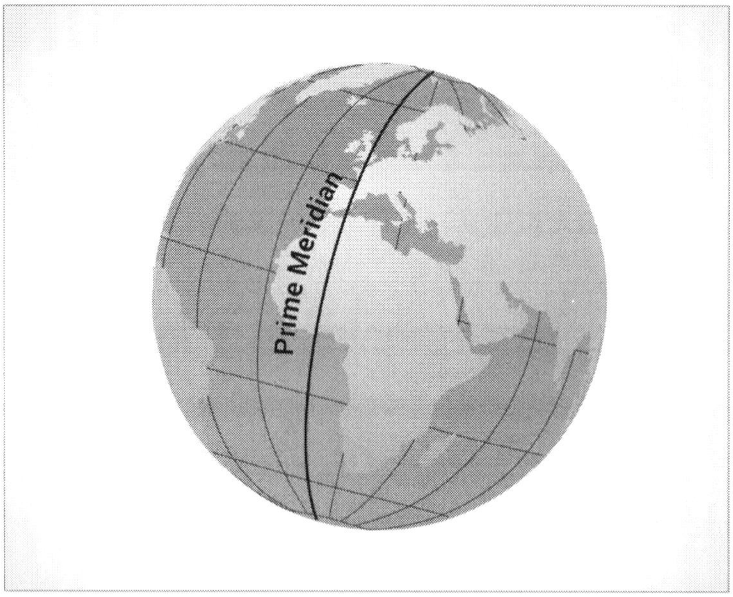

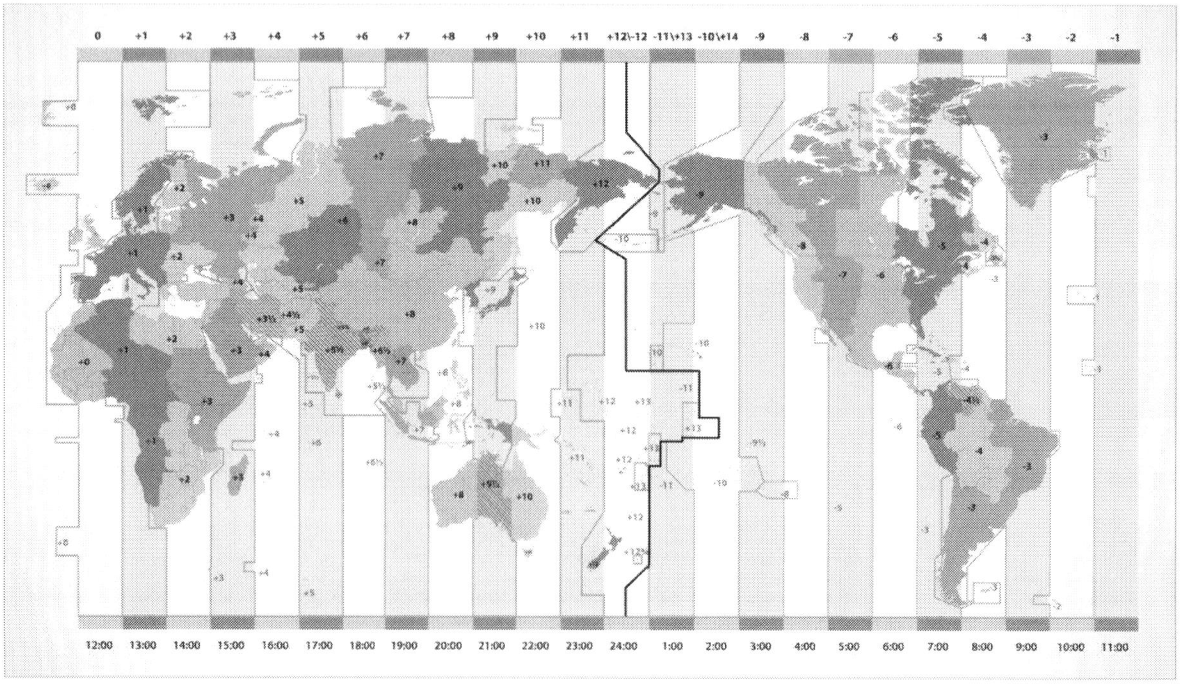

Although world maps are useful in showing the overall arrangement of continents and nations, it is also important at times to look more closely at individual countries because they have unique features that are only visible on more detailed maps.

For example, take the following map of the United States of America. It should be noted that the country is split into multiple states that have their own culture and localized governments. Other countries are often split into various divisions, such as provinces, and while these features are ignored for the sake of clarity on larger maps, they are important when studying specific nations. Individual states can be further subdivided into counties and townships, and they may have their own maps that can be examined for closer analysis.

Finally, one of the first steps in examining any map should be to locate the map's key or legend, which will explain what features different symbols represent on the map. As these symbols can be arbitrary depending on the maker, a key will help to clarify the different meanings.

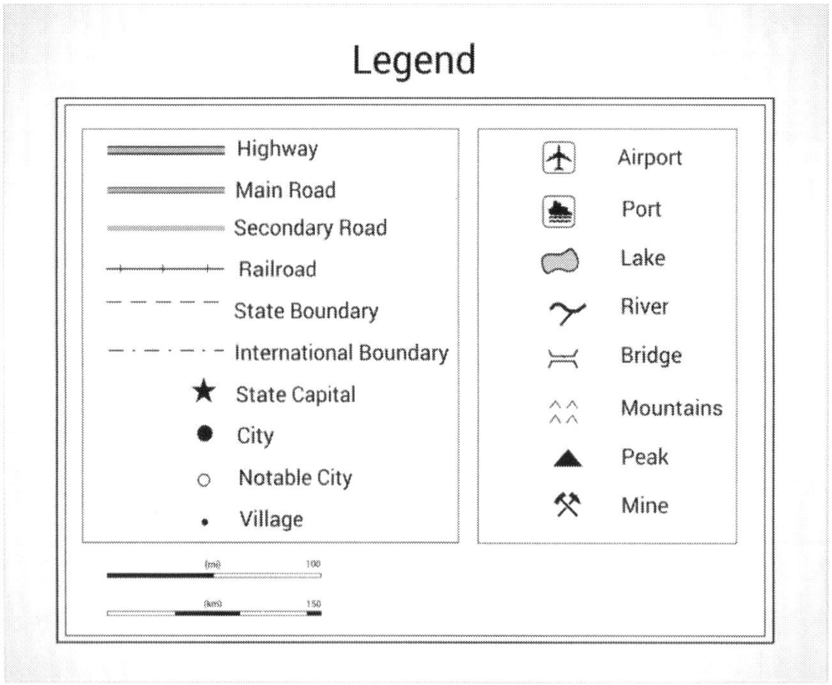

Tools and Technologies Used for a Spatial Perspective

Geographers must employ an array of tools and technologies to adequately analyze environments, cultures, and demographics from a spatial perspective. Maps are important tools because they offer 2D and 3D graphic images that display useful information for understanding the physical and human features of a region. Maps are usually separated into two categories: reference maps and thematic maps. Geographers use reference maps to designate specific locations, highlighting national and physical boundaries. Thematic maps designate spatial distributions of activities, such as weather and climate. Globes differ from maps because they are three-dimensional. Map projections are flat (two-dimensional) projections of the Earth's features.

In the early 2000s, geographers rely on satellite imagery and computer technologies for representing and analyzing features of the Earth. Global positioning system (GPS) technology, which was first implemented in the 1960s, has helped geographers accurately calculate the coordinates of a location via satellite-based trilateration. The information provided by GPS technology is enhanced further by the geographic information systems (GIS) that gather, store, and organize geographic information on computers. Together, GPS and GIS tools have helped usher geography into the 21st century, streamlining how humans acquire, process, and report information from a spatial perspective. GPS and GIS tools have not only influenced the work of scholars and geographers, but they have also dramatically altered how teachers and students approach learning in a social-studies classroom. Teachers and students now have GPS technology at their fingertips with the advent of smartphones, and one major challenge to the current paradigm in education will be finding ways to incorporate this technology into everyday social studies lessons.

Interaction of Physical and Human Systems

Humans have always interacted with nature, and humanity has been shaped by, and, in turn, reshaped environments. Using tools to accomplish things they cannot do on their own, humans have proven highly adaptable to different environments. However, the specific ecosystems have helped to shape human development as individuals and as groups. The earth is highly diverse and has many different ecosystems, each with its own flora and fauna. The specific resources available in different places have, therefore, influenced how humans develop.

Water, in particular, has proved vital in determining the course of human civilizations. As humans require water daily to survive, even more than they do food, proximity to water has always been of utmost necessity. Many human settlements originated adjacent to sources, and only in time expanded to other areas. Water is also essential for the growth of plants, which form a considerable portion of the human diet. In the wild, edible plants grow in places where they can thrive but may not be conveniently located for harvesting by humans. Therefore, humans gradually learned to grow plants themselves in places of their own choice. Humans also diverted water sources to new areas for themselves and to irrigate crops, thus transforming ecosystems.

Another important factor in the relationships between humans and nature has been the role of other animals. From small pests, such as weevils and rodents, to predators, including crocodiles and bears, many species of animals have often posed threats to humans, and conflict increased as humans expanded into environments inhabited by other creatures. On the other hand, animals are invaluable to humans because they can provide sustenance and clothing. This led to hunting and domestication of animal species. Domestication of both plants and animals involves humans breeding species to fit their own needs, which leads to new qualities that would normally not appear in the wild.

However, despite the considerable role that humans can play in altering environments, these changes have remained limited to local levels for much of human history. This does not mean that humans did not affect their ecosystems; some Native American tribes, for instance, used regular fires or hunting methods to maintain environments suitable for their needs. Even so, for much of human existence, nature was seen not simply as an obstacle but rather a power of its own right that was above human interference. Natural phenomena such as severe weather, diseases, and famine all kept human populations in check. Many pantheons of deities center on the gods' roles as arbitrary powers in the natural world, which reflects the lack of influence that humans had in the larger course of environmental changes.

Therefore, natural resources such as water and food were often seen as forces to be respected. Natural environments were recognized as vital regions, and alterations to fully exploit the resources were limited so that the resources could remain adequately sustainable. Riparian customs meant that water was the right of those with immediate access to it, and ownership changed accordingly with who lived nearby. However, increasing industrialization meant that natural resources such as water and lumber became resources that could be commoditized. In addition, appropriation gave water rights to those individuals or businesses that had first used the resource instead of being based on physical proximity.

Another instrumental change in the relationship between humans and nature is the increasing global connections worldwide. In many cases, earlier changes to environments occurred at local levels, with travel between different regions requiring considerable time and effort. The ability to travel around the world quickly has sharply altered that dynamic. Many local ecosystems, and the human cultures that developed accordingly, originated in separate circumstances that created unique plants and animals.

Now products from one part of the world can be transported to entirely different environments and create new exchanges of goods. In some cases, the transferred species escape into the wild, and they often have traits for which the local environments are not prepared. This can result in invasive species that quickly grow and overpower native species.

A key symbol of artificial environments created by humans since early civilization has been the city, which is a human center of habitation that exists separate from the countryside around it. The creation of cities usually requires significant changes to the environment in which it is located, and the city must provide for the needs of residents without being compromised by nature. Yet the city has always remained connected to the rest of the world and to nature. Because a city generally lacks the capacity for agriculture and few natural resources are located within its confines, urban populations rely on resources from outlying areas for nourishment. The city, in turn, acts as a processing center for nearby settlements and offers rural workers and farmers the opportunity to sell their goods to a larger market.

Furthermore, the city, while an artificial construct, is still an environment in its own right. Although many species of animals have perished with the creation of cities, others, such as coyotes and pigeons, have adapted to urban life, thereby creating new ecosystems within cities. Natural connections within cities used to be stronger and more common because people would raise livestock within the city and regularly reuse garbage for livestock feed. While less hygienic, this helped stimulate natural cycles within the city. Recent efforts in many cities to create natural pockets, such as parks and community gardens, have also strengthened the ties between cities and the natural world. In a sense, the city reflects humanity's mixed relationship with nature as a whole: while humans continue to reshape the environment, they also remain linked to nature.

Ways Tools and Technological Advances Affect the Environment

Technology and technological change cannot be readily understood if not analyzed through the lens of environmental change. All technological shifts have natural geographic consequences. For example, industrialization, agriculture, and urbanization have affected the environment are the forces behind climate change. Technology, however, is not wholly negative. In many ways, technological change has helped sustain larger global, national, and urban populations, which has allowed humankind to reach greater heights in terms of scientific advancement.

Movement of People

People migrate for a variety of reasons. Geographers typically categorize migration into two major groups: emigration and immigration. Emigration occurs when a person or entire group of people move *from* a location. Immigration occurs when a person or entire group of people move *to* a location. Immigrants and emigrants move for physical, cultural, economic, and political reasons. Geographers traditionally separate reasons for migration into push and pull factors. Push factors encourage (or force) people to move from their homes. Pull factors attract people to a location. Political push factors include war, government-induced violence and intimidation, genocide, or oppression. Refugees are those pushed from their home country because of such political factors. Refugees are often forcefully expunged from their home states when new countries are formed or when national boundaries are redrawn. For example, the unification of North Vietnam and South Vietnam after the Vietnam War brought hundreds of thousands of Vietnamese refugees to the United States during the 1970s. Economic push factors include economic depressions or panics.

Other economic forces can be push factors. Deindustrialization in cities in the Industrial North (now called the "Rust Belt") during the 1960s-1980s pushed away many residents from industrial hubs like

Buffalo, Cleveland, Chicago, and Milwaukee. In the 1840s, many Irish citizens were pushed from their homes due to a potato famine. During the Great Depression in the 1930s and 1940s, many from the American Heartland moved away from the economic conditions of the Dust Bowl. An extreme version of an economic push factor would be slaves brought to the Americas to enhance the Triangle Trade of the colonial era. Environmental push factors include flooding, natural disasters, droughts, nuclear contamination, and water contamination. In the Sahel region of North Africa, many have found new lands due to the intense droughts. Similarly, after Hurricane Katrina, many New Orleans residents had to relocate to Houston or Baton Rouge to find refuge from the environmental and economic devastation.

Political pull factors include the lure of democracy, safety, and liberty. In the late 19th and early 20th centuries, millions immigrated to the United States from Europe because they were enamored by freedom and opportunity. Some U.S. residents are moving to Canada because of its healthcare system. Some move to states like Texas because of the promise of no state taxes. Economic pull factors include job creation, higher wages, and low unemployment rates. In the United States, millions were drawn to the Sunbelt from the Rust Belt because industry moved South during the 1960s-1970s with the advent of new air conditioning technologies. Even today, thousands flock to cities in Texas such as Austin, Dallas, and Houston because of a booming job market.

Environmental pull factors include hospitable climates, low chances of natural disasters, and outdoor aesthetics. Each year, thousands flock to Colorado to be closer to the outdoor activities associated with the Rocky Mountains. Many move to dry states like New Mexico and Arizona in order to escape inhospitable conditions for those suffering from respiratory ailments such as allergies or bronchitis.

Transportation and Communication Networks

The globalization of the world economy has been catalyzed by the creation of transportation and communication networks. The interconnection of the world's economies has revolutionized how people acquire, absorb, and communicate knowledge. Technology—in particular, the Internet and social media—has enhanced the ways that people communicate. It has also transformed global economic development, creating what some geographers refer to as the global assembly line, a system of production built upon transnational economic development. The globalized efforts of transnational businesses—businesses that are not confined by national boundaries—have created complex systems of inequality across the globe. The global assembly line has increased industrialization in the Global South while catalyzing deindustrialization in the Global North. As a result, former industrial powerhouses in the North have suffered relative degrees of urban plight.

Meanwhile, developing urban areas in the Global South have become epicenters of low wages and exploitation. The current structure of the global assembly line still benefits developed countries despite their recent battles with deindustrialization. Meanwhile, developing sectors of the globe have witnessed some semblance of economic growth, but not without costs like environmental pollution and low wages for workers. The global assembly line has also forced many regions to the periphery, marginalizing their chances of reaping the benefits of the global economy. Industrializing nations such as Mexico are still struggling to create solid infrastructure, while remote rural regions of industrializing countries like India lack infrastructure altogether. The landscape of global economic development, therefore, continues to benefit the so-called former industrial powerhouses, such as the United States, Great Britain, Russia, Japan, and China.

Major Regions in the World, Nation, or State

North America
North America is comprised of Canada, the United States, and Mexico. All three are post-colonial nation-states that developed from the global changes in economics and politics during the 1700s and 1800s. Canada and the United States have long been described as developed nations, having gone through the process of industrialization, though they are now entering a new era of deindustrialized economics. A major aspect of the deindustrialized economy is the so-called information economy. This economy is built on information technology, computers, and fiber optics. Since the 1980s, Canada and the United States have relied heavily on the global retail economy and the information economy. Mexico, on the other hand, is traditionally considered to be a developing nation that relies on factory work and industrialization. Mexico is slowly becoming a major player in the global economy, thanks to beneficial trade deals such as NAFTA.

Latin America (Central America, the Caribbean, and South America)
The region known as Latin America is comprised of Central America, the Caribbean, and South America. The nations of these regions have close ties to the colonial period when they supplied the Spanish, French, English, and Portuguese crowns with crucial resources. Today, nations in this region enjoy their independence thanks to a series of revolutions beginning in the 1700s with the Haitian Revolution. Tourism and agricultural production continue to play a crucial role in the economic development of Latin America. Nevertheless, some nations have entered an era of intense industrialization. Brazil can now be considered one of the leading developing nations of Latin America. Other nations, such as Nicaragua and El Salvador, continue to be marginalized by global economics. Still other nations, such as Cuba, have entered a new era of economic relations following the end of diplomatic tensions with the United States.

Europe
Europe has entered a new era of socio-political development following the economic changes brought about by the European Union (EU). Traditionally a hub for colonialism, Europe has entered a post-colonial era of global economics, which reinvigorated the importance of regional economic relations. Created in 1999, the EU brought together several European nations under a common currency: the euro. The euro has not only brought about economic benefits, but also political benefits to marginal nation-states such as Greece. Nevertheless, the EU has been the subject of political debate, culminating in the recent Brexit, which legitimized the United Kingdom's decision to leave the European Union as of June 23, 2016. This decision makes the future of the region uncertain.

Russia
Previously the political epicenter of the communist Soviet Union, Russia has once again become a player in the global economy under the expansionist tactics of President Vladimir Putin. He has reinvigorated the Russian stronghold over former Soviet states and emphasized Russia becoming a self-sustaining powerhouse of energy resources. As tense relations with the United States and NAFTA threaten to reheat the Cold War, Russia aims to capitalize on resource booms in Siberia and the Caspian coast. Recent reports also indicate that Russia has its eyes focused on the resource-rich territory of the Arctic Circle. Historically, Russia continues to convey itself as an aggressive superpower that answers only to what is best for Moscow and its people.

Middle East
The Middle East has experienced a long history of conflict, as many nations vie for diplomatic supremacy in the region. The oil-rich countries of the Middle East are now, in many ways, facing their greatest

conflict as the war in Syria and the growing power of ISIS threaten regional stability. Increased anti-Semitism and a renewed Israeli-Palestinian conflict threaten to undo decades of attempts at peaceful diplomatic relations. The Middle East continues to be one of the economic epicenters of an oil-dependent world, but growing income gaps, sporadic revolutions, and increased populations threaten the status quo. Russia and the West have renewed interest in the region as conflicts continue in Iraq, Afghanistan, and Syria. The spirit of Islam also seems to be at stake in the wake of ISIS's violent acts and the increasingly Islamophobic sentiment of the West. As Syrian, Iraqi, and Kurdish refugees scatter across the globe, they have been met, at times, with anti-Islamic fervor.

India and South Asia

Rampant urbanization has made India and South Asia a region wrought with overpopulation. India and South Asia have developed into hubs for industry and technology, but not without a cost. Billions of residents in the region are exposed to the devastating effects of pollution and poor infrastructure. Additionally, the income gap has widened, and the region has become relatively destabilized due to India's recent attempts at demonetization. Nevertheless, expect this region to continue to be an important sector of the global economy in the 21st century.

China

China and the Asia-Pacific region face their own industrialism and overpopulation issues. During the late 20th and early 21st centuries, China has joined Japan and South Korea as a global powerhouse in the region. Like India, China's struggles with overpopulation and industrial development come with struggles to maintain infrastructure and limit pollution. Yet, this rapid economic expansion has also made China a leader in private engineering and public works, as the nation rapidly develops high-rise skyscrapers and superhighways. The whole Asia-Pacific region, which includes Australasia, has become a magnet for wealth and economic development.

Government and Civics

Nature, Purpose, and Forms of Government

The United States of America's government, as outlined by the Constitution, is designed to serve as a compromise between democracy and preceding monarchical systems. The American Revolution brought independence from Britain and freedom from its aristocratic system of governance. On the other hand, the short-lived Articles of Confederation revealed the significant weaknesses of state-based governance with limited national control. By dividing power between local, state, and federal governments, the United States can uphold its value of individual liberties while, nevertheless, giving a sense of order to the country.

While the federal government manages the nation as a whole, state governments address issues pertaining to their specific territory. In the past, states claimed the right, known as nullification, to refuse to enforce federal laws that they considered unconstitutional. However, conflicts between state and federal authority, particularly in the South in regard to first, slavery, and later, discrimination, have led to increased federal power, and states cannot defy federal laws. Even so, the Tenth Amendment limits federal power to those specifically granted in the Constitution, and the rest of the powers are retained by the states and citizens. Therefore, individual state governments are left in charge of decisions with immediate effects on their citizens, such as state laws and taxes. Like the federal government, state governments consist of executive, judicial, and legislative branches, but the exact configuration of those branches varies between states. For instance, while most states follow the bicameral structure of Congress, Nebraska has only a single legislative chamber. State governments have considerable authority within their states, but they cannot impose their power on other states, nor can they secede from the United States.

Local governments, which include town governments, county boards, library districts, and other agencies, are especially variable in their composition. They often reflect the overall views of their state governments but also have their own values, rules, and structures. Generally, local governments function in a democratic fashion, although the exact form of government depends on its role. Depending on the location within the state, local government may have considerable or minimal authority based on the population and prosperity of the area; some counties may have strong influence in the state, while others may have a limited impact.

Native American tribes are treated as dependent nations that answer to the federal government but may be immune to state jurisdiction. As with local governments, the exact form of governance is left up to the tribes, which ranges from small councils to complex systems of government. Other U.S. territories, including the District of Columbia (site of Washington, D.C.) and acquired islands, such as Guam and Puerto Rico, have representation within Congress, but their legislators cannot vote on bills.

Rights and Responsibilities of Citizenship in a Democracy

Citizens living in a democracy have several rights and responsibilities to uphold. The first duty is that they uphold the established laws of the government. In a democracy, a system of nationwide laws is necessary to ensure that there is some degree of order. Therefore, citizens must try to obey the laws and also help enforce them because a law that is inadequately enforced, such as early civil rights laws in the South, is almost useless. Optimally, a democratic society's laws will be accepted and followed by the community as a whole.

However, conflict can occur when an unjust law is passed. For instance, much of the civil rights movement centered around Jim Crow laws in the South that supported segregation between black and whites. Yet these practices were encoded in state laws, which created a dilemma for African Americans who wanted equality but also wanted to respect the law. Fortunately, a democracy offers a degree of protection from such laws by creating a system in which government leaders and policies are constantly open to change in accordance with the will of citizens. Citizens can influence the laws that are passed by voting for and electing members of the legislative and executive branches to represent them at the local, state, and national levels.

This, however, requires citizens to be especially vigilant in protecting their liberties because they cannot depend solely on the existing government to meet their needs. To assert their role in a democracy, citizens should be active voters and speak out on issues that concern them. Even with these safeguards, it is possible for systems to be implemented that inhibit active participation. For instance, many southern states had laws that prevented blacks from voting. Under such circumstances, civil rights leaders felt that they had no choice but to resist the laws in order to defend their personal rights. Once voting became possible, civil rights groups strove to ensure that their votes counted by changing state and national policy.

An extension of citizens' voting rights is their ability to run as elected officials. By becoming leaders in the government, citizens can demonstrate their engagement and help determine government policy. The involvement of citizens as a whole in the selection of leaders is vital in a democracy because it helps to prevent the formation of an elite cadre that does not answer to the public. Without the engagement of citizens who run for office, voters are limited in their ability to select candidates that appeal to them. In this case, voting options would become stagnant, which inhibits the ability of the nation to grow and change over time. As long as citizens are willing to take a stand for their vision of America, America's government will remain dynamic and diverse.

These features of a democracy give it the potential to reshape itself continually in response to new developments in society. In order for a democracy to function, it is of the utmost importance that citizens care about the course of politics and be aware of current issues. Apathy among citizens is a constant problem that threatens the endurance of democracies. Citizens should have a desire to take part in the political process, or else they simply accept the status quo and fail to fulfill their role as citizens. Moreover, they must have acute knowledge of the political processes and the issues that they can address as citizens. A fear among the Founding Fathers was the prevalence of mob rule, in which the common people did not take interest in politics except to vote for their patrons; this was the usual course of politics in the colonial era, as the common people left the decisions to the established elites. Without understanding the world around them, citizens may not fully grasp the significance of political actions and thereby fail to make wise decisions in that regard. Therefore, citizens must stay informed about current affairs, ranging from local to national or global matters, so that they can properly address them as voters or elected leaders.

Furthermore, knowledge of the nation's history is essential for healthy citizenship. History continues to have an influence on present political decisions. For instance, Supreme Court rulings often take into account previous legal precedents and verdicts, so it is important to know about those past events and how they affect the current processes. It is especially critical that citizens are aware of the context in which laws were established because it helps clarify the purpose of those laws. For instance, an understanding of the problems with the Articles of Confederation allows people to comprehend some of the reasons behind the framework of the Constitution. In addition, history as a whole shapes the course of societies and the world; therefore, citizens should draw on this knowledge of the past to realize the full consequences of current actions. Issues such as climate change, conflict in the Middle East, and civil rights struggles are rooted in events and cultural developments that reach back centuries and should be addressed.

Therefore, education is a high priority in democracies because it has the potential to instill generations of citizens with the right mind-set and knowledge required to do their part in shaping the nation. Optimally, education should cover a variety of different subjects, ranging from mathematics to biology, so that individuals can explore whatever paths they wish to take in life. Even so, social studies are especially important because students should understand how democracies function and understand the history of the nation and world. Historical studies should cover national and local events as well because they help provide the basis for the understanding of contemporary politics. Social studies courses should also address the histories of foreign nations because contemporary politics increasingly has global consequences. In addition, history lessons should remain open to multiple perspectives, even those that might criticize a nation's past actions, because citizens should be exposed to diverse perspectives that they can apply as voters and leaders.

Key Documents and Speeches in U.S. History

With more than two hundred years of history, American leaders have produced a number of important documents and speeches. One of the most essential is the Declaration of Independence, which the Second Continental Congress ratified on July 4, 1776. Although many historians and politicians have drawn upon the words of the Declaration to demonstrate the American ideal of freedom, most of them focus on the preamble, which focuses on the necessity of fair government and the right to overthrow tyrants. The main body of the document consists of a set of grievances against King George III. Still, this document was instrumental in American history because it asserted American independence from Great Britain. Even so, it is important to note that the Declaration did not immediately lead to the United States; the document does not outline the government of the soon-to-be independent colonies, and independence would not become reality until Britain agreed.

The colonies' first blueprint for government was the Articles of Confederation, which was ratified in 1777. The document declared that the confederacy would be called the United States of America and that the individual states would have "a firm league of friendship" with each other. The emphasis on friendship and cooperation highlights how the confederation was a voluntary effort that states could follow or ignore as they saw fit. Still, the document also revealed the importance of obeying decisions made by Congress as a whole; while this was not very effective during the confederation period, the framework would live on to a degree in the following Constitution.

Much like the Declaration of Independence, the 1787 Constitution of the United States is most remembered for the preamble, which takes a more philosophical approach. However, the body of the Constitution is highly complex, and it covers the framework and responsibilities of the different branches of the federal government and the limits to state power. These details are very important and help to define the key institutions within the government. To resolve later issues not addressed in the Constitution, the fifth article in the document establishes a process to modify the government, and the first ten amendments are known as the *Bill of Rights*. Under the Tenth Amendment, powers not specifically allotted to Congress by the Constitution are reserved for the people and to individual states.

George Washington was the first president of the United States, and his administration set many precedents for the nation, particularly with his Farewell Address. In it, he noted the rise of regional feelings, and he urged citizens to uphold their duty to the nation above sectionalism because he felt that America was strongest when united. The issue of regional conflicts and national identity would become increasingly important in years to come, especially during the Civil War. Washington also argued against intervention in European affairs, and this warning would become the cornerstone for advocates of American isolation. On the other hand, his advice that political parties are detrimental to democracy failed to halt the development of the party system.

Washington's fears about sectional conflict were confirmed at the start of the Civil War, when the southern states violently seceded from the Union. As the president during that tumultuous time, Abraham Lincoln was seen by many to embody the Union as a whole. This can be demonstrated through his Gettysburg Address in November of 1863. After the difficult and bloody Battle of Gettysburg ended in a Union victory, crowds gathered for the dedication of the Soldiers' National Cemetery. Although he was not the main speaker of the event, Lincoln's short yet eloquent speech proved to be the most significant. Drawing upon the Declaration of Independence's assertion that "all men are created equal," he argued that the current war was a test of that ideal. More than that, he emphasized the importance of the United States as a whole and argued that it must endure as a Union for the sake of the world.

Earlier that year in January, Lincoln had already indicated his opposition to slavery through the Emancipation Proclamation. Although it was an executive order instead of a law passed by Congress, this document was not challenged by the courts and helped determine the objectives of the Civil War. The proclamation asserted that all slaves in Confederate territories were free. One must note that some southern states remained in the Union, and therefore, were not affected by this proclamation. Even so, the order helped establish a basis for later laws and amendments that would end slavery in the United States.

Another presidential attempt to set a new precedent for American policy was Woodrow Wilson's Fourteen Points, which were outlined in a speech he gave to Congress in 1918 after the United States had entered World War I. Wilson saw the United States as a protector of democracy in the world and said that we could reform world policy by fighting in the war. For instance, Wilson called for an end to private negotiations, which had contributed to the secret alliances behind the war. Most of all, he argued for nations to come together in an international body to determine world policies. The negotiations after the war only partially fulfilled Wilson's ambitions by creating a weak League of Nations, but his vision of U.S. involvement in global affairs would become a key aspect of American foreign policy.

Even as the United States began playing a more active role on the international stage of politics, internal issues such as civil rights remained important, as shown in Martin Luther King Jr.'s "I Have a Dream" speech. A leader in the civil rights movement, King gave his speech as part of the 1963 March on Washington. Drawing on Lincoln's past speech at Gettysburg, King argued that America's journey to true equality was not over yet. His references to biblical passages gave the speech a spiritual tone, but he also mentioned specific locations across the nation to signify how local struggles were tied with national consequences. By emphasizing his optimism, King's speech reflects not only civil rights activism but also the American dream of freedom and progress.

Legislative, Executive, and Judicial Branches

The federal government, which is in charge of laws that affect the entire nation, is split into three main branches: executive, judicial, and legislative. It is important to realize that the three segments of the federal government are intended to stand as equal counterparts to the others, and that none of them are "in charge." The executive branch centers on the president, the vice president, and the cabinet. The president and vice president are elected every four years. Also known as the commander-in-chief, the president is the official head of state and serves as the nation's head diplomat and military leader. The vice president acts as the president of the Senate in the legislative branch, while the president appoints members of the cabinet to lead agencies, including the Treasury and Department of Defense. However, the president can only sign and veto laws and cannot initiate them himself.

Instead, the legislative branch, specifically Congress, proposes and debates laws. Congress is bicameral because it is divided into two separate legislative houses. Each state's representation in the House of Representatives is determined proportionally by population, with the total number of voting seats limited to 435. The Senate, in contrast, has only two members per state and a total of one hundred senators. Members of both houses are intended to represent the interests of the constituents in their home states and to bring their concerns to a national level. Ideas for laws, called bills, are proposed in either chamber and then are voted upon according to the body's rules; should the bill pass the first round of voting, the other legislative chamber must approve it before it can be sent to the president. Congress also has a variety of other powers, such as the rights to declare war, collect taxes, and impeach the president.

The judicial branch, though it cannot pass laws itself, serves to interpret the laws. At the federal level, this is done through several tiers of judicial bodies. At the top, the Supreme Court consists of judges appointed by the president; these judges serve for life, unless they resign from their position or are removed by Congress for improper behavior. The Supreme Court's decisions in trials and other judgments rest on the justices' interpretations of the Constitution and enacted laws. As the Constitution remains fundamental to the American legal system, the Supreme Court's rulings on how laws follow or fail to uphold the Constitution have powerful implications on future rulings. Beneath the Supreme

Court, there are a number of other federal judicial bodies—courts of appeals, district courts, and courts of special jurisdiction.

Electoral System

As members of a democracy, U.S. citizens are empowered to elect most government leaders, but the process varies between branch and level of government. Presidential elections at the national scale use the Electoral College system. Rather than electing the president directly, citizens cast their ballots to select electors, who generally vote for a specific candidate, that represent each state in the college. Legislative branches at the federal and state level are also determined by elections, albeit without an Electoral College. In some areas, judges are elected, but in other states judges are appointed by elected officials. It should also be noted that the two-party system was not built into the Constitution but gradually emerged over time.

Protection of Citizens' Rights Under the United States Constitution

The U.S. Constitution is a series of written rules defining the power of the U.S. government and the rights of U.S. citizens. Written in 1787 to create a stronger national government, it is the world's oldest working constitution. It gave Americans more rights than any other country had previously given its people. Collectively referred to as the Bill of Rights, the first ten amendments to the Constitution were added to protect the individual rights of U.S. citizens and to keep the federal government from wielding too much control. These are rights such as *freedom of speech*, *freedom of religion*, *freedom of the press*, and *right to a fair trial*. The Constitution has been amended twenty-seven times in order to accommodate changes and updates. Some of these amendments were made to be more inclusive to the wide range of American citizens. For example, the 14th Amendment, adopted in 1868, abolished slavery and stated that all citizens must be treated equally under Constitutional law and allowed the same protection within each state.

Economics

Scarcity

Economies, by nature, have limited access to certain resources, which creates a conflict between supply and demand. Scarcity occurs when the demand for a product exceeds its availability. Scarcity in part depends on the choices of individuals as they determine which products they want more than others. Choices, in turn, are influenced by the perceived costs of pursuing certain options over others. The costs and benefits of specific choices often differ depending on the individuals' perceptions of the options. When people believe that a certain service's or product's benefits outweigh its necessary costs, they may choose to pay more for the desired benefits. It is important to realize that the laws of supply and demand are not absolute, and they may fluctuate depending on the situation.

Characteristics of Currency

Currency describes the monetary unit that's commonly used within a nation or union of nations. Examples include the Indian rupee, the U.S. dollar, the Canadian dollar, the Japanese yen, the Swiss franc, the Russian ruble, the South Korean won, the Egyptian pound, the Norwegian krone, and the euro. Within each nation, these currencies maintain an absolute value. On a global scale, these currencies maintain a relative value, based on global economic development and prowess. Currencies are traded among nations in the global exchange, and their absolute and relative values can increase or decrease based on factors in global politics and economics.

Currency isn't confined to coins and paper notes. Credit is a component of national and global currency systems. Credit is a form of borrowing money to be repaid later, though it usually accrues interest over time. Loans—both secured (e.g., home loans and car loans) and unsecured (e.g., student loans, credit cards, and personal bank loans)—are examples of credit systems that affect national and global currency rates. Failure to pay back credit cards or loans typically leads to poor credit ratings, which may affect a person's ability to obtain more credit. In extreme cases, people who fail to pay off credit may have to file for bankruptcy. In the United States the main currency/financial institutions are stock markets, banks, credit unions, and the Federal Reserve System. Banks are owned by small groups of investors who hold or loan money based on the expectation that they'll earn a return on their investments. Stock markets are the overarching financial structure of the United States economy that serve as a mechanism for buying and selling company stocks; stock markets also describe significant increases and decreases in corporate finances. Credit unions are owned collectively by members rather than private investors. This means all information, responsibilities, and resources are shared. The Federal Reserve System is a central banking system that allows government officials and financial experts to consult and influence the creation of national, regional, and local banking policies. The Federal Reserve System maintains reserves of money to lend to banks.

Effects of Economics on Population, Resources, and Technology

Economics are closely linked with the flow of resources, technology, and population in societies. The use of natural resources, such as water and fossil fuels, has always depended in part on the pressures of the economy. A supply of a specific good may be limited in the market, but with sufficient demand the sellers are incentivized to increase the available quantity. Unfortunately, the demand for certain objects can often be unlimited, and a high price or limited supply may prevent consumers from obtaining the product or service. If the sellers succumb to the consumers' demand and continue to exploit a scarce resource, supply could potentially be exhausted.

The resources for most products, both renewable and nonrenewable, are finite. This is a particularly difficult issue with nonrenewable resources, but even renewable resources often have limits: organic products such as trees and animals require stable populations and sufficient habitats to support those populations. Furthermore, the costs of certain decisions can have detrimental effects on other resources. For example, industrialization provides economic benefits in many countries but also has had the negative effect of polluting surrounding environments; the pollution, in turn, often eliminates or harms fish, plants, and other potential resources.

The control of resources within an economy is particularly important in determining how resources are used. While the demand may change with the choices of consumers, the range of supply depends on the objectives of the people producing the goods. They determine how much of their supply they allot for sale, and in the case of monopolies, they might have sole access to the resource. They might choose to limit their use of the resources or instead gather more to meet the demand. As they pay for the products, consumers can choose which sellers they rely on for the supply. In the case of a monopoly, though, consumers have little influence over the company's decision because there is no alternative supplier. Therefore, the function of supply within an economy can drastically influence how the resources are exploited.

The availability of resources, in turn, affects the human population. Humans require basic resources such as food and water for survival, as well as additional resources for healthy lifestyles. Therefore, access to these resources helps determine the survival rate of humans. For much of human existence, economies have had limited ability to extract resources from the natural world, which restricted the growth rate of populations. However, the development of new technologies, combined with increasing demand for certain products, has pushed resource use to a new level. On the one hand, this led to higher living standards that ensured that fewer people would die. However, this has also brought mass population growth. Admittedly, countries with higher standards of living often have lower birthrates. Even so, the increasing exploitation of resources has sharply increased the world's population as a whole to unsustainable levels. The rising population leads, in turn, to more demand for resources that cannot be met. This creates poverty, reduced living conditions, and higher death rates. As a result, economics can significantly influence local and world population levels.

Technology is also intricately related to population, resources, and economics. The role of demand within economies has incentivized people to innovate new technologies that enable societies to have a higher quality of life and greater access to resources. Entrepreneurs expand technologies by finding ways to create new products for the market. The Industrial Revolution, in particular, illustrates the relationship between economics and technology because the ambitions of businessmen led to new infrastructure that enabled more efficient and sophisticated use of resources. Many of these inventions reduced the amount of work necessary for individuals and allowed the development of leisure activities, which in turn created new economic markets. However, economic systems can also limit the growth of technology. In the case of monopolies, the lack of alternative suppliers reduces the incentive to meet and exceed consumer expectations. Moreover, as demonstrated by the effects of economics on resources, technology's increasing ability to extract resources can lead to their depletion and create significant issues that need to be addressed.

Government's Role in Economics and the Impact of Economics on Government

Governments have considerable influence over the flow of economies, which makes it important to understand the relationships between them. When a government has full control over the economic decisions of a nation, it is called a command system. This was the case in many absolute monarchies such as eighteenth-century France; King Louis XIV built his economy on the concept of mercantilism, which believed that the state should manage all resources, particularly by accumulating gold and silver. This system of economics discouraged exports and thereby limited trade.

In contrast, the market system is guided by the concept of capitalism, in which individuals and businesses have the freedom to manage their economic decisions. This allows for private property and increases the opportunities for entrepreneurship and trade. Early proponents of capitalism emphasized *laissez-faire* policies, which means "let it be," and argued that the government should not be involved with the economy at all. They believe the market is guided by the concept of self-interest and that individuals will optimally work for their personal success. However, individuals' interests do not necessarily correlate with the needs of the overall economy. For instance, during a financial recession, consumers may decide to save up their money rather than make purchases; doing so helps them in the short run but further reduces demand in a slumping economy. Therefore, most capitalist governments still assert a degree of control over their economies while still allowing for private business.

Likewise, many command system economies, such as monarchical France, still relied heavily on private businesses maintained by wealthy businessmen. With the end of most absolute monarchies, communism has been the primary form of command system economies in the modern era. Communism is a form of socialism that emphasizes communal ownership of property and government control over production. The high degree of government control gives more stability to the economy, but it also creates considerable flaws. The monopolization of the economy by the government limits its ability to respond to local economic conditions because certain regions often have unique resources and needs. With the collapse of the Soviet Union and other communist states, command systems have been largely replaced with market systems.

The U.S. government helps to manage the nation's economy through a market system in several ways. First and foremost, the federal government is responsible for the production of money for use within the economy; depending on how the government manages the monetary flow, it may lead to a stable economy, deflation, or inflation. Second, state and federal governments impose taxes on individuals, corporations, and goods. For instance, a tariff might be imposed on imports in order to stimulate demand for local goods in the economy. Third, the government can pass laws that require additional regulation or inspections. In addition, the government has passed antitrust laws to inhibit the growth of private monopolies, which could limit free growth in the market system. Debates continue over whether the government should take further action to manage private industries or reduce its control over the private sector.

Just as governments can affect the direction of the economy, the state of the economy can have significant implications on government policies. Financial stability is critical in maintaining a prosperous state. A healthy economy will allow for new developments that contribute to the nation's growth and create jobs. On the other hand, an economic crisis, such as a recession or depression, can gravely damage a government's stability. Without a stable economy, business opportunities plummet, and people begin to lose income and employment. This, in turn, leads to frustration and discontent in the population, which can lead to criticism of the government. This could very well lead to demands for new leadership to resolve the economic crisis.

The dangers of a destabilized economy can be seen with the downfall of the French monarchy. The mercantilist approach to economics stifled French trade. Furthermore, regional aristocracies remained exempt from government taxes, which limited the government's revenues. This was compounded by expensive wars and poor harvests that led to criticism of King Louis XIV's government. The problems persisted for decades, and Louis XVI was forced to convene the Estates-General, a legislative body of representatives from across France, to address the crisis. The economic crises at the end of the eighteenth century were critical in the beginning of the French Revolution. Those financial issues, in turn, at least partially stemmed from both the government's control of the economy through mercantilism and its inability to impose economic authority over local regions.

Types of Productive Resources and the Role of Money as a Resource

Productive resources are the means used by a society to succeed and survive. The four types are:

- Natural resources—the raw materials taken from the land, such as corn, beef, lumber, water, oil, and iron.
- Human resources—the human labor, both mental and physical, that are required to produce goods.

- Capital resources—the man-made physical resources used to create products, such as machinery, tools, buildings, and equipment.

- Entrepreneurship—the capability and motivation to cultivate, organize, and oversee the other three resources into a business venture.

Money functions as a method of exchange to obtain goods or services. It replaced the barter system, which was often considered inefficient and disorganized. Economists referred to the barter system as a double coincidence of wants since trades between parties were not always considered equal. Prices of goods are determined by supply and demand. *Inflation* occurs when people have money to spend, but not enough goods can be produced or imported to meet their demand for a product, which causes prices to rise. The amount of money issued by government-controlled central banks and the prices of leading commodities, such as oil, can also affect inflation. *Deflation* is when people save their money and spend less, leaving stores with surplus goods, which causes prices to drop.

Practice Questions

1. Which of the following correctly lists the Thirteen Colonies?
   a. Connecticut, Delaware, Georgia, Maryland, Massachusetts, New Hampshire, New Jersey, New York, North Carolina, Pennsylvania, Rhode Island, South Carolina, Virginia
   b. Carolina, Connecticut, Delaware, Maryland, Massachusetts, New Hampshire, New Jersey, New York, Ohio, Pennsylvania, Rhode Island, Virginia, West Virginia
   c. Connecticut, Delaware, Georgia, Maine, Massachusetts, New Hampshire, New Jersey, New York, North Carolina, South Carolina, Pennsylvania, Vermont, Virginia
   d. Canada, Connecticut, Delaware, Georgia, Florida, Maryland, Massachusetts, New Hampshire, New York, North Carolina, Rhode Island, South Carolina, Virginia

2. Which of the following was NOT an issue contributing to the American Revolution?
   a. Increased taxes on the colonies
   b. Britain's defeat in the French and Indian War
   c. The stationing of British soldiers in colonists' homes
   d. Changes in class relations

3. The election of a presidential candidate from which party led to the Civil War?
   a. Democrat
   b. Whig
   c. Republican
   d. Federalist

4. Which of the following was NOT an important invention in the twentieth century?
   a. Radio
   b. Telegraph
   c. Television
   d. Computers

5. Which of the following sets comprises a primary cause and effect of the American Revolution?
   a. A cause was the taxation of the colonies, and an effect was the civil rights movement.
   b. A cause was the Declaration of Independence, and an effect was the Constitution.
   c. A cause was the French and Indian War, and an effect was the Bill of Rights.
   d. A cause was the debate over slavery, and an effect was the Seven Years' War.

6. What are the two main parts of the federal legislative branch?
   a. President and vice president
   b. Federal and state
   c. District court and court of appeals
   d. Senate and House of Representatives

7. What was a concern that George Washington warned of in his Farewell Address?
   a. The danger of political parties
   b. To be prepared to intervene in Europe's affairs
   c. The abolition of slavery
   d. To protect states' rights through sectionalism

8. What is NOT a responsibility for citizens of democracy?
   a. To stay aware of current issues and history
   b. To avoid political action
   c. To actively vote in elections
   d. To understand and obey laws

9. Which of the following statements is true?
   a. Times zones are defined by their latitude.
   b. Eastern and Western hemispheres are defined by the prime meridian.
   c. A place is constant, while a location is changeable with the movement of people.
   d. A continent is one of six especially large landmasses in the world.

10. Which of the following statements is true?
   a. Water usage has largely shifted from appropriation to riparian.
   b. Native Americans lived in harmony with nature by never disrupting it.
   c. Cities are fully isolated environments.
   d. Invasive species can have catastrophic impacts on ecosystems.

11. Which of the following are reasons that geography is important to the examination of history?
   I. Historians make use of maps in their studies to get a clear picture of how history unfolded.
   II. Knowing the borders of different lands helps historians learn different cultures' interactions.
   III. Geography is closely linked with the flow of resources, technology, and population in societies.
   IV. Environmental factors, such as access to water and proximity of mountains, help shape the course of civilization.
      a. I, II, and III only
      b. II, III, and IV only
      c. I, II, and IV only
      d. I, III, and IV only

12. Which of the following statements is true?
   a. All Native American tribes are matrilineal.
   b. Japan is struggling to manage its high birthrate.
   c. Shi'a Muslims traditionally follow imams.
   d. Mexico's culture is deeply tied to its Protestant roots.

13. Which of the following advancements was NOT invented by Greek culture?
   a. The alphabet
   b. The Hippocratic Oath
   c. Democratic government
   d. Theater

14. Which of the following was an important development in the twentieth century?
   a. The United States and the Soviet Union officially declared war on each other in the Cold War.
   b. The League of Nations signed the Kyoto Protocol.
   c. World War I ended when the United States defeated Japan.
   d. India violently partitioned into India and Pakistan after the end of colonialism.

15. Which of the following is NOT an example of cross-cultural interactions?
    a. Egyptian and Mayan pyramids
    b. The Spanish language
    c. Styles of sushi
    d. Study of Chinese culture

16. Which of the following is true?
    a. The barter system no longer exists.
    b. Economic resources can be divided into four categories: natural, capital, manufactured, and nonrenewable.
    c. Individuals help to determine the scarcity of items through their choices.
    d. According to the law of supply, as the price of a product increases, the supply of the product will decrease.

17. What is NOT an effect of monopolies?
    a. Promote a diverse variety of independent businesses
    b. Inhibit developments that would be problematic for business
    c. Control the supply of resources
    d. Limit the degree of choice for consumers

18. Which method is NOT a way that governments manage economies in a market system?
    a. Laissez-faire
    b. Mercantilism
    c. Capitalism
    d. Self-interest

19. Which of the following nations did NOT establish colonies in what would become the United States?
    a. Italy
    b. England
    c. France
    d. Spain

20. Which of the following statements about the U.S. Constitution is true?
    a. It was signed on July 4, 1776.
    b. It was enacted at the end of the Revolutionary War.
    c. New York failed to ratify it, but it still passed by majority.
    d. It replaced the Articles of Confederation.

21. Which of the following locations was NOT subjected to American imperialism?
    a. Philippines
    b. Puerto Rico
    c. Canada
    d. Guam

22. What is a power that Congress has?
    a. To appoint the cabinet
    b. Right of nullification
    c. To impeach the president
    d. To interpret laws through courts

23. Which of the following is true?
  a. The Emancipation Proclamation ended slavery in the United States.
  b. President Wilson called for the foundation of the United Nations in his Fourteen Points.
  c. The Constitution of 1787 and the Bill of Rights were ratified simultaneously.
  d. The Declaration of Independence was primarily concerned with the colonists' complaints against King George III.

24. *The entire Roman Empire was destroyed in the fifth century A.D.* Is this statement true or false?
  a. True; it was conquered by barbarians in that era.
  b. True; it was destroyed by a civil war during that time period.
  c. False; the western half survived as the Holy Roman Empire.
  d. False; the eastern half, known as the Byzantine Empire, survived until 1453 A.D.

25. Which of the statements about the United Nations is false?
  a. It ensured the continuance of an alliance between the United States and Soviet Union.
  b. It was based on the idea for the League of Nations.
  c. It helps to promote human rights.
  d. It includes many former colonies from around the world.

26. Which of the following gentlemen was not instrumental in leading the charge for discussion at the Constitutional Convention held in Philadelphia in 1787?
  a. George Washington
  b. Alexander Hamilton
  c. Thomas Jefferson
  d. James Madison

27. Which American Indian tribe led a nomadic lifestyle and lived in teepees that were easily moved from place to place?
  a. Plains
  b. Southwest
  c. Eastern
  d. Northwest

28. What was Britain's first permanent settlement in North America?
  a. Plymouth, Massachusetts
  b. Roanoke, Virginia
  c. Jamestown, Virginia
  d. L'Anse Meadows, Newfoundland

29. What was the controlling act imposed by the British on American colonists that taxed imported lead, glass, paints, paper, and tea, and prompted the colonies to unite against British rule?
  a. The Stamp Act
  b. The Sugar Act
  c. The Currency Act
  d. The Townsend Act

30. Where did the first shot of the American Revolution take place?
   a. At the Boston Massacre
   b. During the Boston Tea Party
   c. On Lexington Green
   d. At the Battle of Trenton

31. The Revolutionary War's final battle took place on October 19, 1781, when British General Lord Cornwallis surrendered to Washington's troops at what location?
   a. Yorktown, Virginia
   b. Valley Forge, Pennsylvania
   c. Trenton, New Jersey
   d. Saratoga, New York

32. What important U.S. structure was burned during the War of 1812?
   a. The Washington Monument
   b. Independence Hall
   c. The White House
   d. The Statue of Liberty

33. Who was elected President of the Confederate States of America during the Civil War?
   a. Robert E. Lee
   b. Jefferson Davis
   c. William T. Sherman
   d. Abraham Lincoln

34. The period of business and industrial growth from 1876 through the turn of the twentieth century was deemed by author Mark Twain as what?
   a. Manifest Destiny
   b. The Columbian Exchange
   c. The New Deal
   d. The Gilded Age

35. When did World War I begin?
   a. 1915
   b. 1917
   c. 1914
   d. 1918

36. Which of the following countries was a U.S. ally during World War II?
   a. The Soviet Union
   b. Italy
   c. Germany
   d. Japan

37. The North Atlantic Treaty Organization (NATO) was formed between which countries or regions?
   a. Canada, the U.S., and South America
   b. Western Europe, the U.S., and Canada
   c. The U.S., Western Europe, Canada, and the Soviet Union
   d. Asia, the U.S., and Western Europe

38. Which of these events was not a driving force for the passage of the Civil Rights Act in 1964?
  a. *Brown vs. the Board of Education*
  b. Freedom rides
  c. The G.I. Bill
  d. The Montgomery bus boycott

39. What program launched by the U.S. government under President Ronald Reagan was designed to shield the U.S. from nuclear attack by the Soviet Union?
  a. The Strategic Arms Limitation Talks (SALT I and II)
  b. The Strategic Defense Initiative (SDI)
  c. The Iran-Contra Affair
  d. *Glasnost*

40. After the terrorist attacks initiated by Islamic fundamentalist Osama bin Laden on September 11, 2001, President George W. Bush ordered bombing raids on various locations in what country in an attempt to bring down bin Laden and his al-Qaeda network?
  a. Afghanistan
  b. Iraq
  c. Kuwait
  d. Pakistan

41. What are the two largest rivers in the U.S. called?
  a. The Mississippi and the Colorado
  b. The Mississippi and the Missouri
  c. The Missouri and the Ohio
  d. The Mississippi and the Ohio

42. What is used to pinpoint location on a map?
  a. Scale and longitude
  b. Contour lines and scale
  c. Latitude and longitude
  d. Latitude and contour lines

43. Under America's democratic form of government, which of the following are citizens not obligated to do?
  a. Obey the law
  b. Pay taxes
  c. Serve on a jury if asked to do so
  d. Vote in elections

44. How many times has the U.S. Constitution been amended in order to accommodate changes and updates?
  a. Fourteen
  b. Eighteen
  c. Twenty-one
  d. Twenty-seven

45. What is interaction of consumers, households, and companies within individual markets and the relationships between them called?

a. Macroeconomics
b. Microeconomics
c. Boom and bust
d. Economic output

46. What are the types of productive resources used to create products, such as machinery, tools, buildings, and equipment called?

a. Natural resources
b. Human resources
c. Capital resources
d. Entrepreneurship

47. What is the business sector of the economy that provides consumer or business services, including industries such as entertainment, travel and tourism, and banking called?

a. Primary
b. Secondary
c. Tertiary
d. Quaternary

48. Consumers must make choices regarding the goods and services to buy with their limited income. By purchasing one good or service, they are giving up the chance to purchase another. This is referred to as which of the following?

a. The circular flow model
b. Opportunity cost
c. Savings account
d. Assets

49. Which of the following is one way teachers can move beyond traditional direct instruction in the social studies classroom?

a. Textbook work
b. Lectures
c. PowerPoints
d. Field experiences

50. Which of the following geographic tools best allows teachers and students to use satellite technology in the classroom?

a. Globes
b. GPS
c. Timelines
d. Map projections

51. Which of the following represents the Florida state economy?

a. It has strong ties to the aerospace industry.
b. It is a Rust Belt state that has experienced decades-long bouts with deindustrialization.
c. It has historically relied on ranching.
d. It has benefitted from the Mexican national period.

52. The following should be implemented in EC-6 social studies classrooms for the benefit of student learning:

a. Differentiated assessments
b. Field experiences
c. Project-based learning
d. All of the above.

53. What is the difference between a primary source and a secondary source?

a. Secondary sources are usually fictional, while primary sources are always true.
b. Primary sources are context-specific, first-hand accounts, and secondary sources usually synthesize primary sources with some historical distance.
c. Secondary sources are almost always first-hand accounts, while primary sources are second-hand fictional testimonies.
d. There are no major differences between primary sources and secondary sources.

54. Which of the following is a pre-colonial Native American tribe in Florida?

a. Seminoles
b. Karankawas
c. Witchitas
d. All of the above

55. What countries controlled Florida during the era of European colonization?

a. Spain, France, and the United States
b. Spain, Mexico, and the United States
c. Spain, Cuba, and the United States
d. Spain, Portugal, and the United States

Answer Explanations

1. A: Carolina is divided into two separate states—North and South. Maine was part of Nova Scotia and did not become an American territory until the War of 1812. Likewise, Vermont was not one of the original Thirteen Colonies. Canada remained a separate British colony. Finally, Florida was a Spanish territory. Therefore, by process of elimination, *A* is the correct list.

2. B: Britain was not defeated in the French and Indian War, and, in fact, disputes with the colonies over the new territories it won contributed to the growing tensions. All of the other options were key motivations behind the Revolutionary War.

3. C: Abraham Lincoln was elected president as part of the new Republican Party, and his plans to limit and potentially abolish slavery led the southern states to secede from the Union.

4. B: Out of the four inventions mentioned, the first telegraphs were invented in the 1830s, not in the twentieth century. In contrast, the other inventions had considerable influence over the course of the twentieth century.

5. C: The Declaration of Independence occurred during the American Revolution, so it should therefore be considered an effect, not a cause. Similarly, slavery was a cause for the later Civil War, but it was not a primary instigator for the Revolutionary War. Although a single event can have many effects long into the future, it is also important to not overstate the influence of these individual causes; the civil rights movement was only tangentially connected to the War of Independence among many other factors, and therefore it should not be considered a primary effect of it. The French and Indian War (also known as the Seven Years' War) and the Bill of Rights, on the other hand, were respectively a cause and effect from the American Revolution, making Choice *C* the correct answer.

6. D: The president and vice president are part of the executive branch, not the legislative branch. The question focuses specifically on the federal level, so state government should be excluded from consideration. As for the district court and the court of appeals, they are part of the judicial branch. The legislative branch is made up of Congress, which consists of the House of Representatives and the Senate.

7. A: George Washington was a slave owner himself in life, so he did not make abolition a theme in his Farewell Address. On the other hand, he was concerned that sectionalism could potentially destroy the United States, and he warned against it. Furthermore, he believed that Americans should avoid getting involved in European affairs. However, one issue that he felt was especially problematic was the formation of political parties, and he urged against it in his farewell.

8. B: To avoid involvement in political processes such as voting is antithetical to the principles of a democracy. Therefore, the principal responsibility of citizens is the opposite, and they should be steadily engaged in the political processes that determine the course of government.

9. B: Time zones are determined by longitude, not latitude. Locations are defined in absolute terms, while places are in part defined by the population, which is subject to movement. There are seven continents in the world, not six. On the other hand, it is true that the prime meridian determines the border for the Eastern and Western hemispheres.

10. D: Riparian water usage was common in the past, but modern usage has shifted to appropriation. While often practicing sustainable methods, Native Americans used fire, agriculture, and other tools to shape the landscape for their own ends. Due to the importance of trade in providing essential resources to cities, a city is never truly separated from the outside world. However, invasive species are a formidable threat to native environments, making *D* the correct answer.

11. C: I, II, and IV only. Historians make use of maps in their studies to get a clear picture of how history unfolded, knowing the borders of different lands helps historians learn different cultures' interactions, and environmental factors, such as access to water and the proximity of mountains, help determine the course of civilization. The phrase "Geography is closely linked with the flow of resources, technology, and population in societies" is a characteristic of economics.

12. C: While many Native American tribes are matrilineal, not all of them are. Japan is currently coping with an especially low birthrate, not a high one. Mexico's religion, like that of Spain, is primarily Roman Catholic rather than Protestant. On the other hand, Shi'a Islam is based on the view that imams should be honored as Muhammad's chosen heirs to the Caliphate, making *C* correct.

13. A: Although Greeks used the alphabet as the basis for their written language, leading to a diverse array of literature, they learned about the alphabet from Phoenician traders. All the other options, in contrast, were invented in Greece.

14. D: It is important to realize that the Cold War was never an official war and that the United States and the Soviet Union instead funded proxy conflicts. The Kyoto Protocol was signed by members of the United Nations, as the League of Nations was long since defunct. While Japan was a minor participant in World War I, it was not defeated by America until World War II. The correct answer is *D*: India's partition between Hindu India and Islamic Pakistan led to large outbreaks of religious violence.

15. A: Although Egyptian and Mayan civilizations are an interesting subject for comparisons, the two cultures never interacted. The other answers are all examples of interactions between different cultures; a study of Chinese culture, for instance, would require examination of the multiple ethnic groups throughout China.

16. C: Although monetary systems were invented to solve problems with barter systems, it is wrong to assume that barter systems have ceased to exist; bartering remains a common practice throughout the world, albeit less common than money. The four main categories for economic resources are land, labor, capital, and entrepreneurship. The law of supply says that supplies will increase, not decrease, as prices increase. The correct answer is *C,* as scarcity is determined by human choice.

17. A: Rather than competition, a monopoly prevents other businesses from offering a certain product or service to consumers.

18. B: Mercantilism, which is built on the vision of full government control over the economy, is a hallmark of command system economies. Laissez-faire, capitalism, and self-interest, in contrast, are all fundamental concepts behind the market system.

19. A: England, France, and Spain all established North American colonies that would later be absorbed into the United States, but Italy, despite Christopher Columbus' role as an explorer, never established a colony in America.

20. D: The Constitution was signed in 1787; the Declaration of Independence was signed in 1776. It was successfully ratified by all the current states, including New York. Finally, the Articles of Confederation was established at the end of the American Revolution; the Constitution would replace the articles years later due to issues with the government's structure.

21. C: Although American forces made several early attempts to take Canada from Britain, the United States was never able to successfully seize this territory. On the other hand, the United States did control the Philippines, Puerto Rico, and Guam.

22. C: The executive branch determines the cabinet, while the judicial branch has the responsibility of interpreting the Constitution and laws. Even so, the legislative branch can check the president's power by impeaching him.

23. D: The Emancipation Proclamation only freed slaves in Confederate-held territories; southern states still loyal to the Union kept their slaves for the time being. Although Wilson succeeded in instituting the League of Nations, the United Nations would not emerge until decades later. The Bill of Rights was ratified after the Constitution to provide additional protection for individual liberties. However, it is true that the main body of the Declaration of Independence consisted of grievances that the colonies had against British rule.

24. D: While it is true that Rome fell to barbarians in the fifth century A.D., it would be inaccurate to say the Roman Empire had been completely destroyed. The Byzantine Empire considered itself the heir of the Roman Empire. The western sections, on the other hand, certainly collapsed; the later Holy Roman Empire tried to draw on Rome's past glory but was not a true successor.

25. A: Based on the prior League of Nations, the United Nations included many nations in postcolonial Africa and Asia and worked to support human rights. However, it failed to maintain the World War II alliance between the United States and the Soviet Union, leading to the unofficial Cold War.

26. C: At the time of the Constitutional Convention, Thomas Jefferson was in Paris serving as America's foreign minister to France. George Washington led the meeting, and Alexander Hamilton and James Madison set the tone for debate, rendering *A*, *B*, and *D* incorrect.

27. A: Plains Indians followed the buffalo across the prairies, living in tent-like teepees that were easily moved from place to place. Choice *B* is incorrect because Indians in the Southwest relied on farming for much of their food and built adobes, which are houses made out of dried clay or earth. Indians in the Eastern and Northwest sections of North America survived by hunting, gathering, farming, and fishing, and lived in wooden longhouses, plank houses, or wigwams. Thus, Choices *C* and *D* are incorrect.

28. C: Established in 1607, Jamestown, Virginia was the first permanent British settlement in the New World. Plymouth was founded a bit later in 1620 when a group of Pilgrims founded the first permanent European settlement in New England, making Choice *A* incorrect. Choice *B* is incorrect because although the Roanoke Colony was founded in 1585, it isn't considered permanent – the colony's leader, John White, went back to England for supplies two years later, and he returned to find that all of the colonists had mysteriously disappeared. Choice *D* is incorrect because L'Anse Meadows was an area in Newfoundland that was briefly settled by Scandinavian Vikings around 1000 A.D.

29. D: The British issued the Townsend Act in 1767, which taxed imported lead, glass, paints, paper, and tea, and increased the colonists' anger and further strained the relationship between England and the colonies. Choice *A*, the Stamp Act of 1765, taxed printed items, including playing cards and newspapers printed in the colonies. Choice *B*, the Sugar Act of 1764, placed import duties on items such as molasses, sugar, coffee, and wine. Choice *C*, the Currency Act, banned the issuing of paper money in the colonies and mandated the use of gold in business dealings.

30. C: The first shot took place on Lexington Green. When the British heard that colonists were stockpiling weapons they sent troops to Concord to seize them. However, a group of approximately seventy Minutemen confronted the British soldiers on Lexington green. British troops killed five protesting colonists during the Boston Massacre in 1770, but this is not considered the first shot of the Revolution. Thus, Choice *A* is incorrect. Choice *B* is incorrect because the Boston Tea Party was when colonists dumped 342 chests of expensive tea into the Boston Harbor in defiance of the tea tax. The Revolution had already started when the Battle of Trenton took place on December 25, 1776, making Choice *D* incorrect.

31. A: British General Lord Cornwallis surrendered to Washington's troops at Yorktown, Virginia. No battles occurred at Valley Forge, but Washington's troops suffered major losses as a result of starvation, disease, and exposure to the cold, making Choice *B* incorrect. Choice *C* is incorrect because the Battle of Trenton was the first major battle of the Revolution, which occurred when Washington led his troops across the Delaware River to wage a surprise attack on British and Hessian soldiers stationed in Trenton on December 25, 1776. Choice *D,* Saratoga, New York, was the site of a major victory by General John Burgoyne in October 1777 and prompted European countries to help support the American cause.

32. C: British soldiers burned the White House during the War of 1812. Neither the Washington Monument nor the Statue of Liberty – Choices *A* and *D* – were built at the time, and Philadelphia's Independence Hall, Choice *B*, escaped conflict during this war.

33. B: Jefferson Davis was elected president of the Confederate States of America in November 1861. Choice *A*, General Robert E. Lee, was the leader of the Confederate Army. Choice *C*, William T. Sherman, was a union general famous for his march through Georgia and the burning of Atlanta in 1864. Choice *D*, Abraham Lincoln, was President of the U.S. during the Civil War.

34. D: This period was called the Gilded Age since it appeared shiny and golden on the surface, but was fueled by undercurrents of corruption led by big businessmen known as robber barons. Choice *A*, Manifest Destiny, is the concept referring to the pursuit and acquisition of new lands by the U.S., which led to the purchase of Alaska from Russia in 1867 and the annexation of Hawaii in 1898. The Columbian Exchange, Choice *B*, was an era of discovery, conquest, and colonization of the Americas by the Europeans. The New Deal, Choice *C*, was a plan launched by President Franklin Delano Roosevelt to help rebuild America's economy after the Great Depression.

35. C: World War I began in 1914 when a Serbian assassin killed Archduke Franz Ferdinand of Austria and prompted Austria-Hungary to declare war on Serbia. 1915, Choice *A*, is the year when German submarines sank the passenger ship *Lusitania*, killing 128 Americans and leading many to support U.S. efforts to enter the war. 1917, Choice *B*, is the year the U.S. entered World War I, declaring war on Germany. 1918, Choice *D*, signaled the end of the war when American troops helped defeat the German army that September. Fighting ended in November after Germany signed a peace agreement.

36. A: The Soviet Union was invaded by Germany in 1941 and allied with Britain and subsequently the U.S. President Roosevelt, British Prime Minister Winston Churchill, and Soviet director Joseph Stalin met in 1945 to plan their final assault on Germany and discuss postwar strategies. Germany aligned with Italy and Japan in 1940 to form the Axis Alliance. Their goal was to establish a German empire in Europe and place Japan in control over Asia. Thus, Choices *B*, *C*, and *D* are incorrect.

37. B: The North Atlantic Treaty Organization (NATO) was formed between Western Europe, Canada, and the U.S. in defense of Soviet hostility after the Soviet Union introduced Communism into Eastern Europe. The Soviet Union countered by creating the Warsaw Pact.

38. C: The G.I. Bill was a government program started in the 1950s that gave military veterans a free education. In the revolutionary 1954 case, *Brown vs. the Board of Education,* the Supreme Court ruled that school segregation was illegal, thereby setting the Civil Rights Movement in motion, making Choice *A* incorrect. *Freedom Rides*, Choice *B*, and the Montgomery bus boycott, Choice *D*, were among the non-violent protests against segregation that took place in the U.S. in the 1960s.

39. B: President Reagan advocated *peace through strength*, building up the U.S. military and launching the Strategic Defense Initiative (SDI), also called *Star Wars*. Choice *A*, the Strategic Arms Limitation Talks (SALT I and II), negotiated between 1972 and 1979, resulted in limits on nuclear weapons for both the U.S. and Russia. Choice *C*, the Iran-Contra Affair, was a scandal involving the secret sale of weapons to Iran in exchange for American hostages. Choice *D*, *Glasnost*, was a policy of political openness launched by Soviet leader Mikhail Gorbachev.

40. A: Afghanistan was the site of the bombing raids. Bush invaded Iraq, Choice *B*, in 2003 when Iraqi dictator Saddam Hussein defied the terms of the truce agreed upon in 1991 after the Gulf War. Kuwait, Choice *C*, was invaded by Iraq in 1990, sparking the Gulf War. Pakistan, Choice *D*, is where Osama bin Laden was killed by a group of Navy SEALs under orders from President Obama.

41. B: The Mississippi and the Missouri are the two largest rivers in the U.S., winding through the Great Plains in the center of the country. The Colorado and Ohio Rivers are about half the length of the Mississippi and Missouri.

42. C: Latitude – imaginary lines covering the globe from east to west – and longitude – imaginary lines running north to south – are used to pinpoint location on a map. Scale is used to show the relationship between the map measurements and the equivalent distance on the world's surface. Contour lines are used to show detailed elevation on a map.

43. D: Under America's democratic form of government, voting is a *right*, but it is not an *obligation*. U.S. citizens are *obliged* to obey the law, pay taxes, and serve on a jury if asked to do so, making Choices *A*, *B*, and *C* incorrect.

44. D: There are twenty-seven amendments to the U.S. Constitution. The 14th Amendment was adopted in 1868 to abolish slavery. The 18th Amendment was passed in 1919 and prohibited the production and sale of alcoholic beverages, but the 21st Amendment repealed it in 1933.

***45.* B:** Microeconomics looks at the interplay of consumers, households, and companies within individual markets and the relationships between them. Macroeconomics, Choice *A*, is the study of entire economies. Booms and busts, Choice *C*, are terms used to describe the cyclical nature of economic activity, typically prompted by extreme changes in the economy. Economic output, Choice *D*, is the total amount of goods and services produced by an *economy.*

46. C: Capital resources are the man-made physical resources used to create products, such as machinery, tools, buildings, and equipment. Natural resources, Choice *A*, are raw materials taken from the land, such as corn, beef, lumber, water, oil, and iron. Human resources, Choice *B*, refer to the human labor—both mental and physical—required to produce goods. Entrepreneurship, Choice *D*, is the capability and motivation to cultivate, organize, and oversee the other three resources into a business venture.

47. C: The tertiary sector provides consumer or business services, including industries such as entertainment, retail sales, and restaurants. The primary sector, Choice *A*, takes raw materials from the Earth, such as coal, timber, copper, and wheat. The secondary sector, Choice *B*, converts raw materials into goods, such as textile manufacturing, food processing, and car manufacturing. The quaternary sector, Choice *D*, provides informational and knowledge services, such as education, business consulting, and financial services.

48. B: Opportunity cost is the term used to describe the choices that determine how consumers spend or save their money. Choice *A*, the circular flow model, is used by economists to describe the movement of supply, demand, and payment between businesses and consumers. A savings account, Choice *C*, is considered low-risk because the bank will pay the saver a low interest rate to keep it safe. Assets, Choice *D*, are valuable items purchased by investors in the hopes that they will increase in worth over time and yield returns or profits.

49. D: Field experiences. The FTCE guide recommends that teachers move beyond traditional, direct instruction to enhance student learning and better prepare students for work in secondary school and college. Field experiences can enhance student learning by exposing them to real-world objects, ideas, and issues. Field experiences prepare students to become young social scientists who can carry out qualitative and quantitative research.

50. B: GPS uses satellite technology to analyze and display geographic features. In an increasingly technological world, students must know how to use GPS technology to their advantage in the classroom. Other tools, such as globes, timelines, and map projections can also be useful, but none of these employ satellite technology.

51. A: Florida has had long-standing ties to the aerospace industry and has been a hub for NASA. Florida is a Sunbelt state, not a Rust Belt state, so Choice *B* is incorrect. Florida is not traditionally a ranching state, so Choice *C* is also incorrect. Finally, Florida was never under Mexican control, so Choice *D* is also incorrect.

52. D: All of the above. The FCTE guide recommends that differentiated assessments, field experiences, and project-based learning should be implemented in EC-6 social-studies classrooms. Differentiated assessments are crucial for reaching and evaluating all learning types. Through exposure to real-world artifacts, ideas, and issues, field experiences enhance student knowledge. Project-based learning prepares EC-6 social science students for projects in secondary school, college, and the real world.

53. B: Primary sources are context-specific, first-hand accounts, and secondary sources usually synthesize primary sources with some historical distance. Choice *A* is incorrect because both primary and secondary sources can be fictional or realistic. Choice *C* is wrong for two reasons. First, it confuses the fact that primary sources are first-hand accounts and secondary sources can be second-hand testimonies. Second, secondary sources aren't always fictional. Choice *D* is incorrect because primary sources and secondary sources are drastically different in scope and context.

54. A: Seminoles. Seminoles were an indigenous group that lived in Florida during the pre-colonial and colonial eras. Choices *A* (Karankawas) and *B* (Witchitas) are incorrect because these Native Americans didn't live in Florida. Choice *D* is therefore incorrect.

55. A: Spain, France, and the United States all had footholds in the Florida peninsula during the era of European colonization. Spain had the strongest foothold in Florida prior to the U.S. purchase of the Florida territory via the Adams-Onis Treaty of 1819. Spain colonized Florida between the 1500s and 1800s. France also briefly colonized Florida between 1562 and 1565 when a French Huguenot colony was established on the peninsula. Choices *B, C,* and *D* are incorrect because Mexico, Cuba, and Portugal didn't possess colonial control over Florida.

Science

Nature of Science

Systems, Models, Changes, and Scale's Role in Science and Technology

Visual representation and hands on-learning through the development of models is critical for students' conceptual understanding at a young age. A *system* is a set of smaller things that work together to form a larger whole. A Styrofoam ball model can demonstrate the role of planets in the larger solar system. Verbal discussion of ecosystems and food chains isn't as effective as drawing pictures of food chains and watching and discussing video clips of feeding relationships. Illustrating how plants need nutrients in their soil could be emphasized by an experiment such as the one described above.

The *scale* of science simply means its breadth, and for students to gain perspective of scale, they need models. For example, a class project involving constructing a globe would be a meaningful activity to show the land to water ratio of the Earth. Discussing destruction of rainforests and how this changes the Earth's environment by using magic markers to color affected areas on the globe is another way to show the scope of science.

A project at the University of North Texas investigated conservation habits and their effect on water bills. Children wore a bracelet to remind themselves of a promise they made to turn off the water when they brushed their teeth. Their conservation habit involved using a toothbrush that gave a signal after two minutes from starting to brush. Then, after a significant portion of time (a month or more), students had their parents bring in their water bills, and they measured and graphed the consumption decrease from month to month. The project extended further in that it actually obtained the entire city's water consumption levels, and the data indeed showed that the small changes made at home resulted in a significant conservation of water. Including technological resources into science lessons provides the opportunity for deeper understanding.

Scientific Investigation Skills and Communication

<u>Hypothesis</u>
Valid experiments must start with a valid hypothesis. There must be one independent variable for any scientific question and a measurable dependent variable that is used to investigate the question. The *hypothesis* is a statement that explains how changing the independent variable would affect the dependent variable, and is often stated as an *if (independent variable plus verb), then (dependent variable plus verb)* sentence. At the early childhood level, before developing a hypothesis, it's important to emphasize valid dependent variables.

Dependent variables must be measurable. Common dependent variables include mass (measured with a balance or scale), length (measured with a ruler), and volume (measured with a graduated cylinder or the more familiar tablespoons, cups, and pints for young students).

It is also important to develop an independent variable with at least two known conditions. The *normal condition* is called the control group, and other conditions different from the control group are called *experimental groups*.

For example, a simple experiment could entail investigating how fertilizer affects plant growth.

Here are examples of valid hypotheses that collect quantitative data:

- If fertilizer is added to the soil, then plant height will increase.
- If fertilizer is added to the soil, then the number of leaves on the plant will increase.

Here are examples of invalid hypotheses:

- If fertilizer is added to the soil, then the plant will grow better.
- If the plant soil changes, then the plant will grow better.

Notice in the valid hypothesis that there's a clear independent variable: the addition of fertilizer to soil. Also, both dependent variable options are quantitative and can be measured. Height can be measured with a ruler, and the number of leaves can be measured by counting.

The invalid hypotheses contain immeasurable changes. "Growing better" isn't specific enough and can't be measured. "Soil changes" isn't specific enough and could involve many different changes, including amount of soil, type of fertilizer, or amount of fertilizer.

Variable Development

After developing a valid hypothesis with specific changes and measurements, the details of the experiment must be confirmed before developing a procedure. That means defining constants, a control group, experimental groups, and measurement methods/devices.

With the proposed hypothesis in mind (*If fertilizer is added to the soil, then plant height will increase),* several constants should be defined. The type of plant is important. Some plants grow faster than others, so all the plants included in the experiment should be of the same type (Wisconsin fast plants are an excellent choice). The brand and amount of soil should be the same; the shape and type of pot should be the same; and the amount of watering and light exposure should be consistent between all test groups. If any one of these factors is different, it will be impossible to tell which factor caused an observable change as opposed to the independent variable. The independent variable (the addition of fertilizer) should be the only changed factor.

A control group is also important to include in all experiments. In this case, the control group would be soil with no added fertilizer. There would be no way to know if the fertilizer was actually helpful unless the experiment included the unaffected condition. Including at least two experimental conditions of the manipulated variable is important if it is desirable to see varying amounts of change. Good options in this case would be to include soil with 5% fertilizer and 10% fertilizer.

The dependent variable should be something easy for young students to measure. In this experiment, a good dependent variable is length. It's important for children to know that the measurement should consist of stretching out the plant and measuring its length with a string, then using the ruler to measure the length of the straightened string. This method of measurement will account for possible drooping and will be more accurate. Discussing with students why such a procedure is important offers an opportunity for students to analyze and come up with the reason for this measuring procedure on their own, enhancing their high-level analysis skills.

Finally, it's important to include multiple trials of each test group—in this case multiple seeds in each fertilizer condition. Students must be able to have confidence in their results; some experiments inevitably go wrong through forces of nature (such as a dud seed), so this is a critical part of any experiment.

Procedure

Developing a procedure could be a class process. For this particular experiment, several parameters should be kept in mind:

- The experiment should last for at least a week so the plants have a chance to grow.
- Water and light should be a critical part of plant care and should be uniform in all conditions.
- The string/ruler measurement system is important.

Example procedure:

Day 1

1. Place 2 cups of soil without fertilizer (0% fertilizer)* into the pot.
2. Add five seeds in the pattern exemplified below.

3. Pour ½ cup of tap water over seeds.
4. Sprinkle ¼ cup of soil over watered seeds.
5. Place the group name on the pot (label the pot appropriately).
6. Repeat steps #1-5 with:
7. Low fertilizer mix (5% fertilizer)*
8. High fertilizer mix (10% fertilizer)*
9. Lastly, put the pots in the light box.

*For young students, percentages are a concept that can be omitted, depending on their level. The purpose of this experiment is teaching the scientific process (not math), so "no fertilizer," "low fertilizer," and "high fertilizer" are sufficient experimental group descriptions.

Days 2-14

10. Water the plants with 1/3 cup of water every school day.
11. Day 14: Carefully pull each plant out of the soil. Carefully stretch it out and measure its length with a piece of string. Then measure the piece of string against a ruler and record the value.

At the early elementary level, it's important to know that qualitative data based on the senses (sight, taste, touch, smell, hearing) should be used in investigation as well as quantitative data (numerical data). As a class, discussing data about plants such as color, number and size of leaves, and root structure adds to the learning experience.

Developing the procedure as a class has many benefits. There is opportunity for students to make choices and further discussion. For example, if they want to use only one seed, it's a good opportunity to talk about the importance of multiple trials.

<u>Data Collection and Results</u>

At a young age, students will need guidance with data collection as well as communicating results. A great way to model data collection is having a data table on the blackboard and asking each group to walk up and fill in their data. Teachers should be sure to guide them so they know where to put their numbers. For example:

	Plant height (cm)					
Amount of Fertilizer	**Group 1**	**Group 2**	**Group 3**	**Group 4**	**Group 5**	**Average**
None						
Low						
High						

If students aren't familiar with the concept of averaging, it might be more appropriate to do that for them and instead to place on the board a simplified table like the one below (with mock data):

	Plant Height (cm)*
No fertilizer	5
Medium Fertilizer	12
High Fertilizer	19

*Note that figures are rounded to the nearest integer. Rounding is fine for early childhood experiments and a good point of discussion. More advanced students can write numbers to the tenths place in their data collection.

A concept that students should eventually develop on their own is how to make and present a graph; however, this should be modeled by the teacher for younger students by giving them the actual graph on paper for them to color. For older or more advanced students, an empty graph without the data bars would be sufficient, so students can draw and color the bars themselves. Teachers should emphasize to students that the independent variable should be the x-axis and that the dependent variable should be the y-axis so the results are easy to interpret.

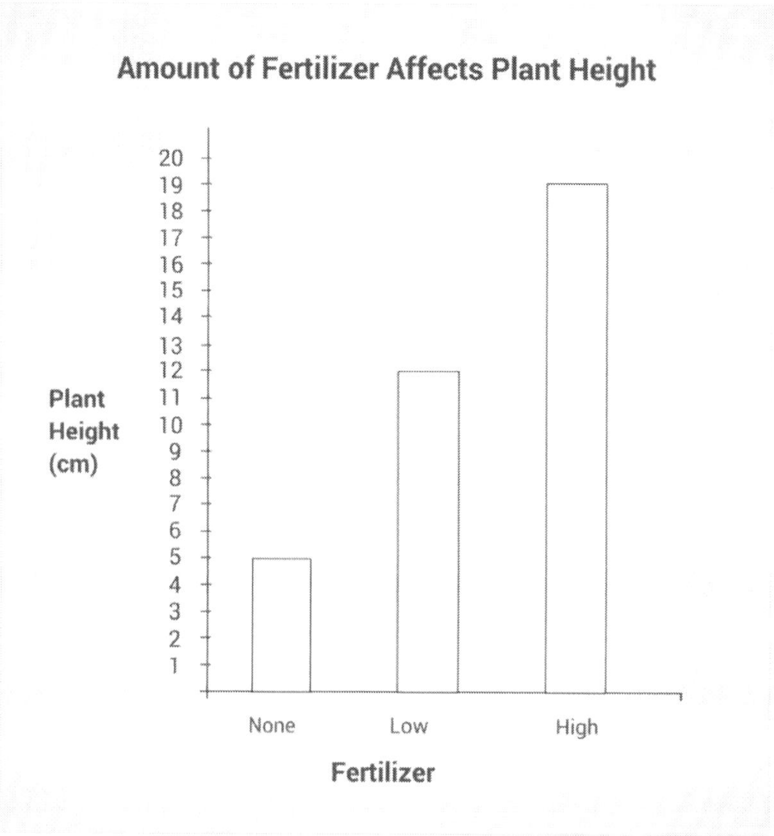

Communicating the results with a graph is simple because either the fertilizer affected the plants or it didn't, and the trend in the graph will illustrate the answer. A simple conclusion sentence can be written to wrap up the investigation. Students should decide whether the hypothesis was proven true or false, such as, "*When fertilizer was added to the soil, plant growth increased*."

Science as an Inquiry

Science begins with questions—it is difficult to have an answer when there are no questions. A great source of inquiry for scientists has been weather. The study of weather is called meteorology. Meteorologists measure temperature, air pressure, wind speed, wind direction, and humidity, all in hopes of predicting how and where air and water vapor will move and behave. These questions inspire meteorologists to use weather balloons and satellites to study weather and make educated guesses. As knowledge grows, technologies also improve and facilitate better weather forecasting. The impressive Doppler radar has provided scientists with meaningful data since the 1980s, allowing them to better predict the weather with more certainty.

Supporting Conclusions with Tools and Representations

Science is a process that always begins with a question or a problem. For early childhood, students must be able to perform experiments, collect quantitative and qualitative data, and communicate results visually and verbally.

The classic scientific process can be demonstrated by the development of modern genetics. Why offspring resemble parents is the question that led Gregor Mendel to experiment with pea plants and ultimately elucidate the mechanism behind heredity. Mendel proposed that there were two alleles per trait, and that an organism receives one allele from each parent. He proposed that there was a dominant allele and a recessive allele, and an organism's appearance is determined by the presence of the overpowering dominant allele. After many experiments with pea plants, Mendel found that round seeds were dominant over wrinkled seeds because if the round allele was present (even if the wrinkled allele was present), the organism appeared round.

He replicated his data not only with seed shape, but also with leaf color and plant height, among other traits, and consistently noticed that dominant alleles were overpowering.

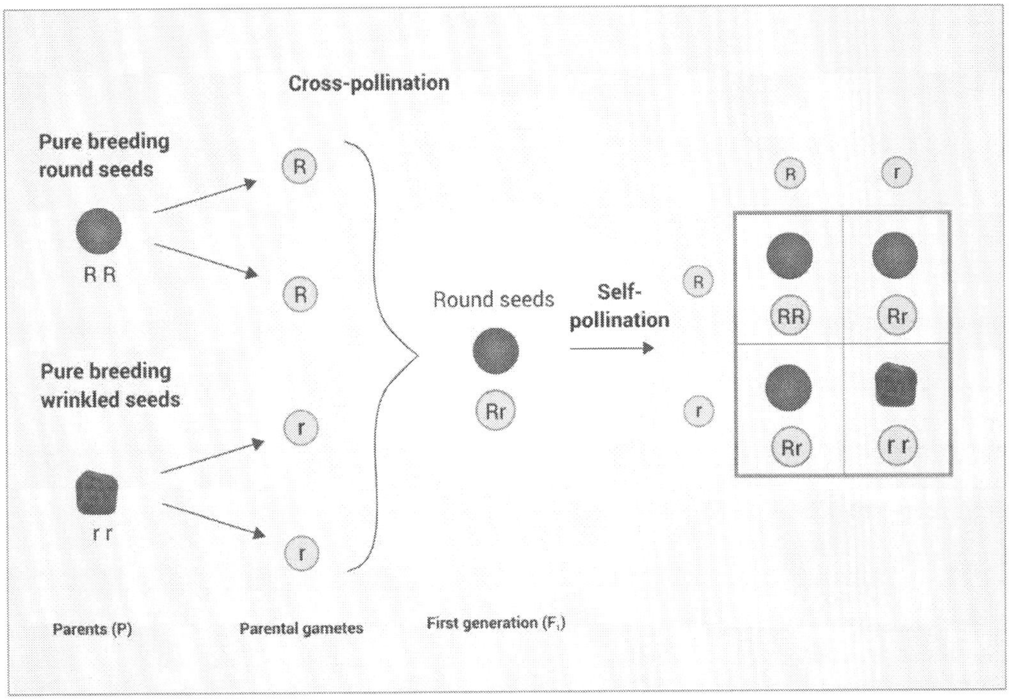

Phenotype: 3:1 round:wrinkled

Genotype: 1 RR : 2 Rr : 1 rr

Like any scientist, Mendel analyzed the question via valid experimentation and multiple trials. He performed thousands of crosses of pea plants and observed data that supported the dominant/recessive/two genes per trait idea. After the results confirming the predicted ratio, he confidently concluded that traits are determined by dominant and recessive alleles, and that every individual has two genes per trait.

In the late 1800s and early 1900s, Mendel's ideas were rejected because the prevailing idea was that an individual's traits were simply a blend of his or her parents' traits.

Modern genetics confirms that humans are diploid, meaning that they have two chromosomes and therefore two genes for every trait, which affirms Mendel's notion of heredity. A karyotype—a picture of all of an organism's chromosomes—is visual proof that has become possible with modern tools.

Mendel's journey exemplifies the scientific process and experimental development: problem/question, hypothesis, valid experimentation, data collection, multiple trials, and conclusions. Scientific conclusions are continually tested as technology advances. For example, Mendel's pea plant conclusions were retested and validated by visualization of chromosomes with modern microscopes.

Science as an Endeavor, Process, and Career

People of all cultures around the world utilize science in order to explore questions and find solutions to problems. The systematic process of designing, conducting, and analyzing experiments is universally known and respected. These processes are time-consuming and require specific knowledge and skills. Therefore, the pursuit of science is its own career path, with many smaller paths for each respective area of study (i.e., life sciences, chemical sciences, physical sciences). Of course, each of those paths splits into even more refined areas and requires much study and dedication. Men and women alike pursue scientific questions; some are driven by pure curiosity and others are compelled by finding a faster, or even a more economical way, of performing a task or producing an object.

Not all ideas, methods, or results are popular or accepted by society. Thus, the pursuit of science is often riddled with controversy. This has been an underlying theme since the early days of astronomical discovery. Copernicus was excommunicated from his religious establishment when he announced the belief that the sun, not the Earth, was the controlling body of the heavens known to humans at the time. Despite his having documented observations and calculations, those opposed to his theory could not be convinced. Copernicus experienced great ridicule and suffering due to his scientific research and assertions. In addition, other scientists have faced adverse scrutiny for their assertions including Galileo, Albert Einstein, and Stephen Hawking. In each case, logical thought, observations, and calculations have been used to demonstrate their ideas, yet opposition to their scientific beliefs still exists.

The possibilities for careers involving science range from conducting research, to the application of science and research (engineering), to academia (teaching). All of these avenues require intensive study and a thorough understanding of the respective branch of science and its components. An important factor of studying and applying science is being able to concisely and accurately communicate knowledge to other people. Many times this is done utilizing mathematics or even through demonstration. The necessity of communicating ideas, research, and results brings people from all nationalities together. This often lends to different cultures finding common ground for research and investigation, and opens lines of communication and cooperation.

Unifying Process of Science

Following the scientific method, and keeping to the standards of proper research and reporting, lends to easier communication of data and results. When information can be conveyed to multiple audiences in a manner of common understanding (i.e., mathematics), it increases the possibilities for the use of such information. Having other scientists understand an idea can also lead to further experimentation and discovery in that area. This leads to the further organization of information and a deeper understanding of our universe.

It is more systematic to group, sort, and organize information for commonalities in order to increase understanding. The organization of groups can also serve as a reference point when attempting to identify other members of that group. For instance, a newly discovered type of rock can be compared to known rocks and then better categorized as to its uses or properties, based upon how it appears and responds in experiments, when measured against known rocks. This occurs regularly when varying crystal rock structures are developed for use in super-cooled or super-conductive experiments because certain properties are more useful with regard to conduction and strength. In order to have knowledge and access to this type of variation of information, societies are formed and people from all over the world find ways to communicate and share in the scientific endeavor.

The communication of research can further questions and explorations across the world. This common goal of reaching new discoveries or uses for the application of science can bring people together. Oftentimes, the quest for scientific discovery is spawned by competition or the race to create something before another society or country. Examples of this include the race to explore space, the race for nuclear armaments, and the race to create and cure strains of deadly bacteria. In these situations, the urge to push scientific discovery ahead may not be for the most humanitarian motives; however, oftentimes these research prompts result in accidental discoveries that can solve other problems. The discoveries of vaccinations, stronger materials such as plastics, and cleaner forms of energy through superconducting crystals have all been accidental discoveries along the way of competitive scientific research. Whatever the motive for scientific discovery, it can be seen as a common thread across many nations with a potential to create unity through its demand for structure and organization.

Physical Sciences

Physical and Chemical Properties

In the physical sciences, it is important to break things down to their simplest components in order to truly understand why they act and react the way they do. It may seem burdensome to separate out each part of an object or to diagram each movement made by an object, but these methods provide a solid basis for understanding how to accurately depict the motion of objects and then correctly predict their future movements.

Everything around us is composed of different materials. To properly understand and sort objects, we must classify what types of materials they comprise. This includes identifying the foundational properties of each object such as its reaction to chemicals, heat, water, or other materials. Some objects might not react at all and this is an important property to note. Other properties include the physical appearance of the object or whether it has any magnetic properties. The importance of being able to sort and classify objects is the first step to understanding them.

Matter: anything that has mass and takes up space

Substance: a type of matter that cannot be separated out into new material through a physical reaction

Elements: substances that cannot be broken down by either physical or chemical reactions. Elements are in the most basic form and are grouped by identified properties using the Periodic Table. The periodic table groups elements based on similar properties. Metallic elements, inert elements, and transition elements are a few categories used to organize elements on the periodic table. New elements are added as they are discovered or created, and these newer elements tend to be heavier, fall into the metal section of the periodic table, and are often unstable. Examples of elements include carbon, gold, and helium.

Atoms: the building blocks of all elements. Atoms are the smallest particles of matter that retain their identities during chemical reactions. Atoms have a central nucleus that includes positively charged protons, and neutrons, which carry no charge. Atoms are also surrounded by electrons that carry a negative charge. The amount of each component determines what type of atom is formed when the components come together. For example, two hydrogen atoms and one oxygen atom can bond together to form water, but the hydrogen and oxygen atoms still remain true to their original identities.

Mass: the measure of how much of a substance exists in an object. The measure of mass is not the same as weight, area, or volume.

Physical Properties vs. Chemical Properties

Both physical and chemical properties are used to sort and classify objects:

Physical properties: refers to the appearance, mass, temperature, state, size, or color of an object or fluid; a physical change indicates a change in the appearance, mass, temperature, state, size or color of an object or fluid.

Chemical properties: refers to the chemical makeup of an object or fluid; a chemical change refers to an alteration in the makeup of an object or fluid and forms a new solution or compound.

Reversible Change vs. Non-Reversible Change

Reversible change (physical change) is the changing of the size or shape of an object without altering its chemical makeup. Examples include the heating or cooling of water, change of state (solid, liquid, gas), the freezing of water into ice, or cutting a piece of wood in half.

When two or more materials are combined, it is called a mixture. Generally, a mixture can be separated out into the original components. When one type of matter is dissolved into another type of matter (a solid into a liquid or a liquid into another liquid), and cannot easily be separated back into its original components, it is called a solution.

States of matter refers to the form substances take such as solid, liquid, gas, or plasma. Solid refers to a rigid form of matter with a flexed shape and a fixed volume. Liquid refers to the fluid form of matter with no fixed shape and a fixed volume. Gas refers to an easily compressible fluid form of matter with no fixed shape that expands to fill any space available. Finally, plasma refers to an ionized gas where electrons flow freely from atom to atom.

> Examples: A rock is a solid because it has a fixed shape and volume. Water is considered to be a liquid because it has a set volume, but not a set shape; therefore, you could pour it into different containers of different shapes, as long as they were large enough to contain the existing volume of the water. Oxygen is considered to be a gas. Oxygen does not have a set volume or a set shape; therefore, it could expand or contract to fill a container or even a room. Gases in fluorescent lamps become plasma when electric current is applied to them.

Matter can change from one state to another in many ways, including through heating, cooling, or a change in pressure.

Changes of state are identified as:

- Melting: solid to liquid
- Sublimation: solid to gas
- Evaporation: liquid to gas
- Freezing: liquid to solid
- Condensation: gas to liquid
- Non-reversible change (chemical change): When one or more types of matter change and it results in the production of new materials. Examples include burning, rusting, and combining solutions. If a piece of paper is burned it cannot be turned back into its original state. It has forever been altered by a chemical change.

Homogenous Mixtures and Heterogeneous Mixtures

When a material can be separated by physicals means (such as sifting it through a colander), it is called a *mixture*. Mixtures are categorized into two types: *heterogeneous* and *homogeneous*. Heterogeneous mixtures have physically distinct parts, which retain their different properties. A mix of salt and sugar is an example of a heterogeneous mixture. With heterogenous mixtures, it is possible that different samples from the same parent mixture may have different proportions of each component in the mixture. For example, in the sugar and salt mixture, there may be uneven mixing of the two, causing one random tablespoon sample to be mostly salt, while a different tablespoon sample may be mostly sugar.

A homogeneous mixture, also called a *solution*, has uniform properties throughout a given sample. An example of a homogeneous solution is salt fully dissolved in warm water. In this case, any number of samples taken from the parent solution would be identical.

Potential Energy vs. Kinetic Energy

Potential energy (gravitational potential energy, or PE) is stored energy, or energy due to an object's height above the ground. Kinetic energy (KE) is the energy of motion. If an object is moving, it has some amount of kinetic energy.

Consider a rollercoaster car sitting still on the tracks at the top of a hill. The rollercoaster has all potential energy and no kinetic energy. As it travels down the hill, the energy transfers from potential energy into kinetic energy. At the bottom of the hill, where the car is going the fastest, it has all kinetic energy, but no potential energy. If energy losses to the environment (friction, heat, sound) are ignored, the amount of potential energy at the top of the hill equals the amount of kinetic energy at the bottom of the hill.

Energy

The term *energy* typically refers to an object's ability to perform work. This can include a transfer of heat from one object to another, or from an object to its surroundings. Energy is usually measured in Joules. There are two main categories of energy: renewable and non-renewable.

Renewable: energy produced from the exhaustion of a resource that can be replenished. Burning wood to produce heat, then replanting trees to replenish the resource is an instance of using renewable energy.

Non-renewable: energy produced from the exhaustion of a resource that cannot be replenished. Burning coal to produce heat would be an example of a non-renewable energy. Although coal is a natural resource found in/on the earth that is mined or harvested from the earth, it cannot be regrown or replenished. Other examples include oil and natural gas (fossil fuels).

Temperature is measured in degrees Celsius (C) or Kelvin (K). Temperature should not be confused with heat. Heat is a form of energy: a change in temperature or a transfer of heat can also be a measure of energy. The amount of energy measured by the change in temperature (or a transfer) is the measure of heat.

Heat energy (thermal energy) can be transferred through the following ways:

<u>Conduction</u>
Conduction is the heating of one object by another through the actual touching of molecules, in order to transfer heat across the objects involved. A spiral burner on an electric stovetop heats from one molecule touching another to transfer the heat via conduction.

<u>Convection</u>
Heat transfer due to the movement/flow of molecules from areas of high concentration to ones of low concentration. Warmer molecules tend to rise, while colder molecules tend to sink. The heat in a house will rise from the vents in the floor to the upper levels of the structure and circulate in that manner, rising and falling with the movement of the molecules. This molecular movement helps to heat or cool a house and is often called convection current.

<u>Radiation</u>
The sun warms the earth through radiation or radiant energy. Radiation does not need any medium for the heat to travel; therefore, the heat from the sun can radiate to the earth across space.

<u>Greenhouse Effect</u>
The sun transfers heat into the earth's atmosphere through radiation traveling in waves. The atmosphere helps protect the earth from extreme exposure to the sun, while reflecting some of the waves continuously within the atmosphere, creating habitable temperatures. The rest of the waves are meant to dissipate out through the atmosphere and back into space. However, humans have created pollutants and released an overabundance of certain gasses into the earth's atmosphere, causing a layer of blockage. So, the waves that should be leaving the atmosphere continue to bounce back upon the earth repeatedly, thus contributing to global warming. This is a negative effect from the extra re-radiation of the sun's energy and causes planetary overheating.

This additional warming is not something easily or quickly reversed. Because the rate of reflection within the atmosphere only multiplies the more a light wave is bounced around, it will take a concerted effort to undue past reflectance and stop future reflectance of the light waves in the earth's atmosphere. Once the re-reflectance occurs, it duplicates exponentially, along with the additional compounding of more waves. Each degree the atmospheric temperature increases has a profound effect on the delicate balance of our planet, including the melting of polar ice caps, the rise of tidal currents—which cause strong weather systems—and the depletion of specific ecosystems necessary to sustain certain species of animals or insects, to name a few.

Energy can be harnessed to operate objects, and this energy is obtained from various sources such as electricity, food, gasoline, batteries, wind, and sun. For example, wind turbines out in a field are turned by the natural power of the wind. The turbines then store that energy internally in power cells; that stored energy can be used to power the lights on a farm or run machinery.

Mechanical Energy

Mechanical energy is the sum of the potential energy plus the kinetic energy in a system, minus energy lost to non-conservative forces. Often, the effects of non-conservative forces are small enough that they can be ignored. The total mechanical energy of a system is conserved or always the same. The amount of potential energy and the amount of kinetic energy can vary to add up to this total, but the total mechanical energy in the situation remains the same.

$$ME = PE + KE$$

$$Mechanical\ Energy = Potential\ Energy + Kinetic\ Energy$$

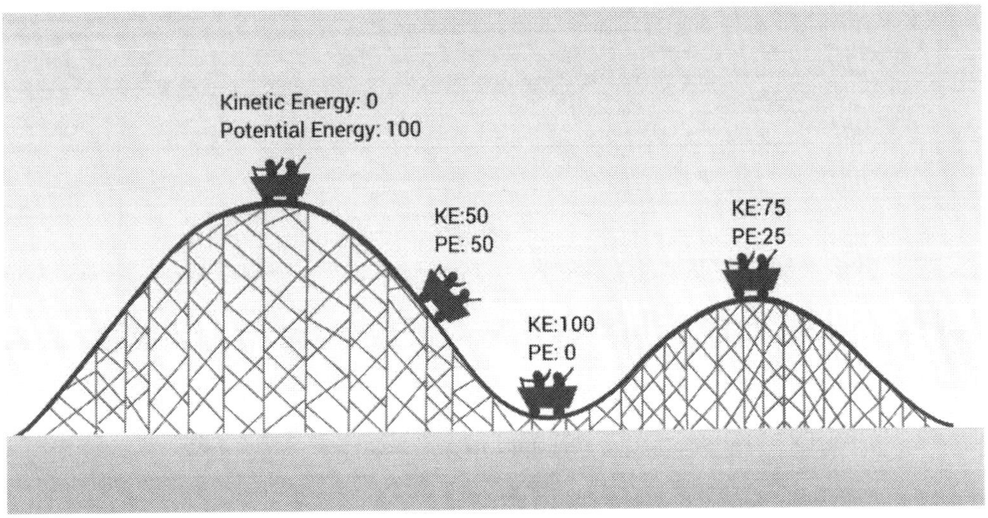

An illustration of a rollercoaster going down a hill demonstrates this point. At the top of the hill a label of $ME = PE$ describes the rollercoaster, halfway down the hill the label $ME = \frac{1}{2}PE + \frac{1}{2}KE$ describes the rollercoaster, and at the bottom of the hill, $ME = KE$ describes the rollercoaster.

Remember, energy can transfer or change forms, but it cannot be created or destroyed. This transfer can take place through waves (including light waves and sound waves), heat, impact, etc.

Simple Machines

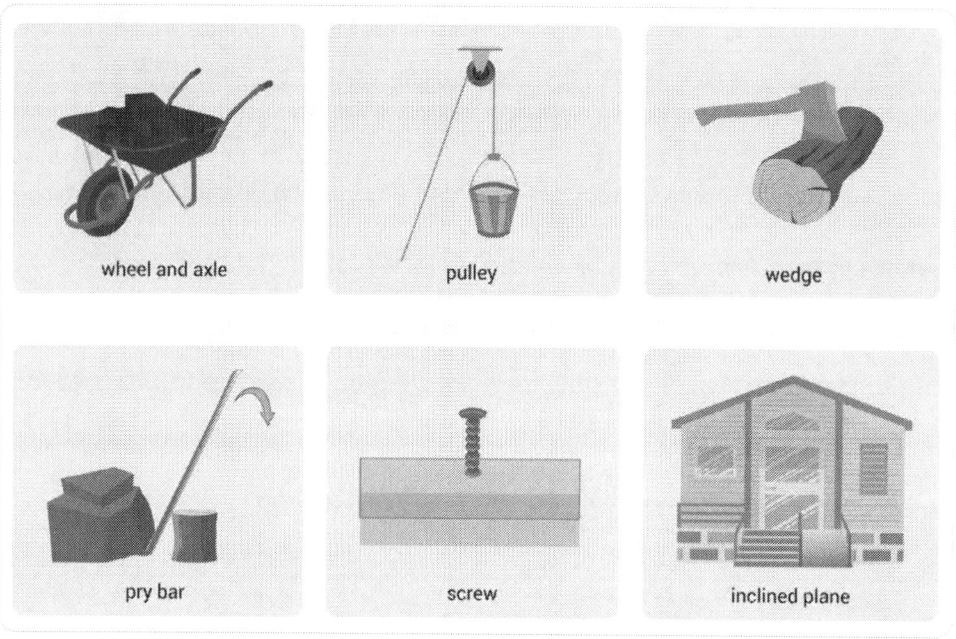

The use of simple machines can help by requiring less force to perform a task with the same result. This is also referred to as mechanical advantage.

Trying to lift a child into the air to pick an apple from a tree would require less force if the child was placed on the end of a teeter-totter and the adult pushed the other end of the teeter-totter down, in order to elevate the child to the same height to pick the apple. In this instance, the teeter-totter is a lever and provides a mechanical advantage to make the job easier.

Interactions of Energy

There is a fundamental law of thermodynamics (the study of heat and movement) called Conservation of Energy. This law states that energy cannot be created or destroyed, but rather energy is transferred to different forms involved in a process. For instance, a car pushed beginning at one end of a street will not continue down that street forever; it will gradually come to a stop some distance away from where it was originally pushed. This does not mean the energy has disappeared or has been exhausted; it means the energy has been transferred to different mediums surrounding the car. The frictional force from the road on the tires dissipates some of the energy, the air resistance from the movement of the car dissipates some of the energy, the sound from the tires on the road dissipates some of the energy, and the force of gravity pulling on the car dissipates some of the energy. Each value can be calculated in a number of ways including measuring the sound waves from the tires, measuring the temperature change in the tires, measuring the distance moved by the car from start to finish, etc. It is important to understand that many processes factor into such a small situation, but all situations follow the conservation of energy.

As in the earlier example, the rollercoaster at the top of a hill has a measurable amount of potential energy, and when it rolls down the hill, it converts most of that energy into kinetic energy. There are still additional factors like friction and air resistance working on the rollercoaster and dissipating some of the energy, but energy transfers in every situation.

Electrostatics

Electrostatics is the study of electric charges at rest. A charge comes from an atom having more or fewer electrons than protons. If an atom has more electrons than protons, it has a negative charge. If an atom has fewer electrons than protons, it has a positive charge. It is important to remember that opposite charges attract each other, while like charges repel each other. So, a negative attracts a positive, a negative repels a negative, and similarly, a positive repels a positive. Just as energy cannot be created or destroyed, neither can charge; charge is transferred. This transfer can be done through touch.

If a person wears socks and scuffs their feet across carpeting, they are transferring electrons to the carpeting through friction. If that person then goes to touch a light switch, they will receive a small shock, which is the electrons transferring from the switch to their hand. The person lost electrons to the carpet, which left them with a positive charge; therefore, the electrons from the switch attract to the person for the transfer. The shock is the electrons jumping from the switch to the person's finger.

Another method of charging an object is through induction. Induction is when a charged object is brought near, but not touched to, a neutral conducting object. The charged object will cause the electrons within the conductor to move. If the charged object is negative, the electrons will be induced away from the charged object and vice versa.

Yet another way to charge an object is through polarization. Polarization can be achieved by simply reconfiguring the electrons on an object. If a person were to rub a balloon on their hair, the balloon would then stick to a wall. This is because rubbing the balloon causes it to become negatively charged and when the balloon is held against a neutral wall, the negatively charged balloon repels all of the wall's electrons, causing a positively charged surface on the wall. This type of charge would be temporary, due to the massive size of the wall, and the charges would quickly redistribute.

Electric Current

Electrical current is the process by which electrons carry charge. In order to make the electrons move so that they can carry a charge, a change in voltage must be present. On a small scale, this is demonstrated through the electrons travelling from the light switch to a person's finger in the example where the person scuffed their socks on a carpet. The difference between the switch and the finger caused the electrons to move. On a larger and more sustained scale, this movement would need to be more controlled. This can be achieved through batteries/cells and generators. Batteries or cells have a chemical reaction that takes place inside, causing energy to be released and a charge to be able to move freely. Generators convert mechanical energy into electric energy.

If a wire is run from touching the end of a battery to the end of a light bulb, and then another is run from touching the base of the light bulb to the opposite end of the original battery, the light bulb will light up. This is due to a complete circuit being formed with the battery and the electrons being carried across the voltage drop (the two ends of the battery). The appearance of the light from the bulb is the visible heat caused by the friction of the electrons moving through the filament.

Electric Energy

Electric energy can be derived from a number of sources including coal, wind, sun, and nuclear reactions. Electricity has numerous applications, including being able to transfer into light, sound, heat, or magnetic forces.

Magnetic Forces

Magnetic forces can occur naturally in certain types of materials. If two straight rods are made from iron, they will naturally have a negative end (pole) and a positive end (pole). These charged poles react just like any charged item: opposite charges attract and like charges repel. They will attract each other when set up positive to negative, but if one rod is turned around, the two rods will repel each other due to the alignment of negative to negative and positive to positive.

These types of forces can also be created and amplified by using an electric current.

The relationship between magnetic forces and electrical forces can be explored by sending an electric current through a stretch of wire, which creates an electromagnetic force around the wire from the charge of the current, as long as the flow of electricity is sustained. This magnetic force can also attract and repel other items with magnetic properties. Depending upon the strength of the current in the wire, a smaller or larger magnetic force can be generated around this wire. As soon as the current is cut off, the magnetic force also stops.

Magnetic Energy

Magnetic energy can be harnessed, or controlled, from natural sources or from a generated source (a wire carrying electric current). Magnetic forces are used in many modern applications, including the creation of super-speed transportation. Super-magnets are used in rail systems and supply a cleaner form of energy than coal or gasoline.

Sound/Acoustic Energy

Just like light, sound travels in waves and both are forms of energy. The transmittance of a sound wave produced when plucking a guitar string sends vibrations at a specific frequency through the air, resulting in one's ear hearing a specific note or sets of notes that form a chord. If the same guitar is plugged into an electric amplifier, the strength of the wave is increased, producing what is perceived as a "louder" note. If a glass of water is set on the amplifier, the production of the sound wave can also be visually observed in the vibrations in the water. If the guitar were being plucked loudly enough and in great succession, the force created by the vibrations of the sound waves could even knock the glass off of the amplifier.

Waves can travel through different mediums. When they reach a different material (i.e., light traveling from air to water), they can bend around and through the new material. This is called refraction.

If one observes a straw in half a glass of water from above, the straw appears to be bent at the height of the water. The straw is still straight, but the observation of light passing from air to water (different materials) makes the straw seem as though it bends at the water line. This illusion occurs because the human eye can perceive the light travels differently through the two materials. The light might slow down in one material, or refract or reflect off of the material, causing differences in an object's appearance.

In another example, imagine a car driving straight along a paved road. If one or two of the tires hit the gravel along the side of the road, the entire car will pull in that direction, due to the tires in the gravel now traveling slower than the tires on the paved road. This is what happens when light travels from one medium to another: its path becomes warped, like the path of the car, rather than traveling in a straight line. This is why a straw appears to be bent when the light travels from water to air; the path is warped.

When waves encounter a barrier, like a closed door, parts of the wave may travel through tiny openings. Once a wave has moved through a narrow opening, the wave begins to spread out and may cause interference. This process is called diffraction.

Earth and Space

Characteristics of Geologic Formations

Rocks cover the surface of Earth. Igneous rock comes from the molten, hot, liquid magma circulating beneath Earth's surface in the upper mantle. Through vents called volcanoes, magma explodes or seeps onto the Earth's surface. Magma is not uniform; it varies in its elemental composition, gas composition, and thickness or viscosity. There are three main types of volcanoes: shield, cinder, and composite.

Shield volcanoes are the widest because their thin magma flows out of a central crater calmly and quietly, like a gentle fountain. This flowing magma results in layers of solid lava. The slow flow results in a convex hill that spans a wide area.

Like shield volcanoes, *cinder volcanoes* typically have a central crater and thin lava. In contrast to shield volcanoes, they are small, cone-shaped hills with steep sides. They are made of volcanic debris, or cinders. They are often found as secondary volcanoes near shield and composite volcanoes. In cinder volcanoes, the central vent spews lava that shatters into rock and debris and settles around it, resulting in its characteristic cone shape. Cinder volcanoes are surrounded by ashy, loose, magma dust.

Composite volcanoes (also called stratovolcanoes) are the most common and the tallest type of volcano. Their thick magma gets stuck at the vent, and as more and more builds up, the volcano eventually explodes and removes the clog. These eruptions generate loose debris, and once the plug has been violently expelled, the thick lava oozes out like a fountain. These volcanoes are the most dangerous with their extremely violent behavior and huge height. Most volcanoes are located around cracks in Earth's lithosphere.

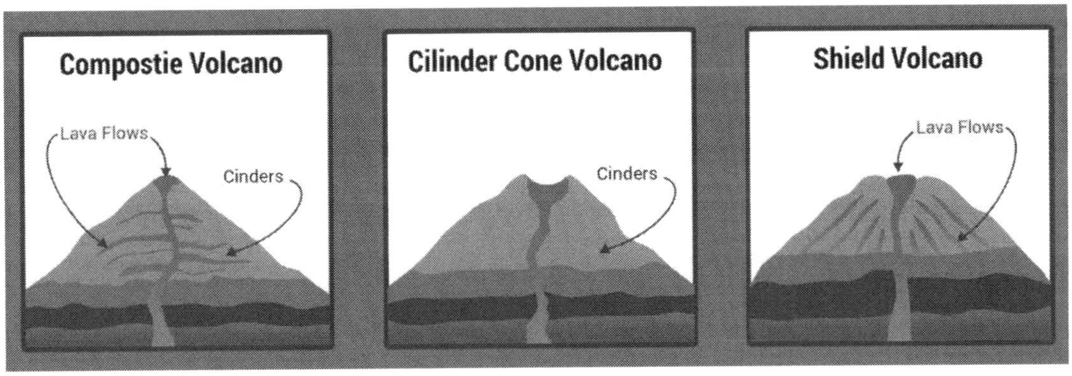

Once magma makes it to the surface, it is called lava. Once it cools, it solidifies into igneous rock. Common examples of igneous rock are obsidian, pumice, and granite. Weathering and erosion result in these rocks becoming soil or sediment and accumulating in layers mostly found in the ocean. These loose sediments settle over time and compress to become a uniform rock in a process called lithification. Examples of sedimentary rock include shale, limestone, and sandstone. As layers are piled atop each other, the bottom rock experiences an intense amount of pressure and transforms into metamorphic rock. Examples of metamorphic rocks are marble and slate. After long periods of time, the metamorphic rock moves closer to the asthenosphere and becomes liquid hot magma. Magma's eventual fate is lava and igneous rock, and the cycle starts anew.

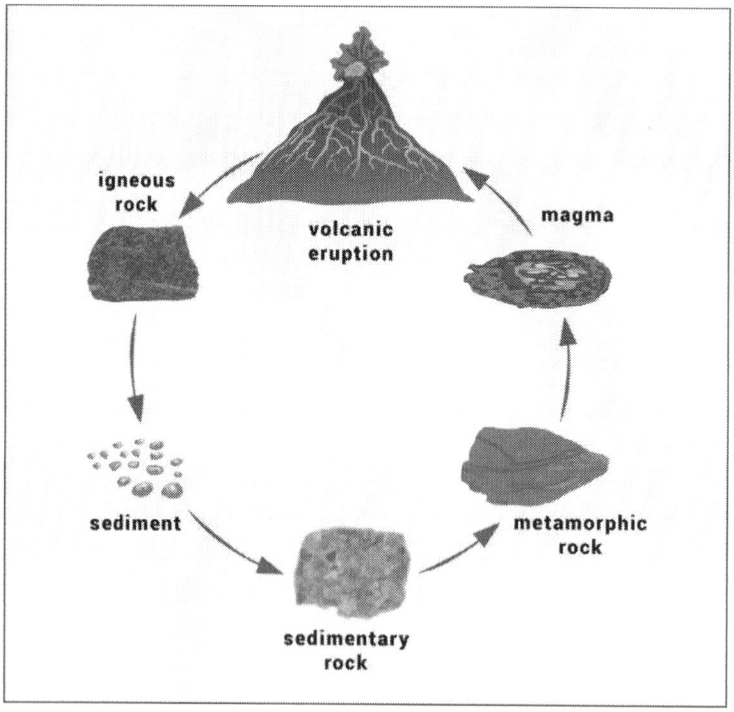

How does magma return to the surface if the lithosphere presses it down? Intense heat from the Earth's core travels to the upper mantle via convection. Convection involves thermal energy (heat) that converts into kinetic energy (movement), resulting in rapidly circulating molecules. Convection moves heat energy through fluids. In a pot of boiling water, the water closest to the burner becomes hot, causing its particles to move faster. Faster-moving molecules have more space between them and become less dense, so they rise. Some will vaporize, and some hit the cool air and slow down, becoming dense and sinking. Likewise, Earth's interior particles undergo convection (the heat source being the nuclear fission from the core), and the rock in the upper mantle will acquire so much kinetic energy that magma will be expelled from underneath Earth to the surface.

There are seven or eight major plates in the lithosphere and several minor plates. These tectonic plates explain the changing topography, or shape, of earth.

There are three types of boundaries between plates: divergent, convergent, and transform. All boundaries can be sites of volcanic activity. A *divergent boundary* occurs when plates separate. Lava fills in the space the plates create and hardens into rock, which creates oceanic crust. In a *convergent boundary*, if one of the plates is in the ocean, that plate is denser due to the weight of water. The dense ocean plate will slip under the land plate, causing a subduction zone where the plate moves underneath. Where plates converge on land, the continental crusts are both lighter with a similar density, and as a result they will buckle together and create mountains.

In *transform boundaries*, adjacent plates sliding past each other create friction and pressure that destroy the edges of the boundary and cause earthquakes. Transform boundaries don't produce magma, as they involve lateral movement.

Just as plates pushing together cause mountains, *canyons* are deep trenches caused by plates moving apart. Weather and erosion from rivers and precipitation run-off also create canyons. *Deltas* form when rivers dump their sediments and water into oceans. They are triangular flat stretches of land that are kind of like a triangular spatula; the handle represents the river and the triangle represents the mouth of a delta.

Sand dunes are another landform caused by wind or waves in combination with the absence of plants to hold sand in place. These are found in sandy areas like the desert or the ocean.

Rocks, Soil, and Fossils

Rocks are solid blocks composed of a combination of minerals. There are three different types of rocks: igneous, sedimentary, and metamorphic.

Igneous rocks are formed from magma in the Earth's mantle or lava that has cooled after volcanic eruptions. *Sedimentary rocks* are little pieces of igneous rocks that break off and then they combine in layers many times at the bottom of oceans. *Metamorphic rocks* are the rocks underneath layers and layers of either sedimentary or igneous rocks that meld together and transform due to the pressure of the layers and the heat radiating upward from the Earth's core.

The differences in the appearances of rocks are called their *physical properties*. Some are shiny and some are dull. Others are hard and don't scratch easily, while still others are soft and can be scratched. They come in a range of colors, and some are even metallic. Many rocks can be found every day in houses. Igneous rocks, like granite, are found on many kitchen countertops, and pumice stones are used in foot care. Metamorphic rock, such as marble, is often found in bathroom countertops. Limestone, a sedimentary rock, is commonly found in cement. See the example below:

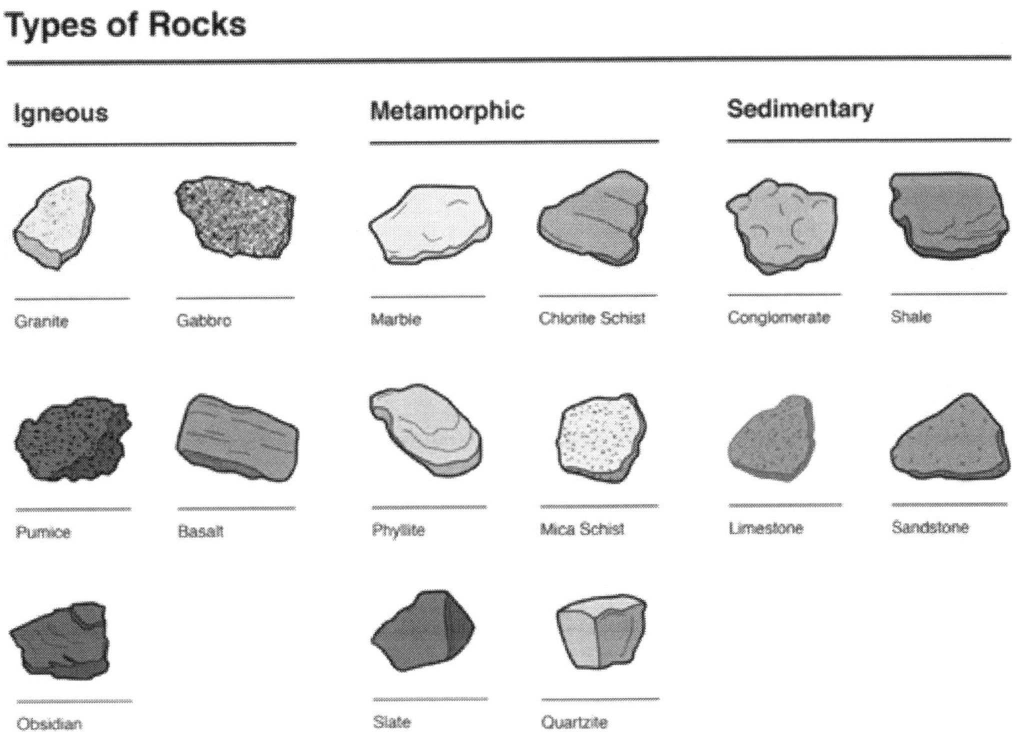

To demonstrate the differences between rocks, activities in the classroom could involve taking qualitative data on the rocks while having a theme of the day. For example, igneous rock formation can be demonstrated by making erupting papier-mâché volcanoes. On that day, the class could be full of igneous rocks. Students can use their senses to record properties of the rocks and the proximity and connection to the volcano will help them remember that igneous rocks come from lava.

In order to connect metamorphic rocks to the concept that they are changed due to heat and pressure, metamorphic rocks can be scattered around the room with a stack of books over each one. Students can temporarily remove the "pressure" and examine the look and feel of the rock, recording qualitative data.

Students can investigate sedimentary rocks by digging for buried sedimentary rocks in a sandbox. The physical properties of the rocks can be recorded, and the proximity to the sand communicates that sedimentary rocks are formed by the erosion of subsequent compression of layers of sediment from other rocks. Precipitation and the water cycle results in the weathering and breakdown of rocks. Erosion involves runoff that carries them away to where they pile up into the layers of sediments that form sedimentary rock.

Fossils show Earth's changing history and are trapped in sedimentary rocks. The lower the fossil, the older the organism because it has been buried deeper and deeper over time.

There is an entire field of science called *paleontology* that specifically studies fossils. Fossils can be completely intact organisms, like the mosquito preserved in the sap in the movie *Jurassic Park*. Fossils can also include remnants of an organism left behind, such as bones and teeth. Structures like these have remained intact due to minerals seeping inside and preserving them like the process that occurs in petrified wood. *Trace fossils* like a footprint are also considered fossils even though they aren't actual remains—they are simply evidence that the organism was there.

Using the sandbox to hunt for fossils will enhance the learning experience. If students also get their hands dirty with soil, the next day, they can compare and contrast soil with sand. While sedimentary rock is the result of erosion and compaction of sediments, soil is the result of weathered rock mixing with decomposing dead organisms to form a loose mix conducive to plant growth. Liquid flows in soil, and air seeps through it as well. Sedimentary rock does not have the same amount of vulnerability to liquids and gases.

Water Cycle, Weather, and Climate

Earth has changed dramatically since its birth around 4.6 billion years ago. Several processes have caused these changes, including the water cycle, the rock cycle, convection, and plate tectonics.

The water cycle is the cycling of water between its three physical states: solid, liquid, and gas. The sun is a critical component of the water cycle because its thermal energy heats up surface liquid water so much that parts of it evaporate. Transpiration is a similar process that occurs when the sun evaporates water from plant pores called stomata. As water vapor rises into the atmosphere through evaporation and transpiration, it eventually condenses and forms clouds heavy with liquid water droplets. The liquid (or solid ice or snow) will precipitate back to Earth, collect on land, and either be absorbed by soil or run-off to the oceans and lakes where it will accumulate, circulate, and evaporate once again.

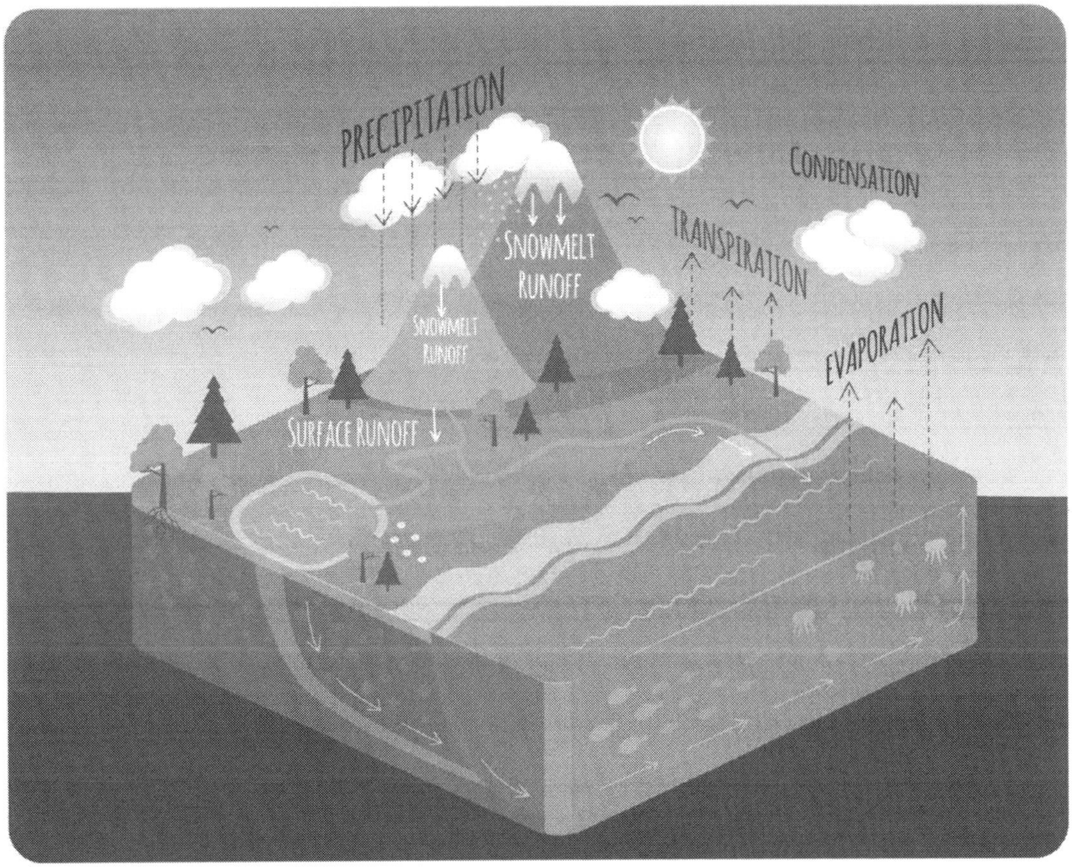

Clouds are condensed water vapor, which is water that has cooled from a gas to liquid, like the droplets on the outside of a glass of lemonade on a hot summer day. That water on the glass is water vapor that cooled enough to slow down the moving particles so that they become denser, forming a liquid. In the sky, water vapor combines in different ways so clouds appear in different forms. Cloud height, shape, and behavior results in a variety of different types:

- High Clouds
  - Cirrus: wispy and thread-like
  - Cirrostratus: like cirrus clouds, but wider and thicker sheets. They have a halo effect where sunlight and moonlight refract through.

Cirrocumulus: a cross between cirrus and cirrostratus clouds. These have rows of round puffs like a cotton-ball stretched out.

Contrails: clouds made by jets

- Mid-Clouds

  Altostratus: thick, stretched clouds that block sunlight and are blue-grayish in color

  Nimbostratus: a thick altostratus cloud accompanied by rain

  Altocumulus: layered rolls of clouds

- Low-Clouds

  Cumulus: white, round, puffy clouds

  Stratus: wide, thick, stretched-out, gray clouds that may cause drizzle

  Fog: lazy stratus clouds that have drooped so low that they reach Earth's surface

  Cumulonimbus: the angry cloud that brings thunderstorms, hail, and tornadoes. It looks like a thick mountain.

  Stratocumulus: stretched-out grayish, puffy, cumulus clouds

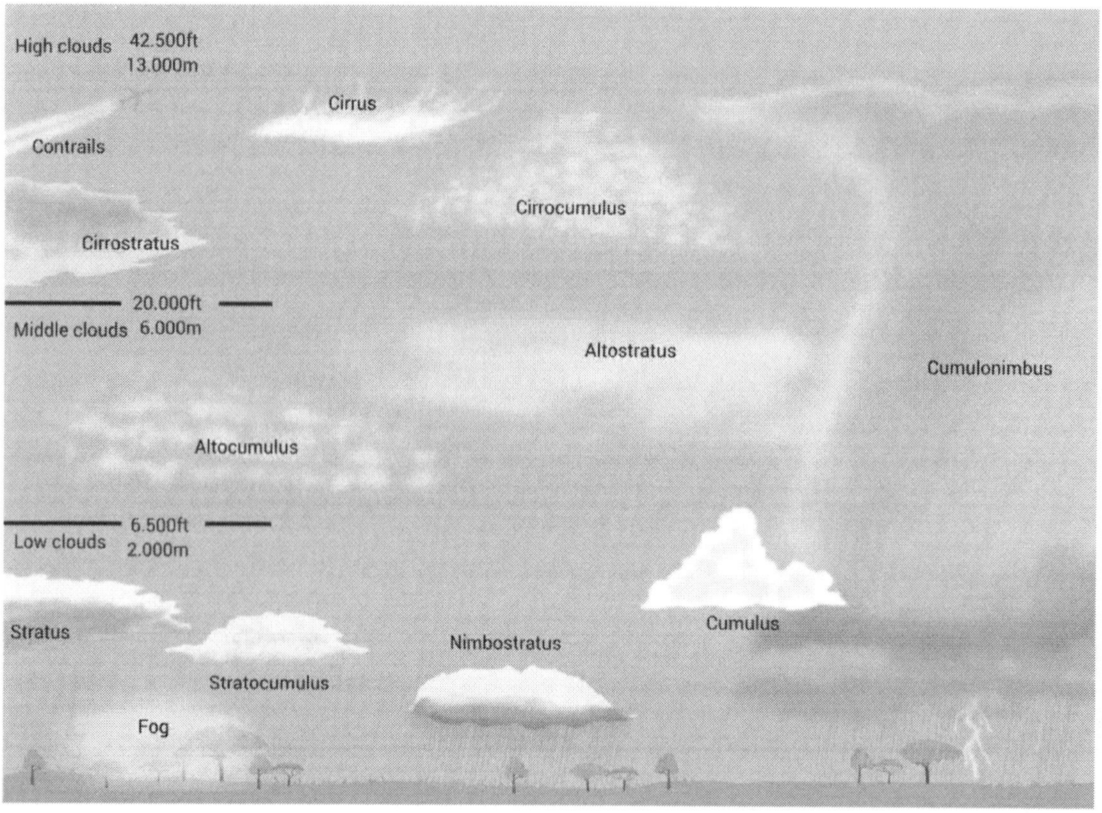

Precipitation comes in many different forms:

- *Rain* occurs due to water vapor condensing on dust particles in the troposphere. As more and more water condenses, the drops will eventually enlarge and accumulate mass, becoming so heavy that they fall to Earth.

- If the temperature is above the freezing point, the water falls as rain. Rain can freeze on the ground if the temperature on Earth's surface is colder than that of the troposphere. Freezing rain causes extremely dangerous driving conditions due to the slickness of the ice.

- *Sleet* freezes on its way down as opposed to freezing upon impact. Sleet starts as ice that melts as it falls through the atmosphere due to hitting spots of warmer temperature, and then it freezes again before hitting the ground.

- *Hail* is precipitation of balls of ice. Hail begins as ice at very cold temperatures in the atmosphere. Instead of precipitating sheets of ice like sleet storms, hailstorms precipitate ice that looks like rocks because hail is formed during thunderstorms. The massive winds throw hail up and down so more and more water vapor condenses and freezes on the original ice. Layer upon layer of ice combine, creating hail sometimes as large as golf balls.

- *Snow* forms as loosely packed ice crystals. Snow is less dangerous than the other frozen forms of precipitation and can produce beautiful snowflakes.

Even though seasons have predictable temperatures, there can be significant differences day to day. In the troposphere, the Sun's heat is trapped by the blanket of greenhouse gases and creates warm, low-pressure air. Because warm gas particles move faster and have less space between them, they are less dense than colder air, and they rise. Cool air moves below the warm air. This atmospheric movement is called general circulation and is the source of wind. Earth's spinning motion also causes wind.

Weather depends in a large part on temperature. Earth's equator is closest to the sun and receives more heat, so this area of earth is significantly warmer than the poles (Arctic and Antarctic). This warm air can form huge bubbles, as can the colder air at the poles. When warm air and cold air meet, the boundary is called a front. Fronts can be the site of extreme weather like thunderstorms, which are caused by water particles in clouds quickly rubbing against each other and transferring electrons, creating positive and negative regions. Lightning occurs when there is a massive electric spark due to the electrical current within a cloud, between two clouds, and even between a cloud and the ground.

While seasons are predictable trends in temperatures over a few months, climate describes the average weather and temperature patterns for a particular area over a long period of time, upwards of thirty years. While *fall* describes a season and *rain* describes weather, *rainforest* describes a climate. The climate of a rainforest, due to its proximity to the equator and oceans, consists of warm temperatures with humid air.

Even more extreme weather includes tornadoes and hurricanes. Tornadoes are spinning winds that can exceed 300 miles per hour and are caused by changing air pressure and quick winds. Hurricanes, typhoons, and tropical cyclones (the same phenomenon with different regional names) are storms with spinning winds that form over the ocean. Hurricanes are caused by warm ocean water quickly evaporating and rising to a colder, lower-pressure portion of the atmosphere. The fast movement of the warm air starts a cyclone around a central origination point (the eye of the storm). Blizzards are also caused by the clash of warm air and cold air. They occur when the cold Arctic air moves toward warmer air and involve massive amounts of snow.

Precipitation and run-off are constantly affecting the surface of Earth, as the run-off weathers rocks or breaks them down from the original bedrock into pieces called regolith. Regolith sizes range from microscopic to large and quickly form either soil or sediment. *Weathering* is the process of breaking rock while *erosion* is the process of moving rock. Weathering can be caused by both physical and chemical changes. Mechanical forces such as roots growing, animal contact, wind, and extreme weather cause weathering. Another cause is the water cycle, which includes flowing water, moving glaciers, and liquid ice seeping into rocks and cracking them as water freezes and expands. Chemical weathering actually transforms the regolith into clay and soft minerals. One consequence of chemical weathering is corrosive acid rain.

Renewable Sources of Energy

A research area closer to home is the attempt to utilize renewable resources for energy production rather than burning fossil fuels. Fossil fuels are organic compounds from dead organisms (hundreds of millions of years old) that, when burned, produce energy. Through the pressure from rock layers above them, the heat emanating from the earth's mantle, and decomposition, these once-living organisms transform into oil, coal, and natural gas. Fossil fuels provide energy for the modern world, but there is a strong push to find other ways to harness energy. One reason is that there is a finite amount of fossil fuels. As the population grows, the supply of fossil fuels could simply run out. Another problem is that fossil fuels are burned in a process called combustion, which releases carbon dioxide. Excess carbon dioxide in the atmosphere causes a phenomenon known as global warming. The thickened carbon dioxide blanket (greenhouse gas) holds in more heat, which is changing the biosphere. Finally, fossil fuel combustion releases pollution (harmful molecules like carbon monoxide) into the atmosphere; this too negatively affects the biosphere.

Scientists are interested in finding renewable sources of energy, such as:

Wind: Converting kinetic energy from wind into electrical energy using windmills (turbines) is inexpensive.

Solar: Converting light energy from the sun using solar cells and panels is a more expensive option than wind energy, and effective storage solutions need to be developed for extended cloudy days.

Geothermal: Converting heat energy that water picks up from the earth's surface into electricity requires expensive power stations that can only exist at geographical locations where water and heat converge (close to hot springs, for example).

Hydroelectric: Converting kinetic energy from running water to electrical energy using water turbines has a major drawback. Hydroelectric power requires dams to hold water (to slow down its movement to maximize the energy production), which are expensive and can damage ecosystems.

Biofuels/Biomass: Converting potential energy from decomposing organic material that does not require millions of years to develop is currently expensive and also has the potential to damage ecosystems.

Sun-Earth-Moon System

The heat from the sun as well as the orbit and position of earth cause seasons. As discussed, earth rotates around the sun and spins on an axis. Earth is slightly tilted on its side. An imaginary line around the middle called the equator splits the earth into the northern and southern hemispheres.

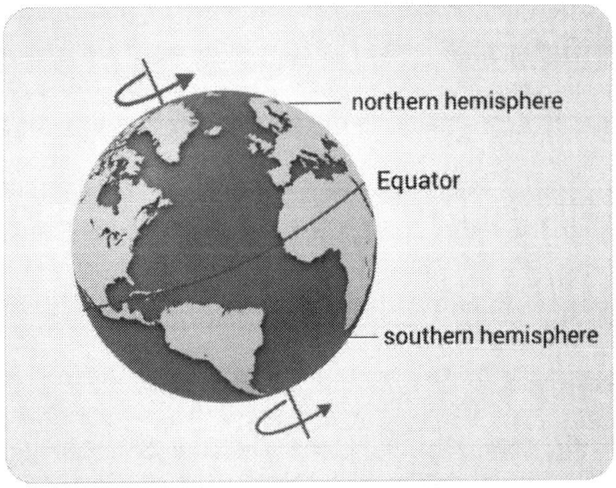

To understand seasons and the heating of the planet, refer to this picture:

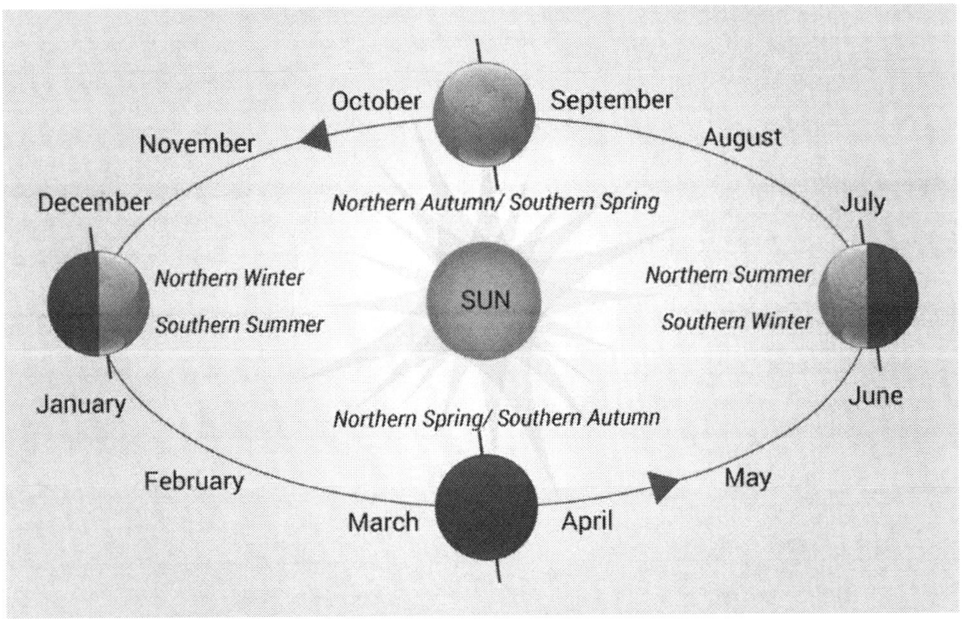

Observing July, these facts are apparent:

Earth is tilted so that the northern hemisphere is pointing towards the sun. The southern hemisphere is pointed away.

Because the north is tilted toward the sun, it gets more daylight in July than the southern hemisphere.

These observations explain why in July, the northern hemisphere experiences summer while the southern hemisphere experiences winter.

Notice in December that the opposite is true: the southern hemisphere gets more daylight compared to the northern hemisphere.

In spring and fall, both the north and the south get around the same sun exposure; therefore, those seasons have milder temperatures.

As the earth rotates, the distribution of light slowly changes, which explains why seasons gradually change. In June, the northern hemisphere experiences the summer solstice, the day with the most daylight. As the earth continues to orbit, its days will get shorter and shorter until the winter solstice, the shortest day of the year. Equinoxes occur in the fall and the spring and represent the days when the amount of daylight and darkness are relatively equal.

Just as the earth orbits the sun, the moon orbits the earth. The moon is much closer to earth than the sun. And even though the moon is so close to the earth, the moon contains no life because it lacks water and an atmosphere. Without greenhouse gases to blanket the sun's heat, temperatures on the moon are very low at night.

The moon is visible from the earth because it reflects sunlight at certain points in its orbit. The moon's orbit has a predictable pattern. It has two main phases, waxing and waning. When the moon is waxing, it goes from a new moon to a full moon. Notice that only the left side of the moon is dark during the waxing phase. The waning phase goes from full moon to new moon. Only the right side of the moon is dark when it is waning.

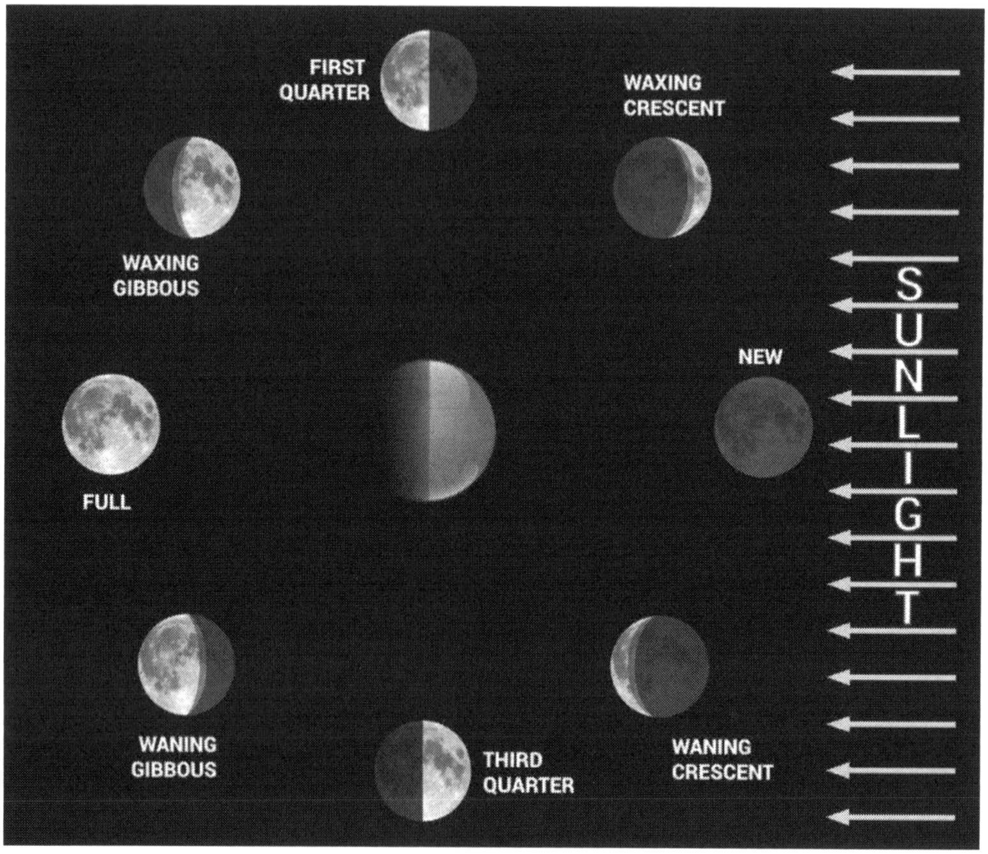

This picture shows that when the moon is behind the earth, then the moon's entire surface is reflected and we see a full moon. When the moon is between the earth and the sun, it is invisible at night, which is called a *new moon*.

Half-moons are visible when the moon and the earth are in a line that is perpendicular to the direction of sunlight. Only half of the moon reflects light to the earth at night, as seen in the figure above.

A moon that looks larger than a half moon is called a *gibbous moon*, and a moon that looks smaller is called a *crescent moon*.

Eclipses occur when the earth, the sun, and the moon are all aligned—the earth blocks the others from seeing each other. If they are perfectly lined up, a total eclipse happens, and if they are only a little lined up, there is a partial eclipse.

There are two types of eclipses: lunar and solar. A lunar eclipse occurs when the earth interrupts the sun's light reflecting off of the full moon. Earth will then cast a shadow on the moon, and particles in earth's atmosphere refract the light so some reaches the surface of the moon, causing the moon to look yellow, brown, or red.

During a new moon, when the moon is between the earth and the sun, the moon will interrupt the sunlight, casting a shadow on earth. This is called a solar eclipse.

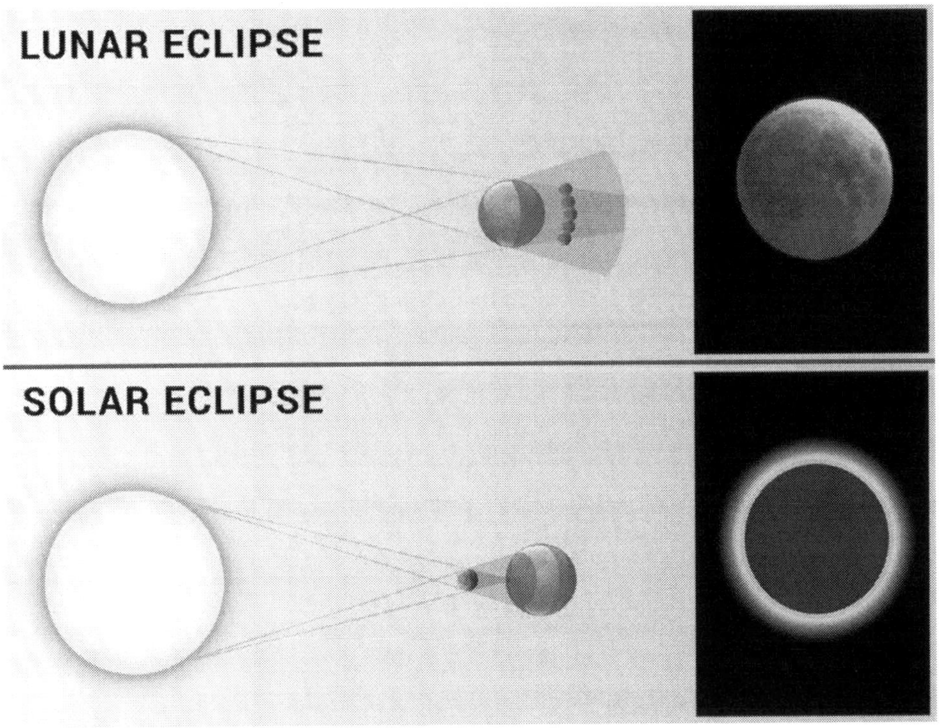

The moon also affects ocean tide due to gravity. Earth is much larger than the moon and has a very significant gravitational force that keeps us on the ground even though it is spinning very quickly. The moon is much smaller than earth, but because it is so close, it has a pulling effect on earth's oceans. When it is closest to earth, it pulls the water more, resulting in high tide. When the moon is farthest from earth, it pulls the ocean less and is called low tide.

Earth and the Universe

Earth is part of a solar system that rotates around a star. Our solar system is a miniscule portion of the universe; the Sun is just one star, and there are more stars in the universe than there are grains of sands on Earth. Almost every existing star belongs to a galaxy, clusters of stars, rocks, ice, and space dust. Between galaxies there is nothing, just darkness. There could be as many as a hundred billion galaxies. There are three main types of galaxies: spiral, elliptical, and irregular.

The majority of galaxies are spiral galaxies, with a large, central galactic bulge, which is a cluster of older stars. They look like a disk with arms circulating stars and gas. Elliptical galaxies have no particular rotation pattern. They can be spherical or extremely elongated and do not have circulating arms. Irregular galaxies have no pattern and can vary significantly in size and shape.

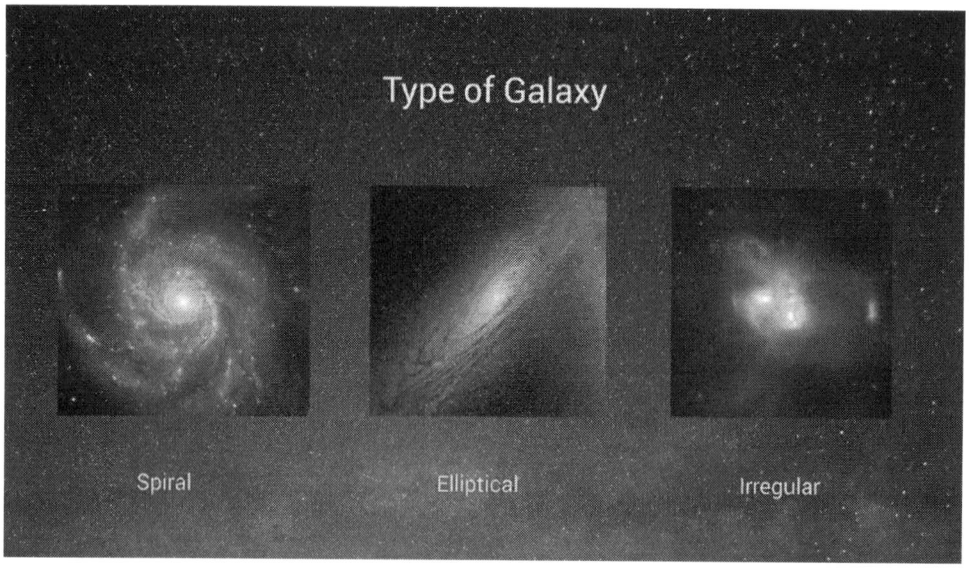

Earth's galaxy, the Milky Way, is a spiral galaxy and contains hundreds of billions of stars.

Pre-stars form from nebulas, clouds of gas and dust that can combine to form two types of small stars: brown and red dwarves. Stars produce enormous amounts energy by combining hydrogen atoms to form helium via nuclear fusion. Brown dwarves don't have enough hydrogen to undergo much fusion and fizzle out. Red dwarves have plenty of gas (hydrogen) to undergo nuclear fusion and mature into white dwarves. When they use all of their fuel (hydrogen), a burst of energy expands the star into a red giant. Red giants eventually condense into a white dwarf, which is a star approaching the end of its life.

Stars that undergo nuclear fusion will run out of gas quickly and burst in violent explosions called supernovas. This burst releases as much energy in a few seconds as the Sun will release in its entire lifetime. The particles from the explosion will condense into the smallest type of star, a neutron star; this will eventually condense into a black hole, which has such a high amount of gravity that not even light energy can escape.

Earth's sun is currently a red dwarf; it is early in its life cycle. As the center of Earth's solar system, the Sun has planets and space debris (rocks and ice) orbiting around it. The various forms of space debris include:

Comet: made of rock and ice with a tail due to the melting ice

Asteroid: a large rock orbiting a star. The asteroid belt lies between Mars and Jupiter and separates the smaller rocky planets (Mercury, Venus, Earth, and Mars) from the larger, gassy planets (Jupiter, Saturn, Uranus, and Neptune). Pluto is not considered a planet anymore due to its small size and distance from the Sun.

Meteoroid: a mini-asteroid with no specific orbiting pattern

Meteor: a meteoroid that has entered Earth's atmosphere and starts melting due to the warmth provided by our insulating greenhouse gases. These are commonly known as "falling stars."

Meteorite: a meteor that hasn't completely burned away and lands on Earth. One is believed to have caused the Cretaceous mass extinction.

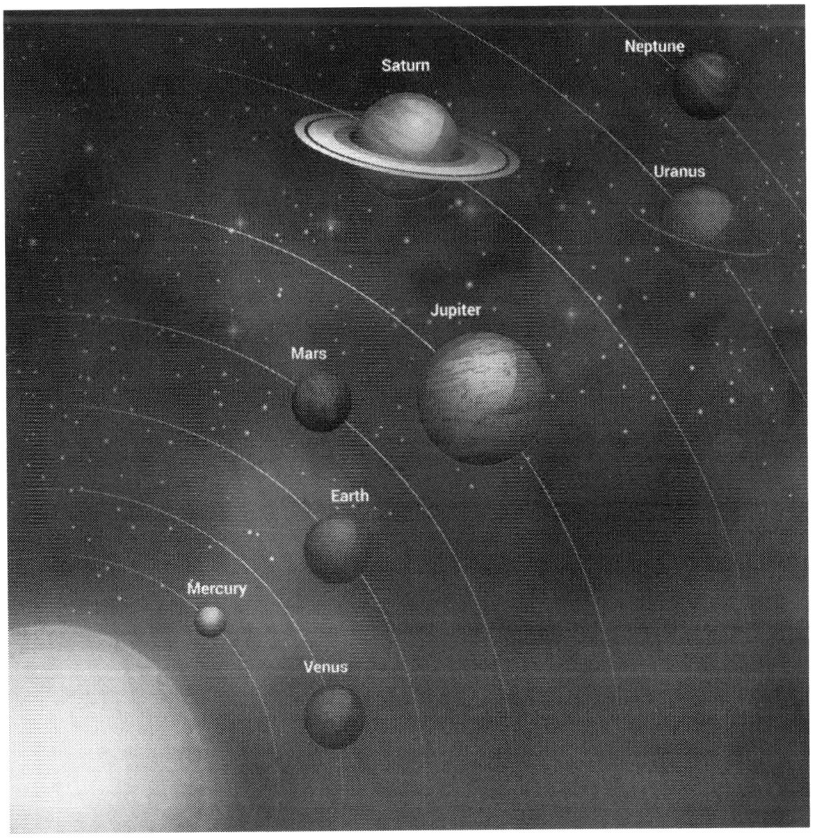

Each planet travels around the Sun in an elliptic orbit. The time it takes for one complete orbit is considered a year. The gravity of the massive Sun keeps the planets rotating, and the farther the planets are from the Sun, the slower they move and the longer their orbits. Earth's journey is little bit over 365 days a year. Because Mercury is so close to the Sun, one year for Mercury is actually only 88 Earth days. The farthest planet, Neptune, has a year that is about 60,255 Earth days long. Planets not only rotate around the Sun, but they also spin like a top. The time it takes for a planet to complete one spin is considered one day. On Earth, one day is about 24 hours. On Jupiter, one day is about nine Earth hours, while a day on Venus is 241 Earth days.

Planets may have natural satellites that rotate around them called moons. Some planets have no moons and some have dozens. In 1969, astronaut Neil Armstrong became the first man to set foot on Earth's only moon.

Space Exploration

One of the largest areas of scientific research is space exploration. Of course, people have always wondered about the universe, but the United States didn't make space research a priority until the 1940s and 1950s "space race" with the Soviet Union. In 1957, Russia launched a satellite called Sputnik, which fueled the intense competition between the two countries. In space research, the question that accelerated space exploration was "How can man travel into space safely?" This question fueled the creation of NASA (the National Aeronautics and Space Administration) on October 1, 1958.

NASA research continues today. They observe the sky, launch satellites and telescopes into space, and study the data collected. Currently, there are a multitude of satellites and land vehicles or "rovers" on Mars collecting data with the hope of one day finding a way for humans to live there. In fact, the target date for human occupation on Mars is somewhere in the 2030s.

Life Science

Characteristics of Living and Non-Living Things

There are several common traits among all living organisms, including:

- They are comprised of cells
- The contain DNA, the genetic code of life
- They grow and develop
- They reproduce
- They need food for energy
- They maintain homeostasis
- They react to their surroundings
- They evolve as a population

There are two types of cells that make up living things: simple bacterial cells (prokaryotes) and the complicated cells of protists, fungi, plants, and animals (eukaryotes). All of these have a set of instructions, DNA, which codes for the proteins that allow organisms to grow. In the case of bacteria and single-celled eukaryotes, there is simple development, such as creating structures like DNA, ribosomes (protein factories), and a cell membrane. Bacteria do not have complex development because they simply divide once and make a new organism; however, multicellular organisms develop more complex structures—for examples, humans have hearts, stomachs, brains, etc. A human starts as one cell called a *zygote*. In nine months, that zygote has developed so much that it has all the internal organs needed to support life.

Organisms cannot live without energy to fuel the necessary reactions to grow and develop. They get the energy they need either by making it themselves (if they are producers/autotrophs like plants) or consuming it (like animals and fungi) from an outside source. Not only do organisms use that food to grow and develop, but they also use it to stay healthy and maintain homeostasis. For example, the human body has a constant temperature of 98.6 degrees. If the temperature goes above that, the body starts to sweat to cool off. Much below that temperature, the body will shiver in order to generate energy to heat up. For survival, all organisms must be highly regulated to function, kind of like a car. Every single part has to work together in harmony in order to function properly.

Living things, such as humans, respond to their surroundings. If someone hears a loud noise, his or her head turns toward it. If something gets thrown at one's face, the person blink. Even plants grow towards sunlight. Living things also evolve as a population. Humans today are nothing like our ancestors of long ago because as a species, humans had to continually adapt to the Earth's changing environment.

An extensive explanation of these characteristics of life is beyond an early childhood curriculum, but it's helpful for the teacher to know them because delineating living and nonliving objects can be tricky. A teacher needs to know why fire, a dead grasshopper, and a robot are not alive, because these are common student misconceptions. Although a fire can grow, it does not have DNA. Although a dead grasshopper is made of cells and has DNA, it can't grow or reproduce. A robot doesn't have DNA and isn't made of cells, although it can react to its environment. Conversely, some students don't believe that plants are alive because they don't walk around. To illustrate that they are alive, simple experiments can be used to show that they can reproduce, develop, and grow, such as planting seeds and using light-boxes to show that plants grow toward light.

Teachers must be able to explain that not all organisms move. Plants are alive because they are made of cells, have DNA, grow independently, and meet all of the other characteristics of life. Tiny germs are alive for the same reasons.

These nuances are complicated, but young students should be able to explain that living things grow and nonliving things don't. They should be able to identify mushrooms, plants, and animals as living, and fire, desks, and robots as nonliving.

Prokaryotes, Viruses, and Eukaryotes

Every living organism is made up of cells. And these cells come in various shapes and sizes, depending on the organism. There are two types of cells: prokaryotes and eukaryotes. The big difference between them is that eukaryotes have a nucleus and prokaryotes do not. The structures that will be focused on for this section will be:

Bacteria	Protist, Fungus, Plant, Animal
DNA Ribosomes Cytoplasm Cell Membrane Cell Wall	DNA Ribosomes Cytoplasm Cell Membrane Cell Wall (except animal cells) Unique structures Nucleus Mitochondria Chloroplasts (only autotrophs, or organisms that can produce their own food. Only protists and plants are producers).

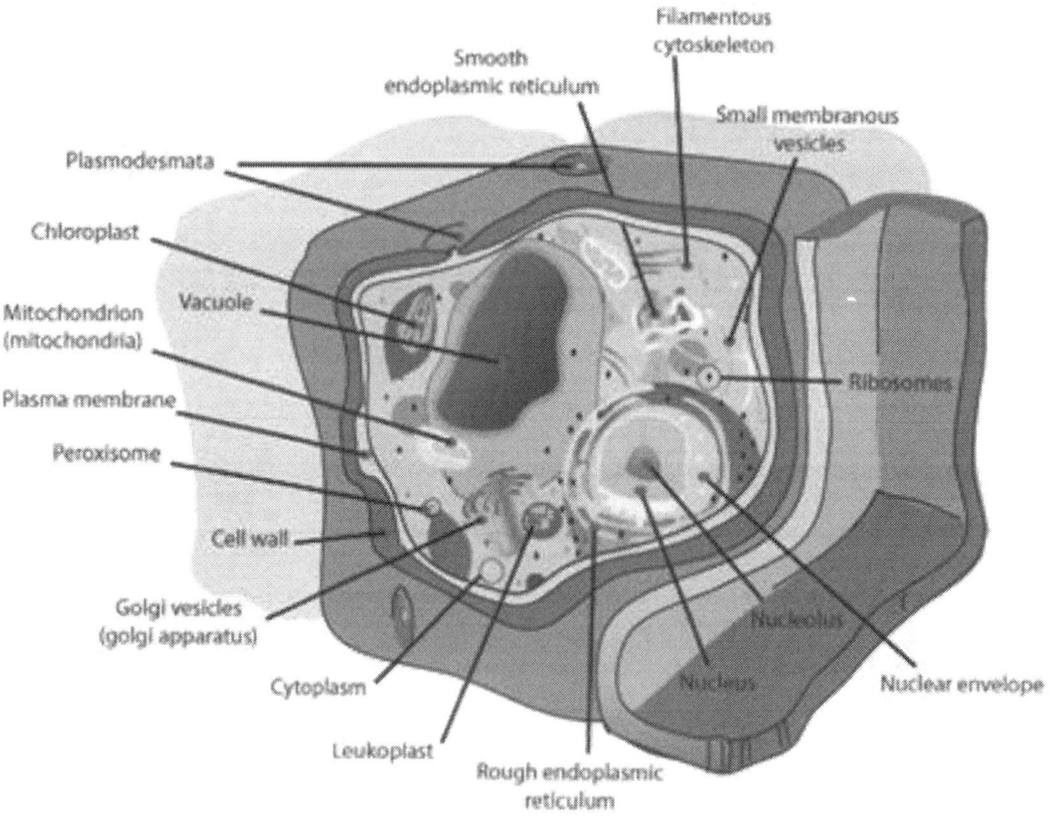

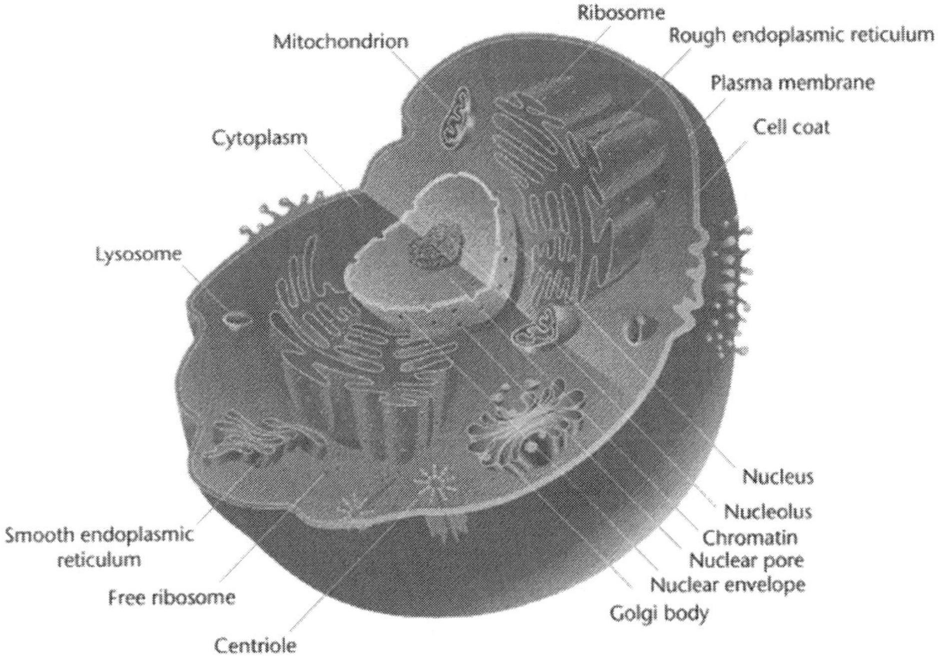

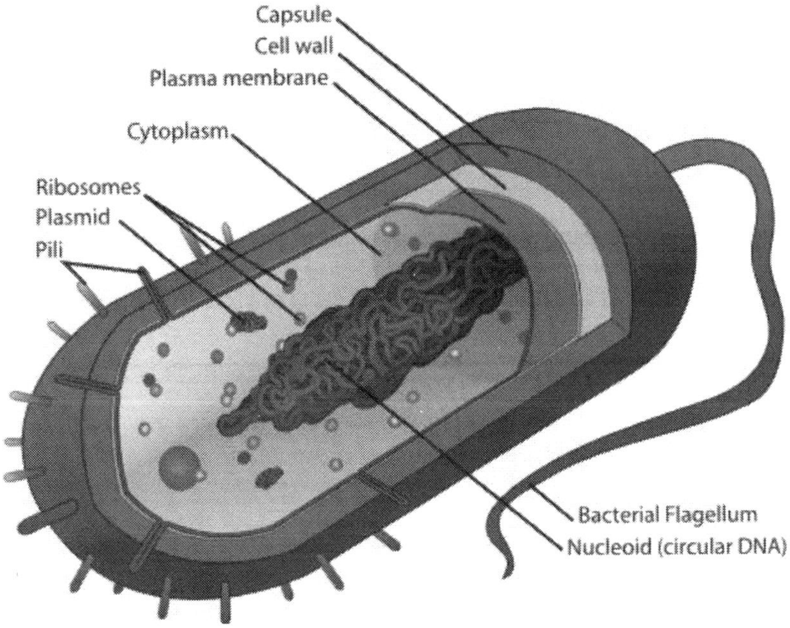

Like all cells, bacterial cells contain DNA, the genetic material that gives instructions for every single structure and process that the cell undergoes. DNA is a code made up of four letters: A (adenine), T (thymine), G (guanine), and C (cytosine). There are billions of these letters in DNA, and the order of these letters tells a cell exactly what to do and how to do it (just like reading a book of instructions).

Because DNA doesn't do anything on its own, all cells must have a means of decoding DNA and turning it into the structure, which is the function of ribosomes—they are protein-makers. If DNA is like a recipe, then the ribosomes are like the chef.

DNA and ribosomes sit in a fluid called cytoplasm, which contains a cytoskeleton (a network of proteins) that holds them in place. All cells need a covering to contain everything inside—these are called cell membranes in animals or cell walls for plant cells.

Bacteria can also have a capsule and a flagellum, which are all external structures. A capsule is sticky and causes bacteria to cluster with other cells or on food. Only about 50 percent of bacteria can move, and those that do often have a flagellum, which is a whip-like structure like a tadpole's tail.

Viruses are commonly thought of as living organisms, but many scientists argue they aren't for two reasons: (1) they are not cells, and (2) they cannot reproduce by themselves. Both qualities are required for an organism to be considered alive. Viruses are unique in that they require a host in order to make proteins and reproduce, because viruses don't have all of the complex tools of a living cell. When a virus has infected a host, it acts like a living organism—it moves and reproduces—but outside of a host, it does nothing. A virus can survive outside of a host, but it cannot reproduce. Scientists are still trying to properly define a virus, so we can currently say that viruses are not like bacteria or any other living thing.

Eukaryotic cells are more complex than prokaryotic cells. They make up all the organisms in the kingdoms protist, fungus, plant, and animal. Eukaryotic cells are also larger than prokaryotes and contain a nucleus and other organelles.

Eukaryotic cells hold their DNA inside a nucleus in pieces called chromosomes. Chromosomes are a cell's way of organizing long strands of DNA in twisted-up bundles. Imagine a room filled with rolls of toilet paper compared to a room that has all of those rolls unraveled and thrown everywhere; it would be a mess!

Other important organelles include chloroplasts and mitochondria. Chloroplasts can be found in cells called autotrophs, which can convert sunlight into energy. Plants are autotrophs. Mitochondria are little energy factories found in almost every type of cell. They use chemical reactions to make little packets of energy that can be used by other parts of the cell.

Classification of Living Things

Due to the speciation that has occurred over the last 3.5 billion years since life first appeared, the variety of organisms is astronomical. Scientists have identified about 2 million species, and they suspect that there are at least 8 million others out there.

A man named Carolus Linnaeus developed a naming system to try to create some order in classifying all species. For example, the classification of humans through the seven levels, from all-inclusive to the most specific, looks like this:

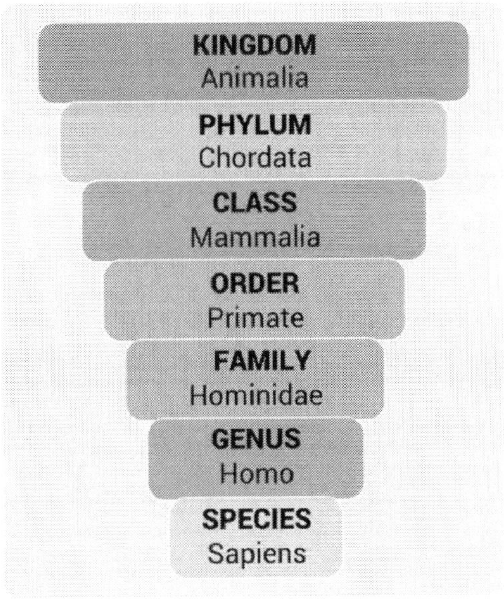

One benefit of this universal naming system is that because some organisms have different common names, like the roly-poly and doodlebug, or the cougar and panther, it allows scientists to have a common language. Due to the sheer magnitude of species, scientists need the seven levels, but when referring to organisms, their official names are just the last two: genus and species. Humans are simply referred to as *Homo sapiens*. This two-name system is called binomial nomenclature.

There are currently six kingdoms, although the prokaryotes (simpler cells) used to be lumped together into one kingdom called Monera. Currently, there are two prokaryotic kingdoms, Archaebacteria and Eubacteria.

<u>Archaebacteria</u>
Prokaryotes that have a cell membrane made of fats. They live in harsh places including extremely hot areas (volcanic vents or hot springs) and extremely salty locations (Utah's Salt Lake). These are the rarest prokaryotes.

<u>Eubacteria</u>
Common bacteria that have a cell membrane made of a protein-carbohydrate blend. They make up the vast majority of existing prokaryotes. An example is staphylococcus.

<u>Protista</u>
This kingdom consists of eukaryotes. Most are unicellular. This kingdom is the most diverse and can be divided into three types: fungus-like (including slime-molds), plant-like (including algae), and animal-like (including amoeba). Some scientists believe that there is so much diversity within the kingdom that they should be split into separate kingdoms, but so far they remain in one group.

Animal-like protists are heterotrophs (they do not make their own food), and plant-like protists are autotrophs (they make their own food). Fungus-like protists are heterotrophs. Like actual fungi, these organisms externally digest their food by acting as parasites and decomposers. Animal-like protists ingest their food via phagocytosis (cell eating) or by absorbing it.

Depending on the particular protists, some produce asexually via mitosis and others reproduce sexually.

<u>Fungi</u>
Fungi are eukaryotic heterotrophs that digest their food externally. Many of them, including common mushrooms and toadstools, act as decomposers by breaking down dead organisms then absorbing the broken down nutrients. Other fungi accomplish ingestion as parasites feeding off of living organisms, as in the case of a yeast infection. All fungi are multicellular with one exception—yeast. Fungi have cell walls made of a complex carbohydrate called chitin. Most fungi reproduce sexually and asexually.

<u>Plantae</u>
Plants are multicellular autotrophs like daisies, roses, and pine trees. They are closely related to the aquatic producer, algae, but different in that algae don't contain true roots, stems, or leaves. Plants are photosynthesizers, and their cells have surrounding cell walls made of the starch cellulose.

<u>Animalia</u>
Animals are multicellular heterotrophs, like fungi, except that animals move and internally ingest their food by consuming it. Animals are the only kingdom to not have cells with cell walls due to their flexibility and ability to move. The animal kingdom is very diverse and includes humans, jellyfish, and spiders, as well as all sorts of other organisms.

Cellular Organization

Prokaryotes contain ribosomes, DNA, cytoplasm, a cell membrane, a cytoskeleton, and a cell wall. Eukaryotes vary between kingdoms but contain all of these structures except a cell wall because animal cells require so much mobility. Large, land-dwelling animals typically compensate with an exoskeleton (like insects) or an endoskeleton (like humans and other mammals, reptiles, and birds) for structure.

All bacterial cells are unicellular (existing as just one cell). Almost all types of protist and some species in fungi kingdom are unicellular, but they still have the complicated organelles of eukaryotes. A few protists, almost all fungi, and all plants and animals are multicellular. Multicellularity leads to development of structures that are perfectly designed for their function.

Cells combine to form tissue. Tissue combines to form organs. Organs combine to form organ systems, and organ systems combine to form one organism. The structures of all of these combinations allow for the maximum functionality of an organism, as demonstrated by the nervous system.

A neuron is a cell in the nervous system designed to send and receive electrical impulses. Neurons have dendrites, which are sensors waiting to receive a message. Neurons also have an axon, a long arm that sends the message to the neighboring neuron. The axon also has insulation known as myelin that speeds the message along. Many neurons combine to form a nerve, the tissue of the nervous system, which is like a long wire. The structure of this nerve is perfect—it is a long cable whose function is to send signals to the brain so the brain can process the information and respond. Nerve tissue combines with other tissue to form the brain, a complex structure of many parts.

The brain also has glands (epithelial tissue) that release hormones to control processes in our body. The brain and spinal cord together form the central nervous system that controls the stimulus/response signaling in our body. The nervous system coordinates with the circulatory system to make our heart beat, the digestive system to control food digestion, the muscular system to move an arm, the respiratory system to facilitate breathing, and all other body systems to make the entire organism functional. Cells are the basic building block in our bodies, and their structure is critical for their function and the function of the tissues, organs, and systems that they comprise.

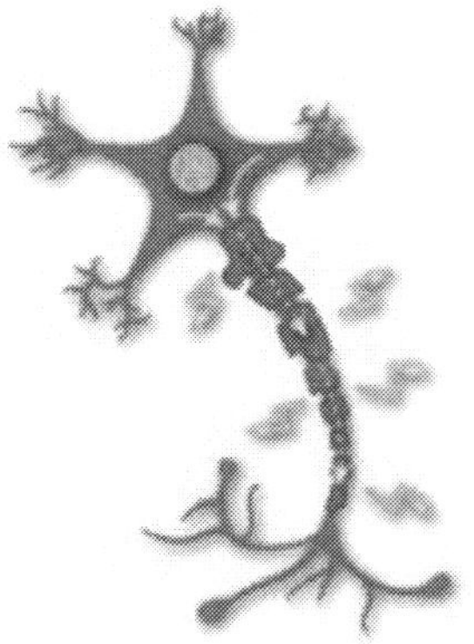

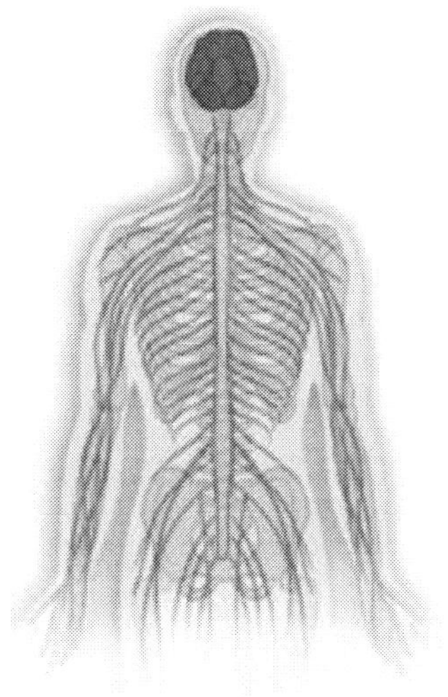

In the graphic above, the left depicts a neuron, and the right depicts the nervous system. A neuron is a nerve cell, and it is the basic building block of the nervous system. Cell, tissue, organ, and organ system structure are critical for function. The following table lists organ systems in the human body:

Name	**Function**	**Main organs**
Nervous	Detect stimuli and direct response	Brain and spinal cord
Circulatory	Pump blood to deliver oxygen to cells so they can perform cellular respiration	Heart
Respiratory	Breathe in oxygen (reactant for cellular respiration) and release carbon dioxide waste	Lungs
Muscular	Movement	Heart and muscles
Digestive	Break down food so that glucose can be delivered to cells for energy	Stomach, small intestine, lots of others
Skeletal	Support and organ protection	All sorts of joints, skull, ribcage

Heredity: Passing Genes Across Generations

All living things are a product of their DNA, specifically portions of their DNA called genes that code for different characteristics.

Learned behavior is not affected by DNA and is not hereditable. Changes in appearance like a woman painting her toenails, a bird whose feathers accidentally fall out due to a tornado, or a person getting a scar are also not heritable. Heritable characteristics are those coded by DNA like eye color, hair color, and height.

A man named Gregor Mendel is considered the father of genetics. He was a monk and a botanist, and through extensive experiments with pea plants, he figured out a great deal about heredity.

Our genetic code comes in pairs. Each chromosome contains many genes, and since we have one chromosome from our mom and one chromosome from our dad, we have two copies of each gene. Genes come in different forms called alleles. The two alleles work together, and when the cell reads them and follows their instructions, the way an organism looks or behaves is called a trait. For some traits, there are only two alleles: a dominant allele and a recessive allele. Even though eye color is a bit more complicated, pretend that brown eyes are dominant over blue eyes, and there are the only two alleles:

- B = Brown eyes
- b = blue eyes

A child inherits these alleles from his parents. There are three possible combinations a child can inherit, dependent on his parents' alleles:

- BB (homozygous dominant)
- Bb (heterozygous)
- bb (homozygous recessive)

The combination of genes above will determine the trait in the offspring. If the child gets any combination with a B, the more powerful allele, his eyes will be brown. Only the bb combination will give the child blue eyes. In this example, the combination of alleles is called a genotype, and the actual eye color the child has is called a phenotype.

Natural Selection and Evolution

Genetic variation is the key for a process called natural selection, which is commonly referred to as evolution. Charles Darwin is known as the father of evolution. He was a naturalist on a ship that voyaged around the world. Darwin collected samples and made extensive observations, and his theory of natural selection had several important components:

Natural selection can only happen in a population. Evolution is not something that occurs in one organism. Evolution occurs when a whole population, like horses, changes significantly over long periods of time.

There must be genetic variation. Without genetic variation, changes in phenotype are impossible; everything would be a clone of each other.

Natural selection doesn't occur without competition for food, water, shelter, space, and mates. If there is no competition, no genes are favored over others, so evolution doesn't occur.

Limited resources cause the survival of the fittest—individuals with genes for traits that make them the most fit for their environment will have more offspring and pass on their genes. Those without those traits will not live as long or have as many long-living offspring, so their genes will not be passed on.

Descent with modification is the last part of natural selection. This means that populations change over long periods of time. Sometimes entirely new populations emerge; sometimes populations simply cannot survive in their environment and they go extinct; and sometimes species change in appearance or behavior. This is the case with horses.

An early ancestor of horses was a small animal with toes instead of hooves. The early horses that were bigger and had more muscle mass were better able escape predators; so were those early horses who had more padding on their feet, which over time evolved into a very thick fingernail, that we would recognize as a hoof. The animals with these traits survived to pass these favorable genes to their offspring.

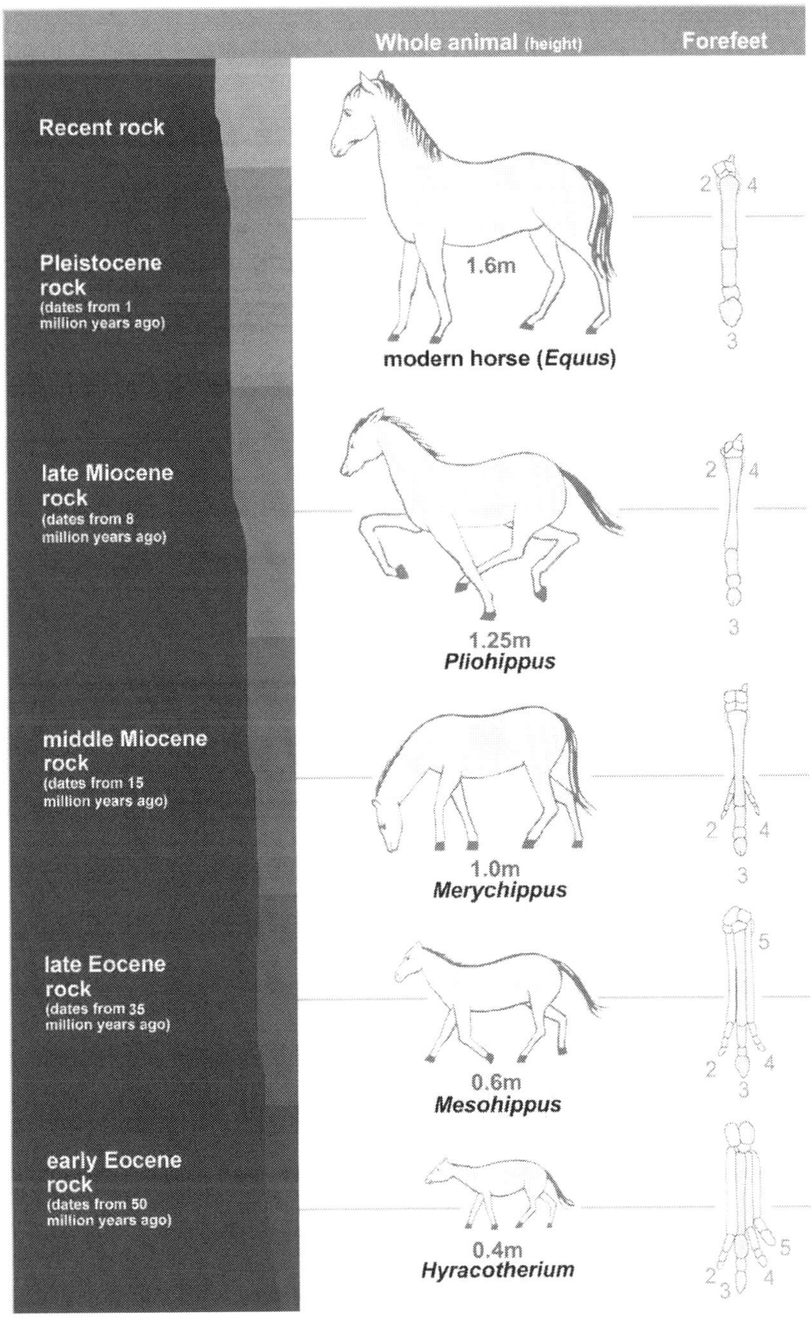

The evolution of the horse shows all components of natural selection:

Change occurred across a population, not one individual animal.

The horses of long ago had different genes; none of them looked like the modern horse. Over time, mutations caused new genes and new traits. These new traits include increased size and replacing toes with hooves.

Horses that couldn't outrun predators perished. Bigger horses with hooves were likelier to escape and survive.

Horses with the "small" and "no hoof" genes didn't survive as often to pass on their genes.

Over many generations, the smaller horses became extinct, while larger horses with better fitness evolved into a new species.

Fitness depends on different environments. For example, think about the variety of plants and their unique characteristics:

Cactus: Over time, the cactus evolved for life in the desert, where there is little rainfall. Spines protect the cactus from hungry herbivores and also act as leaves with tiny stomata. Stomata are little holes in leaves that let carbon dioxide in and oxygen out. They also act as the site of transpiration, which is a significant source of water loss in plants. By having such skinny leaves, there are fewer stomata, allowing cacti to better conserve their water.

Venus flytrap: Many think the Venus flytrap is an animal because it eats live animals, but it is actually a plant with green, glucose producing leaves. The reason it catches flies is because of an adaptation that evolved after years of living in an ecosystem with soil that lacked nitrogen. The nitrogen-poor soil resulted in plants that could obtain the element in other ways.

Rose: The thorny spikes on a rose's stem are an adaptation that deters predators from eating it.

Pine tree: As a cactus has needle-like spines, pines have thin leaves for the same reason. They have typically grown in dry climates, so over time, the smaller surface area of the leaf prevents water loss.

The variety of the animal kingdom can also be explained by evolution. The following adaptations illustrate how fitness in different environments can look very different:

Ducks: Their webbed feet not only help them swim faster in order to catch food, but also help them swim away from predators. Double duty!

Walking sticks: These bugs look exactly like sticks. Camouflage is a useful adaptation to avoid predators used by a variety of different organisms.

Sharks: Check out the rows and rows of sharp teeth on sharks. The carnivorous fish are the ultimate predators, and it makes sense that those with the most teeth will be more successful hunters and better survivors.

Fossil evidence has been found in sedimentary rocks, and observations using fossils support small changes over time. Fossils have helped scientists piece together the history of the world, including discovering extinct species and learning how species have evolved.

Fossil evidence has shed a significant amount of insight on human origins. In 1974, 40 percent of a single ancient human skeleton was discovered. Scientists named their discovery Lucy. Due to the symmetry of the body and the similarity between the right and left sides, scientists were able to figure out about 75 percent of Lucy's total skeletal structure. Scientists revealed that Lucy was 3.5 feet tall. At first, due to her small stature, she was thought to be a child. However, upon analysis of her teeth, they found that all of her teeth were permanent, so they revised their conclusion. Noting her hip structure supported a wide opening for the birth canal, they concluded she was a woman. In 1999, a fossil of the same species was discovered and named Selam. The skeletal remains of Selam are nearly as complete as Lucy's, but this skeleton came from a child, as analysis showed she still had her baby teeth.

Both fossils showed evidence that the organism walked upright. These conclusions were drawn from extensive analysis and comparisons. As these fossils' hip structure and larger heel resemble those in humans, Lucy and her species are considered bipeds, meaning that they walked on two legs (instead of hunched over with dragging arms like chimpanzees). Humans are considered more closely related to these ancient fossil species than to modern primates.

Other evidence for evolution comes from analyzing similarities and differences between genes and traits of different species. Humans and chimpanzees share about 95 percent of the same genes, and humans and bananas have about 50 percent of their genes in common. That alone is strong evidence for the notion that all species come from an original common ancestor that evolved in many different directions.

Physical similarities in homologous structures (similar location and function) also point towards a common ancestor. That humans, cats, dogs, and bears all have a similar bone structure and organization suggest they are more closely related to each other than with birds, whose bones are so different in structure that they actually have a completely different function. Vestigial (unused) structures also suggest change over time. Whales have a pelvis, although it is small and nonfunctional.

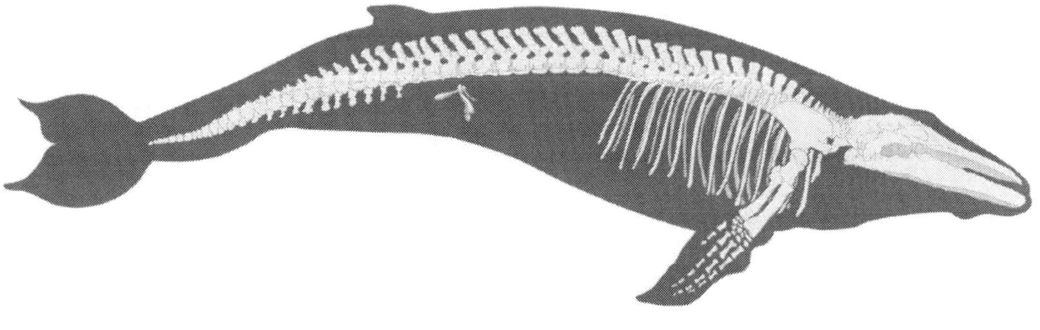

Interdependence of Organisms

The biosphere has layers and layers of complexity:

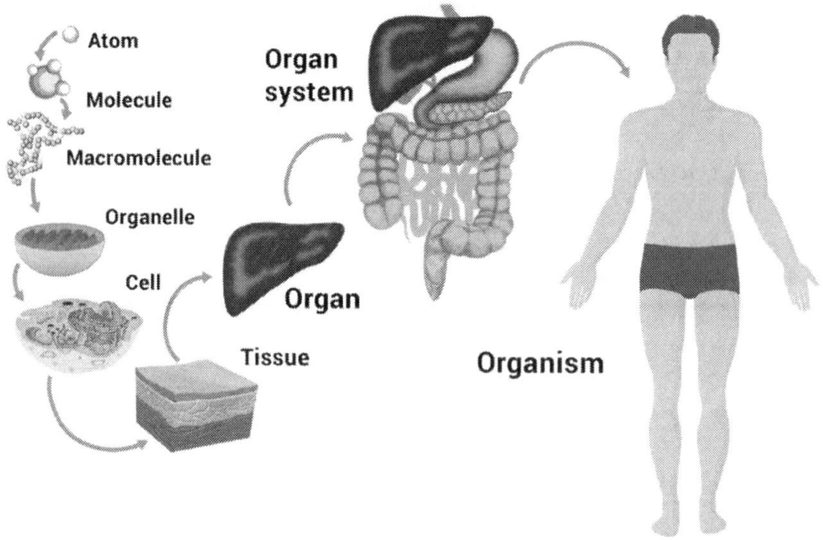

All organisms work together so that life can exist. An organism represents one of a species, like the fish below, and all organisms serve a particular function. The fish's niche is to eat aquatic producers and excrete waste that acts as fertilizer.

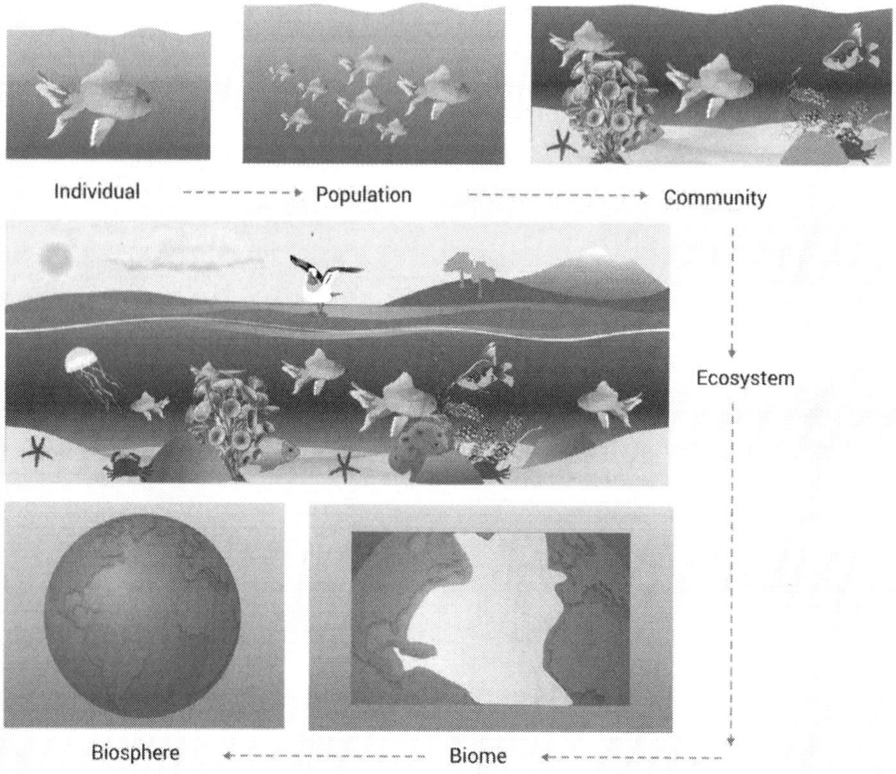

This fish is just one organism within a population. A population represents multiple individuals living in the same habitat. The community includes every biotic factor (living organism) within an ecosystem, in this case, the fish, jellyfish, algae, crab, bacteria, etc. An ecosystem includes all the biotic factors as well as the abiotic, which includes anything non-living—for the fish, that's a rock, a shipwreck, and a nearby glacier. For biomes, add weather and climate into the mix. The biosphere is all of Earth, which is the combination of all biomes.

We already discussed that producers (plants, protists, and even some bacteria) photosynthesize and make the food that provides energy required for all chemical reactions to occur and therefore all life to exist. A non-photosynthesizer must find and eat food, and this feeding relationship can be visualized in food chains. Consider this food chain:

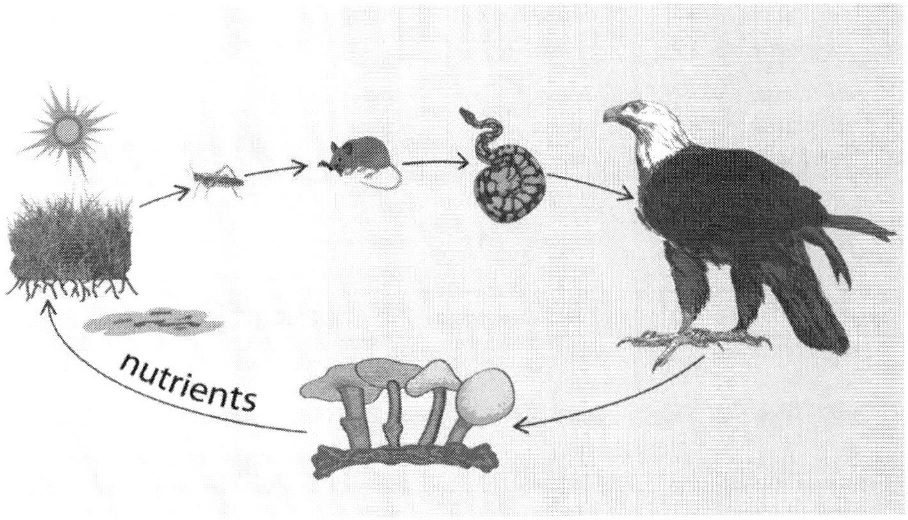

The true source of the energy for every living organism is the sun. Plants absorb the sun's energy to make glucose and are on the first trophic level (feeding level). The grasshopper on the second trophic level is an example of an herbivore and is a primary consumer, as he is the first eater in the food chain. Unfortunately, he receives only 10 percent of the energy that the plant absorbed (this is known as the 10 percent rule) because the other 90 percent of energy was either used by the plant to grow or will be lost as heat. The mouse on the third trophic level is the secondary consumer, or second eater. Food chains are not as inclusive as food webs, which show all feeding relationships in an ecosystem. Looking at this food chain suggests that mice are carnivores (eaters of animals), but mice also eat berries and plants, so they are actually considered omnivores (eaters of both plants and animals). The mouse only gets 10 percent of the energy from the grasshopper, which is actually only 1 percent of the original energy provided by the Sun. The snake on the fourth trophic level is a carnivore, as is the hawk on the highest trophic level.

The arrows in the food chain show the transfer of energy, and fungi as well as bacteria act as decomposers, which break down organic material. Decomposers act at every trophic level because they feed on all organisms; they are non-discriminating omnivores. Decomposers are critical for life, as they recycle the atoms and building blocks of organisms.

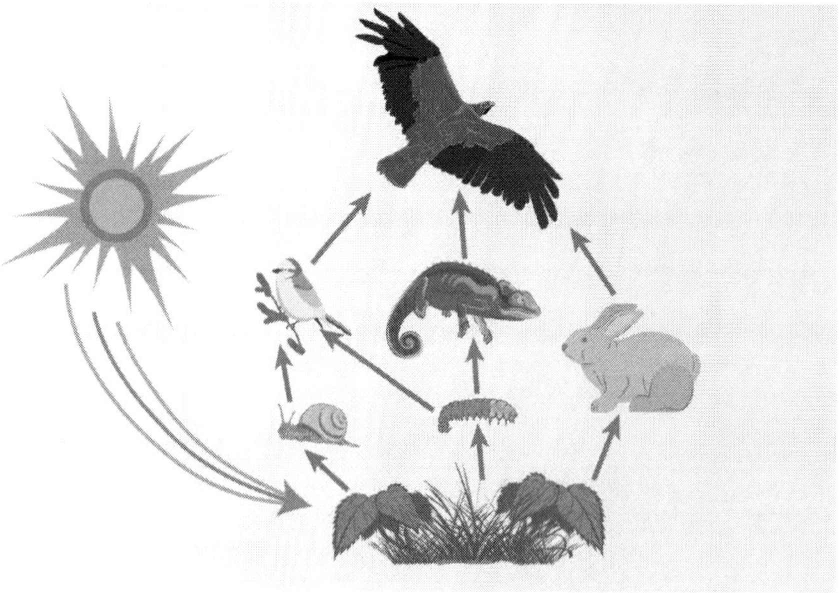

Feeding relationships and predator-prey relationships (hunter-hunted, like the hawk and the rabbit in the food web above) are not the only relationships in an ecosystem. There also can be competition within and between species. For example, in the food chain above, the rabbit and snail both eat grass, showing a relationship called competition, when two organisms want the same thing. Other relationships include symbiotic relationships, which represent two species living together. Symbiosis comes in three varieties:

Mutualism: an arrangement where both organisms help each other. An example is the relationship between birds and flowers. When birds consume the nectar that the flower produces, pollen rubs on the bird's body so that when it travels to a neighboring plant, it helps with fertilization. The plant helps the bird by providing food, and the bird helps the plant by helping it reproduce. This is a win-win.

Parasitism: when one organism is hurt while the other is helped. Fleas and dogs are a prime example. Fleas suck the dog's blood, and dogs are itchy and lose blood. This is a win-lose.

Commensalism: when one organism is helped and the other is neither harmed nor helped. For example, barnacles are crusty little creatures that attach themselves to whales. They don't feed on the whale like a parasite. Instead, they use the whale to give them a free ride so they have access to food. The whales don't care about the barnacles. This is a win-do not care.

Photosynthesis in the Chloroplast Provides Energy

Any producer must have a chloroplast in order to convert light energy into food, usually in the form of a carbohydrate. Chloroplasts are organelles that look like little green beans because they contain the pigment chlorophyll, which is able to absorb the sunlight's energy in the form of photons, or light rays.

Some prokaryotes are also photosynthetic, and although they don't have a chloroplast because they're too simple and don't contain organelles, they have a pigment in order to make their own food.

Plants need water and sunlight to live. Plants suck up water from their roots. The sunlight they need is absorbed by the chlorophyll in chloroplasts, which are clustered and concentrated in their leaves. Interestingly, the chlorophyll actually is able to absorb every color of light except for green, which is why leaves look green: they reflect green light. If the roots take in water and the leaves take in carbon dioxide and sunlight energy, why are stems important? The stems in plants are an example of how structure helps function. The stem is like a skeleton for plants; it holds the leaves high so they can be closer to the sun.

Plants are critical for life on earth because they absorb the energy from the sun and invest it in the bonds that make sugar. Sugar passes through the food chain to provide energy for all living organisms. Plants and other autotrophs can make their own energy, while heterotrophs (which cannot make their own energy) consume the sugar, break it down, and convert it into usable energy with their mitochondria.

Cellular Respiration in the Mitochondria

The glucose that provides energy does nothing by itself; it is the bonds between atoms holding these complex glucose molecules together that hold the energy. When the molecule is intact, the bonds between them hold energy in the form of potential energy. When the bonds are broken, that potential energy is released and becomes available to the workers in the cell to perform chemical reactions.

The process of cellular respiration breaks the bonds in an organelle called the mitochondria in eukaryotes (protists, fungi, plants, animals).

Note that the equation for cellular respiration is the almost exact opposite of photosynthesis:

$$C_6H_{12}O_6 + 6O_2 \rightarrow 6CO_2 + 6H_2O + 36ATP$$

The only difference between the above equation and photosynthesis is the new product: ATP. ATP is a conversion of light energy into usable pockets of energy that provide energy to all the workers in cells that do the chemical reactions. While glucose is like a $100 bill with lots of energy in its bonds, ATP is like one hundred $1 bills that can be invested here and there as needed.

Bacteria do not have mitochondria, so they perform different reactions in their cytoplasm that produce much less energy (2ATP).

Organisms Need Food for More than Just Energy

When we eat a hamburger, we're eating more than carbohydrates; we're also eating proteins and fats. Plants provide more than just carbohydrates when we eat them; they also are able to use the light energy to make proteins, fats, and, of course, their DNA, because if they didn't have DNA, they'd have no instructions to grow. The following organic compounds and their atoms don't magically appear in organisms—life has to either grab the nutrients from soil or seeds or eat them.

- Carbohydrates, proteins, fats, and DNA/RNA have carbon, hydrogen, and oxygen
- DNA, proteins, and fats also have phosphorous
- DNA and proteins also have nitrogen
- Proteins also can have sulfur

Plants need all of these elements to make food. Where do they get them? Remember that earth's atmosphere is a conglomerate of different gases, including nitrogen. Bacteria in the soil are able to convert that nitrogen into a usable form, and the roots of plants absorb the critical nitrogen. Carbon and oxygen get into the plant via photosynthesis (carbon dioxide), as does the element hydrogen, because plants take in water, which contains hydrogen. Phosphorous and sulfur are absorbed in plants through soil. Since heterotrophs cannot make their own food, they have to eat an autotroph (or eat something that ate an autotroph) in order to obtain these critical elements.

Cycles are a recurring pattern in science, and making food is no exception. When living things die, fungi and bacteria act as decomposers and break down the material. That's actually why dead things and rotten meat smell bad; the decomposers have broken them down so much that gases containing carbon, oxygen, phosphorous, nitrogen, and even smelly sulfur are released. Remember that sulfur is heavy in protein, and eggs are protein-rich. It makes sense that rotten eggs have an unpleasant smell as they release sulfur because they're mostly protein. Once living things decompose, all the elements eventually recycle back to the atmosphere or to the soil, and the atoms are available to construct molecules once again.

Practice Questions

1. At what point in its swing does a pendulum have the most mechanical energy?
   a. At the top of its swing, just before going into motion
   b. At the bottom of its swing, in full motion
   c. Halfway between the top of its swing and the bottom of its swing
   d. It has the same amount of mechanical energy throughout its path

2. What does the scientific method describe?
   a. How to review a scientific paper
   b. How to organize a science laboratory
   c. The steps utilized to conduct an inquiry into a scientific question
   d. How to use science to earn money in society

3. The energy of motion is also referred to as what?
   a. Potential energy
   b. Kinetic energy
   c. Solar energy
   d. Heat energy

4. Burning a piece of paper is what type of change?
   a. Chemical change
   b. Physical change
   c. Sedimentary change
   d. Potential change

5. A ramp leading up to a loading dock would be considered which type of simple machine?
   a. Screw
   b. Lever
   c. Inclined plane
   d. Pulley

6. Who is credited for simplifying the laws of motion?
   a. Einstein
   b. Hawking
   c. Copernicus
   d. Newton

7. The heat transfer due to the movement of gas molecules from an area of higher concentration to one of lower concentration is known as what?
   a. Conduction
   b. Convection
   c. Solarization
   d. Radiation

8. Which of the following is true of an object at rest on earth?
   a. It has no forces acting upon it.
   b. It has no gravity acting upon it.
   c. It is in transition.
   d. It is in equilibrium.

9. When researching a problem in science, what are the best sources to use?
   a. People you have seen on television
   b. Anyone with a Ph.D.
   c. Accredited laboratories and universities
   d. Any source with an internet webpage

10. What is a change in state from a solid to a gas called?
    a. Evaporation
    b. Melting
    c. Condensation
    d. Sublimation

11. The forces acting upon an object can be illustrated using what?
    a. A Venn diagram
    b. A periodic table
    c. A force diagram
    d. A stress-strain diagram

12. Which is not a form of Energy?
    a. Light
    b. Sound
    c. Heat
    d. Mass

13. A projectile at a point along its path has 30 Joules of potential energy and 20 Joules of kinetic energy. What is the total mechanical energy for the projectile?
    a. 50 Joules
    b. 30 Joules
    c. 20 Joules
    d. 10 Joules

14. What factors can prompt scientific inquiry and progress?
    a. Curiosity
    b. Competition
    c. Greed
    d. All of the above

15. Which of the following is considered a force?
    a. Weight
    b. Mass
    c. Acceleration
    d. Gravity

16. Why would a pencil appear to bend at the water line in a glass of water?
   a. The wood of the pencil becomes warped from being in the water.
   b. It appears to bend because of the refraction of light traveling from air to water.
   c. The pencil temporarily bends because of its immersion into separate mediums.
   d. The reflection of the light from water to a human's pupil creates the illusion of a warping object.

17. Which of the following is NOT one of Newton's three laws of motion?
   a. Inertia: an object at rest tends to stay at rest, and an object in motion tends to stay in motion
   b. $E = mc^2$
   c. For every action there is an equal and opposite reaction
   d. $F = ma$

18. The law of the conservation of energy states which of the following?
   a. Energy should be stored in power cells for future use.
   b. Energy will replenish itself once exhausted.
   c. Energy cannot be created or destroyed.
   d. Energy should be saved because it can run out.

19. Which of the following is true regarding magnets?
   a. Opposite charges attract
   b. Like charges attract
   c. Opposite charges repel
   d. Like charges do not repel or attract

20. Running electricity through a wire generates which of the following?
   a. A gravitational field
   b. A frictional field
   c. An acoustic field
   d. A magnetic field

21. When an ice skater spins on one skate in a circle, what happens if they extend their arms out like the letter "T"?
   a. They spin faster.
   b. They spin slower.
   c. They stop spinning.
   d. Nothing changes.

22. For circular motion, what is the name of the actual force pulling toward the axis of rotation?
   a. Centrifugal force
   b. Gravity
   c. Centripetal force
   d. No force is acting.

23. Which is not a method for transferring electrostatic charge?
   a. Polarization
   b. Touch
   c. Election
   d. Induction

24. What does the re-radiation of solar waves trapped in the earth's atmosphere contribute to?
    a. Global warming
    b. Greenhouse effect
    c. Climate change
    d. All of the above

25. Velocity is a measure of which of the following?
    a. Speed with direction
    b. The change in position over the change in time
    c. Meters covered over seconds elapsed
    d. All of the above

26. Which of the following sources of energy are non-renewable?
    a. Wind energy
    b. Solar energy
    c. Fossil fuel energy
    d. Geothermal energy

Use the following image to answer question 27.

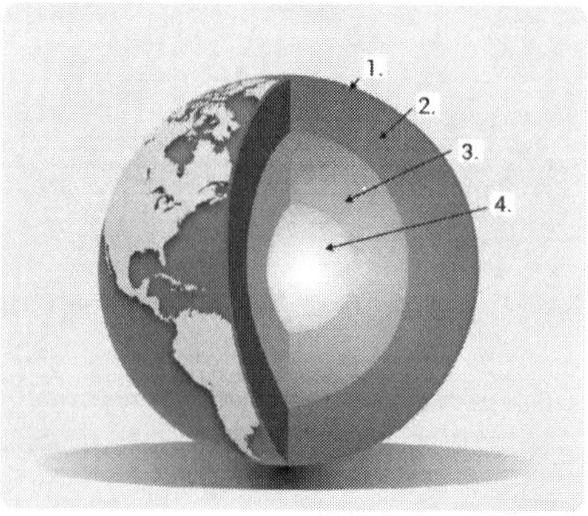

27. Which choice describes layer 4?
    a. Inner core: solid
    b. Inner core: liquid
    c. Outer core: solid
    d. Outer core: liquid

28. Which type of rock accumulates in layers at the bottom of the ocean due to run-off?
    a. Igneous
    b. Sedimentary
    c. Metamorphic
    d. Minerals

29. The water cycle involves phase changes. Which example below is evaporation?
    a. Clouds forming in the sky
    b. Rain, snow, or ice storms
    c. River water flowing to the ocean
    d. Sunlight's effect on morning dew

30. Which of the following is NOT directly caused by tectonic plate movement?
    a. Spreading of the ocean floor
    b. Earthquakes
    c. Mountain formation
    d. Precipitation

31. Which of the following statements is false?
    a. Magma circulates in the upper mantle.
    b. All volcanoes have explosive eruptions.
    b. Igneous rocks are formed by crystallized lava.
    c. Igneous rocks recycle and form magma.

Use the following image to answer questions 32 and 33.

32. Which fossil is the oldest?
    a. Dinosaur head
    b. Seashell
    c. Skeleton
    d. Grass

33. The fossils in the figure are embedded in which type of rock?
    a. Metamorphic
    b. Igneous
    c. Sedimentary
    d. Magma

Use the following image to answer question 34.

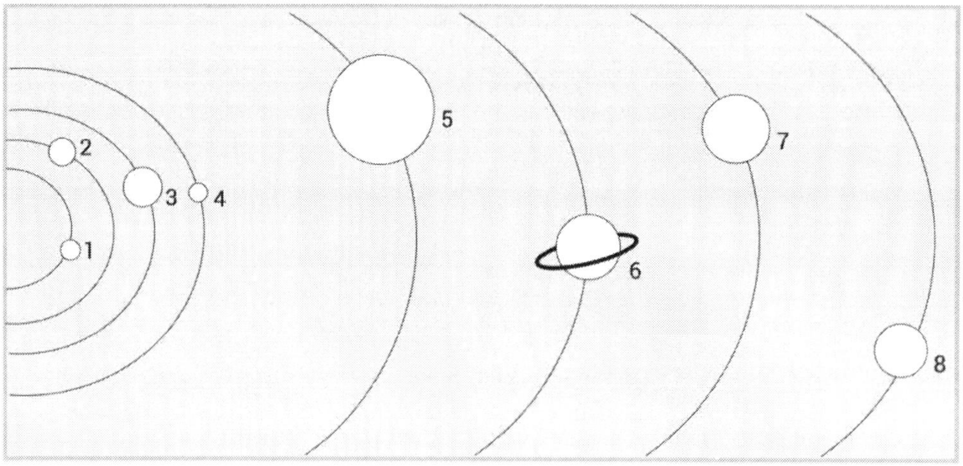

34. Where is the asteroid belt located in the figure above?
    a. Between structures #2 and #3
    b. Between structures #3 and #4
    c. Between structures #4 and #5
    d. Between each planet

35. Why is a year on Mars shorter than a year on Jupiter?
    a. Mars is much smaller than Jupiter.
    b. Mars is a rocky planet, while Jupiter is made of gas.
    c. Mars has a smaller orbit around the Sun.
    d. Mars is inside the asteroid belt.

Use the following image to answer question 36.

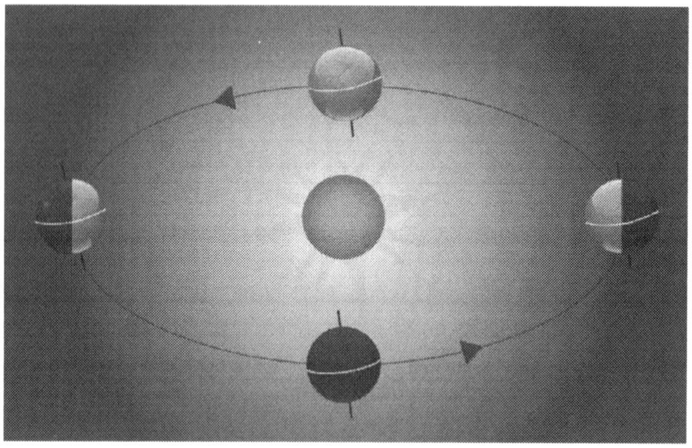

36. The figure above illustrates earth's orbit around the sun. What season is it where the red dot is located?
    a. Summer
    b. Winter
    c. Fall
    d. Spring

37. Which statement(s) are true about the phases of the moon?
    a. Full moons are farther away from the sun than new moons.
    b. Crescent moons are smaller than half moons.
    c. Gibbous moons are larger than half moons.
    d. All of the above are true.

38. Why are greenhouse gases important?
    a. They allow UV rays to penetrate the troposphere.
    b. They insulate earth and keep it warm.
    c. They reflect light so that the sky looks blue.
    d. They form clouds and directly participate in the water cycle.

39. How is a theory different from a hypothesis?
    a. Theories are predictions based on previous research, and hypotheses are proven.
    b. Hypotheses can change, while theories cannot.
    c. Theories are accepted by scientists, while hypotheses remain to be proven.
    d. Hypotheses are always wrong, while theories are always true.

40. Which scientist is correctly paired with what he or she studies?
    a. Paleontologist: earth's crust
    b. Meteorologist: fossils
    c. Seismologist: earthquakes
    d. Geologist: weather

41. What part of most plants performs photosynthesis?
    a. Root
    b. Stem
    c. Leaf
    d. Flower

42. Which definition describes an ecosystem?
    a. One individual organism
    b. Rocks, soil, and atmosphere within an area
    c. All the organisms in a food web
    d. All living and nonliving things in an area

Use the following image to answer questions 43 and 44.

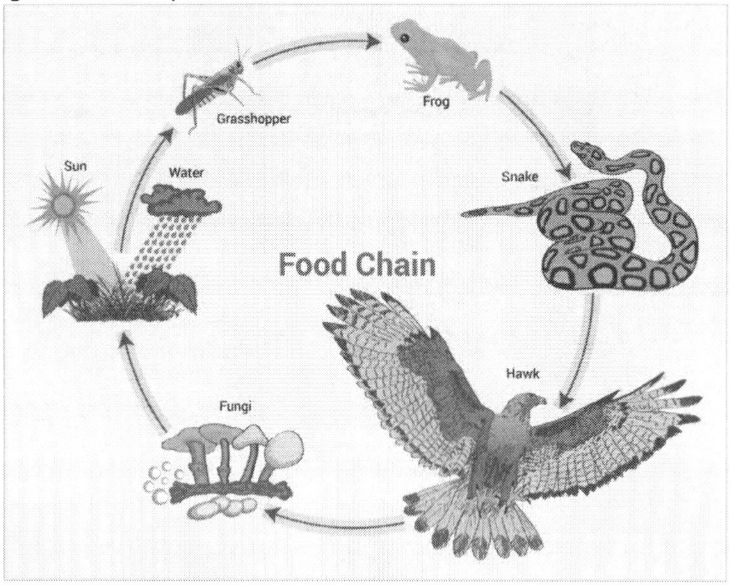

43. Which is the decomposer in the food chain above?
    a. Sun
    b. Grass
    c. Frog
    d. Fungi

44. Which is the herbivore in the food chain above?
    a. Grass
    b. Grasshopper
    c. Frog
    d. Fungi

45. What is a product of photosynthesis?
    a. Water
    b. Sunlight
    c. Oxygen
    d. Carbon Dioxide

46. What is cellular respiration?
    a. Making high-energy sugars
    b. Breathing
    c. Breaking down food to release energy
    d. Sweating

47. Which is true regarding DNA?
    a. It is the genetic code.
    b. It provides energy.
    c. It is single-stranded.
    d. All of the above.

48. Which one of the following can perform photosynthesis?
  a. Mold
  b. Ant
  c. Mushroom
  d. Algae

49. What does NOT happen at stomata?
  a. Carbon dioxide enters.
  b. Water exits due to transpiration.
  c. Oxygen exits.
  d. Glucose exits.

50. Which of the following represents a helpful inherited adaptation?
  a. A male elephant defending his territory by chasing another elephant away.
  b. A female dog that has a permanent strong odor that other male dogs tend to avoid.
  c. A male moose born with bigger horns that enable him to reduce competition for mating.
  d. A monkey learning to peel a banana after several tries.

51. Esther is left-handed. Hand dominance is a genetic factor. If being right-handed is a dominant trait over being left-handed, which of the following cannot be true about Esther's parents?
  a. Her parents are both right-handed.
  b. Her parents are both left-handed.
  c. Only one parent is right-handed.
  d. All of the above can be true.

52. What structures are made by the body's white blood cells that fight bacterial infections?
  a. Antibodies
  b. Antibiotics
  c. Vaccines
  d. Red blood cells

53. Cell -> ___1___ -> ___2___ -> organ system -> organism
Fill in blank #2 with the correct structure and a possible example in the circulatory system.
  a. Organ: heart
  b. Organ: blood vessel
  c. Tissue: heart
  d. Tissue: blood vessel

Use the following image to answer question 54.

54. Ants and aphids are organisms commonly found in nature. The ant doesn't eat the aphid, nor does the aphid eat the ant, so they have a different type of relationship than predator-prey. When aphids feed on plants, they simultaneously secrete a sugary substance that ants like to snack on. Ants in return protect the aphids from predators. What kind of relationship do the ant and the aphid demonstrate?
   a. Competition
   b. Parasitism
   c. Mutualism
   d. Commensalism

55. Jackson wants to open a dog-training business. He wants to see which dog treat is most effective in training dogs to sit. If he wants to design an experiment testing twenty dogs to figure out which treats to use, what would be a good dependent variable?
   a. Type of food
   b. Time in seconds the dogs sit
   c. How many times the dog wags its tail
   d. Shape of food

Answer Explanations

1. D: It has the same amount of mechanical energy throughout its path. Mechanical energy is the total amount of energy in the situation; it is the sum of the potential energy and the kinetic energy. The amount of potential and kinetic energy both vary by the position of an object, but the mechanical energy remains constant.

2. C: The scientific method refers to how to conduct a proper scientific inquiry, including recognizing a question/problem, formulating a hypothesis, making a prediction of what will happen based on research, experimenting, and deciding whether the outcome confirmed or denied the hypothesis.

3. B: Kinetic energy is energy an object has while moving. Potential energy is energy an object has based on its position or height. Solar energy is energy that comes from the sun. Heat energy is the energy produced from moving atoms, molecules, or ions, and can transfer between substances.

4. A: A chemical change alters the chemical makeup of the original object. When a piece of paper burns it cannot be returned to its original chemical makeup because it has formed new materials. Physical change refers to changing a substance's form, but not the composition of that substance. In physical science, "sedimentary change" and "potential change" are not terms used to describe any particular process.

5. C: An inclined plane is a simple machine that can make it easier to raise or lower an object in height. Simple machines offer a mechanical advantage to performing tasks. While a screw, a level, and a pulley are also simple machines, they would be used to offer a mechanical advantage in other situations.

6. D: Sir Isaac Newton simplified the laws of motion into three basic rules, based upon his observations in experimentation and advanced mathematical calculations. Albert Einstein was known for his theories involving electricity and magnetism, relativity, energy, light, and gravitational waves. Stephen Hawking is known for his theories and studies of space, dark matter, black holes, and relativity. Copernicus was known for his observations and theories regarding the movements of the planets in our universe; specifically, that the sun was the center of our solar system, not earth.

7. B: Convection is the transfer of heat due to the movement of molecules from an area of higher concentration to that of lower concentration; this is also how heat can travel throughout a house to warm each room. Conduction is the transfer of energy from one molecule to another molecule through actually touching or making contact with each other. Radiation is how the sun warms the earth; no medium is needed for this type of transfer.

8. D: An object at rest has forces acting upon it, including gravitational, normal, and frictional forces. All of these forces are in balance with each other and cause no movement in the object's position. This is equilibrium. An object in constant motion is also considered to be in equilibrium or a state of balanced forces.

9. C: When conducting scientific research, it is best to rely on sources that are known for honest, ethical, and unbiased research and experimentation. Most laboratories and universities must have their work validated through independent means in order to publish or claim results. Anyone can publish things on the Internet—it does not mean their work has been validated, and therefore, their work may not be correct.

10. D: Sublimation is a change in state from a solid to a gas. Evaporation is a change in state from a liquid to a gas, melting is a change in state from a solid to a liquid, and condensation is a change in state from a gas to a liquid.

11. C: A force diagram shows all of the forces acting upon an object in a situation. The direction of arrows pointing around the object shows the direction of each force. A Venn diagram is used to show mathematical sets, a periodic table shows how the elements are categorized, and a stress-strain diagram is used in engineering.

12. D: Mass refers to the amount or quantity there is of an object. Light, sound, and heat are all forms of energy that can travel in waves.

13. A: The mechanical energy is the total (or sum) of the potential energy and the kinetic energy at any given point in a system.

$ME = PE + KE; 50\,Joules = 30\,Joules + 20\,Joules$

14. D: Scientific inquiry can be prompted by simple curiosity as to how or why something works. As seen in the race to enter outer space, scientific progress can be driven by competition. Many inventors are motivated by the idea of finding a better, faster, or more economical way of doing or producing something so that they can prosper from their discovery.

15. A: Using Newton's equation for motion, $F = ma$, and substituting gravity in for acceleration (a), the weight, or force could be calculated for an object having mass (m). Weight is a force, mass is the amount of a substance, and acceleration and gravity are rate of speed over time.

16. B: It appears to bend because of the refraction of light traveling from air to water. When light travels from one material to another it can reflect, refract, and go through different materials. Choice *A* is incorrect, as the pencil does not actually become warped but only *appears* to be warped. Choice *C* is incorrect; although the pencil appears to bend because of its immersion into separate mediums where speed is different, the pencil does not become temporarily warped—it only appears to be warped. Choice *D* is incorrect; it is the refraction of light, not reflection. The latter happens within the same medium, which makes the answer choice incorrect.

17. B: While this is Einstein's application of Newton's theory to that of light, it is not one of Newton's original three laws of motion. Newton's three laws are $F = ma$, the law of inertia, and for every action there is an equal and opposite reaction.

18. C: This is a fundamental law of thermodynamics. Energy can only transfer, transform, or travel. The amount of energy in a system is always the same.

19. A: The ends (or poles) of a straight magnet are different charges. One end is positive and one end is negative. Therefore, the positive end of magnet #1 would attract the negative end of magnet #2 and repel magnet #2's positive end.

20. D: When electricity is run through a wire, it is carrying current and current has a charge. Therefore, there is a charge running down the wire, which creates a magnetic field that can attract and repel just like any magnet.

21. B: The ice skater is demonstrating the conservation of angular momentum. This means that the amount of momentum for the situation will remain the same. If the skater is redistributing the mass (their arms), then the angular speed will compensate for that alteration. In this case, the mass is extended out away from the axis of rotation, so the rate of rotation is slowed down. If their arms were brought back in near their body, then the rate of rotation would increase, making the skater spin faster.

22. C: This is the actual force recognized in a rotational situation. The reactive force acting opposite of the centripetal force is named the centrifugal force, but it is not an actual force on its own. A common mistake is to interchange the two terms. But, the real force acting in a rotational situation is pulling in toward the axis of rotation and is called the centripetal force.

23. C: Electric charge can be transferred through touch of one physical object to another, induction by bringing a charged object near another object, and polarization, or the forcing of one charge to the end of an object in a centralized area.

24. D: The solar waves from the sun warm the earth. Many of the waves are meant to reflect back off of the atmosphere to keep the earth warm, and the rest of the waves are meant to reflect back out into space through the atmosphere. This is known as the greenhouse effect. However, when the atmosphere has become too dense (polluted by gases), the waves meant to escape are trapped and re-radiate in the earth's atmosphere, causing an overall warming of the climate, known as global warming.

25. D: Velocity is a measure of speed with direction. To calculate velocity, find the distance covered and the time it took to cover that distance; change in position over the change in time. A standard measurement for velocity is in meters per second (m/s).

26. C: Fossil fuel energy. Wind energy from turbines, solar energy from sun panels, and geothermal energy are all considered renewable and preferable alternatives to fossil fuel, of which there is a limited supply.

The following image is the answer to question 27.

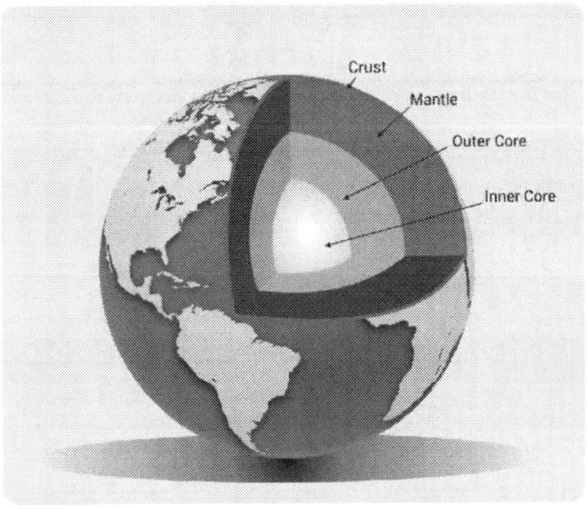

27. A: Inner core: solid. Layer 4 is the inner core; therefore, Choices *C* and *D* are incorrect. The inner core is solid due to the intense pressure upon it, making Choice *B* incorrect.

28. B: Sedimentary. Choice *A* (igneous) is incorrect, because that is crystallized magma found on land. Choice *C* (metamorphic) is incorrect, because that is unified, solid rock close to earth's mantle. Choice *D* (minerals) isn't a type of rock, but what composes rock.

29. D: Sunlight evaporates dew from plants. Choice *A* is incorrect because cloud formation is condensation. Choice *B* is incorrect because rain, snow, and ice storms are different forms of precipitation. Choice *C* is incorrect because rivers flowing into the oceans are examples of run-off.

30. D: Precipitation. Precipitation has nothing to do with plate tectonic theory. Plate movement causes ocean floor spreading, mountain formation, and earthquakes; therefore, all other answer choices are correct.

31. B: All volcanoes have explosive eruptions. This isn't true; shield volcanoes have thin magma that oozes out gently. Choice *A* is correct because magma circulates in the upper mantle. Choice *C* is correct because igneous rock is cooled lava. Choice *D* is correct because igneous rock goes through the rock cycle and will eventually become magma again.

The following image is for questions 32 and 33.

32. B: Seashells. The oldest rock layer is on the bottom. Choice *D* doesn't show a fossil—the grass is a living organism. Choices *A* and *C* show fossils in higher layers, so these are not the correct answers.

33. C: Sedimentary rock. Fossils are only found in sedimentary rock. Igneous rock, metamorphic rock, and liquid magma don't contain fossils, so Choices *A*, *B*, and *D* are incorrect.

The following image is for question 34.

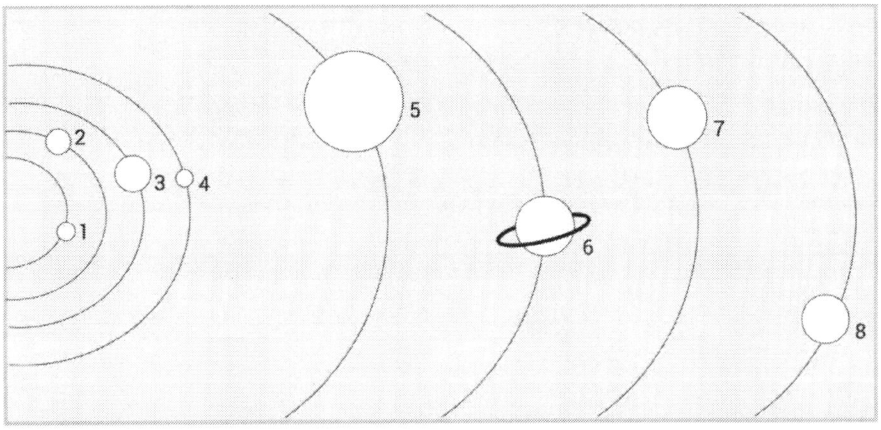

34. C: Between structures #4 and #5. The asteroid belt is rock orbiting between the inner, solid planets and the outer, gassy planets. More precisely, it is between Mars (planet #4) and Jupiter (planet #5). It is not Choice *A* (between Venus and Earth), nor is it Choice *B* (between Earth and Mars). Choice *D* is incorrect since it is not between every planet.

35. C: Mars has a smaller orbit around the Sun. This question requires critical thinking because every answer choice is true, but only one of them has to do with orbiting time. A year is the time it takes a planet to orbit the Sun, and because Mars is closer to the Sun and has a smaller orbit, its year is significantly shorter than a year on Jupiter.

The following image is for question 36.

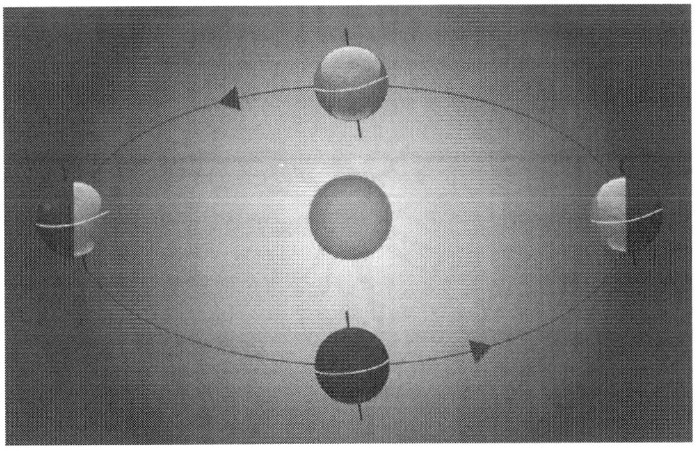

36. B: Winter. Students must identify the lateral equator and know the difference between North and South. They should recognize that because the top hemisphere is tilted away from the Sun; it would be winter at that time. Spring and fall (Choices *D* and *C*) are incorrect because both hemispheres have the same exposure to the sun, and summer (Choice *A*) is incorrect since the top hemisphere is tilted toward the sun.

37. D: All of the above. All choices are correct. New moons are closest to the sun and full moons are farthest (Choice *A*). Crescent moons are smaller than half-moons (Choice *B*), and gibbous moons are larger than half-moons (Choice *C*).

38. B: They insulate earth and keep it warm. Greenhouse gases serve as a blanket and allow earth to exist at livable temperatures. Choice *D* is incorrect because greenhouse gases do not form clouds; clouds are formed by condensed water vapor. Choice *C* is incorrect because while it is true that particles in the atmosphere reflect light so that the sky appears blue, this isn't an important function of the particles in the troposphere. The blue appearance is just cosmetic. Choice *A* is incorrect because ozone in the stratosphere actually prevents UV rays from passing.

39. C: Theories are accepted by scientists, while hypotheses remain to be proven. Choice *A* is incorrect because theories are far more than predictions; they are actually highly supported and accepted as truth. Choice *B* is incorrect because theories can change with new technology and understanding. Choice *D* is also incorrect because theories may not always be true and can change. Also, hypotheses can be and often are supported.

40. C: Seismologist: earthquakes. All other choices have been mixed up. Paleontologists study fossils, meteorologists study weather, and geologists study the earth's crust.

41. C: Leaf. Leaves are the part of the plant that contain chloroplast (due to their green appearance), thus they are the parts that perform photosynthesis. Roots (Choice *A*) suck up water. Seeds and flowers are reproductive structures (Choices *B* and *D*).

42. D: All living and nonliving things in an area. Choice *C* (all the organisms in a food web) describes feeding relationships and not symbiosis. Choice *B* (rocks, soil, and atmosphere in an area) includes nonliving factors in an ecosystem. Choice *A*, one organism, is too small to be considered an ecosystem.

The following image is for questions 43 and 44.

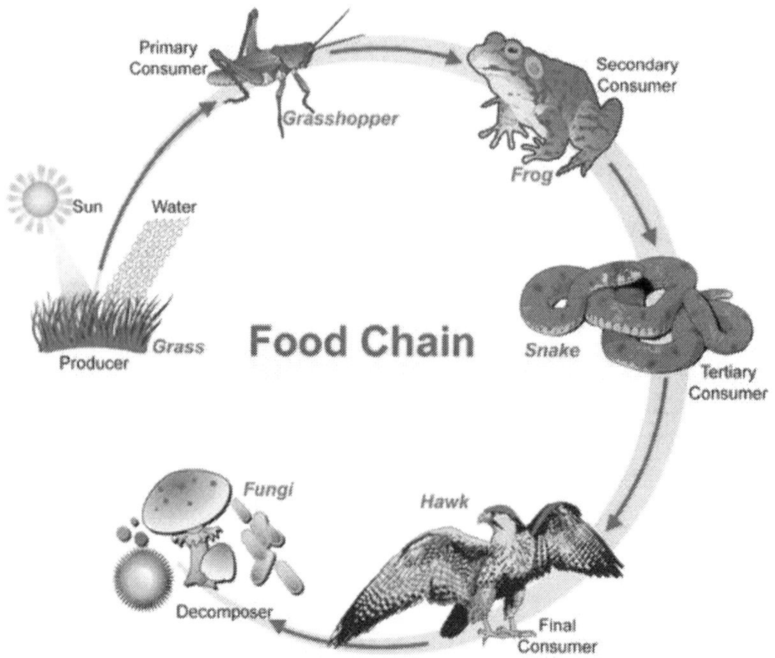

43. D: Fungi. Choice *A* (the sun) is not even a living thing. Grass (*B*) is a producer, and the frog (*C*) is a consumer. The fungi break down dead organisms and are the only decomposer shown.

44. B: Grasshopper. An herbivore is an organism that eats only plants, and that's the grasshopper's niche in this particular food chain. Grass (*A*) is a producer, the frog (*C*) is a consumer, and the fungi (*D*) is a decomposer.

45. C: Oxygen. Water (*A*) is a reactant that gets sucked up by the roots. Carbon dioxide (*D*) is a reactant that goes into the stomata, and sunlight (*B*) inputs energy into the reaction in order to create the high-energy sugar.

46. C: Breaking down food to release energy. Breathing (*B*) is not cellular respiration; breathing is an action that takes place at the organism level with the respiratory system. Making high-energy sugars (*A*) is photosynthesis, not cellular respiration. Perspiration (*D*) is sweating, and has nothing to do with cellular respiration.

47. A: It is the genetic code. Choice *B* is incorrect because DNA does not provide energy—that's the job of carbohydrates and glucose. Choice *C* is incorrect because DNA is double-stranded. Because Choices *B* and *C* are incorrect, Choice *D*, all of the above, is incorrect.

48. D: Algae can perform photosynthesis. One indicator that a plant is able to perform photosynthesis is the color green. Plants with the pigment chlorophyll are able to absorb the warmer colors of the light spectrum, but are unable to absorb green. That's why they appear green. Choices *A* and *C* are types of fungi, and are therefore not able to perform photosynthesis. Fungi obtain energy from food in their environment. Choice *B*, ant, is also unable to perform photosynthesis, since it is an animal.

49. D: Glucose exits. The stomata are pores at the bottom of the leaf, and carbon dioxide enters (it is a reactant for photosynthesis) and oxygen exits (it is a product for photosynthesis), so Choices *A* and *C* are correct. Water exits through the stomata in the process of transpiration, so Choice *B* is correct as well. Glucose is the sugar that is either broken down by the plant for its own energy usage or eaten by other organisms for energy.

50. C: A male moose with horns that enable him to reduce competition for mating. Choices *A* and *D* (elephant and monkey) are not caused by genes. These are learned behaviors from other animals. Choice *B* (smelly dog) is actually a detriment because the dog will be less likely to mate, so she will not pass on her smelly genes.

51. D: All of the above. Let's label *R* as the right-handed allele and *r* as the left-handed allele. Esther has to have the combination rr since she's left-handed. She had to get at least one recessive allele from each parent. So, mom could either be Rr or rr (right-handed or left-handed), and dad can also be Rr or rr. As long as each parent carries one recessive allele, it is possible that Esther is left-handed. Therefore, all answer choices are possible.

52. A: Antibodies. Antibiotics (*B*) fight bacteria, but the body does not make them naturally. White blood cells, not red blood cells (*D*) are the blood cells produced that fight the bacteria. Vaccines (*C*) are given to create antibodies and prevent future illness.

53. A: Organ: Heart. Blank #1 is tissue and blank #2 is organ, so Choices *C* and *D* are automatically incorrect. Blood vessels (*B*) are a type of smooth muscle tissue. The heart is an organ.

The following image is for question 54.

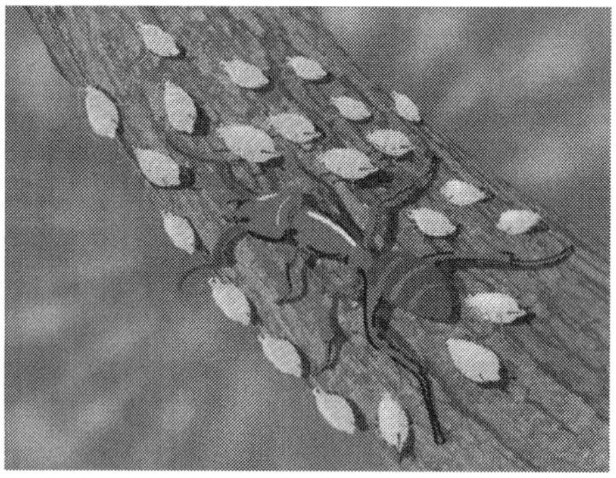

54. C: Mutualism. In the ant-aphid case, both organisms benefit, as the ants are getting food and the aphids are getting protection. Competition (*A*) is when organisms want the same thing (food, water, shelter, space), which is clearly not the case here. Parasitism (*B*) involves one organism getting hurt in the relationship at the expense of the other, while commensalism (*D*) involves an organism that is benefited connected to an indifferent party.

55. B: Time in seconds the dogs sit. This is a better choice than Choice *C* (tail wagging) because it is a measurable, meaningful, and relevant dependent variable. Tail wagging, although quantitative, is not a valid measure of anything. Choices *A* and *D* could be independent variables in the experiment.

Mathematics

Student Thinking and Instructional Practices

Mathematical Concepts to Evaluate Student Solutions

One of the first concepts in elementary mathematics that needs to be mastered is the ability to subitize. Once mastered, the student is able to know how many there are of a quantity without counting each individual piece. They use patterns recognition to do so. For example, they can count by 5s or 10s, group small quantities together, or split up numbers such as knowing 7 can be thought of as the sum of 6 and 1. For example, adding $7 + 9 + 20$ might be rethought as $6 + (1+9) + 20 = 36$. Secondly, transitivity is a property used to build arguments with both equality and inequality. The property of equality states that if $a = b$ and $b = c$, then $a = c$. A transitivity property of inequality is if $a > b$ and $b > c$, then $a > c$.

An iteration is a repetition of a process. In mathematics, it refers to a mathematical operation applied to the result of a previous operation. For example, an output of a function can be plugged back into the function to obtain another output. Again, this output can be plugged in as well. The repetition would be an iterative process. Finally, a tiling exists when individual shapes are placed to fill a flat space with no gaps or overlapping. A tiling is also known as a tessellation. Some can have repeating patterns and some do not. If they repeat, they are known as a periodic tiling. Some can also be symmetric because if it is folded over a line of symmetry, the pattern represents two mirror images.

In the classroom, these concepts should be part of the students' problem-solving abilities. The teacher should recognize when each concept is applicable to a concept, and also recognize when they are being used in their students' solutions.

Problem Structures with Unknowns in All Positions

Traditional methods do not always have to apply when introducing operations in the classroom. For example, there are multiple problem structures when working with multiplication. Consider 6×8. If student did not have the multiplication table memorized, he or she could use the put-together/take-apart method. This involves breaking up the problem into multiplication that is known. In this problem, 8 can be written as the sum of two 4's, or $4 + 4$. The student should know that $6 \times 4 = 24$, and therefore because there are two 4's, the result is found by adding 24 two times. This results in 48. The put-together/take-apart method can also be used in addition. For example, $325 + 417$ could be rewritten as individual addition problems within each place value. Therefore, the problem would be the same as $300 + 400 + 20 + 10 + 5 + 7 = 700 + 30 + 12 = 742$, which might be easier for some students than the traditional approach of adding vertically by digit. A similar methodology can be used for subtraction. Consider $642 - 165$. First, subtract 100 from 642 to obtain 542. Then, 60 is subtracted from 542 to obtain 482. Finally, this amount is reduced by 5. The final answer is 477.

An array/area model is a method that can be used instead of the traditional multiplication techniques. Each number is broken up by place value, and individual multiplication problems are completed within each combination. Here is the problem 65×29 using an area/array model:

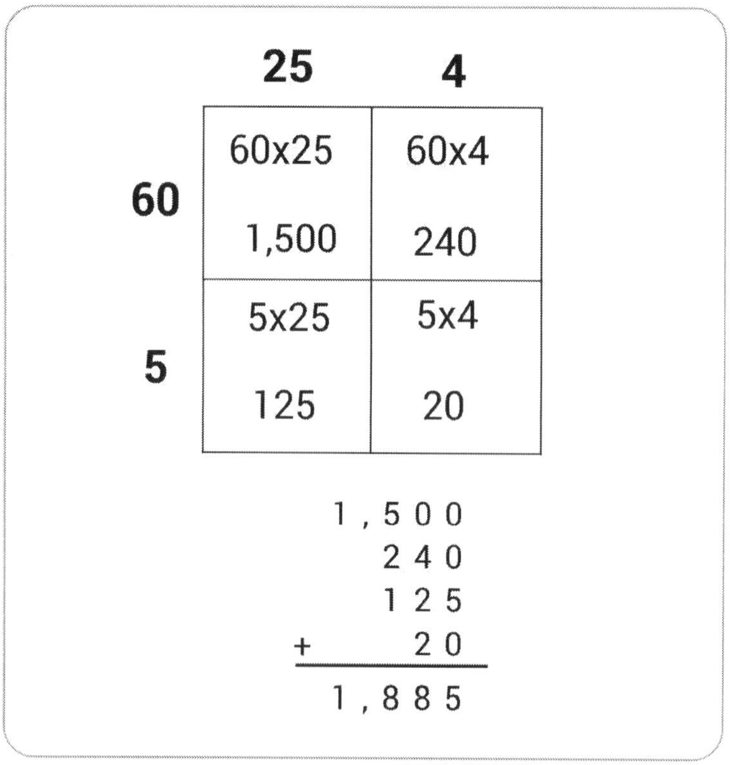

Area models can also be used within division problems. It involves multiplication and subtraction. Here is an example of such a model being used to compute the problem $8580 \div 55 = 156$.

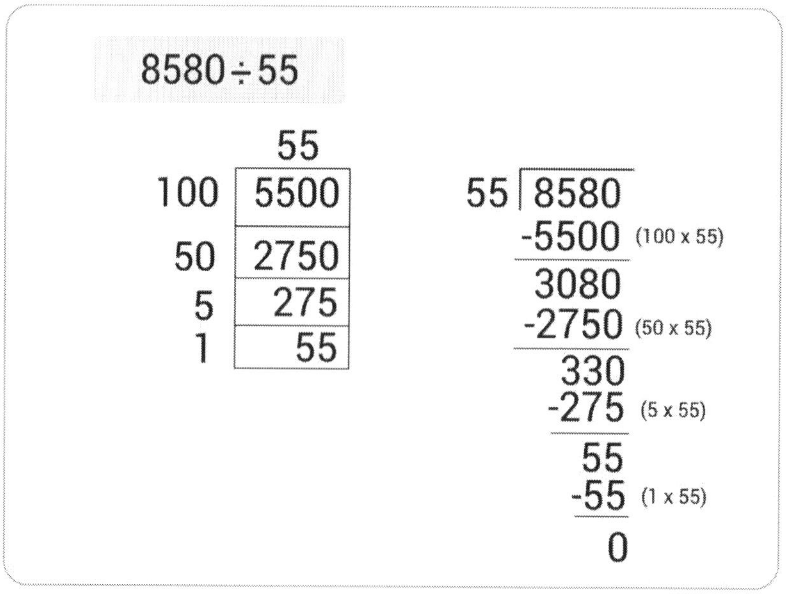

It is up to the teacher to highlight the advantages and disadvantages of the new methods and the traditional methods, and distinguish amongst all the different solving mechanisms to develop students understanding of operations in the most appropriate manner.

Validity of a Student's Mathematical Model

Even though there could be more than one correct approach to solving math problems, there are approaches that are deemed to be either valid and invalid. A standard algorithm refers to the traditional way of doing something. For example, in addition, if the sum of 345 and 746 needed to be found, the standard algorithm would involve adding the ones place, the tens place, and then the hundreds place in the traditional sense. An inventive strategy involves any other strategy besides the traditional approach. In the case of the same addition problem, the numbers could be estimated or decomposed to obtain a result. For example, grouping by 5s, 10s, and 100s would be a nontraditional approach that would result in the same answer. Within the inventive strategies, students are focused more on place value in this example and less on the actual addition of digits. There are many benefits to using inventive strategies, but both techniques must be taught. Inventive strategies might be able to help the students understand the concepts more because they are breaking the problem down further instead of just repeating a process over and over. It might take more time in the classroom to introduce inventive strategies rather than the standard algorithms, but research shows that these methods are less likely to be retaught. Teachers will decide when the students need to use inventive strategies and standard algorithms, and be able to see which type of method was used and if it was valid or not.

Interpreting Individual Student Mathematics Assessment Data

Throughout each school year, teachers can use assessments to guide their lecture, assist in creating their lesson plans, and adapt instructional techniques. Diagnostic tests are given at the beginning of the year. They are used to test each student's skill level before new material is introduced, and teachers can use this information to their advantage. They can use the results to determine if any review of previous material is necessary and determine the skill level of the overall class. Balance is the difficult part of this process. If some students are way behind, it does not benefit those that are advanced to spend a ton of time with review. It is up to teachers to find a good balance at the beginning of the year.

Secondly, formative assessments are used throughout the year. These types of assessments can be in the form of quizzes and tests. For example, a chapter test is an example of a formative assignment. They are used to monitor how well the new material is being understood and retained. They are usually scheduled at regular intervals, and teachers can use their results to determine if any concepts need to be reinforced.

Finally, progress monitoring is a technique teachers can use to evaluate their own teaching effectiveness. They measure the student's effectiveness on all of the skills needed to master that year at regular intervals in the school year. They differ from formative assessments in that the measurement is on an entire skill set, and not just a single unit or chapter from the textbook.

Structured Experiences

Depending on the complexity of the mathematical concept being discussed, group activity might be used as a method of instruction. Group activities allow students to develop skills that are crucial in the real-world, such as time management, communication skills, and working with feedback. Whether to use small or large group activities depends on the cognitive complexity of the task. Cognitive complexity is defined in psychology to be how well people perceive concepts, and in the mathematics classroom this concept would relate to how intricate the students' critical thinking skills are.

For a situation that involves brainstorming or discussing a question or a problem, a small group might be the best option. A small group ensures that each student has an opportunity to voice his or her own opinion. In this situation, students do not have to have clearly defined roles, and the general goal of the task is just a discussion. Larger groups work better for more complex project based assignments. In order for a large group to work best, roles must be clearly defined within the project or problem. For example, one student can be in charge of keeping time, another one can be the recorder, etc. All students will play an integral role in developing the answer to the problem, but the more organized the process is the better. The larger projects allow this scenario to happen. In either case, it is important to organize the classroom in the best way so that each group member is able to see each other.

Analyzing Learning Progressions

Learning progressions are plans that lay out a specific sequence of math skills that students are expected to master as they progress throughout the school year. Given a time frame, such as midyear fifth grade, there is a set of corresponding learning standards. The standards summarize all the topics each student should have mastered at that point in time, and such standards are based on the traditional structure of teaching mathematics. Learning progressions have been developed so that students are working on material that is not too hard or not too easy while preparing them for harder topics that will be taught at the next level. Unless students are in an accelerated class, learning progressions are a structured way to ensure students are getting what they need in the classroom. Each standard builds on the previous one, showing how progression is made as each student masters the concepts being taught.

For example, consider the topic of fractions. In third grade, students should be able to know what a fraction means, graph them on a number line, and compare their quantities. However, they should not be expected to find equivalent fractions, convert to decimals, and add or subtract with common denominators. In fifth grade, they should be able to add or subtract with different denominators, and multiply and divide fractions. As each year is summarized, there is a progression that is seen. Each topic builds on each other, and each student's understanding of fractions develops as time progresses and more concepts are introduced.

Math Fluency

In order to be fluent in math, one must be able to retrieve facts from memory and apply them to processes in a quick, effective, and accurate manner. For a student to be accurate, the concepts applied must be correct and precise. Another component of math fluency is automaticity, which is related to speed. If a student is able to recall the mathematical facts at a rapid pace, he or she has automaticity of the concept. For example, if a student is able to quickly recall the correct multiplication tables, he or she is both accurate and automatic when recalling such information. Each year, there is a different benchmark that a student must maintain given a concept. For example, in first grade, let's say a student is able to complete 10 addition problems in a minute at the beginning of the year. Together, the student and teacher could work towards computing 50 addition problems in a minute midyear and 75 addition problems in a minute at the end of the year. Each amount per minute is known as the rate of completion. As each operation is learned, more benchmarks can be introduced. For example, second grade can focus more on subtraction, and fourth grade can focus more on multiplication and division. Teachers should pass out problem lists with more problems than a student could possibly compute in an allotted time so that a correct amount can be counted. Not only do the problems need to be completed, but they also need to be accurate.

Students demonstrate flexibility throughout critical thinking in the classroom. They need to not just memorize the concepts being discussed, but also to learn how to use the concepts in multiple scenarios. An important part of math fluency is to work with numbers and concepts in different ways, without just recalling and stating concepts. For example, a student will memorize multiplication tables, but there is more to the process that just knowing the answers. Flexibility involves knowing when multiplication is necessary to solve a problem. Consider the area of a rectangle. The multiplication tables would be used to find the area of a rectangle that had a length of 6 inches and width of 9 inches. However, a student needs to understand that multiplication connects the problem to the answer. The memorization of the tables is not useful unless it can be applied to tangible scenarios.

Operations, Algebraic Thinking, Counting and Number in Base Ten

Base-10 Numerals, Number Names, and Expanded Form

Numbers used in everyday life are constituted in a base-10 system. Each digit in a number, depending on its location, represents some multiple of 10, or quotient of 10 when dealing with decimals. Each digit to the left of the decimal point represents a higher multiple of 10. Each digit to the right of the decimal point represents a quotient of a higher multiple of 10 for the divisor. For example, consider the number 7,631.42. The digit one represents simply the number one. The digit 3 represents 3×10. The digit 6 represents $6 \times 10 \times 10$ (or 6×100). The digit 7 represents $7 \times 10 \times 10 \times 10$ (or 7×1000). The digit 4 represents $4 \div 10$. The digit 2 represents $(2 \div 10) \div 10$, or $2 \div (10 \times 10)$ or $2 \div 100$.

A number is written in expanded form by expressing it as the sum of the value of each of its digits. The expanded form in the example above, which is written with the highest value first down to the lowest value, is expressed as: $7{,}000 + 600 + 30 + 1 + .4 + .02$.

When verbally expressing a number, the integer part of the number (the numbers to the left of the decimal point) resembles the expanded form without the addition between values. In the above example, the numbers read "seven thousand six hundred thirty-one." When verbally expressing the decimal portion of a number, the number is read as a whole number, followed by the place value of the furthest digit (non-zero) to the right. In the above example, 0.42 is read "forty-two hundredths." Reading the number 7,631.42 in its entirety is expressed as "seven thousand six hundred thirty-one and forty-two hundredths." The word *and* is used between the integer and decimal parts of the number.

Composing and Decomposing Multi-Digit Numbers

Composing and decomposing numbers aids in conceptualizing what each digit of a multi-digit number represents. The standard, or typical, form in which numbers are written consists of a series of digits representing a given value based on their place value. Consider the number 592.7. This number is composed of 5 hundreds, 9 tens, 2 ones, and 7 tenths.

Composing a number requires adding the given numbers for each place value and writing the numbers in standard form. For example, composing 4 thousands, 5 hundreds, 2 tens, and 8 ones consists of adding as follows: $4{,}000 + 500 + 20 + 8$, to produce 4,528 (standard form).

Decomposing a number requires taking a number written in standard form and breaking it apart into the sum of each place value. For example, the number 83.17 is decomposed by breaking it into the sum of 4 values (for each of the 4 digits): 8 tens, 3 ones, 1 tenth, and 7 hundredths. The decomposed or "expanded" form of 83.17 is $80 + 3 + .1 + .07$.

Place Value of a Given Digit

The number system that is used consists of only ten different digits or characters. However, this system is used to represent an infinite number of values. The place value system makes this infinite number of values possible. The position in which a digit is written corresponds to a given value. Starting from the decimal point (which is implied, if not physically present), each subsequent place value to the left represents a value greater than the one before it. Conversely, starting from the decimal point, each subsequent place value to the right represents a value less than the one before it.

The names for the place values to the left of the decimal point are as follows:

...	Billions	Hundred-Millions	Ten-Millions	Millions	Hundred-Thousands	Ten-Thousands	Thousands	Hundreds	Tens	Ones

*Note that this table can be extended infinitely further to the left.

The names for the place values to the right of the decimal point are as follows:

Decimal Point (.)	Tenths	Hundredths	Thousandths	Ten-Thousandths	...

*Note that this table can be extended infinitely further to the right.

When given a multi-digit number, the value of each digit depends on its place value. Consider the number 682,174.953. Referring to the chart above, it can be determined that the digit 8 is in the ten-thousands place. It is in the fifth place to the left of the decimal point. Its value is 8 ten-thousands or 80,000. The digit 5 is two places to the right of the decimal point. Therefore, the digit 5 is in the hundredths place. Its value is 5 hundredths or $\frac{5}{100}$ (equivalent to .05).

Base-10 System

Value of Digits

In accordance with the base-10 system, the value of a digit increases by a factor of ten each place it moves to the left. For example, consider the number 7. Moving the digit one place to the left (70), increases its value by a factor of 10 ($7 \times 10 = 70$). Moving the digit two places to the left (700) increases its value by a factor of 10 twice ($7 \times 10 \times 10 = 700$). Moving the digit three places to the left (7,000) increases its value by a factor of 10 three times ($7 \times 10 \times 10 \times 10 = 7{,}000$), and so on.

Conversely, the value of a digit decreases by a factor of ten each place it moves to the right. (Note that multiplying by $\frac{1}{10}$ is equivalent to dividing by 10). For example, consider the number 40. Moving the digit one place to the right (4) decreases its value by a factor of 10 ($40 \div 10 = 4$). Moving the digit two places to the right (0.4), decreases its value by a factor of 10 twice ($40 \div 10 \div 10 = 0.4$) or ($40 \times \frac{1}{10} \times \frac{1}{10} = 0.4$). Moving the digit three places to the right (0.04) decreases its value by a factor of 10 three times ($40 \div 10 \div 10 \div 10 = 0.04$) or ($40 \times \frac{1}{10} \times \frac{1}{10} \times \frac{1}{10} = 0.04$), and so on.

Exponents to Denote Powers of 10

The value of a given digit of a number in the base-10 system can be expressed utilizing powers of 10. A power of 10 refers to 10 raised to a given exponent such as 10^0, 10^1, 10^2, 10^3, etc. For the number 10^3, 10 is the base and 3 is the exponent. A base raised by an exponent represents how many times the base is multiplied by itself. Therefore, $10^1 = 10$, $10^2 = 10 \times 10 = 100$, $10^3 = 10 \times 10 \times 10 = 1{,}000$, $10^4 = 10 \times 10 \times 10 \times 10 = 10{,}000$, etc. Any base with a zero exponent equals one.

Powers of 10 are utilized to decompose a multi-digit number without writing all the zeroes. Consider the number 872,349. This number is decomposed to $800{,}000 + 70{,}000 + 2{,}000 + 300 + 40 + 9$. When utilizing powers of 10, the number 872,349 is decomposed to $(8 \times 10^5) + (7 \times 10^4) + (2 \times 10^3) + (3 \times 10^2) + (4 \times 10^1) + (9 \times 10^0)$. The power of 10 by which the digit is multiplied corresponds to the number of zeroes following the digit when expressing its value in standard form. For example, 7×10^4 is equivalent to 70,000 or 7 followed by four zeros.

Rounding Multi-Digit Numbers

Rounding numbers changes the given number to a simpler and less accurate number than the exact given number. Rounding allows for easier calculations which estimate the results of using the exact given number. The accuracy of the estimate and ease of use depends on the place value to which the number is rounded. Rounding numbers consists of:

- Determining what place value the number is being rounded to
- Examining the digit to the right of the desired place value to decide whether to round up or keep the digit
- Replacing all digits to the right of the desired place value with zeros

To round 746,311 to the nearest ten thousands, the digit in the ten thousands place should be located first. In this case, this digit is 4 (7<u>4</u>6,311). Then, the digit to its right is examined. If this digit is 5 or greater, the number will be rounded up by increasing the digit in the desired place by one. If the digit to the right of the place value being rounded is 4 or less, the number will be kept the same. For the given example, the digit being examined is a 6, which means that the number will be rounded up by increasing the digit to the left by one. Therefore, the digit 4 is changed to a 5. Finally, to write the rounded number, any digits to the left of the place value being rounded remain the same and any to its right are replaced with zeros. For the given example, rounding 746,311 to the nearest ten thousand will produce 750,000. To round 746,311 to the nearest hundred, the digit to the right of the three in the hundreds place is examined to determine whether to round up or keep the same number. In this case, that digit is a one, so the number will be kept the same and any digits to its right will be replaced with zeros. The resulting rounded number is 746,300.

Rounding place values to the right of the decimal follows the same procedure, but digits being replaced by zeros can simply be dropped. To round 3.752891 to the nearest thousandth, the desired place value is located (3.75<u>2</u>891) and the digit to the right is examined. In this case, the digit 8 indicates that the number will be rounded up, and the 2 in the thousandths place will increase to a 3. Rounding up and replacing the digits to the right of the thousandths place produces 3.753000 which is equivalent to 3.753. Therefore, the zeros are not necessary and the rounded number should be written as 3.753.

When rounding up, if the digit to be increased is a 9, the digit to its left is increased by 1 and the digit in the desired place value is changed to a zero. For example, the number 1,598 rounded to the nearest ten is 1,600. Another example shows the number 43.72961 rounded to the nearest thousandth is 43.730 or 43.73.

Solving Multistep Mathematical and Real-World Problems

Problem Situations for Operations

Addition and subtraction are *inverse operations*. Adding a number and then subtracting the same number will cancel each other out, resulting in the original number, and vice versa. For example, $8 + 7 - 7 = 8$ and $137 - 100 + 100 = 137$. Similarly, multiplication and division are inverse operations. Therefore, multiplying by a number and then dividing by the same number results in the original number, and vice versa. For example, $8 \times 2 \div 2 = 8$ and $12 \div 4 \times 4 = 12$. Inverse operations are used to work backwards to solve problems. In the case that 7 and a number add to 18, the inverse operation of subtraction is used to find the unknown value ($18 - 7 = 11$). If a school's entire 4th grade was divided evenly into 3 classes each with 22 students, the inverse operation of multiplication is used to determine the total students in the grade ($22 \times 3 = 66$). Additional scenarios involving inverse operations are included in the tables below.

There are a variety of real-world situations in which one or more of the operators is used to solve a problem. The tables below display the most common scenarios.

Addition & Subtraction

	Unknown Result	**Unknown Change**	**Unknown Start**
Adding to	5 students were in class. 4 more students arrived. How many students are in class? $5 + 4 = ?$	8 students were in class. More students arrived late. There are now 18 students in class. How many students arrived late? $8 + ? = 18$ Solved by inverse operations $18 - 8 = ?$	Some students were in class early. 11 more students arrived. There are now 17 students in class. How many students were in class early? $? + 11 = 17$ Solved by inverse operations $17 - 11 = ?$
Taking from	15 students were in class. 5 students left class. How many students are in class now? $15 - 5 = ?$	12 students were in class. Some students left class. There are now 8 students in class. How many students left class? $12 - ? = 8$ Solved by inverse operations $8 + ? = 12 \rightarrow 12 - 8 = ?$	Some students were in class. 3 students left class. Then there were 13 students in class. How many students were in class before? $? - 3 = 13$ Solved by inverse operations $13 + 3 = ?$

	Unknown Total	Unknown Addends (Both)	Unknown Addends (One)
Putting together/ taking apart	The homework assignment is 10 addition problems and 8 subtraction problems. How many problems are in the homework assignment? $10 + 8 = ?$	Bobby has \$9. How much can Bobby spend on candy and how much can Bobby spend on toys? $9 = ? + ?$	Bobby has 12 pairs of pants. 5 pairs of pants are shorts and the rest are long. How many pairs of long pants does he have? $12 = 5 + ?$ Solved by inverse operations $12 - 5 = ?$

	Unknown Difference	Unknown Larger Value	Unknown Smaller Value
Comparing	Bobby has 5 toys. Tommy has 8 toys. How many more toys does Tommy have than Bobby? $5 + ? = 8$ Solved by inverse operations $8 - 5 = ?$ Bobby has \$6. Tommy has \$10. How many fewer dollars does Bobby have than Tommy? $10 - 6 = ?$	Tommy has 2 more toys than Bobby. Bobby has 4 toys. How many toys does Tommy have? $2 + 4 = ?$ Bobby has 3 fewer dollars than Tommy. Bobby has \$8. How many dollars does Tommy have? $? - 3 = 8$ Solved by inverse operations $8 + 3 = ?$	Tommy has 6 more toys than Bobby. Tommy has 10 toys. How many toys does Bobby have? $? + 6 = 10$ Solved by inverse operations $10 - 6 = ?$ Bobby has \$5 less than Tommy. Tommy has \$9. How many dollars does Bobby have? $9 - 5 = ?$

<u>Multiplication and Division</u>

	Unknown Product	Unknown Group Size	Unknown Number of Groups
Equal groups	There are 5 students and each student has 4 pieces of candy. How many pieces of candy are there in all? $5 \times 4 = ?$	14 pieces of candy are shared equally by 7 students. How many pieces of candy does each student have? $7 \times ? = 14$ Solved by inverse operations $14 \div 7 = ?$	If 18 pieces of candy are to be given out 3 to each student, how many students will get candy? $? \times 3 = 18$ Solved by inverse operations $18 \div 3 = ?$

	Unknown Product	Unknown Factor	Unknown Factor
Arrays	There are 5 rows of students with 3 students in each row. How many students are there? $5 \times 3 = ?$	If 16 students are arranged into 4 equal rows, how many students will be in each row? $4 \times ? = 16$ Solved by inverse operations $16 \div 4 = ?$	If 24 students are arranged into an array with 6 columns, how many rows are there? $? \times 6 = 24$ Solved by inverse operations $24 \div 6 = ?$

	Larger Unknown	Smaller Unknown	Multiplier Unknown
Comparing	A small popcorn costs \$1.50. A large popcorn costs 3 times as much as a small popcorn. How much does a large popcorn cost? $1.50 \times 3 = ?$	A large soda costs \$6 and that is 2 times as much as a small soda costs. How much does a small soda cost? $2 \times ? = 6$ Solved by inverse operations $6 \div 2 = ?$	A large pretzel costs \$3 and a small pretzel costs \$2. How many times as much does the large pretzel cost as the small pretzel? $? \times 2 = 3$ Solved by inverse operations $3 \div 2 = ?$

Remainders in Division Problems

If a given total cannot be divided evenly into a given number of groups, the amount left over is the remainder. Consider the following scenario: 32 textbooks must be packed into boxes for storage. Each box holds 6 textbooks. How many boxes are needed? To determine the answer, 32 is divided by 6, resulting in 5 with a remainder of 2. A remainder may be interpreted three ways:

- Add 1 to the quotient
  How many boxes will be needed? Six boxes will be needed because five will not be enough.

- Use only the quotient
  How many boxes will be full? Five boxes will be full.

- Use only the remainder
  If you only have 5 boxes, how many books will not fit? Two books will not fit.

Algebraic Expressions and Equations

An algebraic expression is a statement about an unknown quantity expressed in mathematical symbols. A variable is used to represent the unknown quantity, usually denoted by a letter. An equation is a statement in which two expressions (at least one containing a variable) are equal to each other. An algebraic expression can be thought of as a mathematical phrase and an equation can be thought of as a mathematical sentence.

Algebraic expressions and equations both contain numbers, variables, and mathematical operations. The following are examples of algebraic expressions: $5x + 3, 7xy - 8(x^2 + y)$, and $\sqrt{a^2 + b^2}$. An expression can be simplified or evaluated for given values of variables. The following are examples of equations: $2x + 3 = 7, a^2 + b^2 = c^2$, and $2x + 5 = 3x - 2$. An equation contains two sides separated by an equal sign. Equations can be solved to determine the value(s) of the variable for which the statement is true.

Adding and Subtracting Linear Algebraic Expressions

An algebraic expression is simplified by combining like terms. A term is a number, variable, or product of a number, and variables separated by addition and subtraction. For the algebraic expression $3x^2 - 4x + 5 - 5x^2 + x - 3$, the terms are $3x^2$, -4x, 5, -$5x^2$, x, and -3. Like terms have the same variables raised to the same powers (exponents). The like terms for the previous example are $3x^2$ and -$5x^2$, -4x and x, 5 and -3. To combine like terms, the coefficients (numerical factor of the term including sign) are added and the variables and their powers are kept the same. Note that if a coefficient is not written, it is an implied coefficient of 1 ($x = 1x$). The previous example will simplify to $-2x^2 - 3x + 2$.

When adding or subtracting algebraic expressions, each expression is written in parenthesis. The negative sign is distributed when necessary, and like terms are combined. Consider the following: add $2a + 5b - 2$ to $a - 2b + 8c - 4$. The sum is set as follows: $(a - 2b + 8c - 4) + (2a + 5b - 2)$. In front of each set of parenthesis is an implied positive one, which, when distributed, does not change any of the terms. Therefore, the parentheses are dropped and like terms are combined: $a - 2b + 8c - 4 + 2a + 5b - 2 = 3a + 3b + 8c - 6$.

Consider the following problem: Subtract $2a + 5b - 2$ from $a - 2b + 8c - 4$. The difference is set as follows: $(a - 2b + 8c - 4) - (2a + 5b - 2)$. The implied one in front of the first set of parenthesis will not change those four terms. However, distributing the implied -1 in front of the second set of parenthesis will change the sign of each of those three terms: $a - 2b + 8c - 4 - 2a - 5b + 2$. Combining like terms yields the simplified expression $-a - 7b + 8c - 2$.

Distributive Property

The distributive property states that multiplying a sum (or difference) by a number produces the same result as multiplying each value in the sum (or difference) by the number and adding (or subtracting) the products. Using mathematical symbols, the distributive property states $a(b + c) = ab + ac$. The expression $4(3 + 2)$ is simplified using the order of operations. Simplifying inside the parenthesis first produces 4×5, which equals 20. The expression $4(3 + 2)$ can also be simplified using the distributive property: $4(3 + 2) = 4 \times 3 + 4 \times 2 = 12 + 8 = 20$.

Consider the following example: $4(3x - 2)$. The expression cannot be simplified inside the parenthesis because 3*x* and -2 are not like terms, and therefore cannot be combined. However, the expression can be simplified by using the distributive property and multiplying each term inside of the parenthesis by the term outside of the parenthesis: $12x - 8$. The resulting equivalent expression contains no like terms, so it cannot be further simplified.

Consider the expression $(3x + 2y + 1) - (5x - 3) + 2(3y + 4)$. Again, there are no like terms, but the distributive property is used to simplify the expression. Note there is an implied one in front of the first set of parentheses and an implied -1 in front of the second set of parentheses. Distributing the one, -1, and 2 produces $1(3x) + 1(2y) + 1(1) - 1(5x) - 1(-3) + 2(3y) + 2(4) = 3x + 2y + 1 - 5x + 3 + 6y + 8$. This expression contains like terms that are combined to produce the simplified expression $-2x + 8y + 12$.

Algebraic expressions are tested to be equivalent by choosing values for the variables and evaluating both expressions (see 2.A.4). For example, $4(3x - 2)$ and $12x - 8$ are tested by substituting 3 for the variable *x* and calculating to determine if equivalent values result.

Simple Expressions for Given Values

An algebraic expression is a statement written in mathematical symbols, typically including one or more unknown values represented by variables. For example, the expression $2x + 3$ states that an unknown number (*x*) is multiplied by 2 and added to 3. If given a value for the unknown number, or variable, the value of the expression is determined. For example, if the value of the variable *x* is 4, the value of the expression 4 is multiplied by 2, and 3 is added. This results in a value of 11 for the expression.

When given an algebraic expression and values for the variable(s), the expression is evaluated to determine its numerical value. To evaluate the expression, the given values for the variables are substituted (or replaced) and the expression is simplified using the order of operations. Parenthesis should be used when substituting. Consider the following: Evaluate $a - 2b + ab$ for $a = 3$ and $b = -1$. To evaluate, any variable *a* is replaced with 3 and any variable *b* with -1, producing (3)-2(-1)+(3)(-1). Next, the order of operations is used to calculate the value of the expression, which is 2.

Parts of Expressions

Algebraic expressions consist of variables, numbers, and operations. A term of an expression is any combination of numbers and/or variables, and terms are separated by addition and subtraction. For example, the expression $5x^2 - 3xy + 4 - 2$ consists of 4 terms: $5x^2$, -3*xy*, 4*y*, and -2. Note that each term includes its given sign (+ or $-$). The variable part of a term is a letter that represents an unknown quantity. The coefficient of a term is the number by which the variable is multiplied. For the term 4*y*, the variable is *y* and the coefficient is 4. Terms are identified by the power (or exponent) of its variable.

A number without a variable is referred to as a constant. If the variable is to the first power (x^1 or simply *x*), it is referred to as a linear term. A term with a variable to the second power (x^2) is quadratic and a term to the third power (x^3) is cubic. Consider the expression $x^3 + 3x - 1$. The constant is -1. The linear term is 3*x*. There is no quadratic term. The cubic term is x^3.

An algebraic expression can also be classified by how many terms exist in the expression. Any like terms should be combined before classifying. A monomial is an expression consisting of only one term. Examples of monomials are: 17, 2*x*, and $-5ab^2$. A binomial is an expression consisting of two terms separated by addition or subtraction. Examples include $2x - 4$ and $-3y^2 + 2y$. A trinomial consists of 3 terms. For example, $5x^2 - 2x + 1$ is a trinomial.

Verbal Statements and Algebraic Expressions

An algebraic expression is a statement about unknown quantities expressed in mathematical symbols. The statement *five times a number added to forty* is expressed as $5x + 40$. An equation is a statement in which two expressions (with at least one containing a variable) are equal to one another. The statement *five times a number added to forty is equal to ten* is expressed as $5x + 40 = 10$.

Real world scenarios can also be expressed mathematically. Suppose a job pays its employees $300 per week and $40 for each sale made. The weekly pay is represented by the expression $40x + 300$ where *x* is the number of sales made during the week.

Consider the following scenario: Bob had $20 and Tom had $4. After selling 4 ice cream cones to Bob, Tom has as much money as Bob. The cost of an ice cream cone is an unknown quantity and can be represented by a variable (*x*). The amount of money Bob has after his purchase is four times the cost of an ice cream cone subtracted from his original $\$20 \rightarrow 20 - 4x$. The amount of money Tom has after his sale is four times the cost of an ice cream cone added to his original $\$4 \rightarrow 4x + 4$. After the sale, the amount of money that Bob and Tom have are equal $\rightarrow 20 - 4x = 4x + 4$.

When expressing a verbal or written statement mathematically, it is vital to understand words or phrases that can be represented with symbols. The following are examples:

Symbol	Phrase
+	Added to; increased by; sum of; more than
−	Decreased by; difference between; less than; take away
×	Multiplied by; 3(4,5...) times as large; product of
÷	Divided by; quotient of; half (third, etc.) of
=	Is; the same as; results in; as much as; equal to
x,t,n, etc.	A number; unknown quantity; value of; variable

Use of Formulas

Formulas are mathematical expressions that define the value of one quantity, given the value of one or more different quantities. Formulas look like equations because they contain variables, numbers, operators, and an equal sign. All formulas are equations but not all equations are formulas. A formula must have more than one variable. For example, $2x + 7 = y$ is an equation and a formula (it relates the unknown quantities *x* and *y*). However, $2x + 7 = 3$ is an equation but not a formula (it only expresses the value of the unknown quantity *x*).

Formulas are typically written with one variable alone (or isolated) on one side of the equal sign. This variable can be thought of as the *subject* in that the formula is stating the value of the *subject* in terms of the relationship between the other variables. Consider the distance formula: $distance = rate \times time$ or $d = rt$. The value of the subject variable *d* (distance) is the product of the variable *r* and *t* (rate and time). Given the rate and time, the distance traveled can easily be determined by substituting the values into the formula and evaluating.

The formula $P = 2l + 2w$ expresses how to calculate the perimeter of a rectangle (*P*) given its length (*l*) and width (*w*). To find the perimeter of a rectangle with a length of 3ft and a width of 2ft, these values are substituted into the formula for *l* and *w*: $P = 2(3ft) + 2(2ft)$. Following the order of operations, the perimeter is determined to be 10ft. When working with formulas such as these, including units is an important step.

Given a formula expressed in terms of one variable, the formula can be manipulated to express the relationship in terms of any other variable. In other words, the formula can be rearranged to change which variable is the *subject*. To solve for a variable of interest by manipulating a formula, the equation may be solved as if all other variables were numbers. The same steps for solving are followed, leaving operations in terms of the variables instead of calculating numerical values. For the formula $P = 2l + 2w$, the perimeter is the subject expressed in terms of the length and width. To write a formula to calculate the width of a rectangle, given its length and perimeter, the previous formula relating the three variables is solved for the variable *w*. If *P* and *l* were numerical values, this is a two-step linear equation solved by subtraction and division. To solve the equation $P = 2l + 2w$ for *w*, 2*l* is first subtracted from both sides: $P - 2l = 2w$. Then both sides are divided by 2: $\frac{P-2l}{2} = w$.

Dependent and Independent Variables

A variable represents an unknown quantity and, in the case of a formula, a specific relationship exists between the variables. Within a given scenario, variables are the quantities that are changing. If two variables exist, one is dependent and one is independent. The value of one variable depends on the other variable. If a scenario describes distance traveled and time traveled at a given speed, distance is dependent and time is independent. The distance traveled depends on the time spent traveling. If a scenario describes the cost of a cab ride and the distance traveled, the cost is dependent and the distance is independent. The cost of a cab ride depends on the distance travelled. Formulas often contain more than two variables and are typically written with the dependent variable alone on one side of the equation. This lone variable is the *subject* of the statement. If a formula contains three or more variables, one variable is dependent and the rest are independent. The values of all independent variables are needed to determine the value of the dependent variable.

The formula $P = 2l + 2w$ expresses the dependent variable *P* in terms of the independent variables, *l* and *w*. The perimeter of a rectangle depends on its length and width. The formula $d = rt$ $(distance = rate \times time)$ expresses the dependent variable *d* in terms of the independent variables, *r* and *t*. The distance traveled depends on the rate (or speed) and the time traveled.

Multistep One-Variable Linear Equations and Inequalities

Linear equations and linear inequalities are both comparisons of two algebraic expressions. However, unlike equations in which the expressions are equal, linear inequalities compare expressions that may be unequal. Linear equations typically have one value for the variable that makes the statement true. Linear inequalities generally have an infinite number of values that make the statement true.

When solving a linear equation, the desired result requires determining a numerical value for the unknown variable. If given a linear equation involving addition, subtraction, multiplication, or division, working backwards isolates the variable. Addition and subtraction are inverse operations, as are multiplication and division. Therefore, they can be used to cancel each other out.

The first steps to solving linear equations are distributing, if necessary, and combining any like terms on the same side of the equation. Sides of an equation are separated by an *equal* sign. Next, the equation is manipulated to show the variable on one side. Whatever is done to one side of the equation must be done to the other side of the equation to remain equal. Inverse operations are then used to isolate the variable and undo the order of operations backwards. Addition and subtraction are undone, then multiplication and division are undone.

For example, solve $4(t - 2) + 2t - 4 = 2(9 - 2t)$

Distributing: $4t - 8 + 2t - 4 = 18 - 4t$

Combining like terms: $6t - 12 = 18 - 4t$

Adding $4t$ to each side to move the variable: $10t - 12 = 18$

Adding 12 to each side to isolate the variable: $10t = 30$

Dividing each side by 10 to isolate the variable: $t = 3$

The answer can be checked by substituting the value for the variable into the original equation, ensuring that both sides calculate to be equal.

Linear inequalities express the relationship between unequal values. More specifically, they describe in what way the values are unequal. A value can be greater than (>), less than (<), greater than or equal to (≥), or less than or equal to (≤) another value. $5x + 40 > 65$ is read as *five times a number added to forty is greater than sixty-five.*

When solving a linear inequality, the solution is the set of all numbers that make the statement true. The inequality $x + 2 \geq 6$ has a solution set of 4 and every number greater than 4 (4.01; 5; 12; 107; etc.). Adding 2 to 4 or any number greater than 4 results in a value that is greater than or equal to 6. Therefore, $x \geq 4$ is the solution set.

To algebraically solve a linear inequality, follow the same steps as those for solving a linear equation. The inequality symbol stays the same for all operations *except* when multiplying or dividing by a negative number. If multiplying or dividing by a negative number while solving an inequality, the relationship reverses (the sign flips). In other words, > switches to < and vice versa. Multiplying or dividing by a positive number does not change the relationship, so the sign stays the same. An example is shown below.

Solve $-2x - 8 \leq 22$

Add 8 to both sides: $-2x \leq 30$

Divide both sides by -2: $x \geq -15$

Solutions of a linear equation or a linear inequality are the values of the variable that make a statement true. In the case of a linear equation, the solution set (list of all possible solutions) typically consists of a single numerical value. To find the solution, the equation is solved by isolating the variable. For example, solving the equation $3x - 7 = -13$ produces the solution $x = -2$. The only value for *x* which produces a true statement is -2. This can be checked by substituting -2 into the original equation to check that both sides are equal. In this case, $3(-2) - 7 = -13 \rightarrow -13 = -13$; therefore, -2 is a solution.

Although linear equations generally have one solution, this is not always the case. If there is no value for the variable that makes the statement true, there is no solution to the equation. Consider the equation $x + 3 = x - 1$. There is no value for *x* in which adding 3 to the value produces the same result as subtracting one from the value. Conversely, if any value for the variable makes a true statement, the equation has an infinite number of solutions. Consider the equation $3x + 6 = 3(x + 2)$. Any number substituted for *x* will result in a true statement (both sides of the equation are equal).

By manipulating equations like the two above, the variable of the equation will cancel out completely. If the remaining constants express a true statement (ex. $6 = 6$), then all real numbers are solutions to the equation. If the constants left express a false statement (ex. $3 = -1$), then no solution exists for the equation.

Solving a linear inequality requires all values that make the statement true to be determined. For example, solving $3x - 7 \geq -13$ produces the solution $x \geq -2$. This means that -2 and any number greater than -2 produces a true statement. Solution sets for linear inequalities will often be displayed using a number line. If a value is included in the set (≥ or ≤), a shaded dot is placed on that value and an arrow extending in the direction of the solutions. For a variable > or ≥ a number, the arrow will point right on a number line, the direction where the numbers increase. If a variable is < or ≤ a number, the arrow will point left on a number line, which is the direction where the numbers decrease. If the value is not included in the set (> or <), an open (unshaded) circle on that value is used with an arrow in the appropriate direction.

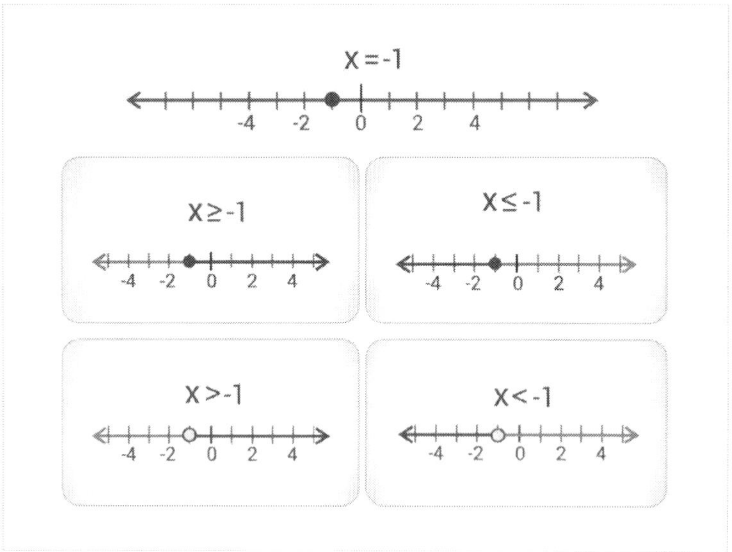

Similar to linear equations, a linear inequality may have a solution set consisting of all real numbers, or can contain no solution. When solved algebraically, a linear inequality in which the variable cancels out and results in a true statement (ex. $7 \geq 2$) has a solution set of all real numbers. A linear inequality in which the variable cancels out and results in a false statement (ex. $7 \leq 2$) has no solution.

Linear Relationships

Linear relationships describe the way two quantities change with respect to each other. The relationship is defined as linear because a line is produced if all the sets of corresponding values are graphed on a coordinate grid. When expressing the linear relationship as an equation, the equation is often written in the form $y = mx + b$ (slope-intercept form) where *m* and *b* are numerical values and *x* and *y* are variables (for example, $y = 5x + 10$). Given a linear equation and the value of either variable (*x* or *y*), the value of the other variable can be determined.

Suppose a teacher is grading a test containing 20 questions with 5 points given for each correct answer, adding a curve of 10 points to each test. This linear relationship can be expressed as the equation $y = 5x + 10$ where *x* represents the number of correct answers and *y* represents the test score. To determine the score of a test with a given number of correct answers, the number of correct answers is substituted into the equation for *x* and evaluated. For example, for 10 correct answers, 10 is substituted for *x*: $y = 5(10) + 10 \rightarrow y = 60$. Therefore, 10 correct answers will result in a score of 60. The number of correct answers needed to obtain a certain score can also be determined. To determine the number of correct answers needed to score a 90, 90 is substituted for *y* in the equation (*y* represents the test score) and solved: $90 = 5x + 10 \rightarrow 80 = 5x \rightarrow 16 = x$. Therefore, 16 correct answers are needed to score a 90.

Linear relationships may be represented by a table of 2 corresponding values. Certain tables may determine the relationship between the values and predict other corresponding sets. Consider the table below, which displays the money in a checking account that charges a monthly fee:

Month	0	1	2	3	4
Balance	$210	$195	$180	$165	$150

An examination of the values reveals that the account loses $15 every month (the month increases by one and the balance decreases by 15). This information can be used to predict future values. To determine what the value will be in month 6, the pattern can be continued, and it can be concluded that the balance will be $120. To determine which month the balance will be $0, $210 is divided by $15 (since the balance decreases $15 every month), resulting in month 14.

Similar to a table, a graph can display corresponding values of a linear relationship.

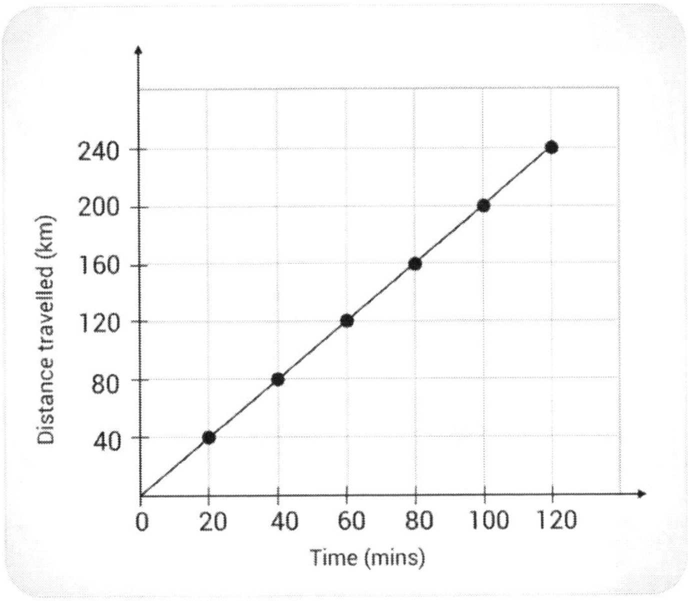

The graph above represents the relationship between distance traveled and time. To find the distance traveled in 90 minutes, the mark for 90 minutes is located at the bottom of the graph. By following this mark directly up on the graph, the corresponding point for 90 minutes is directly across from the 150 kilometer mark. This information indicates that the distance travelled in 90 minutes is 150 kilometers. To predict information not displayed on the graph, the way in which the variables change with respect to one another is determined. In this case, distance increases by 50 kilometers as time increases by 30 minutes. This information can be used to continue the data in the graph or convert the values to a table.

Number and Shape Patterns

Patterns within a sequence can come in 2 distinct forms: the items (shapes, numbers, etc.) either repeat in a constant order, or the items change from one step to another in some consistent way. The core is the smallest unit, or number of items, that repeats in a repeating pattern. For example, the pattern oo▲oo▲o… has a core that is oo▲. Knowing only the core, the pattern can be extended. Knowing the number of steps in the core allows the identification of an item in each step without drawing/writing the entire pattern out. For example, suppose the tenth item in the previous pattern must be determined.

Because the core consists of three items (○○▲), the core repeats in multiples of 3. In other words, steps 3, 6, 9, 12, etc. will be ▲ completing the core with the core starting over on the next step. For the above example, the 9th step will be ▲ and the 10th will be ○.

The most common patterns in which each item changes from one step to the next are arithmetic and geometric sequences. An arithmetic sequence is one in which the items increase or decrease by a constant difference. In other words, the same thing is added or subtracted to each item or step to produce the next. To determine if a sequence is arithmetic, determine what must be added or subtracted to step one to produce step two. Then, check if the same thing is added/subtracted to step two to produce step three. The same thing must be added/subtracted to step three to produce step four, and so on. Consider the pattern 13, 10, 7, 4 . . . To get from step one (13) to step two (10) by adding or subtracting requires subtracting by 3. The next step is checking if subtracting 3 from step two (10) will produce step three (7), and subtracting 3 from step three (7) will produce step four (4). In this case, the pattern holds true. Therefore, this is an arithmetic sequence in which each step is produced by subtracting 3 from the previous step. To extend the sequence, 3 is subtracted from the last step to produce the next. The next three numbers in the sequence are 1, -2, -5.

A geometric sequence is one in which each step is produced by multiplying or dividing the previous step by the same number. To determine if a sequence is geometric, decide what step one must be multiplied or divided by to produce step two. Then check if multiplying or dividing step two by the same number produces step three, and so on. Consider the pattern 2, 8, 32, 128 . . . To get from step one (2) to step two (8) requires multiplication by 4. The next step determines if multiplying step two (8) by 4 produces step three (32), and multiplying step three (32) by 4 produces step four (128). In this case, the pattern holds true. Therefore, this is a geometric sequence in which each step is produced by multiplying the previous step by 4. To extend the sequence, the last step is multiplied by 4 and repeated. The next three numbers in the sequence are 512; 2,048; 8,192.

Although arithmetic and geometric sequences typically use numbers, these sequences can also be represented by shapes. For example, an arithmetic sequence could consist of shapes with three sides, four sides, and five sides (add one side to the previous step to produce the next). A geometric sequence could consist of eight blocks, four blocks, and two blocks (each step is produced by dividing the number of blocks in the previous step by 2).

Conjectures, Predictions, or Generalizations Based on Patterns

An arithmetic or geometric sequence can be written as a formula and used to determine unknown steps without writing out the entire sequence. (Note that a similar process for repeating patterns is covered in the previous section.) An arithmetic sequence progresses by a *common difference*. To determine the common difference, any step is subtracted by the step that precedes it. In the sequence 4, 9, 14, 19 . . . the common difference, or *d*, is 5. By expressing each step as a_1, a_2, a_3, etc., a formula can be written to represent the sequence. a_1 is the first step. To produce step two, step 1 (a_1) is added to the common difference (*d*): $a_2 = a_1 + d$. To produce step three, the common difference (*d*) is added twice to a_1: $a_3 = a_1 + 2d$. To produce step four, the common difference (*d*) is added three times to a_1: $a_4 = a_1 + 3d$. Following this pattern allows a general rule for arithmetic sequences to be written. For any term of the sequence (a_n), the first step (a_1) is added to the product of the common difference (*d*) and one less than the step of the term ($n - 1$): $a_n = a_1 + (n - 1)d$. Suppose the 8th term (a_8) is to be found in the previous sequence. By knowing the first step (a_1) is 4 and the common difference (*d*) is 5, the formula can be used: $a_n = a_1 + (n - 1)d \rightarrow a_8 = 4 + (7)5 \rightarrow a_8 = 39$.

In a geometric sequence, each step is produced by multiplying or dividing the previous step by the same number. The *common ratio*, or (*r*), can be determined by dividing any step by the previous step. In the sequence 1, 3, 9, 27 . . . the common ratio (*r*) is 3($\frac{3}{1} = 3$ or $\frac{9}{3} = 3$ or $\frac{27}{9} = 3$). Each successive step can be expressed as a product of the first step (a_1) and the common ratio (*r*) to some power. For example, $a_2 = a_1 \times r; a_3 = a_1 \times r \times r$ or $a_3 = a_1 \times r^2; a_4 = a_1 \times r \times r \times r$ or $a_4 = a\_1 \times r^3$. Following this pattern, a general rule for geometric sequences can be written. For any term of the sequence (a_n), the first step (a_1) is multiplied by the common ratio (*r*) raised to the power one less than the step of the term ($n - 1$): $a_n = a_1 \times r^{(n-1)}$. Suppose for the previous sequence, the 7th term (a_7) is to be found. Knowing the first step (a_1) is one, and the common ratio (*r*) is 3, the formula can be used: $a_n = a_1 \times r^{(n-1)} \rightarrow a_7 = (1) \times 3^6 \rightarrow a_7 = 729$.

Corresponding Terms of Two Numerical Patterns

When given two numerical patterns, the corresponding terms should be examined to determine if a relationship exists between them. Corresponding terms between patterns are the pairs of numbers that appear in the same step of the two sequences. Consider the following patterns 1, 2, 3, 4 . . . and 3, 6, 9, 12 . . . The corresponding terms are: 1 and 3; 2 and 6; 3 and 9; and 4 and 12. To identify the relationship, each pair of corresponding terms is examined and the possibilities of performing an operation (+, −, ×, ÷) to the term from the first sequence to produce the corresponding term in the second sequence are determined. In this case:

$1 + 2 = 3$ or $1 \times 3 = 3$

$2 + 4 = 6$ or $2 \times 3 = 6$

$3 + 6 = 9$ or $3 \times 3 = 9$

$4 + 8 = 12$ or $4 \times 3 = 12$

The consistent pattern is that the number from the first sequence multiplied by 3 equals its corresponding term in the second sequence. By assigning each sequence a label (input and output) or variable (*x* and *y*), the relationship can be written as an equation. If the first sequence represents the inputs, or *x*, and the second sequence represents the outputs, or *y*, the relationship can be expressed as: $y = 3x$.

Consider the following sets of numbers:

a	2	4	6	8
b	6	8	10	12

To write a rule for the relationship between the values for *a* and the values for *b*, the corresponding terms (2 and 6; 4 and 8; 6 and 10; 8 and 12) are examined. The possibilities for producing *b* from *a* are:

$2 + 4 = 6$ or $2 \times 3 = 6$

$4 + 4 = 8$ or $4 \times 2 = 8$

$6 + 4 = 10$

$8 + 4 = 12$ or $8 \times 1.5 = 12$

The consistent pattern is that adding 4 to the value of a produces the value of b. The relationship can be written as the equation $a + 4 = b$.

Fractions, Ratios, and Integers

Strategies and Algorithms to Perform Operations on Rational Numbers

A rational number is any number that can be written in the form of a ratio or fraction. Integers can be written as fractions with a denominator of 1 ($5 = \frac{5}{1}$; $-342 = \frac{-342}{1}$; etc.). Decimals that terminate and/or repeat can also be written as fractions ($47 = \frac{47}{100}$; $.\overline{33} = \frac{1}{3}$). For more on converting decimals to fractions, see the section *Converting Between Fractions, Decimals,* and *Percent*.

When adding or subtracting fractions, the numbers must have the same denominators. In these cases, numerators are added or subtracted and denominators are kept the same. For example, $\frac{2}{7} + \frac{3}{7} = \frac{5}{7}$ and $\frac{4}{5} - \frac{3}{5} = \frac{1}{5}$. If the fractions to be added or subtracted do not have the same denominator, a common denominator must be found. This is accomplished by changing one or both fractions to a different but equivalent fraction. Consider the example $\frac{1}{6} + \frac{4}{9}$. First, a common denominator must be found. One method is to find the least common multiple (LCM) of the denominators 6 and 9. This is the lowest number that both 6 and 9 will divide into evenly. In this case the LCM is 18. Both fractions should be changed to equivalent fractions with a denominator of 18. To obtain the numerator of the new fraction, the old numerator is multiplied by the same number by which the old denominator is multiplied. For the fraction $\frac{1}{6}$, 6 multiplied by 3 will produce a denominator of 18. Therefore, the numerator is multiplied by 3 to produce the new numerator $\left(\frac{1\times3}{6\times3} = \frac{3}{18}\right)$. For the fraction $\frac{4}{9}$, multiplying both the numerator and denominator by 2 produces $\frac{8}{18}$. Since the two new fractions have common denominators, they can be added $\left(\frac{3}{18} + \frac{8}{18} = \frac{11}{18}\right)$.

When multiplying or dividing rational numbers, these numbers may be converted to fractions and multiplied or divided accordingly. When multiplying fractions, all numerators are multiplied by each other and all denominators are multiplied by each other. For example, $\frac{1}{3} \times \frac{6}{5} = \frac{1\times6}{3\times5} = \frac{6}{15}$ and $\frac{-1}{2} \times \frac{3}{1} \times \frac{11}{100} = \frac{-1\times3\times11}{2\times1\times100} = \frac{-33}{200}$. When dividing fractions, the problem is converted by multiplying by the reciprocal of the divisor. This is done by changing division to multiplication and "flipping" the second fraction, or divisor. For example, $\frac{1}{2} \div \frac{3}{5} \rightarrow \frac{1}{2} \times \frac{5}{3}$ and $\frac{5}{1} \div \frac{1}{3} \rightarrow \frac{5}{1} \times \frac{3}{1}$. To complete the problem, the rules for multiplying fractions should be followed.

Note that when adding, subtracting, multiplying, and dividing mixed numbers (ex. $4\frac{1}{2}$), it is easiest to convert these to improper fractions (larger numerator than denominator). To do so, the denominator is kept the same. To obtain the numerator, the whole number is multiplied by the denominator and added to the numerator. For example, $4\frac{1}{2} = \frac{9}{2}$ and $7\frac{2}{3} = \frac{23}{3}$. Also, note that answers involving fractions should be converted to the simplest form.

Rational Numbers and Their Operations

Irregular Products and Quotients

The following shows examples where multiplication does not result in a product greater than both factors, and where division does not result in a quotient smaller than the dividend.

If multiplying numbers where one or more has a value less than one, the product will not be greater than both factors. For example, $6 \times \frac{1}{2} = 3$ and $0.75 \times 0.2 = .15$. When dividing by a number less than one, the resulting quotient will be greater than the dividend. For example, $8 \div \frac{1}{2} = 16$, because division turns into a multiplication problem, $8 \div \frac{1}{2} \rightarrow 8 \times \frac{2}{1}$. Another example is $0.5 \div 0.2$, which results in 2.5. The problem can be stated by asking how many times 0.2 will go into 0.5. The number being divided is larger than the number that goes into it, so the result will be a number larger than both factors.

Composing and Decomposing Fractions

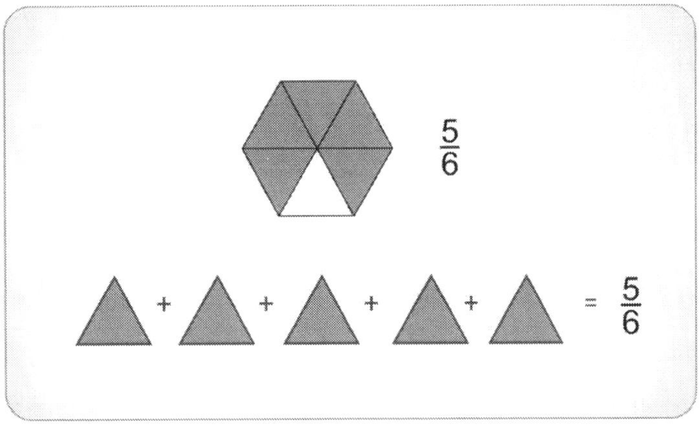

Fractions can be broken apart into sums of fractions with the same denominator. For example, the fraction $\frac{5}{6}$ can be decomposed into sums of fractions with all denominators equal to 6 and the numerators adding to 5. The fraction $\frac{5}{6}$ is decomposed as: $\frac{3}{6} + \frac{2}{6}$; or $\frac{2}{6} + \frac{2}{6} + \frac{1}{6}$; or $\frac{3}{6} + \frac{1}{6} + \frac{1}{6}$; or $\frac{1}{6} + \frac{1}{6} + \frac{1}{6} + \frac{2}{6}$; or $\frac{1}{6} + \frac{1}{6} + \frac{1}{6} + \frac{1}{6} + \frac{1}{6}$.

A unit fraction is a fraction in which the numerator is 1. If decomposing a fraction into unit fractions, the sum will consist of a unit fraction added the number of times equal to the numerator. For example, $\frac{3}{4} = \frac{1}{4} + \frac{1}{4} + \frac{1}{4}$ (unit fractions $\frac{1}{4}$ added 3 times). Composing fractions is simply the opposite of decomposing. It is the process of adding fractions with the same denominators to produce a single fraction. For example, $\frac{3}{7} + \frac{2}{7} = \frac{5}{7}$ and $\frac{1}{5} + \frac{1}{5} + \frac{1}{5} = \frac{3}{5}$.

Decrease in Value of a Unit Fraction

A unit fraction is one in which the numerator is 1 ($\frac{1}{2}, \frac{1}{3}, \frac{1}{8}, \frac{1}{20}$, etc.). The denominator indicates the number of *equal pieces* that the whole is divided into. The greater the number of pieces, the smaller each piece will be. Therefore, the greater the denominator of a unit fraction, the smaller it is in value. Unit fractions can also be compared by converting them to decimals. For example, $\frac{1}{2}$ = 0.5, $\frac{1}{3}$ = $0.\overline{3}$, $\frac{1}{8}$ = 0.125, $\frac{1}{20} = 0.05$, etc.

Use of the Same Whole when Comparing Fractions

Fractions all represent parts of the same whole. Fractions may have different denominators, but they represent parts of the same one whole, like a pizza. For example, the fractions $\frac{5}{7}$ and $\frac{2}{3}$ can be difficult to compare because they have different denominators. The first fraction may represent a whole divided into seven parts, where five parts are used. The second fraction represents the same whole divided into three parts, where two are used. It may be helpful to convert one or more of the fractions so that they have common denominators for converting to equivalent fractions by finding the LCM of the denominator. Comparing is much easier if fractions are converted to the equivalent fractions of $\frac{30}{42}$ and $\frac{28}{42}$. These fractions show a whole divided into 42 parts, where the numerators can be compared because the denominators are the same.

Order of Operations

When reviewing calculations consisting of more than one operation, the order in which the operations are performed affects the resulting answer. Consider $5 \times 2 + 7$. Performing multiplication then addition results in an answer of 17 ($5 \times 2 = 10; 10 + 7 = 17$). However, if the problem is written $5 \times (2 + 7)$, the order of operations dictates that the operation inside the parenthesis must be performed first. The resulting answer is 45 ($2 + 7 = 9$, then $5 \times 9 = 45$).

The order in which operations should be performed is remembered using the acronym PEMDAS. PEMDAS stands for parenthesis, exponents, multiplication/division, and addition/subtraction. Multiplication and division are performed in the same step, working from left to right with whichever comes first. Addition and subtraction are performed in the same step, working from left to right with whichever comes first.

Consider the following example: $8 \div 4 + 8(7 - 7)$. Performing the operation inside the parenthesis produces $8 \div 4 + 8(0)$ or $8 \div 4 + 8 \times 0$. There are no exponents, so multiplication and division are performed next from left to right resulting in: $2 + 8 \times 0$, then $2 + 0$. Finally, addition and subtraction are performed to obtain an answer of 2. Now consider the following example: $6x3 + 3^2 - 6$. Parentheses are not applicable. Exponents are evaluated first, $6 \times 3 + 9 - 6$. Then multiplication/division forms $18 + 9 - 6$. At last, addition/subtraction leads to the final answer of 21.

Properties of Operations

Properties of operations exist that make calculations easier and solve problems for missing values. The following table summarizes commonly used properties of real numbers.

Property	**Addition**	**Multiplication**
Commutative	$a + b = b + a$	$a \times b = b \times a$
Associative	$(a + b) + c = a + (b + c)$	$(a \times b) \times c = a \times (bc)$
Identity	$a + 0 = a; 0 + a = a$	$a \times 1 = a; 1 \times a = a$
Inverse	$a + (-a) = 0$	$a \times \frac{1}{a} = 1; a \neq 0$
Distributive	$a(b + c) = ab + ac$	

The cumulative property of addition states that the order in which numbers are added does not change the sum. Similarly, the commutative property of multiplication states that the order in which numbers are multiplied does not change the product. The associative property of addition and multiplication state that the grouping of numbers being added or multiplied does not change the sum or product, respectively. The commutative and associative properties are useful for performing calculations. For example, $(47 + 25) + 3$ is equivalent to $(47 + 3) + 25$, which is easier to calculate.

The identity property of addition states that adding zero to any number does not change its value. The identity property of multiplication states that multiplying a number by one does not change its value. The inverse property of addition states that the sum of a number and its opposite equals zero. Opposites are numbers that are the same with different signs (ex. 5 and -5; $-\frac{1}{2}$ and $\frac{1}{2}$). The inverse property of multiplication states that the product of a number (other than zero) and its reciprocal equals one. Reciprocal numbers have numerators and denominators that are inverted (ex. $\frac{2}{5}$ and $\frac{5}{2}$). Inverse properties are useful for canceling quantities to find missing values (see algebra content). For example, $a + 7 = 12$ is solved by adding the inverse of 7(-7) to both sides in order to isolate a.

The distributive property states that multiplying a sum (or difference) by a number produces the same result as multiplying each value in the sum (or difference) by the number and adding (or subtracting) the products. Consider the following scenario: You are buying three tickets for a baseball game. Each ticket costs $18. You are also charged a fee of $2 per ticket for purchasing the tickets online. The cost is calculated: $3 \times 18 + 3 \times 2$. Using the distributive property, the cost can also be calculated $3(18 + 2)$.

Representing Rational Numbers and Their Operations

<u>Concrete Models</u>

Concrete objects are used to develop a tangible understanding of operations of rational numbers. Tools such as tiles, blocks, beads, and hundred charts are used to model problems. For example, a hundred chart (10×10) and beads can be used to model multiplication. If multiplying 5 by 4, beads are placed across 5 rows and down 4 columns producing a product of 20. Similarly, tiles can be used to model division by splitting the total into equal groups. If dividing 12 by 4, 12 tiles are placed one at a time into 4 groups. The result is 4 groups of 3. This is also an effective method for visualizing the concept of remainders.

Representations of objects can be used to expand on the concrete models of operations. Pictures, dots, and tallies can help model these concepts. Utilizing concrete models and representations creates a foundation upon which to build an abstract understanding of the operations.

<u>Rational Numbers on a Number Line</u>

A number line typically consists of integers (...3,2,1,0,-1,-2,-3...), and is used to visually represent the value of a rational number. Each rational number has a distinct position on the line determined by comparing its value with the displayed values on the line. For example, if plotting -1.5 on the number line below, it is necessary to recognize that the value of -1.5 is .5 less than -1 and .5 greater than -2. Therefore, -1.5 is plotted halfway between -1 and -2.

Number lines can also be useful for visualizing sums and differences of rational numbers. Adding a value indicates moving to the right (values increase to the right), and subtracting a value indicates moving to the left (numbers decrease to the left). For example, $5 - 7$ is displayed by starting at 5 and moving to the left 7 spaces, if the number line is in increments of 1. This will result in an answer of -2.

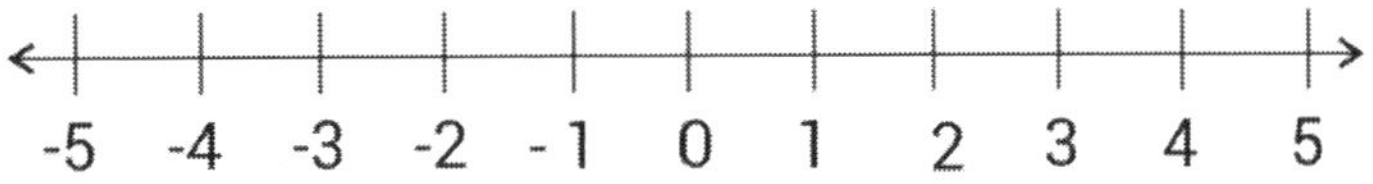

Multiplication and Division Problems

Multiplication and division are inverse operations that can be represented by using rectangular arrays, area models, and equations. Rectangular arrays include an arrangement of rows and columns that correspond to the factors and display product totals.

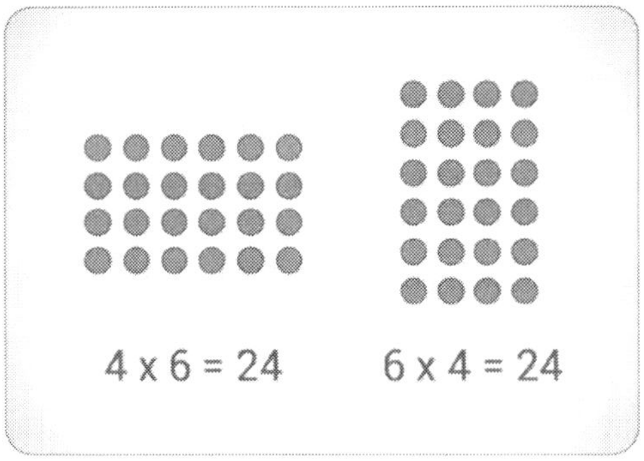

Another method of multiplication can be done with the use of an *area model*. An area model is a rectangle that is divided into rows and columns that match up to the number of place values within each number. For example, $29 \times 65 = 25 + 4$ and $66 = 60 + 5$. The products of those 4 numbers are found within the rectangle and then summed up to get the answer. The entire process is: $(60 \times 25) + (5 \times 25) + (60 \times 4) + (5 \times 4) = 1{,}500 + 240 + 125 + 20 = 1{,}885$.

Here is the actual area model:

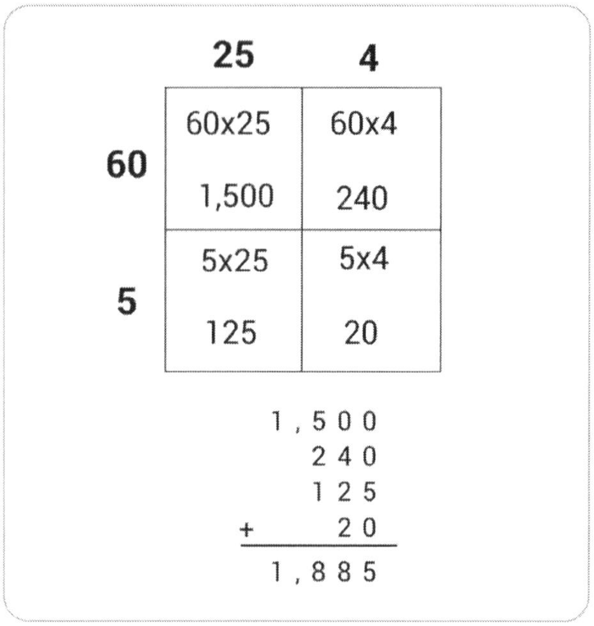

Dividing a number by a single digit or two digits can be turned into repeated subtraction problems. An area model can be used throughout the problem that represents multiples of the divisor. For example, the answer to $8580 \div 55$ can be found by subtracting 55 from 8580 one at a time and counting the total number of subtractions necessary.

However, a simpler process involves using larger multiples of 55. First, $100 \times 55 = 5{,}500$ is subtracted from 8,580, and 3,080 is leftover. Next, $50 \times 55 = 2{,}750$ is subtracted from 3,080 to obtain380.

$5 \times 55 = 275$ is subtracted from 330 to obtain 55, and finally, $1 \times 55 = 55$ is subtracted from 55 to obtain zero. Therefore, there is no remainder, and the answer is $100 + 50 + 5 + 1 = 156$.

Here is a picture of the area model and the repeated subtraction process:

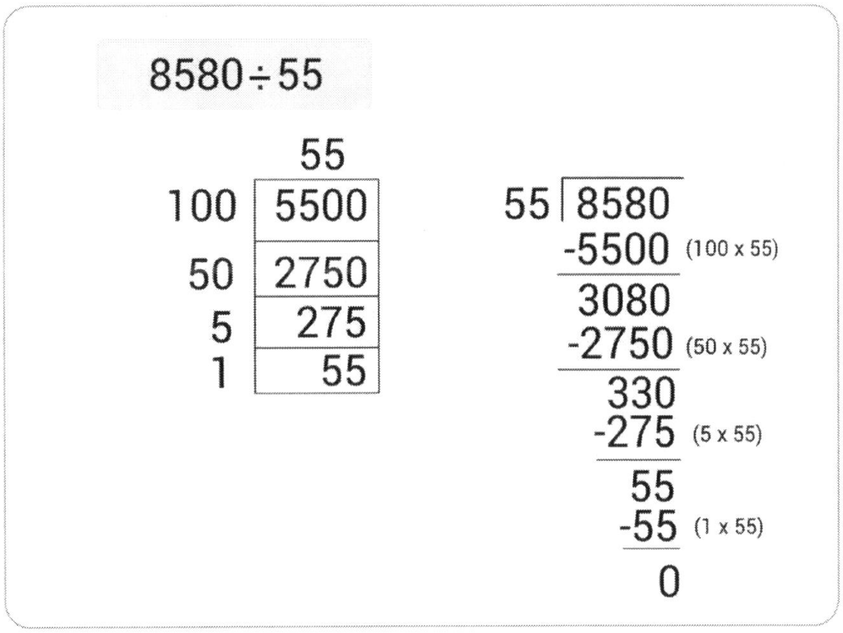

Comparing, Classifying, and Ordering Rational Numbers

Rational numbers are any number that can be written as a fraction or ratio. Within the set of rational numbers, several subsets exist that are referenced throughout the mathematics topics. Counting numbers are the first numbers learned as a child. Counting numbers consist of 1,2,3,4, and so on. Whole numbers include all counting numbers and zero (0,1,2,3,4,...). Integers include counting numbers, their opposites, and zero (...,-3,-2,-1,0,1,2,3,...). Rational numbers are inclusive of integers, fractions, and decimals that terminate, or end (1.7, 0.04213) or repeat ($0.136\overline{5}$).

When comparing or ordering numbers, the numbers should be written in the same format (decimal or fraction), if possible. For example, $\sqrt{49}$, 7.3, and $\frac{15}{2}$ are easier to order if each one is converted to a decimal, such as 7, 7.3, and 7.5 (converting fractions and decimals is covered in the following section). A number line is used to order and compare the numbers. Any number that is to the right of another number is greater than that number. Conversely, a number positioned to the left of a given number is less than that number.

Converting Between Fractions, Decimals, and Percent

To convert a fraction to a decimal, the numerator is divided by the denominator. For example, $\frac{3}{8}$ can be converted to a decimal by dividing 3 by 8 ($\frac{3}{8} = 0.375$). To convert a decimal to a fraction, the decimal point is dropped and the value is written as the numerator. The denominator is the place value farthest to the right with a digit other than zero. For example, to convert .48 to a fraction, the numerator is 48 and the denominator is 100 (the digit 8 is in the hundredths place). Therefore, .48 = $\frac{48}{100}$. Fractions should be written in the simplest form, or reduced. To reduce a fraction, the numerator and denominator are divided by the largest common factor. In the previous example, 48 and 100 are both divisible by 4. Dividing the numerator and denominator by 4 results in a reduced fraction of $\frac{12}{25}$.

To convert a decimal to a percent, the number is multiplied by 100. To convert .13 to a percent, .13 is multiplied by 100 to get 13 percent. To convert a fraction to a percent, the fraction is converted to a decimal and then multiplied by 100. For example, $\frac{1}{5}$ = .20 and .20 multiplied by 100 produces 20 percent.

To convert a percent to a decimal, the value is divided by 100. For example, 125 percent is equal to 1.25 ($\frac{125}{100}$). To convert a percent to a fraction, the percent sign is dropped and the value is written as the numerator with a denominator of 100. For example, 80% = $\frac{80}{100}$. This fraction can be reduced ($\frac{80}{100} = \frac{4}{5}$).

Understanding Proportional Relationships and Percent

Applying Ratios and Unit Rates

A ratio is a comparison of two quantities that represent separate groups. For example, if a recipe calls for 2 eggs for every 3 cups of milk, this is expressed as a ratio. Ratios can be written three ways:

- With the word "to"
- Using a colon
- As a fraction.

In the previous example, the ratio of eggs to cups of milk is written as 2 to 3, 2:3, or $\frac{2}{3}$. When writing ratios, the order is very important. The ratio of eggs to cups of milk is not the same as the ratio of cups of milk to eggs, 3:2.

In simplest form, both quantities of a ratio should be written as integers. These should also be reduced just as a fraction is reduced. For example, 5:10 is reduced to 1:2. Given a ratio where one or both quantities are expressed as a decimal or fraction, multiply both by the same number to produce integers. To write the ratio $\frac{1}{3}$ to 2 in simplest form, both quantities are multiplied by 3. The resulting ratio is 1 to 6.

A problem involving ratios may give a comparison between two groups. The problem may then provide a total and ask for a part, or provide a part and ask for a total. Consider the following: The ratio of boys to girls in the 11th grade class is 5:4. If there are a total of 270 11th grade students, how many are girls? The total number of *ratio pieces* should be determined first. The total number of 11th grade students is divided into 9 pieces. The ratio of boys to total students is 5:9, and the ratio of girls to total students is 4:9. Knowing the total number of students, the number of girls is determined by setting up a proportion: $\frac{4}{9} = \frac{x}{270}$.

A rate is a ratio comparing two quantities expressed in different units. A unit rate is a ratio in which the second quantity is one unit. Rates often include the word *per*. Examples include miles per hour, beats per minute, and price per pound. The word per is represented with a / symbol or abbreviated with the letter *p* and units abbreviated. For example, miles per hour is written as mi/h. When given a rate that is not in its simplest form (the second quantity is not one unit), both quantities are divided by the value of the second quantity. If 99 heartbeats were recorded in $1\frac{1}{2}$ minutes, both quantities are divided by $1\frac{1}{2}$ to determine the heart rate of 66 beats per minute.

Percent

The word percent means per hundred. Similar to a unit rate in which the second quantity is always one unit, a percent is a rate where the second quantity is always 100 units. If the results of a poll state that 47 percent of people support a given policy, this indicates that 47 out of every 100 individuals polled were in support. In other words, 47 per 100 support the policy. If an upgraded model of a car costs 110 percent of the cost of the base model, for every $100 that is spent for the base model, $110 must be spent to purchase the upgraded model. In other words, the upgraded model costs $110 per $100 for the cost of the base model.

When dealing with percentages, the numbers can be evaluated as a value in hundredths. For example, 15 percent is expressed as fifteen hundredths and is written as $\frac{15}{100}$ or 0.15.

Unit-Rate Problems

A rate is a ratio in which two terms are in different units. When rates are expressed as a quantity of one, they are considered unit rates. To determine a unit rate, the first quantity is divided by the second. Knowing a unit rate makes calculations easier than simply having a rate. For example, suppose a 3 pound bag of onions costs $1.77. To calculate the price of 5 pounds of onions, a proportion could show: $\frac{3}{1.77} = \frac{5}{x}$. However, by knowing the unit rate, the value of pounds of onions is multiplied by the unit price. The unit price is calculated: $\$1.77/3lb = \$0.59/lb$. Multiplying the weight of the onions by the unit price yields: $5lb \times \frac{\$0.59}{lb} = \$2.95$. The *lb.* units cancel out.

Similar to unit-rate problems, unit conversions appear in real-world scenarios including cooking, measurement, construction, and currency. Given the conversion rate, unit conversions are written as a fraction (ratio) and multiplied by a quantity in one unit to convert it to the corresponding unit. To determine how many minutes are in $3\frac{1}{2}$ hours, the conversion rate of 60 minutes to 1 hour is written as $\frac{60\ min}{1h}$. Multiplying the quantity by the conversion rate results in $3\frac{1}{2}h \times \frac{60\ min}{1h} = 210\ min$. (The *h* unit is canceled.) To convert a quantity in minutes to hours, the fraction for the conversion rate is flipped to cancel the *min* unit. To convert 195 minutes to hours, $195min \times \frac{1h}{60\ min}$ is multiplied. The result is $\frac{195h}{60}$ which reduces to $3\frac{1}{4}$h.

Converting units may require more than one multiplication. The key is to set up conversion rates so that units cancel each other out and the desired unit is left. To convert 3.25 yards to inches, given that 1yd = 3ft and 12in = 1ft, the calculation is performed by multiplying $3.25\text{ yd} \times \frac{3ft}{1yd} \times \frac{12in}{1ft}$. The *yd* and *ft* units will cancel, resulting in 117in.

<u>Using Proportional Relationships</u>

A proportion is a statement consisting of two equal ratios. Proportions will typically give three of four quantities and require solving for the missing value. The key to solving proportions is to set them up properly. Consider the following: 7 gallons of gas costs $14.70. How many gallons can you get for $20? The information is written as equal ratios with a variable representing the missing quantity $\left(\frac{gallons}{cost} = \frac{gallons}{cost}\right)$: $\frac{7}{14.70} = \frac{x}{20}$. To solve for x, the proportion is cross-multiplied. This means the numerator of the first ratio is multiplied by the denominator of the second, and vice versa. The resulting products are shown equal to each other. Cross-multiplying results in $(7)(20) = (14.7)(x)$. By solving the equation for *x* (see the algebra content), the answer is that 9.5 gallons of gas may be purchased for $20.

Percent problems can also be solved by setting up proportions. Examples of common percent problems are:

a. What is 15% of 25?
b. What percent of 45 is 3?
c. 5 is $\frac{1}{2}$% of what number?

Setting up the proper proportion is made easier by following the format: $\frac{is}{of} = \frac{percent}{100}$. A variable is used to represent the missing value. The proportions for each of the three examples are set up as follows:

a. $\frac{x}{25} = \frac{15}{100}$
b. $\frac{3}{45} = \frac{x}{100}$
c. $\frac{5}{x} = \frac{\frac{1}{2}}{100}$

By cross-multiplying and solving the resulting equation for the variable, the missing values are determined to be:

a. 3.75
b. $6.\overline{6}$%
c. 1,000

Basic Concepts of Number Theory

<u>Prime and Composite Numbers</u>
Whole numbers are classified as either prime or composite. A prime number can only be divided evenly by itself and one. For example, the number 11 can only be divided evenly by 11 and one; therefore, 11 is a prime number. A helpful way to visualize a prime number is to use concrete objects and try to divide them into equal piles. If dividing 11 coins, the only way to divide them into equal piles is to create 1 pile of 11 coins or to create 11 piles of 1 coin each. Other examples of prime numbers include 2, 3, 5, 7, 13, 17, and 19.

A composite number is any whole number that is not a prime number. A composite number is a number that can be divided evenly by one or more numbers other than itself and one. For example, the number 6 can be divided evenly by 2 and 3. Therefore, 6 is a composite number. If dividing 6 coins into equal piles, the possibilities are 1 pile of 6 coins, 2 piles of 3 coins, 3 piles of 2 coins, or 6 piles of 1 coin. Other examples of composite numbers include 4, 8, 9, 10, 12, 14, 15, 16, 18, and 20.

To determine if a number is a prime or composite number, the number is divided by every whole number greater than one and less than its own value. If it divides evenly by any of these numbers, then the number is composite. If it does not divide evenly by any of these numbers, then the number is prime. For example, when attempting to divide the number 5 by 2, 3, and 4, none of these numbers divide evenly. Therefore, 5 must be a prime number.

Factors and Multiples of Numbers

The factors of a number are all integers that can be multiplied by another integer to produce the given number. For example, 2 is multiplied by 3 to produce 6. Therefore, 2 and 3 are both factors of 6. Similarly, $1 \times 6 = 6$ and $2 \times 3 = 6$, so one, 2, 3, and 6 are all factors of 6. Another way to explain a factor is to say that a given number divides evenly by each of its factors to produce an integer. For example, 6 does not divide evenly by 5. Therefore, 5 is not a factor of 6.

Multiples of a given number are found by taking that number and multiplying it by any other whole number. For example, 3 is a factor of 6, 9, and 12. Therefore, 6, 9, and 12 are multiples of 3. The multiples of any number are an infinite list. For example, the multiples of 5 are 5, 10, 15, 20, and so on. This list continues without end. A list of multiples is used in finding the least common multiple, or LCM, for fractions when a common denominator is needed. The denominators are written down and their multiples listed until a common number is found in both lists. This common number is the LCM.

Prime factorization breaks down each factor of a whole number until only prime numbers remain. All composite numbers can be factored into prime numbers. For example, the prime factors of 12 are 2, 2, and 3 ($2 \times 2 \times 3 = 12$). To produce the prime factors of a number, the number is factored and any composite numbers are continuously factored until the result is the product of prime factors only. A factor tree, such as the one below, is helpful when exploring this concept.

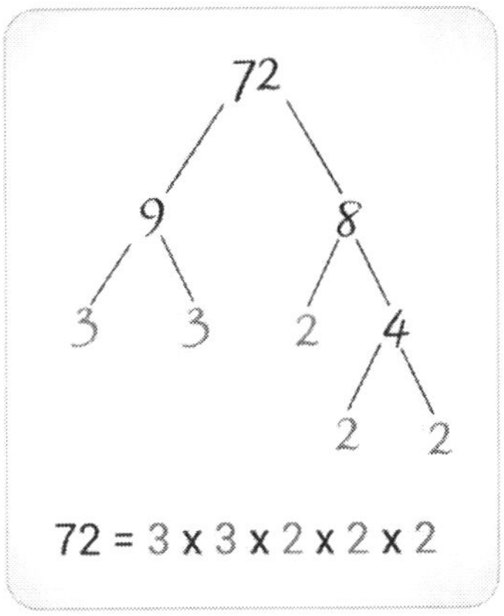

Determining the Reasonableness of Results

When solving math word problems, the solution obtained should make sense within the given scenario. The step of checking the solution will reduce the possibility of a calculation error or a solution that may be *mathematically* correct but not applicable in the real world. Consider the following scenarios:

A problem states that Lisa got 24 out of 32 questions correct on a test and asks to find the percentage of correct answers. To solve the problem, a student divided 32 by 24 to get 1.33, and then multiplied by 100 to get 133 percent. By examining the solution within the context of the problem, the student should recognize that getting all 32 questions correct will produce a perfect score of 100 percent. Therefore, a score of 133 percent with 8 incorrect answers does not make sense and the calculations should be checked.

A problem states that the maximum weight on a bridge cannot exceed 22,000 pounds. The problem asks to find the maximum number of cars that can be on the bridge at one time if each car weighs 4,000 pounds. To solve this problem, a student divided 22,000 by 4,000 to get an answer of 5.5. By examining the solution within the context of the problem, the student should recognize that although the calculations are mathematically correct, the solution does not make sense. Half of a car on a bridge is not possible, so the student should determine that a maximum of 5 cars can be on the bridge at the same time.

Mental Math Estimation

Once a result is determined to be logical within the context of a given problem, the result should be evaluated by its nearness to the expected answer. This is performed by approximating given values to perform mental math. Numbers should be rounded to the nearest value possible to check the initial results.

Consider the following example: A problem states that a customer is buying a new sound system for their home. The customer purchases a stereo for $435, 2 speakers for $67 each, and the necessary cables for $12. The customer chooses an option that allows him to spread the costs over equal payments for 4 months. How much will the monthly payments be?

After making calculations for the problem, a student determines that the monthly payment will be $145.25. To check the accuracy of the results, the student rounds each cost to the nearest ten ($440 + 70 + 70 + 10$) and determines that the total is approximately $590. Dividing by 4 months gives an approximate monthly payment of $147.50. Therefore, the student can conclude that the solution of $145.25 is very close to what should be expected.

When rounding, the place-value that is used in rounding can make a difference. Suppose the student had rounded to the nearest hundred for the estimation. The result ($400 + 100 + 100 + 0 = 600;\ 600 \div 4 = 150$) will show that the answer is reasonable, but not as close to the actual value as rounding to the nearest ten.

Measurement, Data, and Statistics

Elapsed Time, Money, Length, Volume, and Mass

Word problems involving elapsed time, money, length, volume, and mass require determining which operations (addition, subtraction, multiplication, and division) should be performed, and using and/or converting the proper unit for the scenario.

The following table lists key words that can be used to indicate the proper operation:

Addition	Sum, total, in all, combined, increase of, more than, added to
Subtraction	Difference, change, remaining, less than, decreased by
Multiplication	Product, times, twice, triple, each
Division	Quotient, goes into, per, evenly, divided by half, divided by third, split

Identifying and utilizing the proper units for the scenario requires knowing how to apply the conversion rates for money, length, volume, and mass. For example, given a scenario that requires subtracting 8 inches from $2\frac{1}{2}$ feet, both values should first be expressed in the same unit (they could be expressed $\frac{2}{3}$ft & $2\frac{1}{2}$ft, or 8in and 30in). The desired unit for the answer may also require converting back to another unit.

Consider the following scenario: A parking area along the river is only wide enough to fit one row of cars and is $\frac{1}{2}$ kilometers long. The average space needed per car is 5 meters. How many cars can be parked along the river? First, all measurements should be converted to similar units: $\frac{1}{2}$km = 500m. The operation(s) needed should be identified. Because the problem asks for the number of cars, the total space should be divided by the space per car. 500 meters divided by 5 meters per car yields a total of 100 cars. Written as an expression, the meters unit cancels and the cars unit is left: $\frac{500m}{5m/car}$ the same as $500m \times \frac{1\ car}{5m}$ yields 100 cars.

When dealing with problems involving elapsed time, breaking the problem down into workable parts is helpful. For example, suppose the length of time between 1:15pm and 3:45pm must be determined. From 1:15pm to 2:00pm is 45 minutes (knowing there are 60 minutes in an hour). From 2:00pm to 3:00pm is 1 hour. From 3:00pm to 3:45pm is 45 minutes. The total elapsed time is 45 minutes plus 1 hour plus 45 minutes. This sum produces 1 hour and 90 minutes. 90 minutes is over an hour, so this is converted to 1 hour (60 minutes) and 30 minutes. The total elapsed time can now be expressed as 2 hours and 30 minutes.

Measuring Lengths of Objects

The length of an object can be measured using standard tools such as rulers, yard sticks, meter sticks, and measuring tapes. The following image depicts a yardstick:

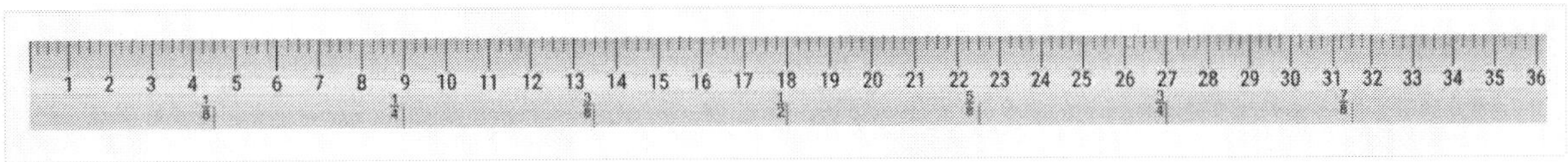

Choosing the right tool to perform the measurement requires determining whether United States customary units or metric units are desired, and having a grasp of the approximate length of each unit and the approximate length of each tool. The measurement can still be performed by trial and error without the knowledge of the approximate size of the tool.

For example, to determine the length of a room in feet, a United States customary unit, various tools can be used for this task. These include a ruler (typically 12 inches/1 foot long), a yardstick (3 feet/1 yard long), or a tape measure displaying feet (typically either 25 feet or 50 feet). Because the length of a room is much larger than the length of a ruler or a yardstick, a tape measure should be used to perform the measurement.

When the correct measuring tool is selected, the measurement is performed by first placing the tool directly above or below the object (if making a horizontal measurement) or directly next to the object (if making a vertical measurement). The next step is aligning the tool so that one end of the object is at the mark for zero units, then recording the unit of the mark at the other end of the object. To give the length of a paperclip in metric units, a ruler displaying centimeters is aligned with one end of the paper clip to the mark for zero centimeters.

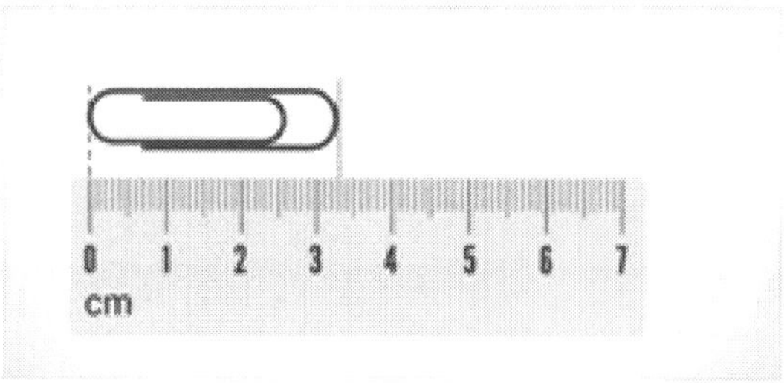

Directly down from the other end of the paperclip is the mark that measures its length. In this case, that mark is two small dashes past the 3 centimeter mark. Each small dash is 1 millimeter (or .1 centimeters). Therefore, the length of the paper clip is 3.2 centimeters.

To compare the lengths of objects, each length must be expressed in the same unit. If possible, the objects should be measured with the same tool or with tools utilizing the same units. For example, a ruler and a yardstick can both measure length in inches. If the lengths of the objects are expressed in different units, these different units must be converted to the same unit before comparing them. If two lengths are expressed in the same unit, the lengths may be compared by subtracting the smaller value from the larger value. For example, suppose the lengths of two gardens are to be compared. Garden A has a length of 4 feet, and garden B has a length of 2 yards. 2 yards is converted to 6 feet so that the measurements have similar units. Then, the smaller length (4 feet) is subtracted from the larger length (6ft): 6ft – 4ft = 2ft. Therefore, garden B is 2 feet larger than garden A.

Relative Sizes of United States Customary Units and Metric Units

The United States customary system and the metric system each consist of distinct units to measure lengths and volume of liquids. The U.S. customary units for length, from smallest to largest, are: inch (in), foot (ft), yard (yd), and mile (mi). The metric units for length, from smallest to largest, are: millimeter (mm), centimeter (cm), decimeter (dm), meter (m), and kilometer (km). The relative size of each unit of length is shown below.

U.S. Customary	Metric	Conversion
12in = 1ft	10mm = 1cm	1in = 254cm
36in = 3ft = 1yd	10cm = 1dm(decimeter)	1m ≈ 3.28ft ≈ 1.09yd
5,280ft = 1,760yd = 1mi	100cm = 10dm = 1m	1mi ≈ 1.6km
	1000m = 1km	

The U.S. customary units for volume of liquids, from smallest to largest, are: fluid ounces (fl oz), cup (c), pint (pt), quart (qt), and gallon (gal). The metric units for volume of liquids, from smallest to largest, are: milliliter (mL), centiliter (cL), deciliter (dL), liter (L), and kiloliter (kL). The relative size of each unit of liquid volume is shown below.

U.S. Customary	Metric	Conversion
8fl oz = 1c	10mL = 1cL	1pt ≈ 0.473L
2c = 1pt	10cL = 1dL	1L ≈ 1.057qt
4c = 2pt = 1qt	1,000mL = 100cL = 10dL = 1L	1gal ≈ 3,785L
4qt = 1gal	1,000L = 1kL	

The U.S. customary system measures weight (how strongly Earth is pulling on an object) in the following units, from least to greatest: ounce (oz), pound (lb), and ton. The metric system measures mass (the quantity of matter within an object) in the following units, from least to greatest: milligram (mg), centigram (cg), gram (g), kilogram (kg), and metric ton (MT). The relative sizes of each unit of weight and mass are shown below.

U.S. Measures of Weight	Metric Measures of Mass
16oz = 1lb	10mg = 1cg
2,000lb = 1 ton	100cg = 1g
	1,000g = 1kg
	1,000kg = 1MT

Note that weight and mass DO NOT measure the same thing.

Time is measured in the following units, from shortest to longest: second (sec), minute (min), hour (h), day (d), week (wk), month (mo), year (yr), decade, century, millennium. The relative sizes of each unit of time is shown below.

- 60sec = 1min
- 60min = 1h
- 24hr = 1d
- 7d = 1wk

- 52wk = 1yr
- 12mo = 1yr
- 10yr = 1 decade
- 100yrs = 1 century
- 1,000yrs = 1 millennium

Conversion of Units

When working with different systems of measurement, conversion from one unit to another may be necessary. The conversion rate must be known to convert units. One method for converting units is to write and solve a proportion. The arrangement of values in a proportion is extremely important. Suppose that a problem requires converting 20 fluid ounces to cups. To do so, a proportion can be written using the conversion rate of 8fl oz = 1c with *x* representing the missing value. The proportion can be written in any of the following ways:

$\frac{1}{8} = \frac{x}{20}\left(\frac{c\ for\ conversion}{fl\ oz\ for\ conversion} = \frac{unknown\ c}{fl\ oz\ given}\right); \frac{8}{1} = \frac{20}{x}\left(\frac{fl\ oz\ for\ conversion}{c\ for\ conversion} = \frac{fl\ oz\ given}{unknown\ c}\right);$

$\frac{1}{x} = \frac{8}{20}\left(\frac{c\ for\ conversion}{unknown\ c} = \frac{fl\ oz\ for\ conversion}{fl\ oz\ given}\right); \frac{x}{1} = \frac{20}{8}\left(\frac{unknown\ c}{c\ for\ conversion} = \frac{fl\ oz\ given}{fl\ oz\ for\ conversion}\right)$

To solve a proportion, the ratios are cross-multiplied and the resulting equation is solved. When cross-multiplying, all four proportions above will produce the same equation: $(8)(x) = (20)(1) \rightarrow 8x = 20$. Dividing by 8 to isolate the variable *x*, the result is *x* = 2.5. The variable *x* represented the unknown number of cups. Therefore, the conclusion is that 20 fluid ounces converts (is equal) to 2.5 cups.

Sometimes converting units requires writing and solving more than one proportion. Suppose an exam question asks to determine how many hours are in 2 weeks. Without knowing the conversion rate between hours and weeks, this can be determined knowing the conversion rates between weeks and days, and between days and hours. First, weeks are converted to days, then days are converted to hours. To convert from weeks to days, the following proportion can be written $\frac{7}{1} = \frac{x}{2}\left(\frac{days\ conversion}{weeks\ conversion} = \frac{days\ unknown}{weeks\ given}\right)$.

Cross-multiplying produces: $(7)(2) = (x)(1) \rightarrow 14 = x$. Therefore, 2 weeks is equal to 14 days. Next, a proportion is written to convert 14 days to hours: $\frac{24}{1} = \frac{x}{14}\left(\frac{conversion\ hours}{conversion\ days} = \frac{unknown\ hours}{given\ days}\right)$. Cross-multiplying produces: $(24)(14) = (x)(1) \rightarrow 336 = x$. Therefore, the answer is that there are 336 hours in 2 weeks.

Measures of Center and Range

The center of a set of data (statistical values) can be represented by its mean, median, or mode. These are sometimes referred to as measures of central tendency. The mean is the average of the data set. The mean can be calculated by adding the data values and dividing by the sample size (the number of data points). Suppose a student has test scores of 93, 84, 88, 72, 91, and 77. To find the mean, or average, the scores are added and the sum is divided by 6 because there are 6 test scores:

$$\frac{93 + 84 + 88 + 72 + 91 + 77}{6} = \frac{505}{6} = 84.17$$

Given the mean of a data set and the sum of the data points, the sample size can be determined by dividing the sum by the mean. Suppose you are told that Kate averaged 12 points per game and scored a total of 156 points for the season. The number of games that she played (the sample size or the number of data points) can be determined by dividing the total points (sum of data points) by her average (mean of data points): $\frac{156}{12} = 13$. Therefore, Kate played in 13 games this season.

If given the mean of a data set and the sample size, the sum of the data points can be determined by multiplying the mean and sample size. Suppose you are told that Tom worked 6 days last week for an average of 5.5 hours per day. The total number of hours worked for the week (sum of data points) can be determined by multiplying his daily average (mean of data points) by the number of days worked (sample size): $5.5 \times 6 = 33$. Therefore, Tom worked a total of 33 hours last week.

The median of a data set is the value of the data point in the middle when the sample is arranged in numerical order. To find the median of a data set, the values are written in order from least to greatest. The lowest and highest values are simultaneously eliminated, repeating until the value in the middle remains. Suppose the salaries of math teachers are: \$35,000; \$38,500; \$41,000; \$42,000; \$42,000; \$44,500; \$49,000. The values are listed from least to greatest to find the median. The lowest and highest values are eliminated until only the middle value remains. Repeating this step three times reveals a median salary of \$42,000. If the sample set has an even number of data points, two values will remain after all others are eliminated. In this case, the mean of the two middle values is the median. Consider the following data set: 7, 9, 10, 13, 14, 14. Eliminating the lowest and highest values twice leaves two values, 10 and 13, in the middle. The mean of these values $\left(\frac{10+13}{2}\right)$ is the median. Therefore, the set has a median of 11.5.

The mode of a data set is the value that appears most often. A data set may have a single mode, multiple modes, or no mode. If different values repeat equally as often, multiple modes exist. If no value repeats, no mode exists. Consider the following data sets:

- A: 7, 9, 10, 13, 14, 14
- B: 37, 44, 33, 37, 49, 44, 51, 34, 37, 33, 44
- C: 173, 154, 151, 168, 155

Set A has a mode of 14. Set B has modes of 37 and 44. Set C has no mode.

The range of a data set is the difference between the highest and the lowest values in the set. The range can be considered the span of the data set. To determine the range, the smallest value in the set is subtracted from the largest value. The ranges for the data sets A, B, and C above are calculated as follows: A: $14 - 7 = 7$; B: $51 - 33 = 18$; C: $173 - 151 = 22$.

Best Description of a Set of Data

Measures of central tendency, namely mean, median, and mode, describe characteristics of a set of data. Specifically, they are intended to represent a *typical* value in the set by identifying a central position of the set. Depending on the characteristics of a specific set of data, different measures of central tendency are more indicative of a typical value in the set.

When a data set is grouped closely together with a relatively small range and the data is spread out somewhat evenly, the mean is an effective indicator of a typical value in the set. Consider the following data set representing the height of sixth grade boys in inches: 61 inches, 54 inches, 58 inches, 63 inches, 58 inches. The mean of the set is 58.8 inches. The data set is grouped closely (the range is only 9 inches) and the values are spread relatively evenly (three values below the mean and two values above the mean). Therefore, the mean value of 58.8 inches is an effective measure of central tendency in this case.

When a data set contains a small number of values either extremely large or extremely small when compared to the other values, the mean is not an effective measure of central tendency. Consider the following data set representing annual incomes of homeowners on a given street: $71,000; $74,000; $75,000; $77,000; $340,000. The mean of this set is $127,400. This figure does not indicate a typical value in the set, which contains four out of five values between $71,000 and $77,000. The median is a much more effective measure of central tendency for data sets such as these. Finding the middle value diminishes the influence of outliers, or numbers that may appear out of place, like the $340,000 annual income. The median for this set is $75,000 which is much more typical of a value in the set.

The mode of a data set is a useful measure of central tendency for categorical data when each piece of data is an option from a category. Consider a survey of 31 commuters asking how they get to work with results summarized below.

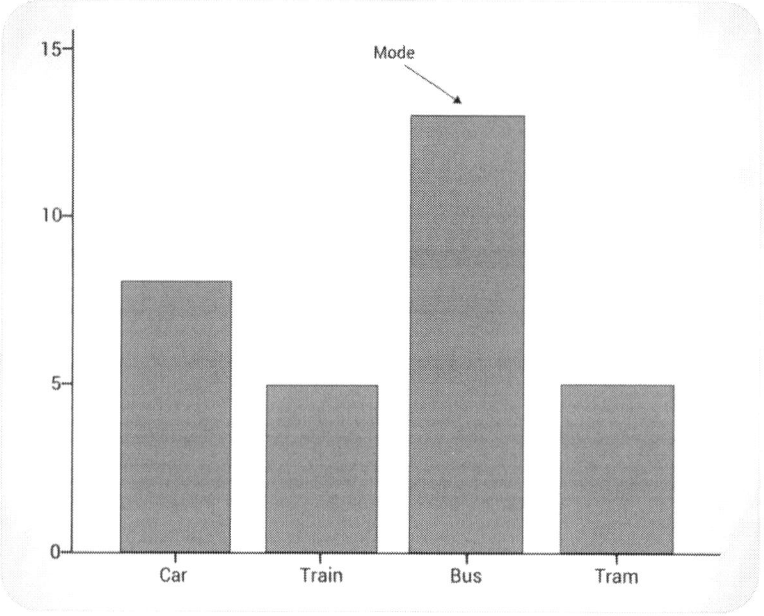

The mode for this set represents the value, or option, of the data that repeats most often. This indicates that the bus is the most popular method of transportation for the commuters.

Effects of Changes in Data

Changing all values of a data set in a consistent way produces predictable changes in the measures of the center and range of the set. A linear transformation changes the original value into the new value by either adding a given number to each value, multiplying each value by a given number, or both. Adding (or subtracting) a given value to each data point will increase (or decrease) the mean, median, and any modes by the same value. However, the range will remain the same due to the way that range is calculated. Multiplying (or dividing) a given value by each data point will increase (or decrease) the mean, median, and any modes, and the range by the same factor.

Consider the following data set, call it set *P*, representing the price of different cases of soda at a grocery store: $4.25, $4.40, $4.75, $4.95, $4.95, $5.15. The mean of set *P* is $4.74. The median is $4.85. The mode of the set is \$4.95. The range is \$0.90. Suppose the state passes a new tax of \$0.25 on every case of soda sold. The new data set, set *T*, is calculated by adding \$0.25 to each data point from set *P*. Therefore, set *T* consists of the following values: \$4.50, \$4.65, \$5.00, \$5.20, \$5.20, \$5.40. The mean of set *T* is \$4.99. The median is \$5.10. The mode of the set is \$5.20. The range is \$.90. The mean, median and mode of set *T* is equal to \$0.25 added to the mean, median, and mode of set *P*. The range stays the same.

Now suppose, due to inflation, the store raises the cost of every item by 10 percent. Raising costs by 10 percent is calculated by multiplying each value by 1.1. The new data set, set *I*, is calculated by multiplying each data point from set *T* by 1.1. Therefore, set *I* consists of the following values: \$4.95, \$5.12, \$5.50, \$5.72, \$5.72, \$5.94. The mean of set *I* is \$5.49. The median is \$5.61. The mode of the set is \$5.72. The range is \$0.99. The mean, median, mode, and range of set *I* is equal to 1.1 multiplied by the mean, median, mode, and range of set *T* because each increased by a factor of 10 percent.

Describing a Set of Data

A set of data can be described in terms of its center, spread, shape and any unusual features. The center of a data set can be measured by its mean, median, or mode. Measures of central tendency are covered in the *Measures of Center and Range* section. The spread of a data set refers to how far the data points are from the center (mean or median). The spread can be measured by the range or the quartiles and interquartile range. A data set with data points clustered around the center will have a small spread. A data set covering a wide range will have a large spread.

When a data set is displayed as a histogram or frequency distribution plot, the shape indicates if a sample is normally distributed, symmetrical, or has measures of skewness or kurtosis. When graphed, a data set with a normal distribution will resemble a bell curve.

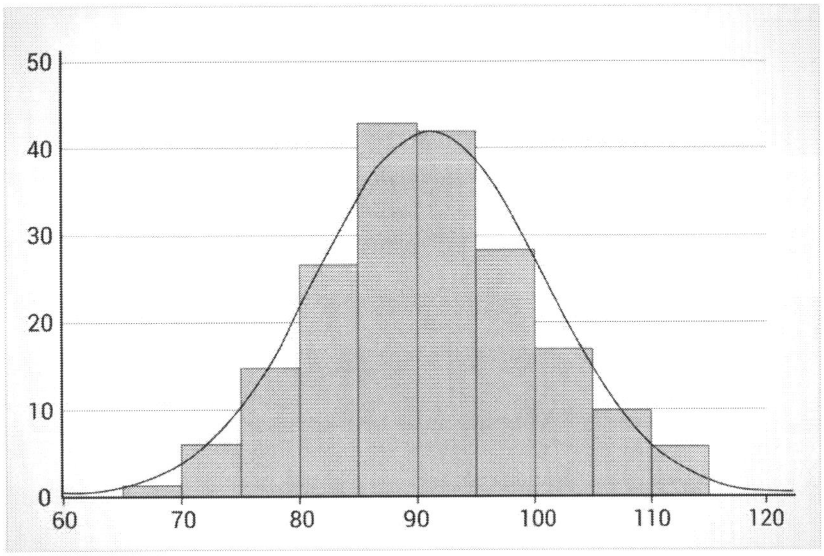

If the data set is symmetrical, each half of the graph when divided at the center is a mirror image of the other. If the graph has fewer data points to the right, the data is skewed right. If it has fewer data points to the left, the data is skewed left.

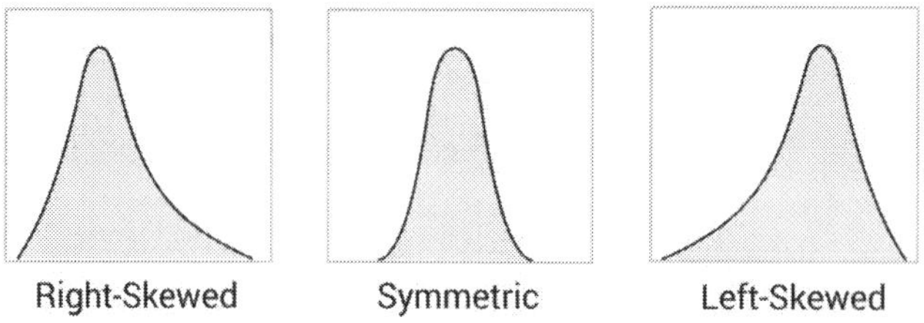

Kurtosis is a measure of whether the data is heavy-tailed with a high number of outliers, or light-tailed with a low number of outliers.

A description of a data set should include any unusual features such as gaps or outliers. A gap is a span within the range of the data set containing no data points. An outlier is a data point with a value either extremely large or extremely small when compared to the other values in the set.

Interpreting Displays of Data

A set of data can be visually displayed in various forms allowing for quick identification of characteristics of the set. Histograms, such as the one shown below, display the number of data points (vertical axis) that fall into given intervals (horizontal axis) across the range of the set. Suppose the histogram below displays IQ scores of students. Each rectangle represents the number of students with scores between a given ten-point span. For example, the furthest bar to the right indicates that five students scored between 130 and 140. Histograms can describe the center, spread, shape, and any unusual characteristics of a data set.

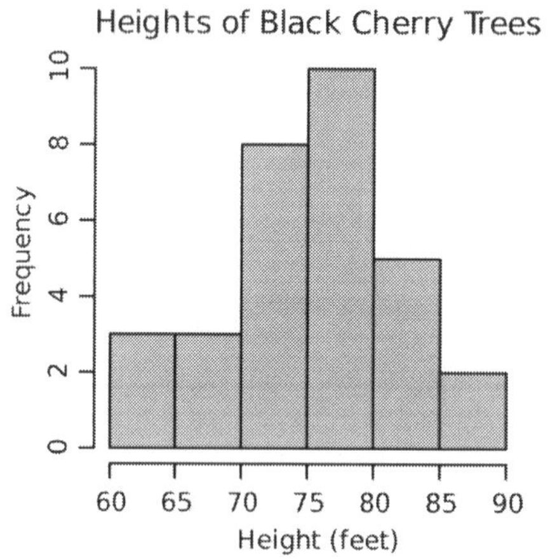

A box plot, also called a box-and-whisker plot, divides the data points into four groups and displays the five number summary for the set, as well as any outliers. The five number summary consists of:

- The lower extreme: the lowest value that is not an outlier
- The higher extreme: the highest value that is not an outlier
- The median of the set: also referred to as the second quartile or Q_2
- The first quartile or Q_1: the median of values below Q_2
- The third quartile or Q_3: the median of values above Q_2

Calculating each of these values is covered in the next section, *Graphical Representation of Data*.

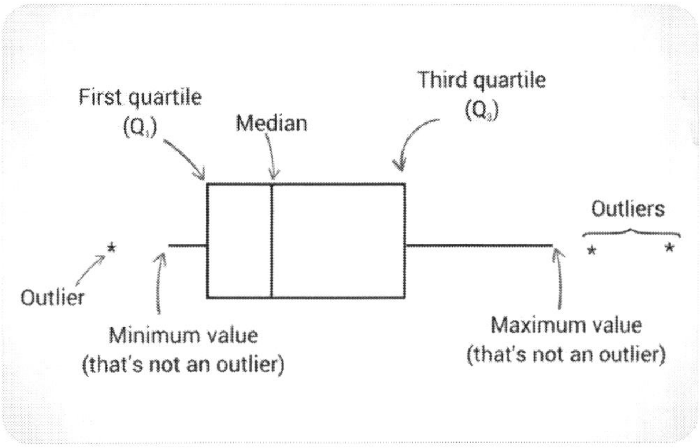

Suppose the box plot displays IQ scores for 12th grade students at a given school. The five number summary of the data consists of: lower extreme (67); upper extreme (127); Q_2or median (100); Q_1 (91); Q_3 (108); and outliers (135 and 140). Although all data points are not known from the plot, the points are divided into four quartiles each, including 25% of the data points. Therefore, 25% of students scored between 67 and 91, 25% scored between 91 and 100, 25% scored between 100 and 108, and 25% scored between 108 and 127. These percentages include the normal values for the set and exclude the outliers. This information is useful when comparing a given score with the rest of the scores in the set.

A scatter plot is a mathematical diagram that visually displays the relationship or connection between two variables. The independent variable is placed on the *x*-axis, or horizontal axis, and the dependent variable is placed on the *y*-axis, or vertical axis. When visually examining the points on the graph, if the points model a linear relationship, or a line of best-fit can be drawn through the points with the points relatively close on either side, then a correlation exists. If the line of best-fit has a positive slope (rises from left to right), then the variables have a positive correlation. If the line of best-fit has a negative slope (falls from left to right), then the variables have a negative correlation. If a line of best-fit cannot be drawn, then no correlation exists. A positive or negative correlation can be categorized as strong or weak, depending on how closely the points are graphed around the line of best-fit.

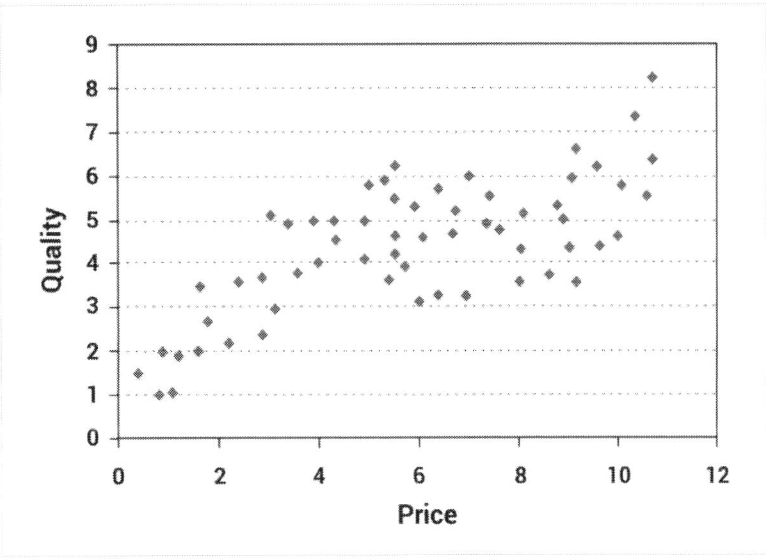

Graphical Representation of Data

Various graphs can be used to visually represent a given set of data. Each type of graph requires a different method of arranging data points and different calculations of the data. Examples of histograms, box plots, and scatter plots are discussed in the previous section *Interpreting Displays of Data*. To construct a histogram, the range of the data points is divided into equal intervals. The frequency for each interval is then determined, which reveals how many points fall into each interval. A graph is constructed with the vertical axis representing the frequency and the horizontal axis representing the intervals. The lower value of each interval should be labeled along the horizontal axis. Finally, for each interval, a bar is drawn from the lower value of each interval to the lower value of the next interval with a height equal to the frequency of the interval. Because of the intervals, histograms do not have any gaps between bars along the horizontal axis.

To construct a box (or box-and-whisker) plot, the five number summary for the data set is calculated as follows: the second quartile (Q_2) is the median of the set. The first quartile (Q_1) is the median of the values below Q_2. The third quartile (Q_3) is the median of the values above Q_2. The upper extreme is the highest value in the data set if it is not an outlier (greater than 1.5 times the interquartile range Q_3 - Q_1). The lower extreme is the least value in the data set if it is not an outlier (more than 1.5 times lower than the interquartile range). To construct the box-and-whisker plot, each value is plotted on a number line, along with any outliers. The *box* consists of Q_1 and Q_3 as its *top* and *bottom* and Q_2 as the dividing line inside the box. The *whiskers* extend from the lower extreme to Q_1 and from Q_3 to the upper extreme.

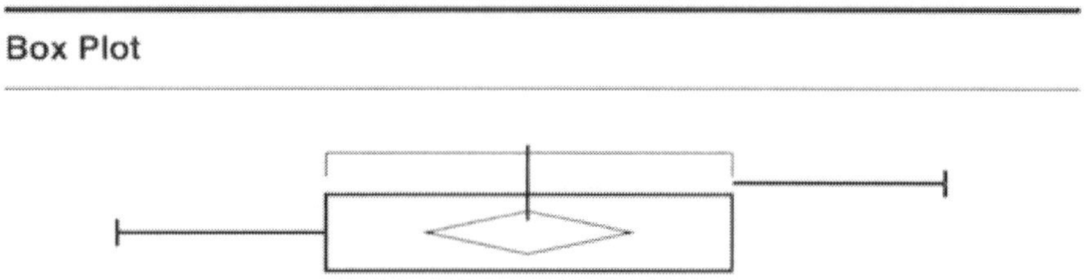

A scatter plot displays the relationship between two variables. Values for the independent variable, typically denoted by *x*, are paired with values for the dependent variable, typically denoted by *y*. Each set of corresponding values are written as an ordered pair (*x*, *y*). To construct the graph, a coordinate grid is labeled with the *x*-axis representing the independent variable and the *y*-axis representing the dependent variable. Each ordered pair is graphed.

Like a scatter plot, a line graph compares variables that change continuously, typically over time. Paired data values (ordered pair) are plotted on a coordinate grid with the *x*- and *y*-axis representing the variables. A line is drawn from each point to the next, going from left to right. The line graph below displays cell phone use for given years (two variables) for men, women, and both sexes (three data sets).

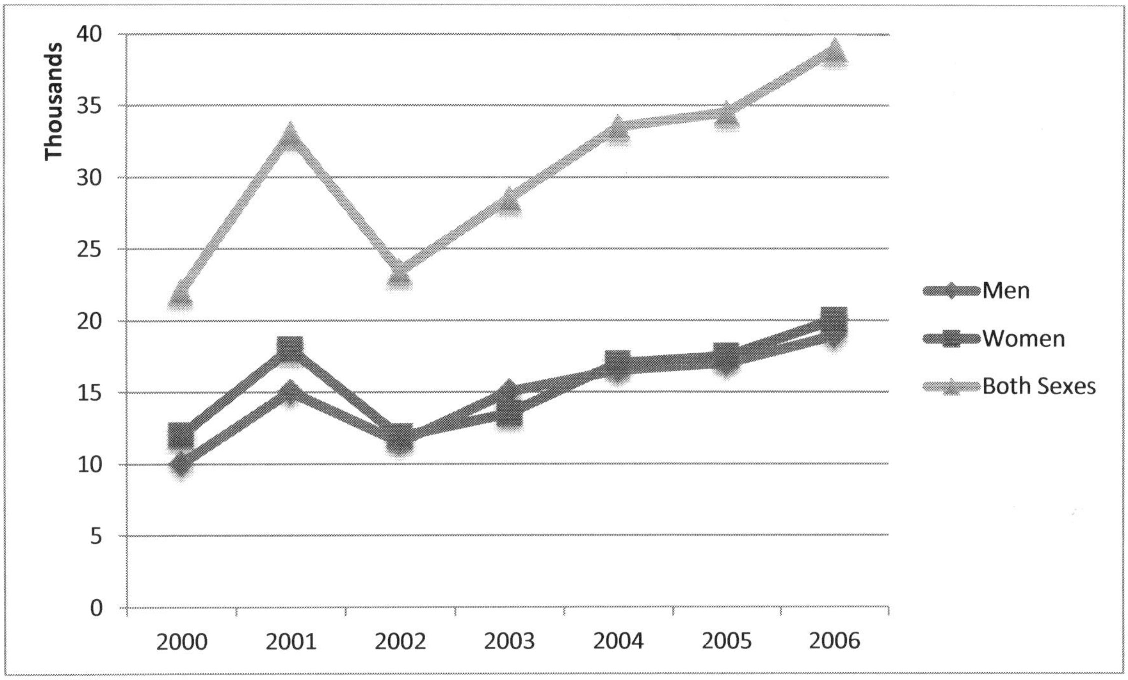

A line plot, also called dot plot, displays the frequency of data (numerical values) on a number line. To construct a line plot, a number line is used that includes all unique data values. It is marked with x's or dots above the value the number of times that the value occurs in the data set.

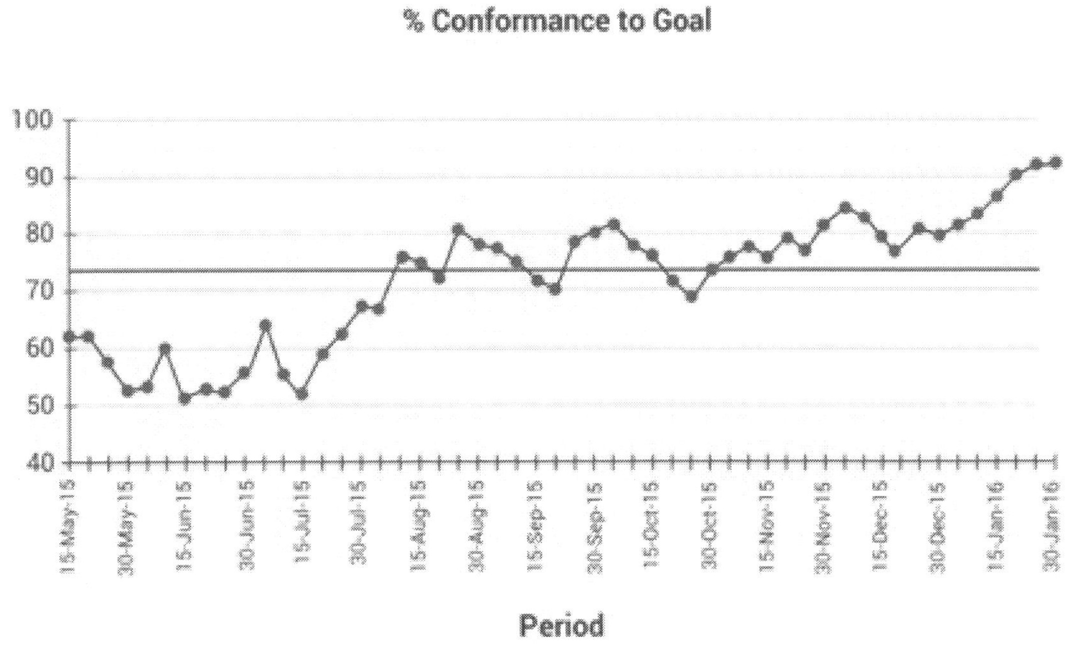

A bar graph looks similar to a histogram but displays categorical data. The horizontal axis represents each category and the vertical axis represents the frequency for the category. A bar is drawn for each category (often different colors) with a height extending to the frequency for that category within the data set. A double bar graph displays two sets of data that contain data points consisting of the same categories. The double bar graph below indicates that two girls and four boys like Pad Thai the most out of all the foods, two boys and five girls like pizza, and so on.

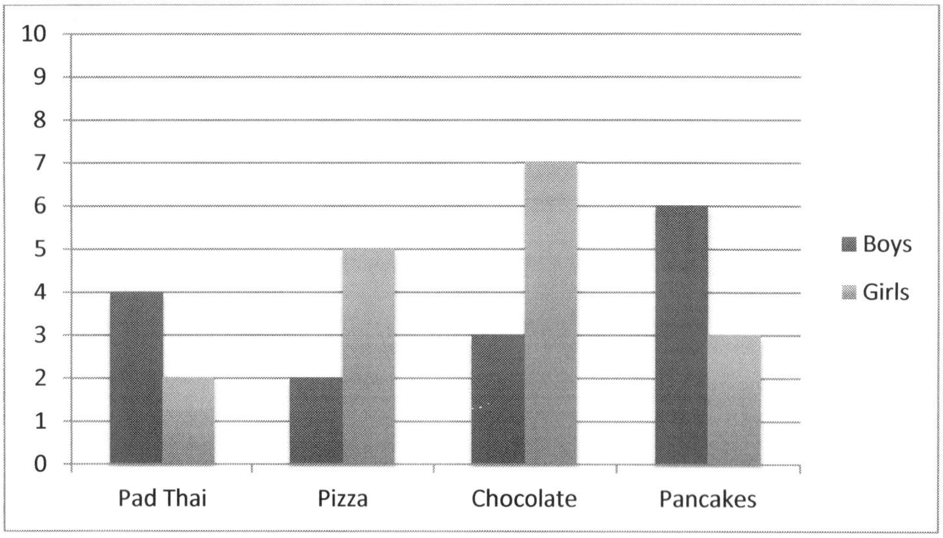

A circle graph, also called a pie chart, displays categorical data with each category representing a percentage of the whole data set. To construct a circle graph, the percent of the data set for each category must be determined. To do so, the frequency of the category is divided by the total number of data points and converted to a percent. For example, if 80 people were asked their favorite pizza topping and 20 responded cheese, then cheese constitutes 25% of the data ($\frac{20}{80} = .25 = 25\%$). Each category in a data set is represented by a *slice* of the circle proportionate to its percentage of the whole.

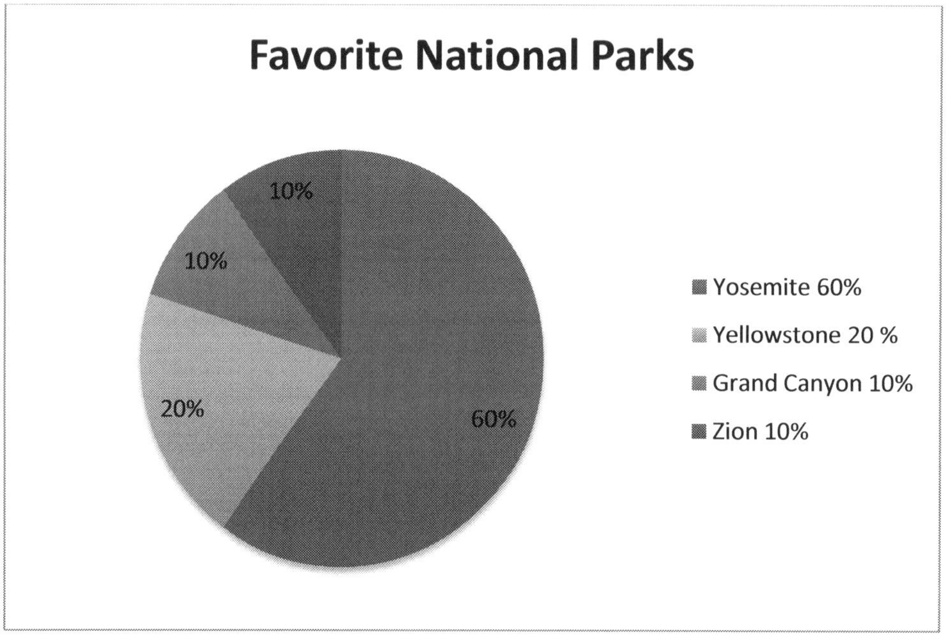

Choice of Graphs to Display Data

Choosing the appropriate graph to display a data set depends on what type of data is included in the set and what information must be displayed. Histograms and box plots can be used for data sets consisting of individual values across a wide range. Examples include test scores and incomes. Histograms and box plots will indicate the center, spread, range, and outliers of a data set. A histogram will show the shape of the data set, while a box plot will divide the set into quartiles (25% increments), allowing for comparison between a given value and the entire set.

Scatter plots and line graphs can be used to display data consisting of two variables. Examples include height and weight, or distance and time. A correlation between the variables is determined by examining the points on the graph. Line graphs are used if each value for one variable pairs with a distinct value for the other variable. Line graphs show relationships between variables.

Line plots, bar graphs, and circle graphs are all used to display categorical data, such as surveys. Line plots and bar graphs both indicate the frequency of each category within the data set. A line plot is used when the categories consist of numerical values. For example, the number of hours of TV watched by individuals is displayed on a line plot. A bar graph is used when the categories consists of words. For example, the favorite ice cream of individuals is displayed with a bar graph. A circle graph can be used to display either type of categorical data. However, unlike line plots and bar graphs, a circle graph does not indicate the frequency of each category. Instead, the circle graph represents each category as its percentage of the whole data set.

Probabilities Relative to Likelihood of Occurrence

Probability is a measure of how likely an event is to occur. Probability is written as a fraction between zero and one. If an event has a probability of zero, the event will never occur. If an event has a probability of one, the event will definitely occur. If the probability of an event is closer to zero, the event is unlikely to occur. If the probability of an event is closer to one, the event is more likely to occur. For example, a probability of $\frac{1}{2}$ means that the event is equally as likely to occur as it is not to occur. An example of this is tossing a coin. To calculate the probability of an event, the number of favorable outcomes is divided by the number of total outcomes. For example, suppose you have 2 raffle tickets out of 20 total tickets sold. The probability that you win the raffle is calculated: $\frac{number\ of\ favorable\ outcomes}{total\ numberof\ outcomes} = \frac{2}{20} = \frac{1}{10}$ (always reduce fractions). Therefore, the probability of winning the raffle is $\frac{1}{10}$ or 0.1.

Chance is the measure of how likely an event is to occur, written as a percent. If an event will never occur, the event has a 0% chance. If an event will certainly occur, the event has a 100% chance. If an event will sometimes occur, the event has a chance somewhere between 0% and 100%. To calculate chance, probability is calculated and the fraction is converted to a percent.

The probability of multiple events occurring can be determined by multiplying the probability of each event. For example, suppose you flip a coin with heads and tails, and roll a six-sided dice numbered one through six. To find the probability that you will flip heads AND roll a two, the probability of each event is determined and those fractions are multiplied. The probability of flipping heads is $\frac{1}{2}\left(\frac{1\ side\ with\ heads}{2\ sides\ total}\right)$ and the probability of rolling a two is $\frac{1}{6}\left(\frac{1\ side\ with\ a\ 2}{6\ total\ sides}\right)$. The probability of flipping heads AND rolling a 2 is: $\frac{1}{2} \times \frac{1}{6} = \frac{1}{12}$.

The above scenario with flipping a coin and rolling a dice is an example of independent events. Independent events are circumstances in which the outcome of one event does not affect the outcome of the other event. Conversely, dependent events are ones in which the outcome of one event affects the outcome of the second event. Consider the following scenario: a bag contains 5 black marbles and 5 white marbles. What is the probability of picking 2 black marbles without replacing the marble after the first pick?

The probability of picking a black marble on the first pick is $\frac{5}{10}\left(\frac{5\ black\ marbles}{10\ total\ marbles}\right)$. Assuming that a black marble was picked, there are now 4 black marbles and 5 white marbles for the second pick. Therefore, the probability of picking a black marble on the second pick is $\frac{4}{9}\left(\frac{4\ black\ marbles}{9\ total\ marbles}\right)$. To find the probability of picking two black marbles, the probability of each is multiplied: $\frac{5}{10} \times \frac{4}{9} = \frac{20}{90} = \frac{2}{9}$.

Geometric Concepts

Lines, Rays, and Line Segments

The basic unit of geometry is a point. A point represents an exact location on a plane, or flat surface. The position of a point is indicated with a dot and usually named with a single uppercase letter, such as point *A* or point *T*. A point is a place, not a thing, and therefore has no dimensions or size. A set of points that lies on the same line is called collinear. A set of points that lies on the same plane is called coplanar.

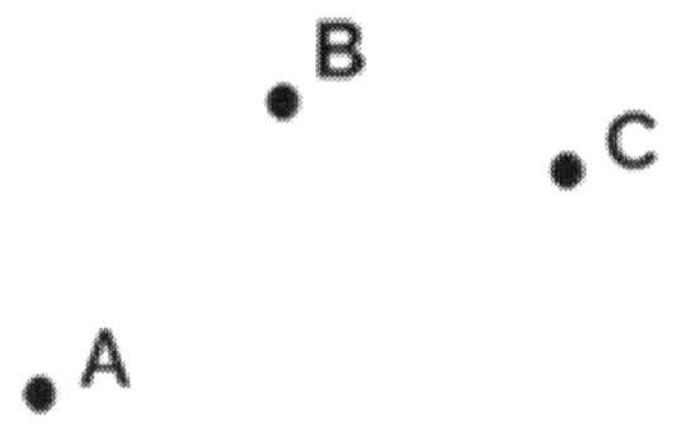

The image above displays point *A*, point *B*, and point *C*.

A line is as series of points that extends in both directions without ending. It consists of an infinite number of points and is drawn with arrows on both ends to indicate it extends infinitely. Lines can be named by two points on the line or with a single, cursive, lower case letter. The two lines below could be named line *AB* or line *BA* or $\overleftrightarrow{AB}$ or $\overleftrightarrow{BA}$; and line *m*.

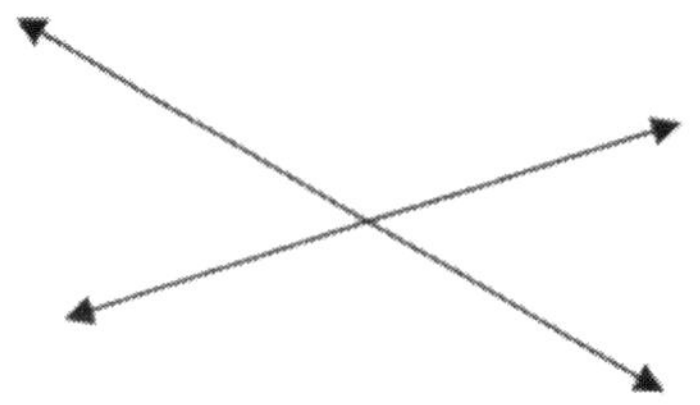

Two lines are considered parallel to each other if, while extending infinitely, they will never intersect (or meet). Parallel lines point in the same direction and are always the same distance apart. Two lines are considered perpendicular if they intersect to form right angles. Right angles are 90°. Typically, a small box is drawn at the intersection point to indicate the right angle.

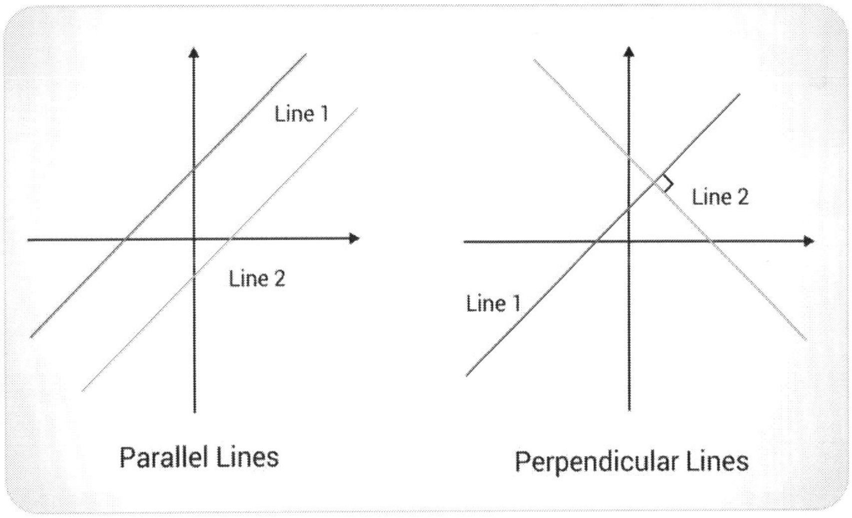

Line 1 is parallel to line 2 in the left image and is written as line 1 || line 2. Line 1 is perpendicular to line 2 in the right image and is written as line 1 $\perp$ line 2.

A ray has a specific starting point and extends in one direction without ending. The endpoint of a ray is its starting point. Rays are named using the endpoint first, and any other point on the ray. The following ray can be named ray *AB* and written $\overrightarrow{AB}$.

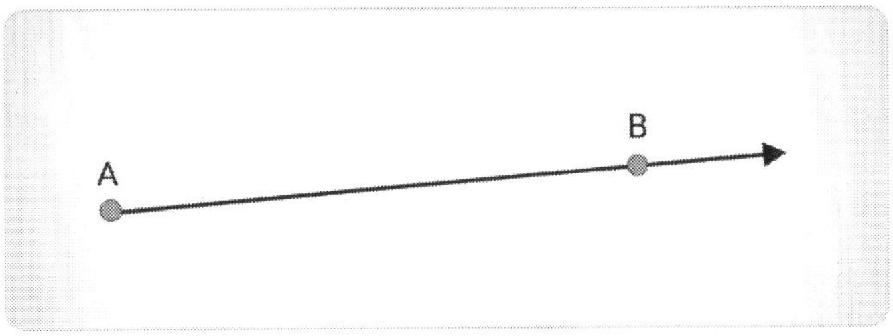

A line segment has specific starting and ending points. A line segment consists of two endpoints and all the points in between. Line segments are named by the two endpoints. The example below is named segment *KL* or segment *LK*, written $\overline{KL}$ or $\overline{LK}$.

Classification of Angles

An angle consists of two rays that have a common endpoint. This common endpoint is called the vertex of the angle. The two rays can be called sides of the angle. The angle below has a vertex at point *B* and the sides consist of ray *BA* and ray *BC*. An angle can be named in three ways:

1. Using the vertex and a point from each side, with the vertex letter in the middle.

2. Using only the vertex. This can only be used if it is the only angle with that vertex.
3. Using a number that is written inside the angle.

The angle below can be written $\angle ABC$ (read angle *ABC*), $\angle CBA$, $\angle B$, or $\angle 1$.

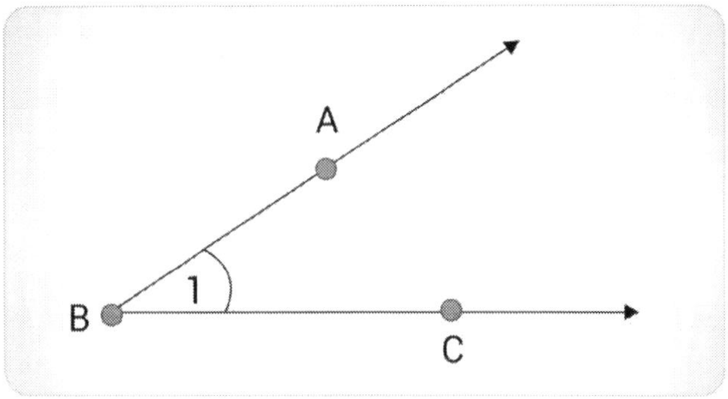

An angle divides a plane, or flat surface, into three parts: the angle itself, the interior (inside) of the angle, and the exterior (outside) of the angle. The figure below shows point *M* on the interior of the angle and point *N* on the exterior of the angle.

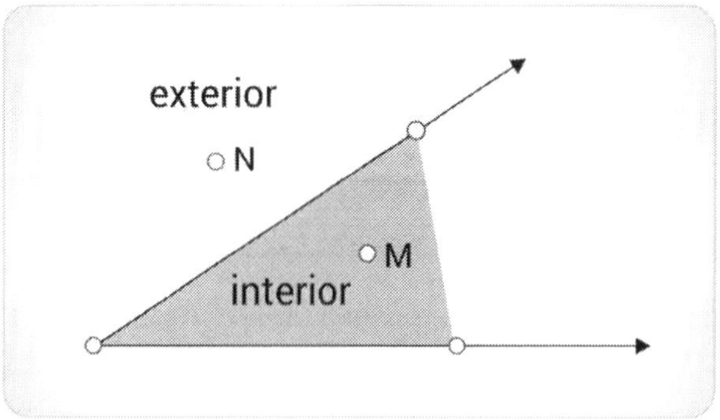

Angles can be measured in units called degrees, with the symbol °. The degree measure of an angle is between 0° and 180° and can be obtained by using a protractor.

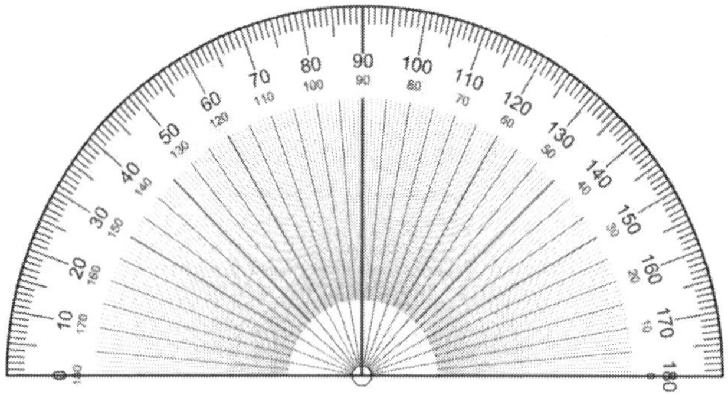

A straight angle (or simply a line) measures exactly 180°. A right angle's sides meet at the vertex to create a square corner. A right angle measures exactly 90° and is typically indicated by a box drawn in the interior of the angle. An acute angle has an interior that is narrower than a right angle. The measure of an acute angle is any value less than 90° and greater than 0°. For example, 89.9°, 47°, 12°, and 1°. An obtuse angle has an interior that is wider than a right angle. The measure of an obtuse angle is any value greater than 90° but less than 180°. For example, 90.1°, 110°, 150°, and 179.9°.

- Acute angles: Less than 90°
- Obtuse angles: Greater than 90°
- Right angles: 90°
- Straight angles: 180°

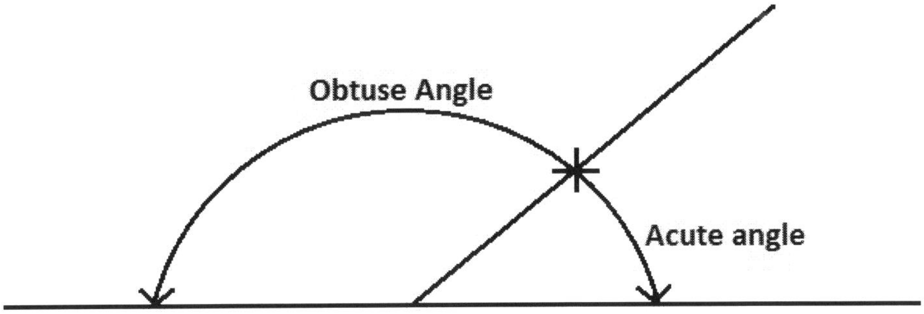

Two- and Three-Dimensional Shapes

A polygon is a closed geometric figure in a plane (flat surface) consisting of at least 3 sides formed by line segments. These are often defined as two-dimensional shapes. Common two-dimensional shapes include circles, triangles, squares, rectangles, pentagons, and hexagons. Note that a circle is a two-dimensional shape without sides.

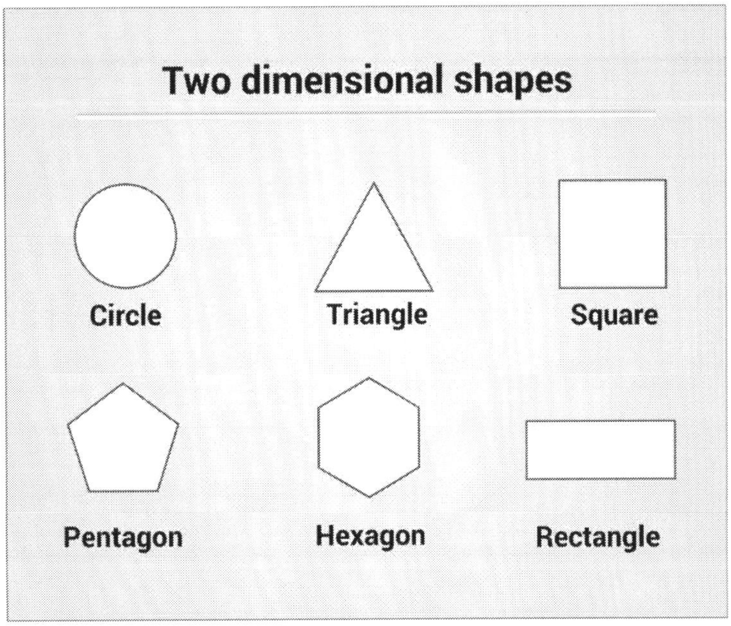

A solid figure, or simply solid, is a figure that encloses a part of space. Some solids consist of flat surfaces only while others include curved surfaces. Solid figures are often defined as three-dimensional shapes. Common three-dimensional shapes include spheres, prisms, cubes, pyramids, cylinders, and cones.

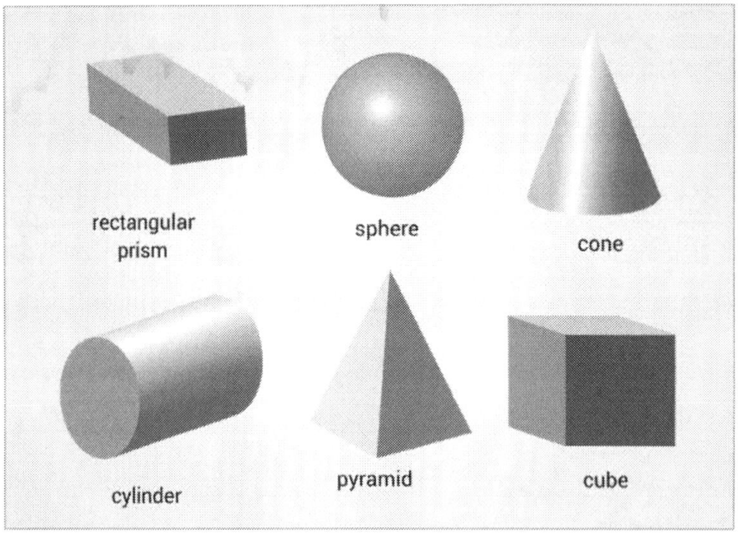

Composing two- or three-dimensional shapes involves putting together two or more shapes to create a new larger figure. For example, a semi-circle (half circle), rectangle, and two triangles can be used to compose the figure of the sailboat shown below.

Similarly, solid figures can be placed together to compose an endless number of three-dimensional objects.

Decomposing two- and three-dimensional figures involves breaking the shapes apart into smaller, simpler shapes. Consider the following two-dimensional representations of a house:

This complex figure can be decomposed into the following basic two-dimensional shapes: large rectangle (body of house); large triangle (roof); small rectangle and small triangle (chimney). Decomposing figures is often done more than one way. To illustrate, the figure of the house could also be decomposed into: two large triangles (body); two medium triangles (roof); two smaller triangles of unequal size (chimney).

Polygons and Solids

A polygon is a closed two-dimensional figure consisting of three or more sides. Polygons can be either convex or concave. A polygon that has interior angles all measuring less than 180° is convex. A concave polygon has one or more interior angles measuring greater than 180°. Examples are shown below.

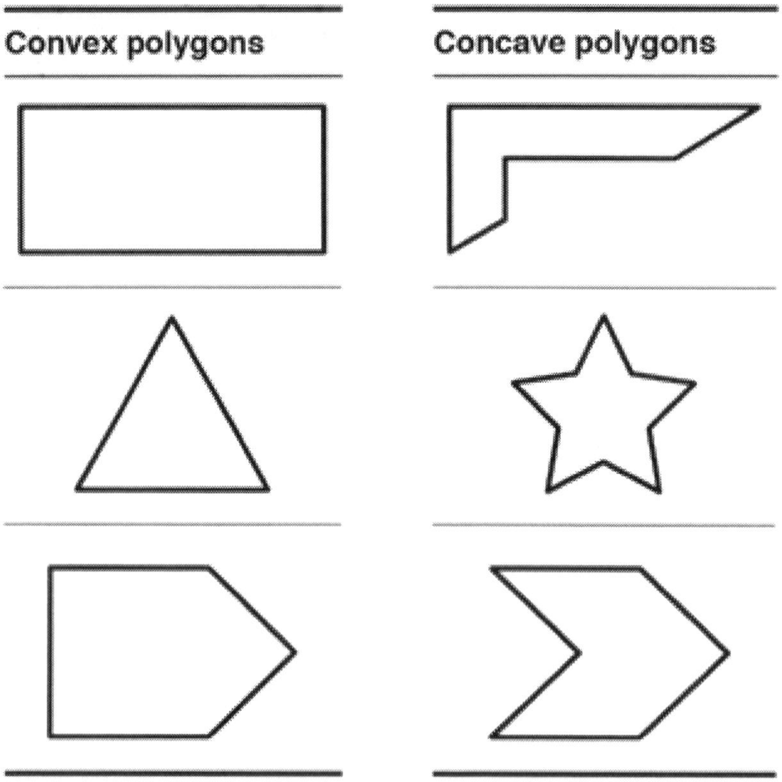

Polygons can be classified by the number of sides (also equal to the number of angles) they have. The following are the names of polygons with a given number of sides or angles:

# of sides	**3**	**4**	**5**	**6**	**7**	**8**	**9**	**10**
Name of polygon	Triangle	Quadrilateral	Pentagon	Hexagon	Septagon (or heptagon)	Octagon	Nonagon	Decagon

Equiangular polygons are polygons in which the measure of every interior angle is the same. The sides of equilateral polygons are always the same length. If a polygon is both equiangular and equilateral, the polygon is defined as a regular polygon.

Triangles can be further classified by their sides and angles. A triangle with its largest angle measuring 90° is a right triangle. A triangle with the largest angle less than 90° is an acute triangle. A triangle with the largest angle greater than 90° is an obtuse triangle. Below is an example of a right triangle.

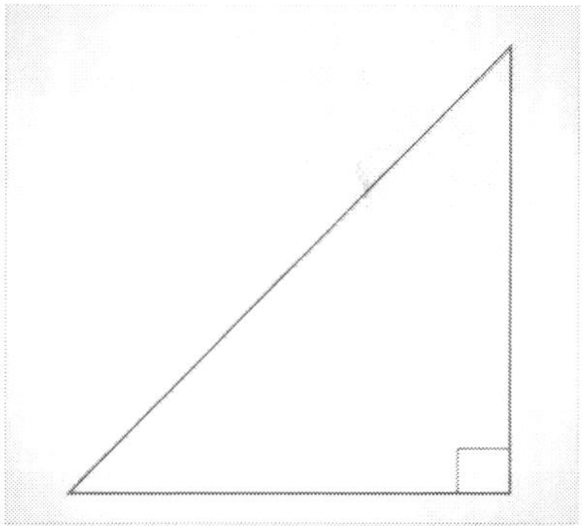

A triangle consisting of two equal sides and two equal angles is an isosceles triangle. A triangle with three equal sides and three equal angles is an equilateral triangle. A triangle with no equal sides or angles is a scalene triangle.

Isosceles triangle:

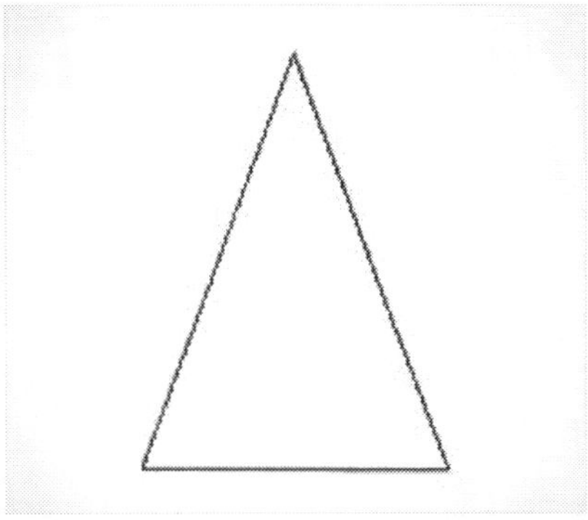

Equilateral triangle:

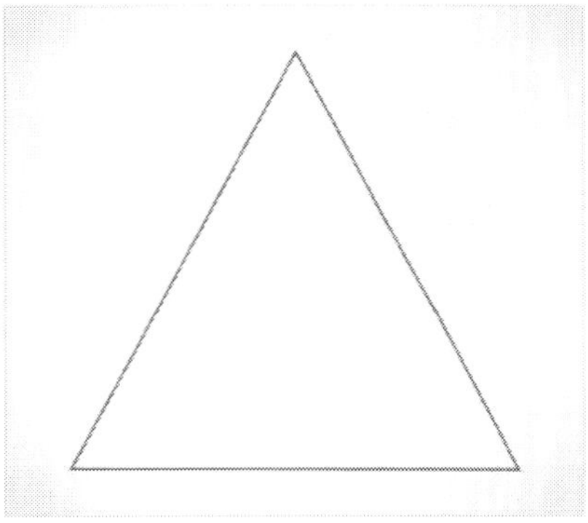

Scalene triangle:

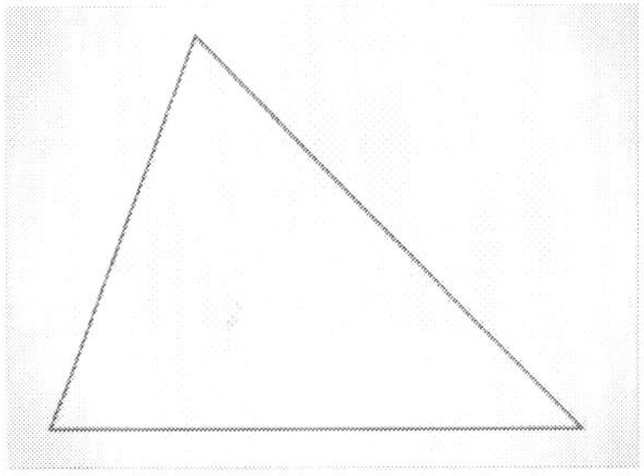

Quadrilaterals can be further classified according to their sides and angles. A quadrilateral with exactly one pair of parallel sides is called a trapezoid. A quadrilateral that shows both pairs of opposite sides parallel is a parallelogram. Parallelograms include rhombuses, rectangles, and squares. A rhombus has four equal sides. A rectangle has four equal angles (90° each). A square has four 90° angles and four equal sides. Therefore, a square is both a rhombus and a rectangle.

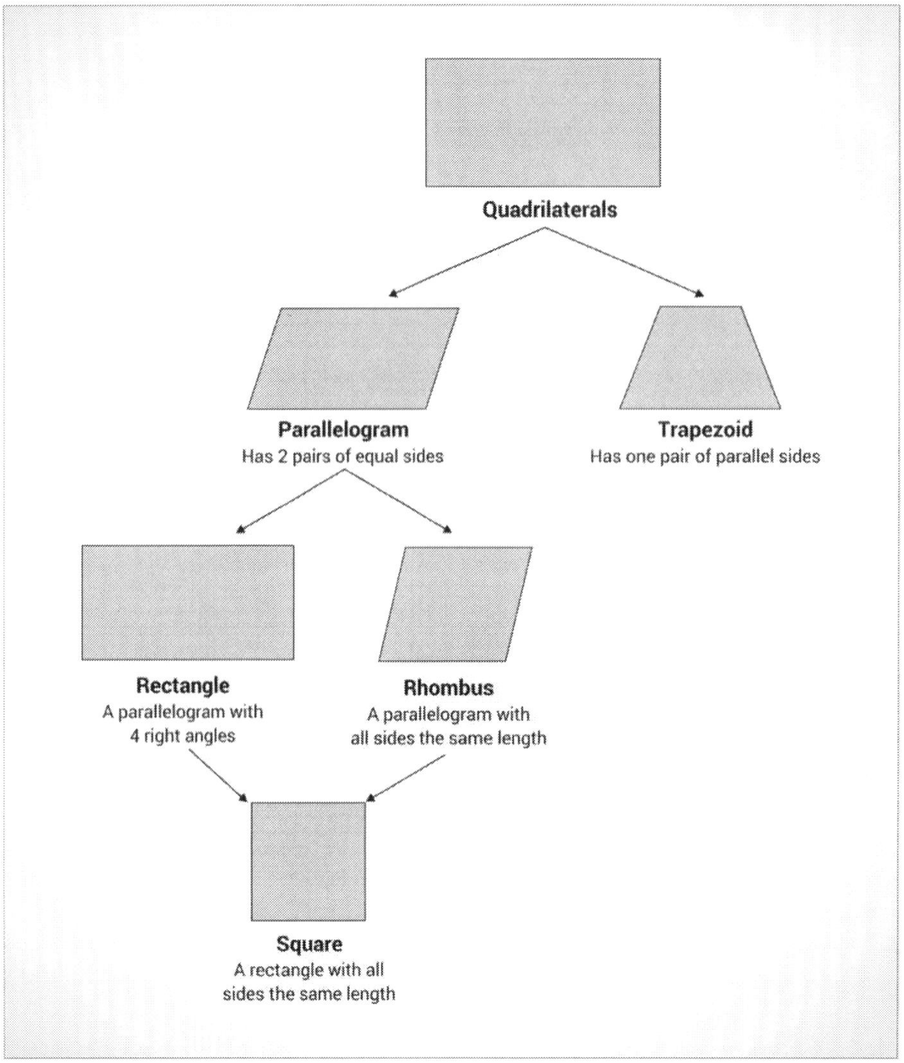

A solid is a three-dimensional figure that encloses a part of space. Solids consisting of all flat surfaces that are polygons are called polyhedrons. The two-dimensional surfaces that make up a polyhedron are called faces. Types of polyhedrons include prisms and pyramids. A prism consists of two parallel faces that are congruent (or the same shape and same size), and lateral faces going around (which are parallelograms). A prism is further classified by the shape of its base, as shown below:

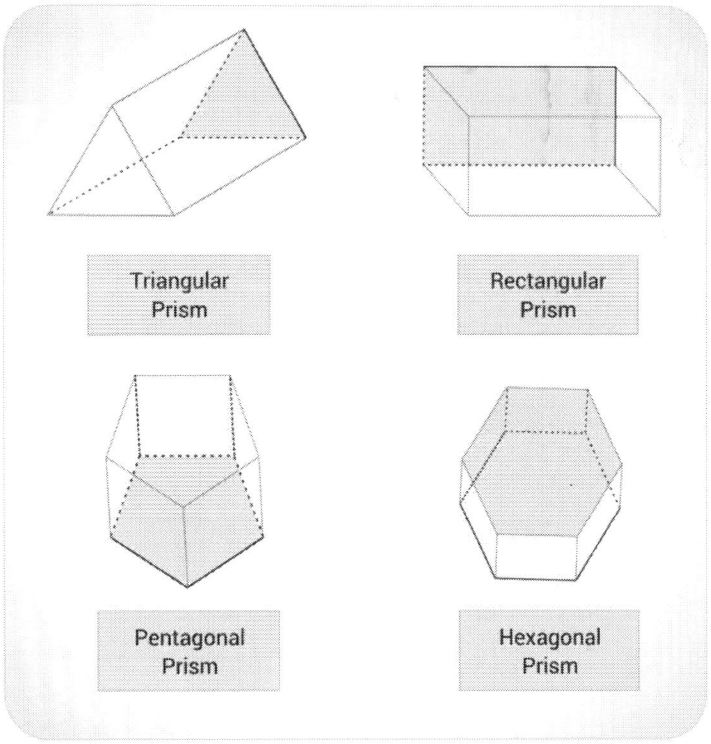

A pyramid consists of lateral faces (triangles) that meet at a common point called the vertex and one other face that is a polygon, called the base. A pyramid can be further classified by the shape of its base, as shown below.

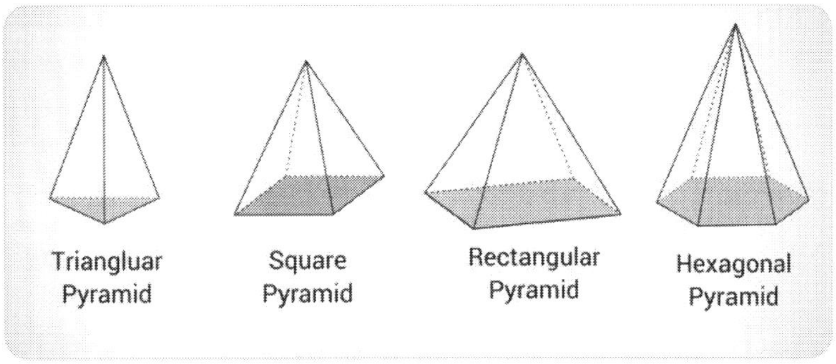

A tetrahedron is another name for a triangular pyramid. All the faces of a tetrahedron are triangles.

Solids that are not polyhedrons include spheres, cylinders, and cones. A sphere is the set of all points a given distance from a given center point. A sphere is commonly thought of as a three-dimensional circle. A cylinder consists of two parallel, congruent (same size) circles and a lateral curved surface. A cone consists of a circle as its base and a lateral curved surface that narrows to a point called the vertex.

Similar polygons are the same shape but different sizes. More specifically, their corresponding angle measures are congruent (or equal) and the length of their sides is proportional. For example, all sides of one polygon may be double the length of the sides of another. Likewise, similar solids are the same shape but different sizes. Any corresponding faces or bases of similar solids are the same polygons that are proportional by a consistent value.

Three-Dimensional Figures with Nets

A net is a construction of two-dimensional figures that can be folded to form a given three-dimensional figure. More than one net may exist to fold and produce the same solid, or three-dimensional figure. The bases and faces of the solid figure are analyzed to determine the polygons (two-dimensional figures) needed to form the net.

Consider the following triangular prism:

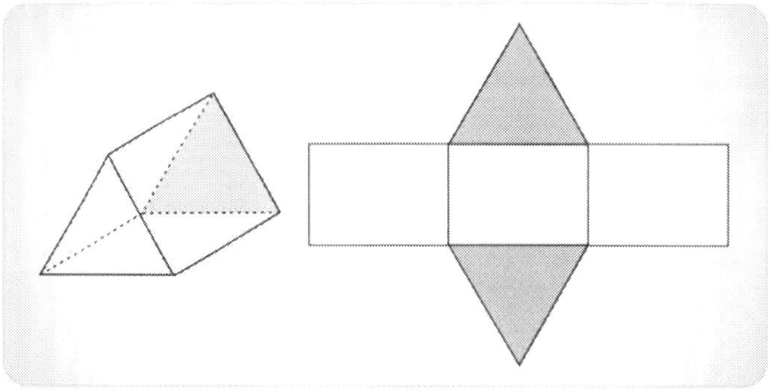

The surface of the prism consists of two triangular bases and three rectangular faces. The net beside it can be used to construct the triangular prism by first folding the triangles up to be parallel to each other, and then folding the two outside rectangles up and to the center with the outer edges touching.

Consider the following cylinder:

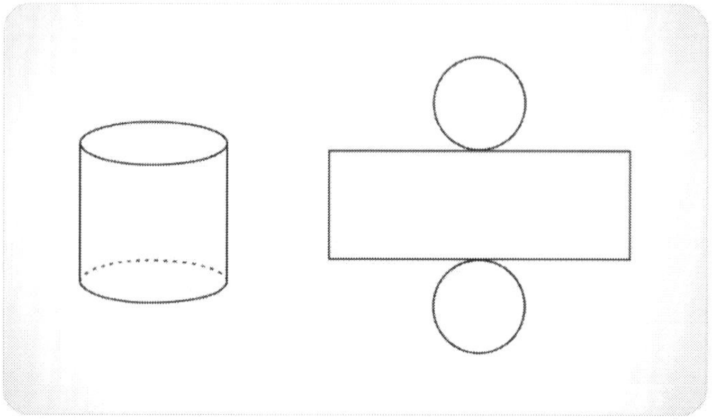

The surface consists of two circular bases and a curved lateral surface that can be opened and flattened into a rectangle. The net beside the cylinder can be used to construct the cylinder by first folding the circles up to be parallel to each other, and then curving the sides of the rectangle up to touch each other. The top and bottom of the folded rectangle should be touching the outside of both circles.

Consider the following square pyramid below on the left. The surface consists of one square base and four triangular faces. The net below on the right can be used to construct the square pyramid by folding each triangle towards the center of the square. The top points of the triangle meet at the vertex.

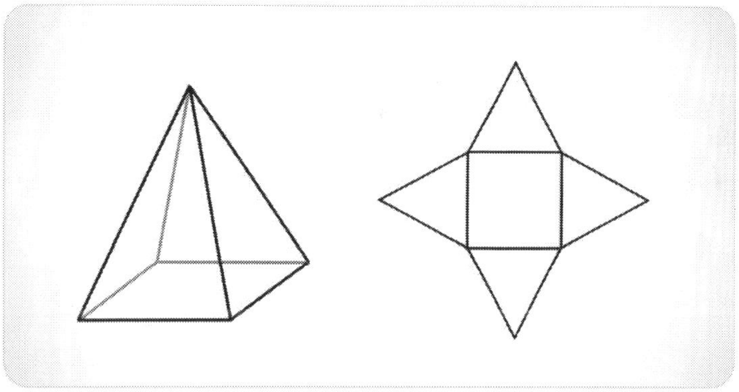

Surface Area of Three-Dimensional Figures

The area of a two-dimensional figure refers to the number of square units needed to cover the interior region of the figure. This concept is similar to wallpaper covering the flat surface of a wall. For example, if a rectangle has an area of 10 square centimeters (written $10cm^2$), it will take 10 squares, each with sides one centimeter in length, to cover the interior region of the rectangle. Note that area is measured in square units such as: square centimeters or cm^2; square feet or ft^2; square yards or yd^2; square miles or mi^2.

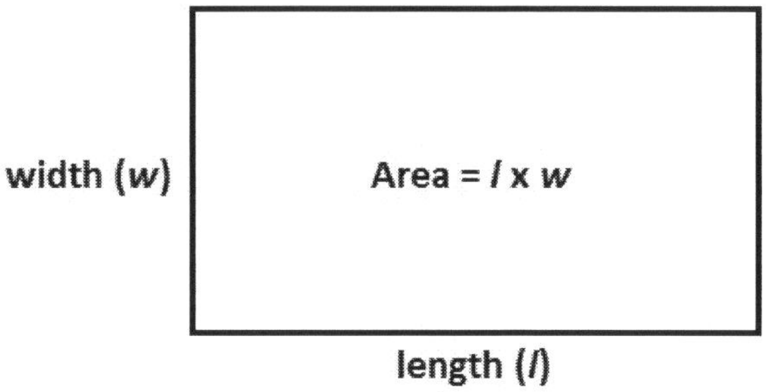

The surface area of a three-dimensional figure refers to the number of square units needed to cover the entire surface of the figure. This concept is similar to using wrapping paper to completely cover the outside of a box. For example, if a triangular pyramid has a surface area of 17 square inches (written $17in^2$), it will take 17 squares, each with sides one inch in length, to cover the entire surface of the pyramid. Surface area is also measured in square units.

Many three-dimensional figures (solid figures) can be represented by nets consisting of rectangles and triangles. The surface area of such solids can be determined by adding the areas of each of its faces and bases. Finding the surface area using this method requires calculating the areas of rectangles and triangles. To find the area (*A*) of a rectangle, the length (*l*) is multiplied by the width (*w*) $\rightarrow A = l \times w$. The area of the rectangle below is calculated: $A = (8cm) \times (4cm) \rightarrow A = 32cm^2$.

To calculate the area (*A*) of a triangle, the product of $\frac{1}{2}$, the base (*b*), and the height (*h*) is found $\rightarrow A = \frac{1}{2} \times b \times h$. Note that the height of a triangle is measured from the base to the vertex opposite of it forming a right angle with the base. The area of the triangle below is calculated: $A = \frac{1}{2} \times (11cm) \times (6cm) \rightarrow A = 33cm^2$.

Consider the following triangular prism, which is represented by a net consisting of two triangles and three rectangles.

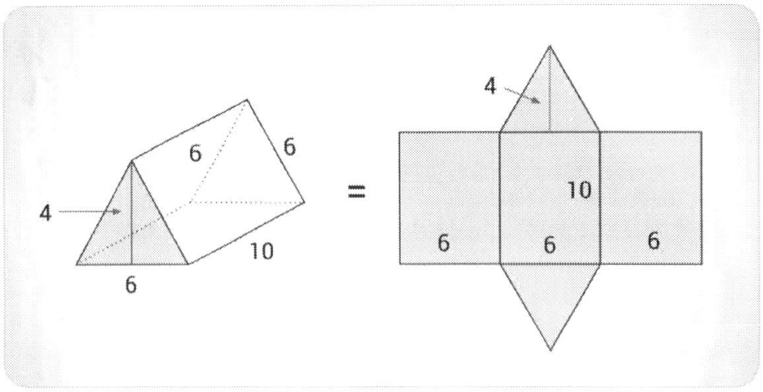

The surface area of the prism can be determined by adding the areas of each of its faces and bases. The surface area (*SA*) = area of triangle + area of triangle + area of rectangle + area of rectangle + area of rectangle.

$$SA = \left(\frac{1}{2} \times b \times h\right) + \left(\frac{1}{2} \times b \times h\right) + (l \times w) + (l \times w) + (l \times w)$$

$$SA = \left(\frac{1}{2} \times 6 \times 4\right) + \left(\frac{1}{2} \times 6 \times 4\right) + (6 \times 10) + (6 \times 10) + (6 \times 10)$$

$$SA = (12) + (12) + (60) + (60) + (60)$$

$$SA = 204 \textit{ square units}$$

Area and Perimeter of Polygons

The perimeter of a polygon is the distance around the outside of the two-dimensional figure. Perimeter is a one-dimensional measurement and is therefore expressed in linear units such as centimeters (*cm*), feet (*ft*), and miles (*mi*). The perimeter (*P*) of a figure can be calculated by adding together each of the sides.

Properties of certain polygons allow that the perimeter may be obtained by using formulas. A rectangle consists of two sides called the length (*l*), which have equal measures, and two sides called the width (*w*), which have equal measures. Therefore, the perimeter (*P*) of a rectangle can be expressed as $P = l + l + w + w$. This can be simplified to produce the following formula to find the perimeter of a rectangle: $P = 2l + 2w$ or $P = 2(l + w)$.

A regular polygon is one in which all sides have equal length and all interior angles have equal measures, such as a square and an equilateral triangle. To find the perimeter of a regular polygon, the length of one side is multiplied by the number of sides. For example, to find the perimeter of an equilateral triangle with a side of length of 4 feet, 4 feet is multiplied by 3 (number of sides of a triangle). The perimeter of a regular octagon (8 sides) with a side of length of $\frac{1}{2}$cm is $\frac{1}{2}cm \times 8 = 4cm$.

The area of a polygon is the number of square units needed to cover the interior region of the figure. Area is a two-dimensional measurement. Therefore, area is expressed in square units, such as square centimeters (cm^2), square feet (ft^2), or square miles (mi^2). The previous section of this unit covered the topic of finding the area of rectangles and triangles. To find the area (*A*) of a parallelogram, the length of the base (*b*) is multiplied by the length of the height (*h*) $\rightarrow A = b \times h$. Similar to triangles, the height of the parallelogram is measured from one base to the other at a 90° angle (or perpendicular).

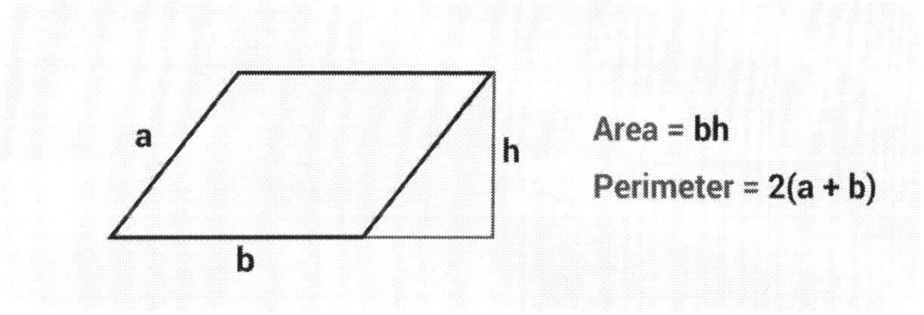

The area of a trapezoid can be calculated using the formula: $A = \frac{1}{2} \times h(b_1 + b_2)$, where *h* is the height and b_1 and b_2 are the parallel bases of the trapezoid.

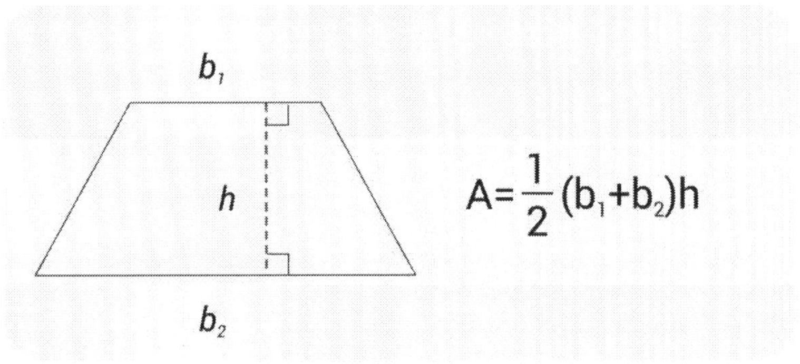

The area of a regular polygon can be determined by using its perimeter and the length of the apothem. The apothem is a line from the center of the regular polygon to any of its sides at a right angle. (Note that the perimeter of a regular polygon can be determined given the length of only one side.) The formula for the area (*A*) of a regular polygon is $A = \frac{1}{2} \times a \times P$, where *a* is the length of the apothem and *P* is the perimeter of the figure. Consider the following regular pentagon:

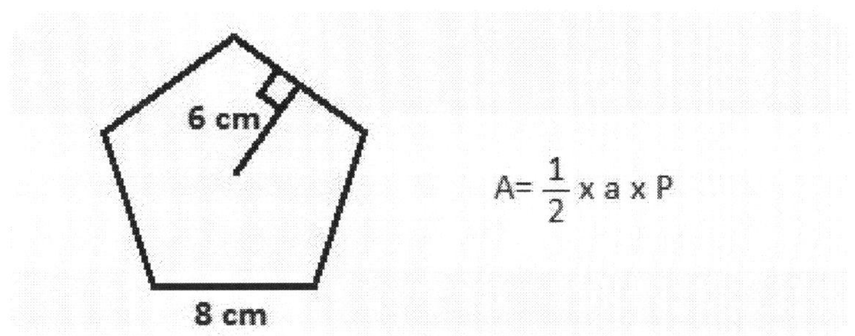

To find the area, the perimeter (*P*) is calculated first: $8cm \times 5 \rightarrow P = 40cm$. Then the perimeter and the apothem are used to find the area (*A*): $A = \frac{1}{2} \times a \times P \rightarrow A = \frac{1}{2} \times (6cm) \times (40cm) \rightarrow A = 120cm^2$. Note that the unit is $cm^2 \rightarrow cm \times cm = cm^2$.

The area of irregular polygons is found by decomposing, or breaking apart, the figure into smaller shapes. When the area of the smaller shapes is determined, the area of the smaller shapes will produce the area of the original figure when added together. Consider the example below:

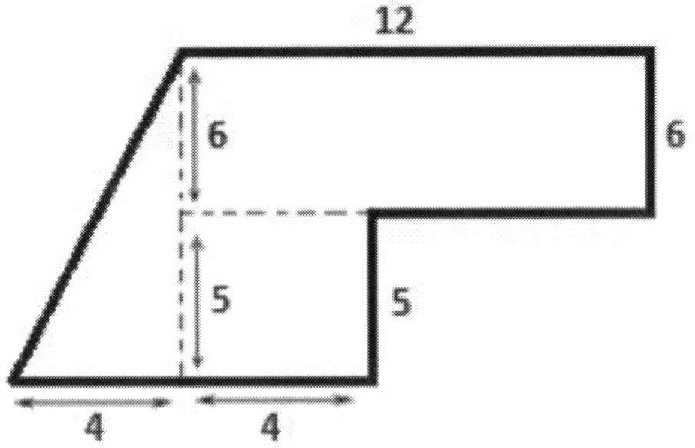

The irregular polygon is decomposed into two rectangles and a triangle. The area of the large rectangle ($A = l \times w \to A = 12 \times 6$) is 72 square units. The area of the small rectangle is 20 square units ($A = 4 \times 5$). The area of the triangle ($A = \frac{1}{2}b \times h \to A = \frac{1}{2}4 \times 11$) is 22 square units. The sum of the areas of these figures produces the total area of the original polygon: $A = 72 + 20 + 22 \to A = 114$ square units.

Right Rectangular Prisms

A right rectangular prism consists of:

- Two congruent (same size and shape) rectangles as the parallel *bases* (top and bottom)
- Two congruent rectangles as the *side* faces
- Two congruent rectangles as the *front and back* faces.

It is called a right prism because the base and sides meet at right angles.

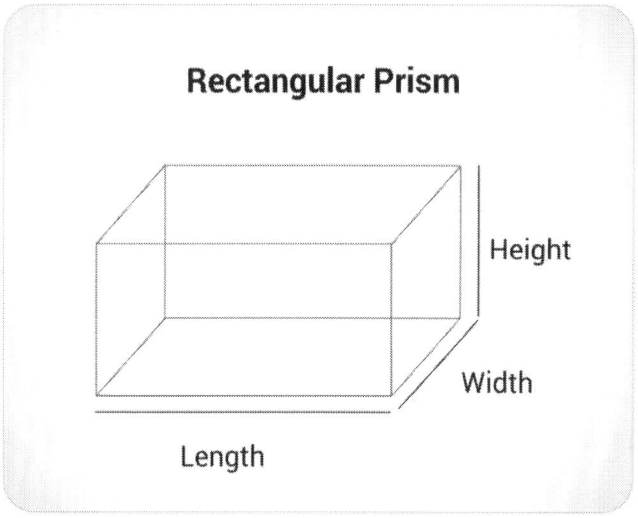

The length and width of the prism is the length and width of the rectangular base. The height of the prism is the measure from one base to the other.

The surface area of three-dimensional figures can be found by adding the areas of each of its bases and faces. The areas of a right rectangular prism are found as follows: two bases $\rightarrow A = l \times w$; front and back faces $\rightarrow A = l \times h$; two side faces $\rightarrow A = w \times h$. The sum of these six areas will equal the surface area of the prism. (Surface area = area of 2 bases + area of front and back + area of 2 sides). This is true for all right rectangular prisms leading to the formula for surface area $SA = 2 \times l \times w + 2 \times l \times h + 2 \times w \times h$ or $SA = 2(l \times w + l \times h + w \times h)$. Given the right rectangular prism below, the surface area is calculated as follows: $SA = 2\left(3\frac{1}{2}\text{ft}\right)\left(2\frac{1}{2}\text{ft}\right) + 2\left(3\frac{1}{2}\text{ft}\right)\left(1\frac{1}{2}\text{ft}\right) + 2\left(2\frac{1}{2}\text{ft}\right)\left(1\frac{1}{2}\text{ft}\right) \rightarrow SA = 35.5\text{ft}^2$

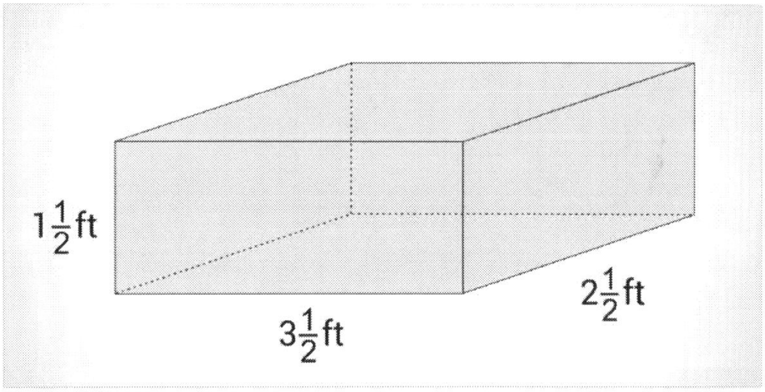

The volume of a solid (three-dimensional figure) is the number of cubic units needed to fill the space that the figure occupies. This concept is similar to filling a box with blocks. Volume is a three-dimensional measurement. Therefore, volume is expressed in cubic units such as cubic centimeters (cm^3), cubic feet (ft^3), and cubic yards (yd^3). If a rectangular prism has a volume of 30 cubic meters ($30m^3$), it will take 30 cubes, each with sides one meter in length, to fill the space occupied by the prism. A simple formula can be used to determine the volume of a right rectangular prism. The area of the base of the prism ($l \times w$) will indicate how many "blocks" are needed to cover the base. The height (h) of the prism will indicate how many "levels" of blocks are needed to construct the prism. Therefore, to find the volume (V) of a right rectangular prism, the area of the base ($l \times w$) is multiplied by the height (h): $V = l \times w \times h$. The volume of the prism shown above is calculated: $V = \left(3\frac{1}{2}\text{ft}\right) \times \left(2\frac{1}{2}\text{ft}\right) \times \left(1\frac{1}{2}\text{ft}\right) \rightarrow V = 13.125\text{ft}^3$

Effects of Changes to Dimensions on Area and Volume

Similar polygons are figures that are the same shape but different sizes. Likewise, similar solids are different sizes but are the same shape. In both cases, corresponding angles in the same positions for both figures are congruent (equal), and corresponding sides are proportional in length. For example, the triangles below are similar. The following pairs of corresponding angles are congruent: $\angle A$ and $\angle D$; $\angle B$ and $\angle E$; $\angle C$ and $\angle F$. The corresponding sides are proportional: $\frac{AB}{DE} = \frac{6}{3} = 2, \frac{BC}{EF} = \frac{9}{4.5} = 2, \frac{CA}{FD} = \frac{10}{5} = 2$. In other words, triangle *ABC* is the same shape but twice as large as triangle *DEF*.

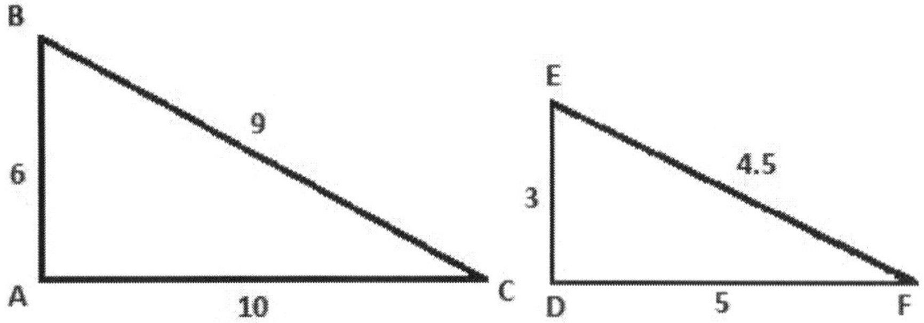

An example of similar triangular pyramids is shown below.

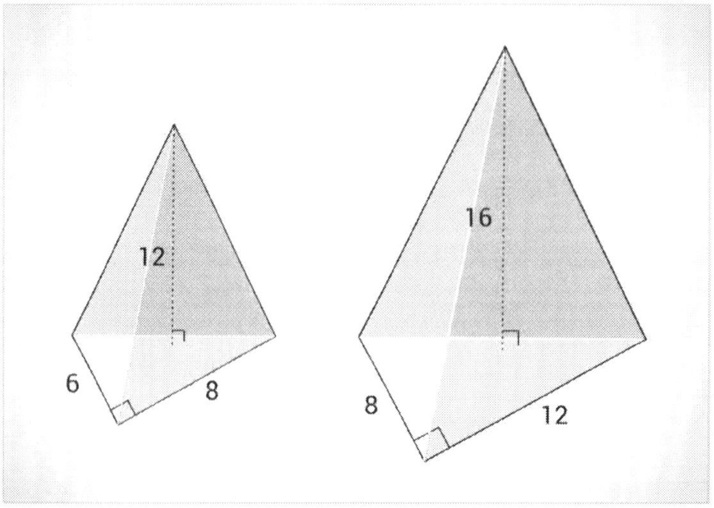

Given the nature of two- and three-dimensional measurements, changing dimensions by a given scale (multiplier) does not change the area of volume by the same scale. Consider a rectangle with a length of 5 centimeters and a width of 4 centimeters. The area of the rectangle is $20cm^2$. Doubling the dimensions of the rectangle (multiplying by a scale factor of 2) to 10 centimeters and 8 centimeters *does not* double the area to $40cm^2$. Area is a two-dimensional measurement (measured in square units). Therefore, the dimensions are multiplied by a scale that is squared (raised to the second power) to determine the scale of the corresponding areas. For the previous example, the length and width are multiplied by 2. Therefore, the area is multiplied by 2^2, or 4. The area of a 5cm × 4cm rectangle is $20cm^2$. The area of a 10cm × 8cm rectangle is $80cm^2$.

Volume is a three-dimensional measurement, which is measured in cubic units. Therefore, the scale between dimensions of similar solids is cubed (raised to the third power) to determine the scale between their volumes. Consider similar right rectangular prisms: one with a length of 8 inches, a width of 24 inches, and a height of 16 inches; the second with a length of 4 inches, a width of 12 inches, and a height of 8 inches. The first prism, multiplied by a scalar of $\frac{1}{2}$, produces the measurement of the second prism. The volume of the first prism, multiplied by $(\frac{1}{2})^3$, which equals $\frac{1}{8}$, produces the volume of the second prism. The volume of the first prism is 8in × 24in × 16in which equals $3{,}072in^3$. The volume of the second prism is 4in × 12in × 8in which equals $384in^3$ ($3{,}072in^3 \times \frac{1}{8} = 384in^3$).

The rules for squaring the scalar for area and cubing the scalar for volume only hold true for similar figures. In other words, if only one dimension is changed (changing the width of a rectangle but not the length) or dimensions are changed at different rates (the length of a prism is doubled and its height is tripled) the figures are not similar (same shape). Therefore, the rules above do not apply.

X-Axis, *Y*-Axis, Origin, and Four Quadrants in the Coordinate Plane

The coordinate plane, sometimes referred to as the Cartesian plane, is a two-dimensional surface consisting of a horizontal and a vertical number line. The horizontal number line is referred to as the *x*-axis, and the vertical number line is referred to as the *y*-axis. The *x*-axis and *y*-axis intersect (or cross) at a point called the origin. At the origin, the value of the *x*-axis is zero and the value of the *y*-axis is zero. The coordinate plane identifies the exact location of a point that is plotted on the two-dimensional surface. Like a map, the location of all points on the plane are in relation to the origin. Along the *x*-axis (horizontal line), numbers to the right of the origin are positive and increasing in value (1,2,3, . . .) and to the left of the origin numbers are negative and decreasing in value (-1,-2,-3, . . .). Along the *y*-axis (vertical line), numbers above the origin are positive and increasing in value and numbers below the origin are negative and decreasing in value.

The *x*- and *y*-axis divide the coordinate plane into four sections. These sections are referred to as quadrant one, quadrant two, quadrant three, and quadrant four, and are often written with Roman numerals I, II, III, and IV. The upper right section is Quadrant I and consists of points with positive *x*-values and positive *y*-values. The upper left section is Quadrant II and consists of points with negative *x*-values and positive *y*-values. The bottom left section is Quadrant III and consists of points with negative *x*-values and negative *y*-values. The bottom right section is Quadrant IV and consists of points with positive *x*-values and negative *y*-values.

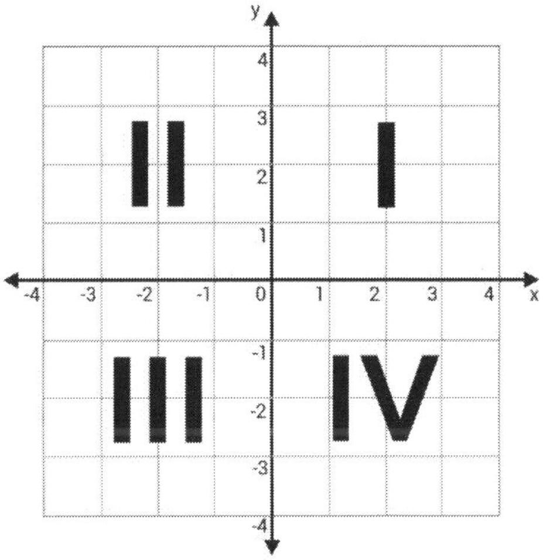

Solving Problems in the Coordinate Plane

The location of a point on a coordinate grid is identified by writing it as an ordered pair. An ordered pair is a set of numbers indicating the *x*-and *y*-coordinates of the point. Ordered pairs are written in the form (*x*, *y*) where *x* and *y* are values which indicate their respective coordinates. For example, the point (3, -2) has an *x*-coordinate of 3 and a *y*-coordinate of -2.

Plotting a point on the coordinate plane with a given coordinate means starting from the origin (0, 0). To determine the value of the *x*-coordinate, move right (positive number) or left (negative number) along the *x*-axis. Next, move up (positive number) or down (negative number) to the value of the *y*-coordinate. Finally, plot and label the point. For example, plotting the point (1, -2) requires starting from the origin and moving right along the *x*-axis to positive one, then moving down until straight across from negative 2 on the *y*-axis. The point is plotted and labeled. This point, along with three other points, are plotted and labeled on the graph below.

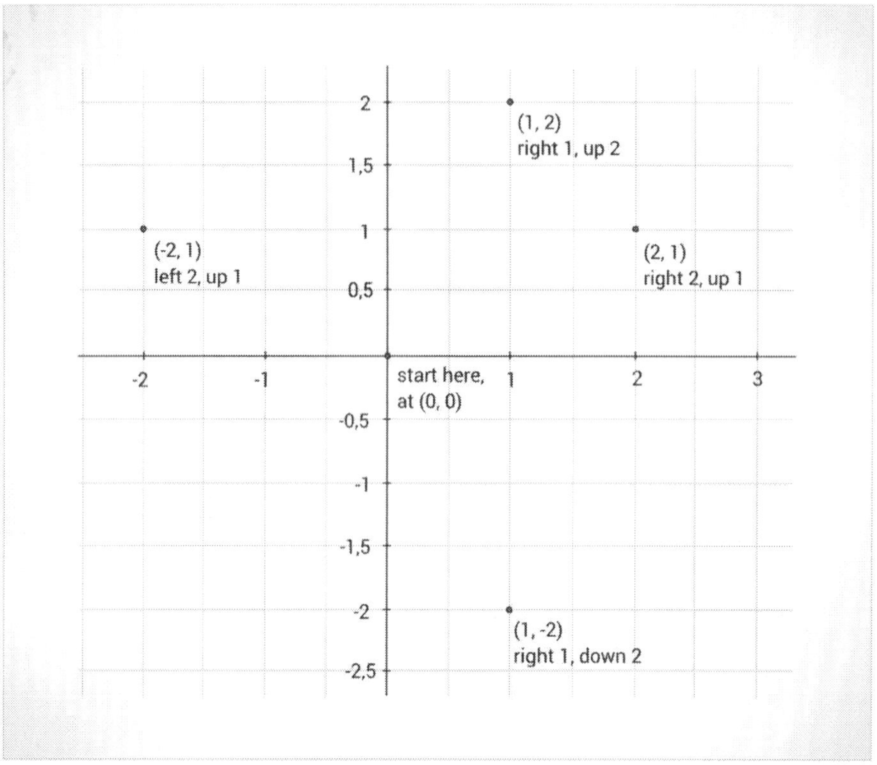

To write the coordinates of a point on the coordinate grid, a line should be traced directly above or below the point until reaching the *x*-axis (noting the value on the *x*-axis). Then, returning to the point, a line should be traced directly to the right or left of the point until reaching the *y*-axis (noting the value on the *y*-axis). The ordered pair (*x*, *y*) should be written with the values determined for the *x*- and *y*-coordinates.

Polygons can be drawn in the coordinate plane given the coordinates of their vertices. These coordinates can be used to determine the perimeter and area of the figure. Suppose triangle *RQP* has vertices located at the points: *R*(-2, 0), *Q*(2, 2), and *P*(2, 0). By plotting the points for the three vertices, the triangle can be constructed as follows:

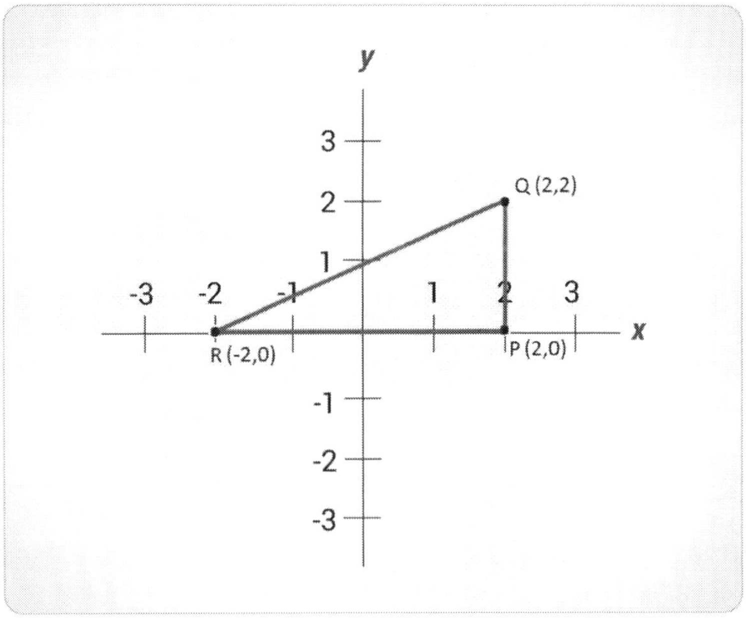

Because points *R* and *P* have the same *y*-coordinates (they are directly across from each other), the distance between them is determined by subtracting their *x*-coordinates (or simply counting units from one point to the other): 2– (-2) = 4. Therefore, the length of side *RP* is 4 units. Because points *Q* and *P* have the same *x*-coordinate (they are directly above and below each other), the distance between them is determined by subtracting their *y*-coordinates (or counting units between them): 2 – 0=2. Therefore, the length of side *PQ* is 2 units. Knowing the length of side *RP*, which is the base of the triangle, and the length of side *PQ*, which is the height of the triangle, the area of the figure can be determined by using the formula $A = \frac{1}{2}bh$.

To determine the perimeter of the triangle, the lengths of all three sides are needed. Points *R* and *Q* are neither directly across nor directly above and below each other. Therefore, the distance formula must be used to find the length of side *RQ*. The distance formula is as follows: $d = \sqrt{(x_2 - x_1)^2 + (y_2 - y_1)^2} \to d$. The perimeter is determined by adding the lengths of the three sides of the triangle.

Practice Questions

1. Which of the following could be used in the classroom to show $\frac{3}{7} < \frac{5}{6}$ is a true statement?
    a. A bar graph
    b. A number line
    c. An area model
    d. Base 10 blocks

2. A teacher is showing students how to evaluate $5 \times 6 + 4 \div 2 - 1$. Which operation should be completed first?
    a. Multiplication
    b. Addition
    c. Division
    d. Subtraction

3. What is the definition of a factor of the number 36?
    a. A number that can be divided by 36 and have no remainder
    b. A number that 36 can be divided by and have no remainder
    c. A prime number that is multiplied times 36
    d. An even number that is multiplied times 36

4. Which of the following is the definition of a prime number?
    a. A number that factors only into itself and 1
    b. A number greater than zero that factors only into itself and 1
    c. A number less than 10
    d. A number divisible by 10

5. What is the next number in the following series: $1, 3, 6, 10, 15, 21, \ldots$?
    a. 26
    b. 27
    c. 28
    d. 29

6. Which of the following is the correct order of operations that could be used on a difficult math problem that contained grouping symbols?
    a. Parentheses, Exponents, Multiplication, Division, Addition, Subtraction
    b. Exponents, Parentheses, Multiplication, Division, Addition, Subtraction
    c. Parentheses, Exponents, Addition, Multiplication, Division, Subtraction
    d. Parentheses, Exponents, Division, Addition, Subtraction, Multiplication

7. The perimeter of a 6-sided polygon is 56 cm. The length of three sides is 9 cm each. The length of two other sides is 8 cm each. What is the length of the missing side?
    a. 11 cm
    b. 12 cm
    c. 13 cm
    d. 10 cm

8. Rewriting mixed numbers as improper fractions can help students perform operations on mixed numbers. Which of the following is a mixed number?

a. $16\frac{1}{2}$

b. 16

c. $\frac{16}{3}$

d. $\frac{1}{4}$

9. If a teacher was showing a class how to round 245.2678 to the nearest thousandth, which place value would be used to decide whether to round up or round down?

a. Ten-thousandth

b. Thousandth

c. Hundredth

d. Thousand

10. Carey bought 184 pounds of fertilizer to use on her lawn. Each segment of her lawn required $12\frac{1}{2}$ pounds of fertilizer to do a sufficient job. If a student were asked to determine how many segments could be fertilized with the amount purchased, what operation would be necessary to solve this problem?

a. Multiplication

b. Division

c. Addition

d. Subtraction

11. Students should line up decimal places within the given numbers before performing which of the following?

a. Multiplication

b. Division

c. Subtraction

d. Exponents

12. Which of the following expressions best exemplifies the additive and subtractive identity?

a. $5 + 2 - 0 = 5 + 2 + 0$

b. $6 + x = 6 - 6$

c. $9 - 9 = 0$

d. $8 + 2 = 10$

13. Which of the following is an equivalent measurement for 1.3 cm?

a. 0.13 m

b. 0.013 m

c. 0.13 mm

d. 0.013 mm

14. Katie works at a clothing company and sold 192 shirts over the weekend. $\frac{1}{3}$ of the shirts that were sold were patterned, and the rest were solid. Which mathematical expression would calculate the number of solid shirts Katie sold over the weekend?

a. $192 \times \frac{1}{3}$

b. $192 \div \frac{1}{3}$

c. $192 \times (1 - \frac{1}{3})$

d. $192 \div 3$

15. Which four-sided shape is always a rectangle?

a. Rhombus

b. Square

c. Parallelogram

d. Quadrilateral

16. A rectangle was formed out of pipe cleaner. Its length was $\frac{1}{2}$ feet and its width was $\frac{11}{2}$ inches. What is its area in square inches?

a. $\frac{11}{4}$ inch^2

b. $\frac{11}{2}$ inch^2

c. 22 inch^2

d. 33 inch^2

17. A teacher cuts a pie into 6 equal pieces and takes one away. What topic would she be introducing to the class by using such a visual?

a. Decimals

b. Addition

c. Fractions

d. Measurement

18. Which item taught in the classroom would allow students to correctly find the solution to the following problem: A clock reads 5:00 am. What is the measure of the angle formed by the two hands of that clock?

a. Each time increment on an analog clock measures 90 degrees.

b. Each time increment on an analog clock measures 30 degrees.

c. Two adjacent angles sum up to 180 degrees.

d. Two complementary angles sum up to 180 degrees.

19. Which of the following represent one hundred eighty-two billion, thirty-six thousand, four hundred twenty-one and three hundred fifty-six thousandths?

a. 182,036,421.356

b. 182,036,421.0356

c. 182,000,036,421.0356

d. 182,000,036,421.356

20. A solution needs 5 mL of saline for every 8 mL of medicine given. How much saline is needed for 45 mL of medicine?

a. $\frac{225}{8}$ mL
b. 72 mL
c. 28 mL
d. $\frac{45}{8}$mL

21. What other operation could be utilized to teach the process of dividing 9453 by 24 besides division?

a. Multiplication
b. Addition
c. Exponents
d. Subtraction

22. What unit of volume is used to describe the following 3-dimensional shape?

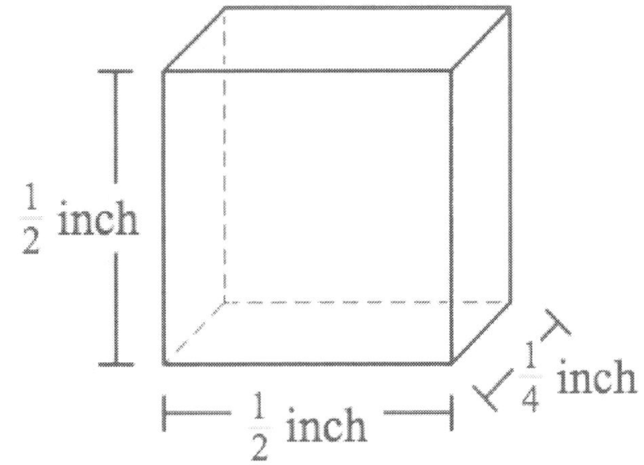

a. Square inches
b. Inches
c. Cubic inches
d. Squares

23. Which common denominator would be used to evaluate $\frac{2}{3}+\frac{4}{5}$?

a. 15
b. 3
c. 5
d. 10

24. What operation are students taught to repeat to evaluate an expression involving an exponent?

a. Addition
b. Multiplication
c. Division
d. Subtraction

25. Which of the following formulas would correctly calculate the perimeter of a legal-sized piece of paper that is 14 inches long and $8\frac{1}{2}$ inches wide?

a. $P = 14 + 8\frac{1}{2}$

b. $P = 14 + 8\frac{1}{2} + 14 + 8\frac{1}{2}$

c. $P = 14 \times 8\frac{1}{2}$

d. $P = 14 \times \frac{17}{2}$

26. Which of the following are units that would be taught in a lecture covering the metric system?

a. Inches, feet, miles, pounds
b. Millimeters, centimeters, meters, pounds
c. Kilograms, grams, kilometers, meters
d. Teaspoons, tablespoons, ounces

27. Which important mathematical property is shown in the expression: $(7 \times 3) \times 2 = 7 \times (3 \times 2)$?

a. Distributive property
b. Commutative property
c. Associative property
d. Multiplicative inverse

28. A grocery store is selling individual bottles of water, and each bottle contains 750 milliliters of water. If 12 bottles are purchased, what conversion will correctly determine how many liters that customer will take home?

a. 100 milliliters equals 1 liter
b. 1,000 milliliters equals 1 liter
c. 1,000 liters equals 1 milliliter
d. 10 liters equals 1 milliliter

29. If a student evaluated the expression $(3 + 7) - 6 \div 2$ to equal 2 on an exam, what error did she most likely make?

a. She performed the operations from left to right instead of following order of operations.
b. There was no error. 2 is the correct answer.
c. She did not perform the operation within the grouping symbol first.
d. She divided first instead of the addition within the grouping symbol.

30. What is the solution to $(2 \times 20) \div (7 + 1) + (6 \times 0.01) + (4 \times 0.001)$?

a. 5.064
b. 5.64
c. 5.0064
d. 48.064

31. A cereal box has a base 3 inches by 5 inches and is 10 inches tall. Another box has a base 5 inches by 6 inches. What formula is necessary for students to use to find out how tall the second box would need to be in order to hold the same amount of cereal?

a. Area of a rectangle
b. Volume of a rectangular solid
c. Volume of a cube
d. Perimeter of a square

32. An angle measures 54 degrees. In order to correctly determine the measure of its complementary angle, what concept is necessary?

a. Two complementary angles make up a right angle.
b. Complementary angles are always acute.
c. Two complementary angles sum up to 90 degrees.
d. Complementary angles sum up to 360 degrees.

33. The diameter of a circle measures 5.75 centimeters. What tool could be used in the classroom to draw such a circle?

a. Ruler
b. Meter stick
c. Compass
d. Yard stick

34. A piggy bank contains 12 dollars' worth of nickels. A nickel weighs 5 grams, and the empty piggy bank weighs 1050 grams. What is the total weight of the full piggy bank?

a. 1,110 grams
b. 1,200 grams
c. 2,250 grams
d. 2,200 grams

35. $\frac{3}{4}$ of a pizza remains on the stove. Katie eats $\frac{1}{3}$ of the remaining pizza. In order to determine how much of the pizza is left, what topic must be introduced to the students?

a. Converting fractions to decimals
b. Subtraction of fractions with like denominators
c. Addition of fractions with unlike denominators
d. Division of fractions

36. Last year, the New York City area received approximately $27\frac{3}{4}$ inches of snow. The Denver area received approximately 3 times as much snow as New York City. How much snow fell in Denver?

a. 60 inches
b. $27\frac{1}{4}$ inches
c. $9\frac{1}{4}$ inches
d. $83\frac{1}{4}$ inches

37. Joshua has collected 12,345 nickels over a span of 8 years. He took them to bank to deposit into his bank account. If the students were asked to determine how much money he deposited, for what mathematical topic would this problem be a good introduction?

a. Adding decimals
b. Multiplying decimals
c. Geometry
d. The metric system

38. Which of the following would be an instance in which ordinal numbers are used in the classroom?

a. Katie scored a 9 out of 10 on her quiz.
b. Matthew finished second in the spelling bee.
c. Jacob missed 1 day of school last month.
d. Kim was 5 minutes late to school this morning.

39. What is the solution to $9 \times 9 \div 9 + 9 - 9 \div 9$?

a. 0
b. 17
c. 81
d. 9

40. A student answers a problem with the following fraction: $\frac{3}{15}$. Why would this be considered incorrect?

a. It is not expressed in decimal form.
b. It is not simplified. The correct answer would be $\frac{1}{5}$.
c. It needs to be converted to a mixed number.
d. It is in the correct form, and there is no problem with it.

41. Which of the following statements is true about the two lines below?

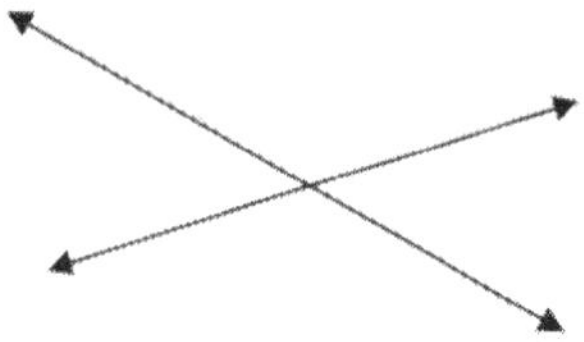

a. The two lines are parallel but not perpendicular.
b. The two lines are perpendicular but not parallel.
c. The two lines are both parallel and perpendicular.
d. The two lines are neither parallel nor perpendicular.

42. Which of the following figures is not a polygon?

a. Decagon
b. Cone
c. Triangle
d. Rhombus

43. What is the area of the regular hexagon shown below?

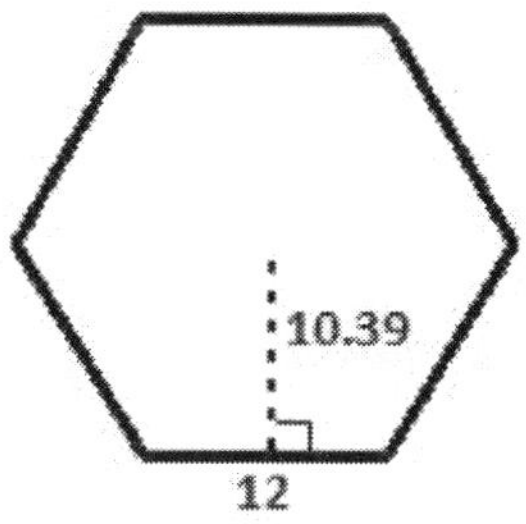

a. 72
b. 124.68
c. 374.04
d. 748.08

44. The area of a given rectangle is 24 centimeters. If the measure of each side is multiplied by 3, what is the area of the new figure?

a. 48cm
b. 72cm
c. 216cm
d. 13,824cm

45. What are the coordinates of the point plotted on the grid?

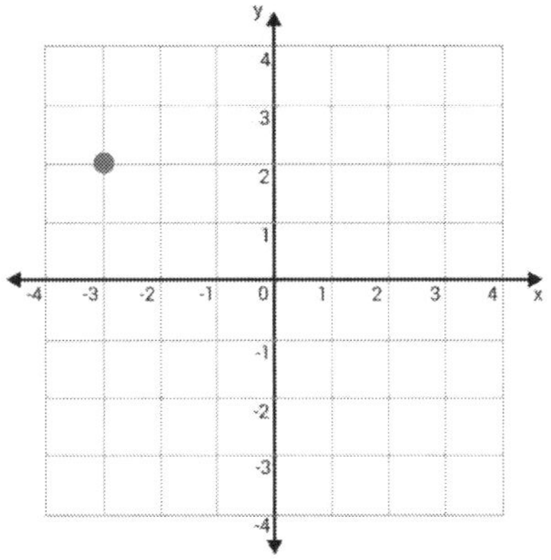

a. (-3, 2)
b. (2, -3)
c. (-3, -2)
d. (2, 3)

46. The perimeter of a 6-sided polygon is 56 cm. The length of three sides is 9 cm each. The length of two other sides is 8 cm each. What is the length of the missing side?

a. 11 cm
b. 12 cm
c. 13 cm
d. 10 cm

47. Katie works at a clothing company and sold 192 shirts over the weekend. $1/3$ of the shirts that were sold were patterned, and the rest were solid. Which mathematical expression would calculate the number of solid shirts Katie sold over the weekend?

a. $192 \times \frac{1}{3}$

b. $192 \div \frac{1}{3}$

c. $192 \times (1 - \frac{1}{3})$

d. $192 \div 3$

48. Which measure for the center of a small sample set is most affected by outliers?

a. Mean
b. Median
c. Mode
d. None of the above

49. Given the value of a given stock at monthly intervals, which graph should be used to best represent the trend of the stock?

a. Box plot
b. Line plot
c. Line graph
d. Circle graph

50. What is the probability of randomly picking the winner and runner-up from a race of 4 horses and distinguishing which is the winner?

a. $\frac{1}{4}$

b. $\frac{1}{2}$

c. $\frac{1}{16}$

d. $\frac{1}{12}$

Answer Explanations

1. B: This inequality can be seen with the use of a number line. $\frac{3}{7}$ is close to $\frac{1}{2}$. $\frac{5}{6}$ is close to 1, but less than 1, and $\frac{8}{7}$ is greater than 1. Therefore, $\frac{3}{7}$ is less than $\frac{5}{6}$.

2. A: Using the order of operations, multiplication and division are computed first from left to right. Multiplication is on the left; therefore, the teacher should perform multiplication first.

3. B: A factor of 36 is any number that can be divided into 36 and have no remainder. $36 = 36 \times 1, 18 \times 2, 9 \times 4, \text{and } 6 \times 6$. Therefore, it has 7 unique factors: 36, 18, 9, 6, 4, 2, and 1.

4. B: A number is prime because its only factors are itself and 1. Positive numbers (greater than zero) can be prime numbers.

5. C: Each number in the sequence is adding one more than the difference between the previous two. For example, $10 - 6 = 4, 4 + 1 = 5$. Therefore, the next number after 10 is $10 + 5 = 15$. Going forward, $21 - 15 = 6, 6 + 1 = 7$. The next number is $21 + 7 = 28$. Therefore, the difference between numbers is the set of whole numbers starting at 2: 2, 3, 4, 5, 6, 7....

6. A: Order of operations follows PEMDAS—Parentheses, Exponents, Multiplication and Division from left to right, and Addition and Subtraction from left to right.

7. C: The perimeter is found by calculating the sum of all sides of the polygon. $9 + 9 + 9 + 8 + 8 + s = 56$, where s is the missing side length. Therefore, 43 plus the missing side length is equal to 56. The missing side length is 13 cm.

8. A: A mixed number contains both a whole number and either a fraction or a decimal. Therefore, the mixed number is $16\frac{1}{2}$.

9. A: The place value to the right of the thousandth place, which would be the ten-thousandth place, is what gets used. The value in the thousandth place is 7. The number in the place value to its right is greater than 4, so the 7 gets bumped up to 8. Everything to its right turns to a zero, to get 245.2680. The zero is dropped because it is part of the decimal.

10. B: This is a division problem because the original amount needs to be split up into equal amounts. The mixed number $12\frac{1}{2}$ should be converted to an improper fraction first. $12\frac{1}{2} = \frac{(12*2)+1}{2} = \frac{23}{2}$. Carey needs determine how many times $\frac{23}{2}$ goes into 184. This is a division problem: $184 \div \frac{23}{2} = ?$ The fraction can be flipped, and the problem turns into the multiplication: $184 \times \frac{2}{23} = \frac{368}{23}$. This improper fraction can be simplified into 16 because $368 \div 23 = 16$. The answer is 16 lawn segments.

11. C: Numbers should be lined up by decimal places before subtraction is performed. This is because subtraction is performed within each place value. The other operations, such as multiplication, division, and exponents (which is a form of multiplication), involve ignoring the decimal places at first and then including them at the end.

12. A: The additive and subtractive identity is 0. When added or subtracted to any number, 0 does not change the original number.

13. B: 100 cm is equal to 1 m. 1.3 divided by 100 is 0.013. Therefore, 1.3 cm is equal to 0.013 mm. Because 1 cm is equal to 10 mm, 1.3 cm is equal to 13 mm.

14. C: $\frac{1}{3}$ of the shirts sold were patterned. Therefore, $1 - \frac{1}{3} = \frac{2}{3}$ of the shirts sold were solid. Anytime "of" a quantity appears in a word problem, multiplication needs to be used. Therefore, $192 \times \frac{2}{3} = \frac{192*2}{3} = \frac{384}{3} = 128$ solid shirts were sold. The entire expression is $192 \times \left(1 - \frac{1}{3}\right)$.

15. B: A rectangle is a specific type of parallelogram. It has 4 right angles. A square is a rhombus that has 4 right angles. Therefore, a square is always a rectangle because it has two sets of parallel lines and 4 right angles.

16. D: Area = length x width. The answer must be in square inches, so all values must be converted to inches. $\frac{1}{2}$ ft is equal to 6 inches. Therefore, the area of the rectangle is equal to $6 \times \frac{11}{2} = \frac{66}{2} = 33$ square inches.

17. C: The teacher would be introducing fractions. If a pie was cut into 6 pieces, each piece would represent $\frac{1}{6}$ of the pie. If one piece was taken away, $\frac{5}{6}$ of the pie would be left over.

18. B: Each hour on the clock represents 30 degrees. For example, 3:00 represents a right angle. Therefore, 5:00 represents 150 degrees.

19. D: There are no millions, so the millions period consists of all zeros. 182 is in the billions period, 36 is in the thousands period, 421 is in the hundreds period, and 356 is the decimal.

20. A: Every 8 ml of medicine requires 5 mL. The 45 mL first needs to be split into portions of 8 mL. This results in $\frac{45}{8}$ portions. Each portion requires 5 mL. Therefore, $\frac{45}{8} \times 5 = \frac{45*5}{8} = \frac{225}{8}$ mL is necessary.

21. D: Division can be computed as a repetition of subtraction problems by subtracting multiples of 24.

22. C: Volume of this three-dimensional figure is calculated using length x width x height. Each measure of length is in inches. Therefore, the answer would be labeled in cubic inches.

23. A: A common denominator must be found. The least common denominator is 15 because it has both 5 and 3 as factors. The fractions must be rewritten using 15 as the denominator.

24. B: A number raised to an exponent is a compressed form of multiplication. For example, $10^3 = 10 \times 10 \times 10$.

25. B: The perimeter of a rectangle is the sum of all four sides. Therefore, the answer is $P = 14 + 8\frac{1}{2} + 14 + 8\frac{1}{2} = 14 + 14 + 8 + \frac{1}{2} + 8 + \frac{1}{2} = 45$ square inches.

26. C: Inches, pounds, and baking measurements, such as tablespoons, are not part of the metric system. Kilograms, grams, kilometers, and meters are part of the metric system.

27. C: It shows the associative property of multiplication. The order of multiplication does not matter, and the grouping symbols do not change the final result once the expression is evaluated.

28. B: $12 \times 750 = 9{,}000$. Therefore, there are 9,000 milliliters of water, which must be converted to liters. 1,000 milliliters equals 1 liter; therefore, 9 liters of water are purchased.

29. A: According to order of operations, the operation within the parentheses must be completed first. Next, division is completed and then subtraction. Therefore, the expression is evaluated as $(3 + 7) - 6 \div 2 = 10 - 6 \div 2 = 10 - 3 = 7$. In order to incorrectly obtain 2 as the answer, the operations would have been performed from left to right, instead of following PEMDAS.

30. A: Operations within the parentheses must be completed first. Then, division is completed. Finally, addition is the last operation to complete. When adding decimals, digits within each place value are added together. Therefore, the expression is evaluated as $(2 \times 20) \div (7 + 1) + (6 \times 0.01) + (4 \times 0.001) = 40 \div 8 + 0.06 + 0.004 = 5 + 0.06 + 0.004 = 5.064$.

31. B: The formula for the volume of a rectangular solid would need to be used. The volume of the first box is $V = 3 \times 5 \times 10 = 150$ cubic inches. The second box needs to hold cereal that would take up the same space. The volume of the second box is $V = 5 \times 6 \times h = 30 \times h$. In order for this to equal 150, h must equal 5 inches.

32. C: The measure of two complementary angles sums up to 90 degrees. $90 - 54 = 36$. Therefore, the complementary angle is 36 degrees.

33. C: A compass is a tool that can be used to draw a circle. The circle would be drawn by using the length of the radius, which is half of the diameter.

34. C: A dollar contains 20 nickels. Therefore, if there are 12 dollars' worth of nickels, there are $12 \times 20 = 240$ nickels. Each nickel weighs 5 grams. Therefore, the weight of the nickels is $240 \times 5 =$ 1,200 grams. Adding in the weight of the empty piggy bank, the filled bank weighs 2,250 grams.

35. B: Katie eats $\frac{1}{3}$ of $\frac{3}{4}$ of the pizza. That means she eats $\frac{1}{3} \times \frac{3}{4} = \frac{3}{12} = \frac{1}{4}$ of the pizza. Therefore, $\frac{3}{4} - \frac{1}{4} = \frac{2}{4} = \frac{1}{2}$ of the pizza remains. This problem involves subtraction of fractions with like denominators.

36. D: 3 must be multiplied times $27\frac{3}{4}$. In order to easily do this, the mixed number should be converted into an improper fraction. $27\frac{3}{4} = \frac{27*4+3}{4} = \frac{111}{4}$. Therefore, Denver had approximately $\frac{3x111}{4} = \frac{333}{4}$ inches of snow. The improper fraction can be converted back into a mixed number through division. $\frac{333}{4} = 83\frac{1}{4}$ inches.

37. B: Each nickel is worth \$0.05. Therefore, Joshua deposited $12{,}345 \times \$0.05 = \$617.25$. Working with change is a great way to teach decimals to children, so this problem would be a good introduction to multiplying decimals.

38. B: Ordinal numbers represent a ranking. Placing second in a competition is a ranking among the other participants of the spelling bee.

39. B: According to the order of operations, multiplication and division must be completed first from left to right. Then, addition and subtraction are completed from left to right. Therefore, $9 \times 9 \div 9 + 9 - 9 \div 9 = 81 \div 9 + 9 - 9 \div 9 = 9 + 9 - 9 \div 9 = 9 + 9 - 1 = 18 - 1 = 17$.

40. B: When giving an answer to a math problem that is in fraction form, it always should be simplified. Both 3 and 15 have a common factor of 3 that can be divided out, so the correct answer is $\frac{3 \div 3}{15 \div 3} = \frac{1}{5}$.

41. D: The two lines are neither parallel nor perpendicular. Parallel lines will never intersect or meet. Therefore, the lines are not parallel. Perpendicular lines intersect to form a right angle (90°). Although the lines intersect, they do not form a right angle, which is usually indicated with a box at the intersection point. Therefore, the lines are not perpendicular.

42. B: Cone. A polygon is a closed two-dimensional figure consisting of three or more sides. A decagon is a polygon with 10 sides. A triangle is a polygon with three sides. A rhombus is a polygon with 4 sides. A cone is a three-dimensional figure and is classified as a solid.

43. C: 374.04. The formula for finding the area of a regular polygon is $A = \frac{1}{2} \times a \times P$ where *a* is the length of the apothem (from the center to any side at a right angle) and *P* is the perimeter of the figure. The apothem *a* is given as 10.39 and the perimeter can be found by multiplying the length of one side by the number of sides (since the polygon is regular): $P = 12 \times 6 \rightarrow P = 72$. To find the area, substitute the values for *a* and *P* into the formula $A = \frac{1}{2} \times a \times P \rightarrow A = \frac{1}{2} \times (10.39) \times (72) \rightarrow A = 374.04$.

44. C: 216cm. Because area is a two-dimensional measurement, the dimensions are multiplied by a scale that is squared to determine the scale of the corresponding areas. The dimensions of the rectangle are multiplied by a scale of 3. Therefore, the area is multiplied by a scale of 3^2 (which is equal to 9): $24cm \times 9 = 216cm$.

45. A: (-3, 2). The coordinates of a point are written as an ordered pair (*x*, *y*). To determine the *x*-coordinate, a line is traced directly above or below the point until reaching the *x*-axis. This step notes the value on the *x*-axis. In this case, the *x*-coordinate is -3. To determine the *y*-coordinate, a line is traced directly to the right or left of the point until reaching the y-axis, which notes the value on the *y*-axis. In this case, the *y*-coordinate is 2. Therefore, the ordered pair is written (-3, 2).

46. C: Perimeter is found by calculating the sum of all sides of the polygon. $9 + 9 + 9 + 8 + 8 + s = 56$, where *s* is the missing side length. Therefore, 43 plus the missing side length is equal to 56. The missing side length is 13 cm.

47. C: $\frac{1}{3}$ of the shirts sold were patterned. Therefore, $1 - \frac{1}{3} = \frac{2}{3}$ of the shirts sold were solid. Anytime "of" a quantity appears in a word problem, multiplication should be used. Therefore, $192 \times \frac{2}{3} = \frac{192 \times 2}{3} = \frac{384}{3} = 128$ solid shirts were sold. The entire expression is $192 \times \left(1 - \frac{1}{3}\right)$.

48. A: Mean. An outlier is a data value that is either far above or far below the majority of values in a sample set. The mean is the average of all the values in the set. In a small sample set, a very high or very low number could drastically change the average of the data points. Outliers will have no more of an effect on the median (the middle value when arranged from lowest to highest) than any other value above or below the median. If the same outlier does not repeat, outliers will have no effect on the mode (value that repeats most often).

49. C: Line graph. The scenario involves data consisting of two variables, month, and stock value. Box plots display data consisting of values for one variable. Therefore, a box plot is not an appropriate choice. Both line plots and circle graphs are used to display frequencies within categorical data. Neither can be used for the given scenario. Line graphs display two numerical variables on a coordinate grid and show trends among the variables.

50. D: $\frac{1}{12}$. The probability of picking the winner of the race is $\frac{1}{4}\left(\frac{number\ of\ favorable\ outcomes}{number\ of\ total\ outcomes}\right)$. Assuming the winner was picked on the first selection, three horses remain from which to choose the runner-up (these are dependent events). Therefore, the probability of picking the runner-up is $\frac{1}{3}$. To determine the probability of multiple events, the probability of each event is multiplied: $\frac{1}{4} \times \frac{1}{3} = \frac{1}{12}$.

FREE Test Taking Tips DVD Offer

To help us better serve you, we have developed a Test Taking Tips DVD that we would like to give you for FREE. **This DVD covers world-class test taking tips that you can use to be even more successful when you are taking your test.**

All that we ask is that you email us your feedback about your study guide. Please let us know what you thought about it – whether that is good, bad or indifferent.

To get your **FREE Test Taking Tips DVD**, email freedvd@studyguideteam.com with "FREE DVD" in the subject line and the following information in the body of the email:

a. The title of your study guide.

b. Your product rating on a scale of 1-5, with 5 being the highest rating.

c. Your feedback about the study guide. What did you think of it?

d. Your full name and shipping address to send your free DVD.

If you have any questions or concerns, please don't hesitate to contact us at freedvd@studyguideteam.com.

Thanks again!

69153204R00158

Made in the USA
Lexington, KY
26 October 2017